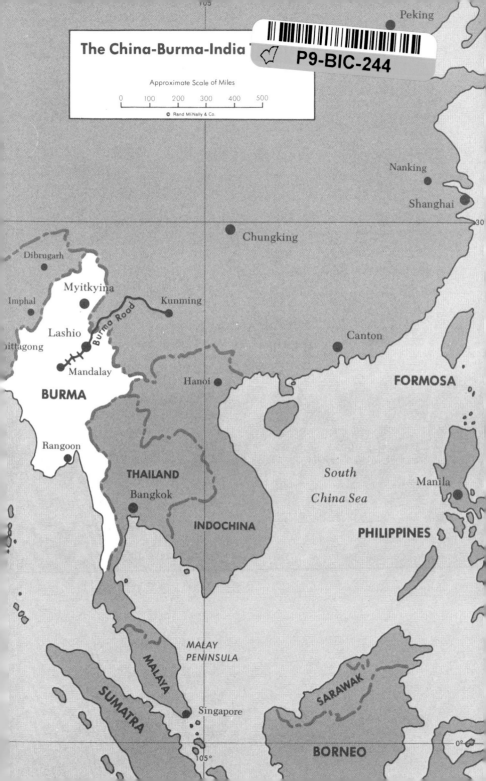

# The China-Burma-India Theater

P9-BIC-244

Approximate Scale of Miles

0    100    200    300    400    500

© Rand McNally & Co.

Peking

Nanking

Shanghai

Chungking

Dibrugarh

Myitkyina

Imphal

Lashio

Kunming

Burma Road

Canton

ittagong

Mandalay

Hanoi

FORMOSA

BURMA

Rangoon

THAILAND

Bangkok

South

China Sea

Manila

INDOCHINA

PHILIPPINES

MALAY
PENINSULA

MALAYA

SARAWAK

SUMATRA

Singapore

BORNEO

# BEHIND
# JAPANESE
With the OSS
in Burma
# LINES

# BEHIND JAPANESE LINES

### With the OSS in Burma

# LINES

## BY RICHARD DUNLOP

RAND McNALLY & COMPANY
CHICAGO · NEW YORK · SAN FRANCISCO

This book is dedicated to Steve Sutton, friend and talented editor, who was lost in the catastrophic crash of a DC-10 airliner at Chicago on May 25, 1979. This was his last book. Through its pages he became an eternal friend of the Kachin people and of the men of Detachment 101. We all feel that our ranks are diminished by his death.

Copyright © 1979 by RAND McNALLY & COMPANY
All rights reserved
Printed in the UNITED STATES of AMERICA
by RAND McNALLY & COMPANY

# CONTENTS

## List of Maps

# Preface

To many readers the following account of the guerrilla war fought against the Japanese army in the jungled mountains of North Burma during World War II will seem as brutal as a pungyi stick thrust into the entrails. But it is the truth of the matter, as told to me by my fellow members of Office of Strategic Services Detachment 101 and as I myself remember it. Sometimes the story is grim and disturbing, sometimes errant and whimsical, deeply sad and tragic, brave and noble, often it is outrageous, humorous, or downright repulsive—but that is the way things were in the Southeast Asian jungles.

I have chosen a narrative style that seems suited to this type of candid history and to the irregular warfare waged behind the Japanese lines by Detachment 101. I have left the more linear approach to the war in Burma to the armchair historians and the political and strategic complexities of the China-Burma-India Theater to scholars. I have presented the "big picture" of the CBI Theater only when it is necessary for an understanding of the OSS mission in Burma.

The Official History of Detachment 101 as jointly prepared by Detachment 101 and the G-2 Section of the Northern Combat Area Command states that the detachment:

> was given the two-fold assignment of espionage and guerrilla warfare in Japanese-occupied Burma. Such an assignment presented staggering difficulties. The country represents the densest kind of jungle terrain and for half the year is rain-sodden and malaria-infested. The Japanese, jungle-wise, made full use of the abundant natural cover; they confined their movement almost entirely to night marches; and employed illogical courses of action to conceal their whereabouts and intentions. A final difficulty is the conspicuousness of white agents in an oriental country.
>
> Under such natural conditions, and against such an enemy, the organization of an army of partisans and agents chosen from among the inhabitants of the country, offered advantages without which the mission could not be accomplished.

In telling the story of Detachment 101 I have tried to give the reader an understanding of the Kachin people who provided most of the partisans and many of the agents and to show why they responded as they did to the Japanese invasion of their homeland. The jungle war that I describe was their war of self-defense and revenge. OSS men could have accomplished very little without them. I have endeavored to bring alive for readers not only the Kachin people but the leeches, the kraits and cobras, the tigers and even weretigers, the heat of the lowland valleys and the cold of the high Himalayan foothills.

The reader should not expect a Kachin jaiwa telling his story around a campfire on a mountainside to have the mental attributes of an Oxford don and should keep in mind that the Kachins and Americans who lived through the experience had no idea at the time that they were making history. In the light of subsequent events in Southeast Asia and of events in Asia yet to happen, the partnership in warfare between the Kachins and Americans, their life together and their friendship and affection for one another, should have great meaning for people in both the East and the West who find it hard to accept the universality of human nature, which can bring together very different peoples in a common venture for their mutual salvation.

My own involvement with the OSS began at Camp Gruber, Oklahoma, when I was summoned out of the field while on maneuvers with my regiment of the 42nd Rainbow Division. The officer's crisp Washington uniform contrasted with my muddy clothing. He glanced at my dossier open before him, asked a few desultory questions and then demanded, "Would you be willing to undertake a dangerous mission behind enemy lines?"

It seemed right out of any number of adventure movies I'd seen as a kid, but theatrical as it might appear, it was also plain that the man, who I later learned was from the Office of Strategic Services, was serious enough.

"Yes, sir," I said, having learned the proper response at the age of twelve at matinees in neighborhood movie theaters back home in Illinois.

Within two weeks I was in Washington, and when my security check was completed, I was put through training, which ranged from cryptography and cryptoanalytics at the OSS headquarters to unorthodox combat techniques in the secret camps in Virginia and Maryland. I met my first 101 man at the Virginia camp. Back from the

Burma jungles, he was one of my instructors, and he distinguished himself by drinking all the shaving lotion in the barracks one morning. He also was a very competent teacher.

When I went through the OSS psychological testing program, I was told at my final interview that I showed a remarkable aptitude for living for long periods with people of another culture and race. Therefore I was not surprised when I was asked to commence Chinese language classes instead of continuing my training for a probable assignment in Europe.

Finally, with five other OSS men detailed for China, I was sent by ship to India. In Calcutta each of us was interviewed by a representative of Detachment 101 and asked if we would be willing to go to Burma instead of China. The 101 man that I had met in training camp in Virginia had impressed me, and I readily agreed to go to Burma. I flew to Chabua, Assam, and was met by an Anglo-Burmese driver in a jeep, who drove me through the jungles, wet with monsoonal rain, to Nazira. That night as I fell asleep in a tent on the periphery of a tea garden I heard my first tiger's coughing roar across the Dikho River. From that moment on I was proud to be a part of Detachment 101. It was autumn, 1944.

In a few weeks I had completed my indoctrination at Nazira, flew to Myitkyina, and soon afterwards went on to the area of Bhamo in a 101 light plane. From that airstrip I walked the rest of the way into the field. At no time did my experiences, fascinating as they were to me, prove either as exciting or as significant as those of many of my fellow 101 men, but I was privileged to be an observer who, with the sensitivity and awareness of a young man who was intended by life to become an author, was to learn firsthand the story of the Kachin people and their extraordinary partnership with the Americans and British of the OSS.

# Acknowledgments

The author is indebted to the three commanders of Detachment 101 of the Office of Strategic Services, Colonel Carl Eifler, Colonel John Coughlin, and Lieutenant General William Raymond Peers. Each in his own distinctive way proved both an inspiration and a rich source of information for the book. General Peers very generously offered both his manuscript on the OSS in Burma and his personal collection of photography for my consideration. The late Major General William J. Donovan, the Director of the Office of Strategic Services, also was a much valued contributor to my understanding of the subject.

Dennis V. Cavanaugh, archivist for the 101 Association, and Harry Hengshoon, known throughout Detachment 101 by his OSS code name of "Skittles," were particularly helpful. The 101 NEWS-LETTER, edited by Dennis Cavanaugh, provided me with valuable anecdotes, drawn from the recollections of the men who served with OSS in Burma. Tom Baldwin and Bill Martin counseled me in my research.

All of my friends and comrades of the detachment assisted me in the preparation of this book, for it became their story. It was mostly a pleasure to share old times together again as we met to talk about the book, but sometimes the memories were very disturbing, for the story is often a grim one. To all of these men I shall always be indebted for their candor. I wish to express my appreciation to Ngai Tawng: though he died in the jungles when still a boy, he had achieved man's estate in his spirit, and his deep insights into his people have marked not only this book but my own life. Last of all I wish to acknowledge my debt to my wife Joan not only for her love and understanding but for her assistance with the research and for creating the index to this book.

New Delhi, India
Sept. 15, 1942

SUBJECT: Letter of Instructions

to    :  Major C. Eifler

1.  You will carry out the general mission given you verbally by
by Gen. Stilwell. You are given complete authority to carry out
these instructions subject only to the restriction that no
important operations will be executed without prior approval
of the Branch office.

2.  10th Air Force and S.O.S. have been directed to give you such
cooperation as is possible from their agencies in Assam. However,
existing facilities as to housing, messing and transportation
are at present inadequate for those agencies and no requests
should be made on them for such assistance. It should be your
aim to operate entirely on your own organizational equipment.

3.  a. The following initial specific mission is given you
    for immediate execution:
    To make plans for denying the use of MIYTKYINA AERODROME to
    the Japanese as an operating field. This is your primary
    mission.  In the accomplishment of this mission, without any
    desire to restrict you, it is desired to indicate that
    destruction on the railroad, the firing of railroad cars
    and the sinking of vessels carrying fuel will all contribute
    to the general success of your operations.  Effective
    destruction of important bridges, such as the R.R. bridge
    near MEZA would reduce rail shipments of gasoline to a
    negligible amount.  You should make a careful estimate of
    the situation and plan on your action, then inform this
    headquarters of your general plan.
    b. Subsequent missions will be given you from time to time,
    but for these you will submit your plans for approval before
    executing them.

4.  Upon arrival in the Assam area you should establish contact
with Mr. B.C.Case who will be directed to cooperate with you.  Mr.
Case is familiar with the area and his knowledge of Burmese and
his connections with the tribesmen should prove invaluable to you

5.  Liaison with British authorities should be initiated to the
end that no possible cause for mutual interference may arise.

6.  It is desired that you keep this headquarters informed as
to your activities by the submission of periodical informal reports.

By Command of Lt. Gen. STILWELL:

                    L.B. THOMPSON,
                    Major, A.G.D.
                    Asst. Adj. General

Memo. for Eifler

2/18/43.

Time factor.

Contact with British ⸢ Continue liaison with 8 A, 4 AC. & S.O.E. ;
Contact with V-force. ⸤ Report their plans, strength & operations.
⸤ act with them according to your judgment

Contact with natives ⸢ Establish friendly relations. Get them
to make reports on jap movements, dis
positions, strength, etc. Set up locations for future supply & chain of communication. Tell them Chinese are with
us. Reassure them about treatment by
chinese. Tell the right ones we will get
them some weapons.

Your own personnel. ⸢ Harass jap communications as far
south as the half-way point between
Mogaung & Katha and east to include
the Myitkyina area. If japs occupy
Sumprabum this will be important.
They should be kept out of Sumprabum
& confined to the immediate vicinity of
Myitkyina. ( Future action south of
Myitkyina will be indicated.)
    Put a group in the Taunggyi —Silem—
Lashio area. Work on the RR. & report
jap moves in the area.

                                        JMB.

# BEHIND
# JAPANESE
With the OSS
in Burma
# LINES

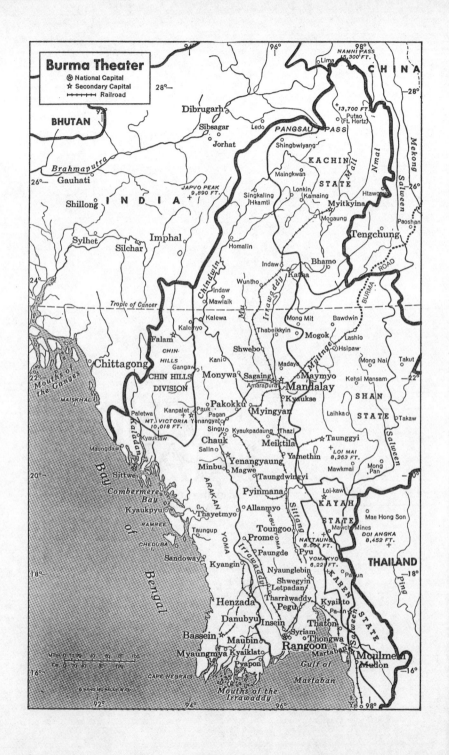

**Burma Theater**

⊕ National Capital
☆ Secondary Capital
┝┼┼┼┼┤ Railroad

BHUTAN

CHINA

NAMNI PASS 15,300' FT.

Dibrugarh

Lima

Sibsagar

Ledo

PANGSAU PASS

Jorhat

Shingbwiyang

+13,700 FT. Putao (Ft. Hertz)

KACHIN

Brahmaputra

Gauhati

Maingkwan

STATE

Htawo

Mali

Nmai

Mekong

Salween

Shillong

INDIA

JAPVO PEAK 9,890 FT.

Singkaling Hkamti

Lonkin

Kamaing

Myitkyina

Mogaung

Paoshan

Sylhet

Silchar

Imphal

Homalin

Indaw

Bhamo

Tengchung

BURMA ROAD

Wuntho

Katha

Chindwin

Indaw

Mawlaik

Mong Mit

Bawdwin

Tropic of Cancer

Kalewa

Mu

Irrawaddy

Myitnge

Chittagong

Kalemyo

Thabeikkyin

Mogok

Lashio

Falam

CHIN HILLS

Shwebo

Hsipaw

Mong Nai

Takut

Gangaw

Kani

Madaya

Mandalay

Kehsi Mansam

CHIN HILLS DIVISION

Monywa

Sagaing

Amarapura

Maymyo

Kyaukse

SHAN

Pakokku

Myingyan

Laihka

STATE

Takaw

Paletwa

Kanpalet

Pauk

Pagan

Yenangyat

Thazi

MT. VICTORIA 10,018 FT.

Singu

Kyaukpadaung

Chauk

Salin

Meiktila

Taunggyi

LOI MAI 8,263 FT.

Kyauktaw

Yamethin

Maungdaw

Minbu

Yenangyaung

Magwe

Mawkmai

Mong Pan

Sittwe

Taungdwingyi

Combermere Bay

Pyinmana

Loi-kaw

Kyaukpyu

Thayetmyo

Allanmyo

KAYAH

Mae Hong Son

RAMREE

Taungup

Toungoo

Prome

Mawchi Mines

STATE

DOI ANGKA 8,452 FT.

CHEDUBA

Sandoway

Kyangin

Paungde

Pyu

NATTAUNG 8,60 FT.

YOMAKYO 6,22 FT.

THAILAND

Nyaunglebin

Shwegyin

Letpadan

Pakun

Henzada

Tharrawaddy

Pegu

Kyaikto

Pa-an

Danubyu

Insein

Thaton

Thongwa

Bassein

Maubin

Syriam

Martaban

Moulmein

Myaungmya

Kyaiklato

Rangoon

Mudon

Pyapon

Gulf of

CAPE NEGRAIS

Martaban

Mouths of the Irrawaddy

Bay of Bengal

ARAKAN YOMA

PEGU YOMA

Irrawaddy

Sittang

Salween

KAREN STATE

Ping

# Prologue

# The Village

A monkey has no feeling for human tragedy. The young Japanese officer hunched back against the bole of a mahogany tree, his left hand clasped around his drawn-up knees, his wounded right hand wrapped in a bloody cloth ripped from his shirt. He kept his eyes on his bare feet. High above in the tangled jungle canopy of interwoven branches and vines a troop of monkeys sported, leaped, and chattered. On a branch above the wounded man one monkey paused to urinate. A shower of droplets descended on him, but he did not stir.

The Japanese continued to study his feet, naked and vulnerable with their toes pressed into the dank jungle floor. They were a city man's feet. The toes were regularly spaced. The thongs of a peasant's sandals had not spread the big toe from the one next to it. There was no callus to show where the leather strap of a countryboy's sandals had rubbed. Encased in Western-style leather shoes, these feet had walked along the Ginza. With his girl on his arm in the Western way, the young man had gazed at the merchandise in the store windows. He had admired the American goods, so clean of line, so practical, so beautiful in their utilitarian, to-be-used-everyday way. Then, in the great cosmopolitan city where young men and women could think of many ways to live, he had been an artist, and the clean American lines had found their way into his paintings. Now the hand that had grasped the brush was bloodied, and by a bullet that had been made in America. His hand throbbed with a strange pain that seemed to emanate from another hand which was not his own, but belonged to someone dear to him.

A trickle of urine ran down the young officer's cheek. He had been thirsty since the night before, when the jungle along the trail had erupted into flashes of gunfire, the sickening chug of a Browning au-

tomatic rifle, the whing-whine of bullets. His tongue captured the
moisture, and it was strangely salt to the taste.

He could stare at his feet no longer. Irresistibly, his eyes were
drawn to the eyes of a slight brown man who, scrunched down on his
heels, sat whittling thin slivers of bamboo. An American officer
scrunched down in similar supple-legged fashion nearby, but the Japanese did not even glance at him. The Americans, those easy-to-like
people of the clean-lined merchandise, didn't worry him. They
abided by the Geneva Convention. But the brown man whittled those
ominous slivers of bamboo, and a gentle and almost womanly smile
turned up the corners of his mouth. His eyes held the eyes of the
Japanese much as the glare of a cobra fascinates the eyes of a shoat.
They did not look fierce or cruel—only dark and brooding.

The Japanese felt his shoulders shiver and his legs tremble invol-
untarily. This brown man with his native longyi tucked in at the waist
was Zhing Htaw Naw, most feared of all the Kachin duwas. There
was no question about it. He remembered him from that day in that
horrible village in what now seemed a lifetime ago. There was no forgetting the fragile, sweet smell of human blood before the stench of
burning houses overwhelmed it.

He knew that some people in the world cruelly force bamboo
slivers beneath a hapless captive's finger- and toenails, but the Kachins' form of torture was far worse. Instead they carefully inserted a
sliver deep into a man's penis. Then they lit the bamboo and watched
the flame creep up to and even into the victim. Remembering the
tales he had heard of these cruel and savage people in the Burma
jungles, the Japanese drew his knees more protectively against his
body. The Kachin saw and understood, and his curious smile broadened almost imperceptibly.

With great force of will the Japanese pulled his eyes away from
the Kachin's gaze. He looked at the American, sandy-haired, shaggy-
bearded, streaks of sweat on his soiled brow. The Japanese could no
longer deny the terrible thirst in his throat. He pointed to his mouth
and then at the roiled river rushing by just beyond a thicket. The
American looked away. He did not seem to notice, but the Japanese
knew he had seen and understood, and before he could look away,
his eyes had betrayed a twinge of sympathy. He, too, must be afraid
of the small brown Kachin. Or at least he did not seem to wish to go
against the will of this brown man, whose fierce people followed him
wherever he led.

Once again the Kachin's gaze captured that of the Japanese. Now the jungle man was slipping his knife into the scabbard at his belt. He laid the slivers out in a neat line before him. Then he stood up with the grace of a rising panther. Erect, he was taller than he had appeared, slender but wiry, his shoulders broad. The Kachin in his American jungle boots padded over to the Japanese. He grasped his neck and pushed him backward so that he could get at a pocket in his pants. He seemed to know exactly what he was looking for as he reached into the captive's pocket and took out a leather wallet, made in America, which had been purchased so long ago on the Ginza.

The wallet was cowhide, and it had always reminded the Japanese of Texas and the cowboy movies that he had seen in the theater near his home when he was a boy. The Kachin released him so that he could sort through the wallet. He drew out a picture of a boy, smiling a boy's eager and confident smile. Despite the dryness of his throat, the Japanese swallowed in anguish. It was his young brother's picture, taken on Boys' Day when the paper carp hung outside the house. The happy memory of that day only a year ago had faded. What remained was the stench of a burning village and of horror beyond any rational comprehension. There was no question at all. The Kachin who impassively studied the boy's face was indeed Zhing Htaw Naw, and he had been in the village.

The terror swelled in the captive's mind as he waited helplessly for the certain insertion of a wicked sliver. He watched the Kachin pad back to where he had left the bamboo. He picked up a section of the hollow stem from which he had sliced the slivers. Then he walked unhurriedly to the river and dipped it into the water. His eyes still had the same unfathomable profundity.

The Japanese straightened his shoulders. He must remember he was a civilized man, superior to this savage, a soldier of his emperor, a man who would not scream or whimper but would suffer and die in stoic silence. He was startled to realize that the Kachin was holding the tube of water out to him. He was even holding it to his lips so that the prisoner, now trembling all over with uncontrollable thirst and the unnerving rush of relief, could drink. The Japanese drank deep. When he was finished, he looked up at the same brown face with its gentle smile, the same eyes. The Kachin put the picture of his young brother back in the wallet and handed it to him.

In a few hours a small powerboat puttered down the river to the bank, and some American soldiers helped the Japanese aboard. They talked to the American officer and the Kachin duwa cheerfully and banteringly, as Americans do, and then set off upstream. The Japanese officer was to be taken to Colonel Joseph Stilwell, Jr., son of the redoubtable Vinegar Joe, who was the intelligence officer for the Northern Combat Area Command. His command post was in a Kachin village in the upper part of the Hukawng Valley. A guerrilla unit of the American-Kachin Rangers, Detachment 101 of the Office of Strategic Services, had captured him in an ambush that had wiped out most of his men, but now he was on his way to the American army. He would be interrogated in strict accordance with the Geneva Convention.

With him in the boat was a tidy package of fresh jungle leaves, moistened so that they would protect the contents. Inside the package were the ears severed from the men whom the officer had led to annihilation. How many Japanese were killed in the ambush? An American officer at NCAC might ask such a question. Simply divide the ears by two, a Kachin would respond. An American might shake his head at the barbarity of it all, but at least he had to admit that the victorious Kachins had not decapitated the dead as they had almost always done before. Progress was being made.

When the boat with its prisoner left the bank, Zhing Htaw Naw raised his carbine to his shoulder and aimed up at the roof of the jungle. His one shot brought a monkey tumbling down at his feet. He deftly slit the dying monkey's throat with the same knife he had used to whittle the bamboo slivers. Holding the furry throat to his mouth, he sucked deeply of the warm blood. That night the American officer and the Kachin devoured a succulent stew of monkey meat and roots dug from the jungle floor. All around them the Kachin hypenlas bedded down. Everybody slept well because the perimeter was secure. The only Japanese soldiers who had not fled the area were the dead ones.

*     *     *

Ngai Tawng's father was a thigh-eating duwa, the youngest son of a thigh duwa, or mag yisha, who under the Kachin laws of ultimogeniture was entitled as headman of his village to a hind leg of every barking deer killed in the jungle near the village and of each bullock slaughtered as a sacrifice. The boy, spear straight and tall for his twelve years, hiding in the thicket of bamboo beside the trail, had a sixteen-year-old sister and a fourteen-year-old brother at home, but as the youngest son he was the uma, who would some day be the duwa of the village to which the trail led.

Ngai Tawng had a Kachin aristocrat's high cheekbones and fine features. His dark eyes were intent, his nose sensed the air, and he canted his head to one side so that his ears could listen. Yet he saw, heard, or smelled nothing.

A moment or two before, he had been running agile and lithe along the trail, but the inexplicable prescience of his mountain and jungle people told him something was wrong. He slipped silently into the bamboo. Now he heard a curious far-off growl. It came from a distant cart track which led into the village from the opposite direction. No matter. It was faraway and could not menace him where he hid by the trail.

Ngai Tawng emerged from the bamboo, and his bare feet, making no sound on the earth, ran again. Soon he would be within the sweet smell of the wood fires of the villagers. Both his stomach and the sun told him that it was time for his mother and sister to be cooking the savory curry made from the jungle fowl he and his brother had shot down with blowguns that morning as they whirred up from the elephant grass that stretched on either side of the trail.

Ngai Tawng kept to the center of the trail because he knew that the tough kunai grass, reaching up to three times his height, could slash his bare legs and arms with its sharp edges. It might also hide a tiger dozing fitfully now that the late afternoon lengthened toward night. A tiger had padded near to the village only the night before, and he and his brother had seen its pugmarks close to where the elongated stone symbol rose in honor of Zhing Htaw Naw, the living phallus, the loving father, and the duwa kaba of all the villages in the district.

Now he was close enough to the village to hear the barking of the dogs and the shouting of children at play. Kachin children hush when an enemy raiding party is known to be in the vicinity, and the villagers kill the dogs so that their barking will not betray the village site. The familiar sounds were reassuring to Ngai Tawng, and the strange dread within him lessened. There was the place where he and his brother had shot the fowl, there were the tiger's marks, and there was the phallic stone. As was the custom of the young boys of the village, Ngai Tawng paused for a moment to embrace the stone. Often when he held his spare body against it, he felt his own small penis rise between his legs, but now there was no response. His

stomach gnawed too much, and there was a strange feeling of menace. At least the stone was in its proper place. As all the Kachins in
the Hukawng believed, the boy knew that the stone would move and
warn the people if there was any impending calamity.

The reassuring thought gave him pause, and he loitered a moment
near the deep ditch that surrounded the thatched-over grave of his
grandfather. Like bright children everywhere, he had a clear memory
of his earliest years, and he recalled the day long ago when the seer
from the village beyond the next had come to select the site of the
grave by divination. To most Kachins a grave, even that of a duwa, is
soon left to return to jungle, but Ngai Tawng had loved his grandfather, the jaiwa, who sang the sagas with his reedy spirit voice, and his
warm affection, and it had been he who had renewed the thatch
shelter.

Again the boy ran, but only to pause for a moment at the
nunshang, the sacred area where once a year the shrines were erected
in honor of the nats. A great sacred banyan tree arched over the circle of stones dedicated to the earth spirits. A tangle of trees crowded
close upon one another, for to cut a tree in the area was forbidden.
Nor could a man or woman be killed in the nunshang, for it was a
refuge protected by the spirits, where any person could find safety.
Even a Shan enemy of the village could hide in the nunshang with
impunity. He might emerge at night to kill village chickens or pigs,
but if he could reach the sanctuary he was safe from even the an-
griest householder who had been robbed. Yet never in Ngai Tawng's
lifetime had there been an enemy hiding in the sanctuary. Now there
were no enemies in the valley, only other friendly Kachin villages,
each following the ancient way of their Jinghpaw people. There had
been no feud since a girl who had been made pregnant by a boy from
another village had died at childbirth. It was her death not her preg-
nancy that was the offense. Even then, the feud had been confined to
the off-season when the paddy was safe in field storehouses. There
had been a cattle raid, but no life had been taken. Then the feud was
settled by the parents of the offending boy.

Ngai Tawng ran on into the village past the familiar thatched
bashas of woven, split bamboo standing on their teak posts out of
reach of prowling tigers. Each house was surrounded by a garden
with its vegetables, medicinal herbs, magic plants, and sometimes
poppies grown for opium. Poppies grew mostly in the gardens of old
people who could count on a pipe to give comfort at the end of a day

against the miseries of the body and the spirit that so often afflicted them.

Only the house of Ngai Tawng's father had a porch in front. It stood high and proud. The boy ran up the entrance ladder, raced past the cooking hearth and into the nadai-hap, the compartment kept sacred to the sky spirit, who was a relative of a distant ancestor. Often at this time, just before the evening meal, Ngai Tawng's father was here before the altar to the sky spirit, but today he had gone to the next village. The boy could hear his mother talking to his sister in her gentle voice. The household was quiet. There were good cooking smells. He looked up into the rafters of the house where the swords and spears from dead relatives were kept above the shrine. They had been there unchanged since Ngai Tawng could remember, gathering ever more soot from the smoke of the cooking fires. Now he found them reassuring. The strange unease quieted within him. He was safe at home.

Then there was the growl again, but now it was nearer. It was not an isolated sound rising and falling from silence back into silence but a sustained, far-off animal noise that grew in intensity as it came nearer, as if some creature were being tortured. Ngai Tawng hurried to the porch of his house and looked down the village street. The first Japanese vehicle came through the bamboo stand at the far end and rolled among the bashas. Dogs howled and ran from the machines and the soldiers who rode in them, their faces grim, their weapons held in readiness. Small children screamed and sought cover. There were a dozen vehicles, or more, and the soldiers sprang down out of them and moved among the houses, brandishing their weapons as if they were magic wands.

Ngai Tawng's brother appeared silently at his side. In his arms he held the flintlock musket that the English commissioner had given to their father so many years ago. A Japanese soldier pointed his weapon at the Kachin boy and fired a chatter of shots. The brother slumped to the porch flooring, and blood from a wound in his hip ran out in a pool. Ngai Tawng stripped off his loose longyi and stuffed it against the place where the bullet had struck to try and stop the blood. All around him the village erupted into women's screams, the crying of children, the shouts of men, the barking of dogs, the loud boom of the villagers' old muzzle-loaders, and the terrible chugging chatter of the Japanese weapons which spit death about them in any direction they were aimed.

At last the blood flow had stopped, and Ngai Tawng snatched up the flintlock that had fallen from his brother's hands. Even as he raised the weapon, a Japanese soldier leaped from the top rung of the entrance ladder and threw him down on the flooring. Then there were other soldiers running past him into the basha. The soldier held Ngai Tawng cruelly against the bamboo. He could hear his mother and sister screaming. He writhed and cried out, and for a moment he tore one arm loose and flailed his clenched fist against his tormentor's strong back. The arm was pinioned once again.

The soldiers were coming out of the basha now. They had snatched firebrands out of the earthen cooking hearth and were tossing them into the thatch to fire the basha. Rough hands seized both Ngai Tawng and his brother and carried them, struggling, down the ladder and into the street.

Ngai Tawng, his arms clamped to his side by the arms of a powerful soldier, even as he kicked and fought to escape, saw that all around him bashas were on fire, and men and youths who had resisted lay dead. There were dead women and girls too, but many others had been forced into the houses where they were screaming in terror and outrage as the soldiers raped them. It was time now to deal with the boys of the village, and as Ngai Tawng watched in horror, his cousin, a cheerful happy boy who always had a ready joke or a piece of mischief on his mind, was thrown down naked before the platform in front of his house where the skull of a bullock sacrificed in the spring still grimaced. His legs were torn apart by the laughing soldiers, and one took a sharp knife and cut his sex away. The soldiers forced open the boy's mouth and pressed the severed penis and testicles into it.

Ngai Tawng heard a deep and sorrowful groan, and for the first time he saw that the soldiers held the duwa kaba himself in bonds. They had brought Zhing Htaw Naw in a vehicle from his own village to see this grizzly insult to his people's seed. At the sight of a son of his people being emasculated the great duwa cried out in grief and anger. One boy after another was brutalized, and Ngai Tawng's brother, now bleeding again from his wound, was among them. Each fought furiously, but not one of them cried out in agony when the knife cut because the duwa kaba's now-smoldering eyes were on each of them. When the soldiers dragged Ngai Tawng forward and threw him down in the dust of the street, he tensed against the bite of the knife. Once the knife had bitten, he thought of seizing it when he could catch the soldier off guard. At first he thought of driving it into his enemy, but now he meant to drive it into his own chest. He would show the duwa kaba how a Kachin boy could die bravely. He would die quickly. He would not die with his blood running between his legs.

Unaccountably the knife did not cut, and Ngai Tawng found the soldier's grip loosen. A strong arm helped him to stand. A firm hand took his jaw and turned his face up, and Ngai Tawng found himself looking into a young Japanese face. He commanded the soldiers to step back. Ngai Tawng stood motionless, unable to run. The Japanese was taking something out of his pocket. It was a small leather case of some sort. He was removing a white square, with a picture of a smiling, happy boy about his own age. The Japanese compared the boy in the picture with Ngai Tawng. His hand briefly caressed the back of Ngai Tawng's neck.

The touch of kindness destroyed the Kachin boy's resolve more than any amount of cruelty could have done, and he broke into sobs. The Japanese shoved Ngai Tawng gently away, and when the boy did not run, he slapped him hard on his buttocks. At last Ngai Tawng realized he was free, and he ran. He sprinted past his burning house, where even in his terror he could see the fire licking around the spears and swords of his ancestors in the rafters. He ran out of the village and into the nunshang. Leaping among the thick tangle of vines, shrubs, and trees, he threw himself full-length upon the damp ground. His heart beat as if it would burst out of his chest and explode among the moldering vegetation. His stomach retched even though it was empty. Then he lay still as if he, too, were dead like so many of the fellow villagers he had known all his life. In the depth of his horror he could still feel the eyes of Zhing Htaw Naw on him, and he knew that he would arise again some time and walk away down the jungle trail. Some day he would make these terrible men in the vehicles suffer in their turn. Now he lay still, though insects crept over him, and a snake slithered over the small of his back. He would lie like a naked baby against the breast of Ga Shadup, the earth spirit who was both mother and father, until he could find the strength to get to his feet and walk down the trail.

*     *     *

He had a pointed nose and a jutting chin, and even after he had shaved, which was very seldom, his face had a dark cast to it. He was a man born to a beard. He wore ragged and soiled khakis and a dilapidated Aussie hat with a pheasant plume stuck into the crown. His stocky body seemed bursting with energy, but at the same time his manner was surprisingly gentle. Father James Stuart belonged to the Columban Order, which had its headquarters in Navan, some twenty miles northwest of Dublin, Ireland.

James Stuart was born on December 7, 1909, in a snug house on Lawford Street in Moneymore, County Derry, in Northern Ireland. His mother and his father, a cattle dealer, presided in an affectionate way over a large family, which was devoutly Catholic. Like other bright and promising lads in the town, Jim decided at an early age to go into the seminary. Family and community alike would be proud of a boy who grew up to be a priest. Young Stuart attended the parish school at Moneymore and then went south to enter the seminary at Navan.

"The Irish are forever longing to be at home but are at the same time forever restless wanderers," remarks Rosemarian Staudacher, Father Stuart's biographer. It was not unexpected that the newly ordained priest would volunteer for missionary service in Burma, halfway around the world. In November, 1936, he arrived with five other Columban priests at Bhamo, on the upper Irrawaddy River, to work with the Kachin people. It was at the bazaar in the Burmese town that he encountered his first Kachins. They had walked down from the high Sinlumkaba Hills east of the valley along the China border to bring baskets of fruits, vegetables, and chickens to trade for cotton flannel, tobacco, tea, and spices. The men wore rectangular skirts and loose jackets. Later Father Stuart was to learn that these skirts were the clothing of the southern Kachins and that those of the northern Kachins were tubular. The women were dressed in bright red, handwoven wool skirts with yellow and black designs. They had leggings of the same design, which reached from their ankles halfway up the calf. Their jackets of black velveteen jingled with silver ornaments. Some had encircled their hips with thin bamboo hoops painted with black lacquer. Both men and women carried handwoven bags dyed with jungle plants and decorated with seeds and with the teeth of both wild animals and men. Each male who had come of age had a razor-sharp, swordlike knife called a dah which dangled from his waist in a scabbard that was often magnificently ornamented. It was said in the bazaar that by swinging his dah in a flashing arc, a

Kachin could cut a man in half, from his shoulders clear to his legs, in one blow.

The Kachins had the oblique eyes and high cheekbones of the Mongolians. Although the men rarely stood more than five-and-a-half feet in height, they were sturdy, lithe, and proud and assured of bearing and had a way of looking the lowland townspeople full in the face. Some anthropologists have compared their appearance to that of the Sherpas of the Himalayans and even to the Apache Indians of the American Southwest, but to Father Stuart they were simply the people he had come to the frontiers of civilization to meet. They lived in a great horseshoe of mountains extending from the Hukawng Valley east along the Tibetan frontier and down the Chinese border as far as the Shan States along the Thai border. Some lived across the Indian border in Assam to the west, and some across the Chinese border in Yunnan to the east. They respected no national boundaries and moved as they willed through a wilderness that was still mainly unexplored. Father Stuart, learning their language and their customs at the Columban Mission, was preparing to go into this wilderness even though Burmese converts and the British civil officers in Bhamo alike warned him that in a region where there were many fierce peoples, the Kachins were the fiercest people of them all.

"Your head will end up on a post outside a village as a sacrifice to the nats," he was told.

In 1939, the young priest took the train to Myitkyina at the headwaters of riverboat navigation on the Irrawaddy, 820 miles north of Rangoon, then the showplace capital of British Burma. The railroad from Rangoon ended there. Hundreds of years earlier Myitkyina had been the capital of the ancient Shan state of Waingmaw, and in early Chinese chronicles it had been mentioned as a place where placer miners washed gold from the river sands. In those times salt was also mined at Myitkyina. In the vast heartland of Asia it was hard to say whether salt or gold was the most precious commodity. When Father Stuart got off the train at the railroad depot, he found himself in a town of fifteen thousand people or so, spread out beside the river, its tin-roofed temples and houses somnolent beneath the shady trees that kept off the hot sun. By then most of the Shans had long since been replaced by Burmese.

As he bought supplies and the necessary gear for a trip into the north, Jim Stuart met Kachins in the bazaar. They spoke the same language as the people he had known in the south, but they were bolder and more direct in their way of saying things. If they were indeed headhunters, they gave no indication. They answered Father Stuart's questions about the enormous wilderness that began a score of miles north of the town where the Irrawaddy was formed by the confluence of the Mali and the Nmai hkas, as the Kachins called the great rivers down which Himalayan snow melt cascaded to the sea, swelling to rushing floods during the torrential monsoons. Then every stream became treacherous to cross, and the trails became quagmires.

"Giant leeches infest the jungles," a Britisher warned the young priest when he learned that he was going to try and penetrate the area called the Triangle, which lies between the Mali Hka and the Nmai Hka. "Best not to be caught out there in the monsoons."

One morning Father Stuart set off into the unknown. For twelve days he traveled north looking for a suitable place to build his mission among the Kachin people. When his provisions ran out, he lived on jungle roots resembling sweet potatoes and on fish and game. Leeches sapped blood from his legs. One wound became so infected and ulcerated that there was nothing to do but return to Myitkyina. In a few weeks, when his wound was healed, he tried again, only to return once more in failure. On the third attempt, with a fellow missionary, Father Dody, he set off once more into the jungles. They were joined by four Kachin boys who were no doubt attracted to Father Stuart's cheerful and warm-hearted ways. It was not uncommon for Kachin boys of thirteen years or more to roam for hundreds of miles through the mountains and jungles exploring both their own emerging manhood and the wild country in which they were to live their lives.

The boys led Father Stuart and Father Dody to the Kachin town of Sumprabum far up the Hukawng Valley. After resting in Sumprabum, the missionary explorers and their young guides set off into the foothills. They walked to the southeast for two days and crossed three mountain ranges, each more precipitous than the other. At last they came to Kajihtu, an idyllic village with an elevation of about thirty-five hundred feet and a delightful climate. Here Father Stuart and Father Dody, helped by the villagers, built their mission of slit bamboo and thatch.

Every morning when he awoke, Father Stuart thanked the Lord for bringing him among the Kachin people, whose cheerful ways had so much appeal. But Father Dody felt differently about living in this remote village. He finally asked to be taken out of the mountains, and young Father Johnny Dunlea took his place. The new arrival had been with Father Stuart for scarcely two months when both the priests came down with typhoid fever. There was no sure cure. If a man was strong enough, he survived. Father Stuart was strong enough, and he survived. But Father Dunlea died in his arms. From then on Father Stuart was alone with the Kachins.

The Kachins proved hard to convert to Christianity, but at the same time they were loyal friends, who accepted the priest and his curious beliefs and strange ways as if he had always been part of their lives. On Father Jim's thirty-second birthday, he was deep in the jungled mountains along the Hukawng Valley when Japanese planes attacked the American base at Pearl Harbor on the faraway island of Oahu. He heard no news of the attack, and if he had, it is not at all likely that he would have expected that the Japanese would ever appear in his remote valley and that he would play an extraordinary role in the events that would unfold.

*          *          *

After their overwhelming victories in South Burma, the Japanese armies swept north in the spring of 1942 to complete the conquest of the country. When Myitkyina fell, Lieutenant General Shinichi Tanaka, the Tiger of Malaya in command of the 18th Division, who had captured Singapore from the British and spearheaded the drive northward through Burma, determined to invade the Hukawng Valley. Burmese and Shan agents in the hire of the Kempi Tai, the Japanese secret police, told the general that the Kachin people, unlike the Burmese and the Shans, were loyal to the former British rulers of the land, and that until they were invaded and destroyed they would always be a source of danger. They would welcome the British back.

The Japanese army, assisted by Burmese army units, moved in strength into the Hukawng. The first Japanese-Burmese attack was ambushed by a small Kachin force armed with shotguns, flintlock rifles, and blowguns. The Japanese and Burmese lost eighty dead, and the Kachins, firing from their jungle, only three. When the Kachins ran out of ammunition, they vanished into the wilderness. It was then possible for the Japanese to advance up the valley, attacking the villages they could reach with their motorized transport. Most of the Kachins lived on inaccessible mountain ridges, but on the valley floor there were several villages that were vulnerable to Japanese attack. One of these was the village where Ngai Tawng's father was the duwa.

It was the Kachin's old enemy, the Shans, who advised the Kempi Tai that the Japanese could terrorize the Kachin mountain warriors into making peace by carrying out ferocious attacks on the lowland villages. Fire, rape, and the mutilation of young boys would intimidate the Kachins into surrender. In a society where sexual freedom among unmarried young people was approved, rape did not hold the terror it aroused in most cultures. It was considered brutal and wrong, but a girl who suffered such an attack suffered little psychological damage. But to destroy the seed of the people even before it could ripen would, on the other hand, have a powerful effect on the Kachins, whose religious beliefs included a pervasive fertility cult that related the fertility of the womb to the fertility of the fields. Kachin leaders, said the Shans, should be taken hostage if possible to witness crimes and report to their people in the mountains that the Japanese were impossible to resist and terrible in their anger.

The Japanese soldiers followed their orders, sometimes in horror and disgust, but often with enthusiasm, surprising village after village. They flayed living men as object lessons, and burned men, women, and children alive in bashas drenched with gasoline. They emasculated the boys except in the large town of Maingkwan, where a more humane commander was content with rounding them all up and shooting them to death.

*     *     *

Father Stuart was at Kajihtu when a Kachin who had escaped the Japanese terror in a village in the southern Hukawng arrived and told his story. He immediately set out to bring help to survivors. Walking the by-now-familiar jungle trails and tracks with a handful of Kachins from the village, the priest encountered old men, women, and children who came out of the jungle to which they had fled.

One of the refugees was Ngai Tawng. The boy had risen before dawn from the leafy floor of the nunshang and without a glance at his still-smoldering village had set off along the trail he had taken only the day before. He moved at a Kachin's swinging run. When his keen nose smelled the awful odor of another burning village at a distance, he left the trail and made a wide detour around it. He lived on jungle fruits. Breaking off a long pole, he knocked down papayas from a tree, making sure to avoid the partially ripened fruit because he knew it still had a bitter flavor. He ate the sharp, tangy berries of the chinbombee. In the afternoon of the second day he came upon a jeco tree, which he climbed eagerly, his feet and thighs grasping the rough bark with something of a monkey's agility. At the very top of the trunk grew the huge fruit, up to nine inches in diameter, succulent and refreshing.

He traveled for several days into the north. At night he scarcely slept for fear of tigers, but when he stepped out of the jungle and confronted Father Stuart and the other refugees he still stood straight and proud and looked the white man who was with people of his own nation square in the eyes. With his knowledge of the Kachins, Father Stuart recognized the rank and quality of the naked boy. His bearing and manner were unmistakable.

"You are the uma of a village," he said with his voice showing both respect and the gentle compassion one would feel for a suffering child.

"If my father still lives, I am the uma," Ngai Tawng replied.

A Kachin standing behind the priest took a cake of cooked rice from his shoulder bag and handed it to the boy. Despite the gnawing in his stomach, Ngai Tawng remembered his manners and offered to share the rice cake with Father Stuart. The priest shook his head, and the boy broke off a tiny piece of the cake and dropped it to the jungle floor as a tribute to the nats. The priest smiled at the pagan boy and hoped that in the course of things he would one day be a Christian. The boy, his mouth now full of rice, smiled back. The tragic course of things was never to permit his conversion, but he was already Father Stuart's friend.

The days that followed were confused. Later, Ngai Tawng was not able to recall the trails and roads that Father Stuart and the refugees followed. Other Kachins from the destroyed villages—mainly children with a scattering of women and old men—came out of the jungle to join them. Finally there were perhaps one hundred. Whatever men and older boys had escaped the Japanese had gone off deeper into the jungles with Zhing Htaw Naw, who had been set free. But the duwa kaba had not reacted precisely as the Japanese had been told he would. As the Kachins in Father Stuart's party all knew, he was already gathering his men from the mountains to fight back against the Japanese. When Ngai Tawng learned one night from a woman that his father had escaped death and was with Zhing Htaw Naw, he felt a fierce joy. Some day he would join his father, and he, too, would make the men in the vehicles die in a cruel and proper fashion.

It was the middle of June before the refugees reached the vicinity of Sumprabum. The monsoons were beginning, and Father Stuart knew he must soon find shelter. The prospect of shepherding women, children, and old people through drenching rains, leeches, and malarial mosquitoes had little appeal. One day a small girl came down with a fever. A huge canker appeared inside each of her cheeks. It was a foul infection of the mucous membranes of her cheeks and lips. Soon she was so exhausted that Ngai Tawng took her on his back and carried her. Within a few days the sore had eaten its way through her face. What only a short time before had been smooth brown skin now fell away as parts of the girl's cheeks disappeared altogether. Though Father Stuart had some medical knowledge, he had no experience with *cancrum oris,* which is virtually unknown among the Kachins. Perhaps it had been brought into North Burma by the Chinese who retreated through the area after the Allied defeat in the south. There is no way of knowing for certain. One afternoon Ngai Tawng tenderly laid the little girl down on a grassy spot by the trail. Father Stuart knew by the compassionate slump of his shoulders that she was dead.

The next day the duwa of Napa, a village in the foothills, met the refugees on the trail.

"My people and those of Byiklau La will come and bring the children to Napa," he said.

Byiklau La was the duwa of Wasathku only a mile away. The two headmen and their people helped the refugees to Napa where they were taken to new bashas built by the villagers. Ngai Tawng, staying in a large room with other boys, slept on a bedroll given to him by the priest. He could look through the cracks in the floor and watch the chickens scratching about in the dirt. He felt at home with the sounds, sights, and smells of a Kachin village all around him. All the refugees began to take heart. The monsoons whirled down on the village. Winds blew branches from the trees, scattered leaves, and drove rain into the houses.

Before long, however, Father Stuart learned that a column of Japanese cavalry was riding down the road toward Napa. He waited alone just outside the village for the Japanese to come. A major cantered at the head of his men. As the Japanese rounded a turn in the road, the major stared with astonishment at the white man who stood in the way. He raised his hand to halt the column. His horse clip-clopped up to Father Stuart. He swung down out of the saddle, unhooked his pistol holster, and stepped up close.

"Are you Chinese?" Father Stuart asked in English, his blue eyes all innocence.

"No, we are Japanese," the major replied in English. "Are you British?"

The major spit fiercely on the ground.

"No. I am Irish."

Father Stuart spit with precision exactly where the major had.

The major glared. He drew his samurai sword and scratched a rough map in the dirt at the white-man's feet. He pointed to the lower part.

"This is England," he said.

Then he pointed to the upper part of the map where by all rights Scotland should have been.

"And this is Ireland. Where are you from?"

Father Stuart indicated with the toe of his boot that he was from Ireland. Then he asked the Japanese for food for the refugees in the village. The major was very possibly the very same officer who had directed much of the horror in the Kachin villages. There was a grim silence.

"We have no food to give you," the major finally said. "You may remain with your refugees, but do not get in our way. You will be watched."

He mounted. With a wave of his arm he gave the order to the column to advance, and the horsemen swung off down the road. Each man in the column glared at the priest in imitation of their commanding officer—except for a young lieutenant. It was the same lieutenant who had spared Ngai Tawng in the village, and as he passed Father Stuart he gave him a look that revealed the anguish in his heart.

In the weeks that followed, Father Stuart often visited the nearby camp established by the Japanese. He begged for food. The major had ideas of his own. He had been told by a Shan informer that a British civil officer, a Colonel Stevenson, had given Father Stuart money to take care of an earlier group of refugees, whom the priest had spirited away to distant Putao before the Japanese seized Myit-kyina. Father Stuart was said to have three thousand rupees in his possession. The young lieutenant was sent with a party of men on

June 19 to demand that two hundred rupees be given to the Japanese army.

"The money is to take care of the children," Father Stuart explained to the officer.

Yet he knew that he could not protest too much against the thievery for fear that the Japanese might then demand the entire sum. He was surprised when the Japanese reached into his own pocket and took out ten rupees and gave them to him.

"You may keep the money for the children," he said in English.

He did not ask again for the two hundred rupees. After he returned to the camp, the lieutenant also sent men carrying three bags of rice for the refugees. In a day or two Ngai Tawng saw him walk into the village. The Japanese looked right at him, his face reddened with emotion, and he glanced sharply away. He demanded to know where he could find Father Stuart.

For at least an hour he talked to the priest. In Tokyo he had been an art student. He had gone to a Baptist Sunday school. Father Stuart must not think that all Japanese people were cruel or indifferent to the plight of refugee children. There was a war, of course. When he climbed down the ladder from Father Stuart's basha, he found Ngai Tawng waiting for him. The boy was leaning on the porch post of a basha across the dusty village street. He pulled the new longyi made for him by a village woman more tightly around himself and stared at the Japanese. The boy said nothing, but when the lieutenant walked back down the village street, his gaze followed him until he had passed out of sight. The Japanese felt his eyes on him the entire way. The boy was as dangerous as a krait, that small but deadly serpent that lived in the jungle. This was the boy he had spared in the village. Perhaps he did so because he looked something like his own brother, but more likely it was because it was too terrible a thing to put an end to a young person who had so much grace and spirit. Now the boy was a living reminder of his own cruelty and a constant threat. Would he tell the Catholic priest about that day in the village?

\*     \*     \*

The plane came in the morning. The Kachins stared upward with awe as it circled around the village. Father Stuart saw the stars of the American air force on its wings. There was no explanation as to where it had come from or why it had flown over Napa. Father

Stuart only knew that he must be the first to tell the Japanese of the plane. He hurried to the camp and asked to see the major.

He told him excitedly that a Japanese plane had swooped over the refugee village.

"No," replied the major. "The plane was American."

"You are wrong," said Father Stuart. "I clearly saw your star on it."

He pointed to the red star on the major's cap.

"The Japanese star is red," said the major. "The white star is American."

There was no question about it. The white priest was either a first-rate idiot or an extremely duplicit man. Why take a chance? He must be put to death. When the priest had gone, the major called the lieutenant to him and ordered him to take four men to Napa and search Father Stuart's basha.

They found Father Stuart living in a structure built by the British, who had left behind a broken radio transmitter when they departed. The radio was in a closet. The Japanese party soon found it. Fortunately, many parts were missing and vital wires had been cut long ago. It was clearly inoperative, but it certainly could be used as an excuse for a firing squad.

The lieutenant stared at Father Stuart for several moments. Then he picked up the transmitter and carried it to the edge of a cliff beyond which there was a sheer drop into the jungle below. He tossed the radio over the edge and watched it crash through the canopy of trees and disappear.

"My major won't even bother to look down there, and my men are loyal to me," he said to Father Stuart.

The days slipped by. The refugees gathered health and strength. Some time earlier, when the Chinese soldiers passed through the Sumprabum area, they had threatened to kill the pigs owned by the villagers at Wasathku. The villagers had chased their pigs into the jungle so the Chinese could not seize them, and now, months later, they roamed free. Byiklau La, the duwa, came to Father Stuart and told him that the refugees could eat all the pigs that they could capture. When Ngai Tawng and the other boys failed to trap the pigs with snares set in the jungle, the priest went again to the Japanese camp. He visited the lieutenant and told him about the pigs.

"Could you give me a rifle?" he asked innocently. "I can then shoot the pigs, and the children will have meat."

"It is against regulations," said the lieutenant.

He could not possibly let the priest have a rifle, but he would lend him a .38 Webley revolver captured from a British officer. In fact, the lieutenant would show the priest how to shoot the gun. That afternoon they went out into the jungle, and the Japanese soldier taught the Irish priest how to discharge the weapon on the downward stroke of the arm for the most accurate aim. Father Stuart brought the revolver back to Napa, but he never did shoot a pig with it. He kept it to use against the first Japanese soldier who turned to violence in the village of the refugees. He was a crack pistol shot, and he had only accepted the officer's instruction to put his suspicions at rest.

Several days later, in the evening, the refugees, young and old, gathered with the villagers to listen to Father Stuart talk. Then they sang old Kachin songs about a fire in the middle of the village compound. The old melodies from the ancient homeland beyond Tibet, the deep voices of the men and the treble of the women and children singing their fanciful descants, sounded out into the surrounding jungle. These were songs of adventure and love. Father Stuart had invited the young officer who had taught him how to shoot to come to the sing. When he arrived, Father Stuart waved him to a position of honor by the fire.

At first he listened to the eerie nasal singing of the savage people around him, but when the priest urged him to sing too, he sang an American song from an old motion picture, *Rose Marie*. He had a baritone voice, and he did his very best to sound like Nelson Eddy. If he hadn't kept singing "Rosalie, I love you," instead of "Rose Marie," and if his tongue hadn't tripped over the tricky English words, he might have carried it off. No mind. When he finished singing, the Kachins all laughed and applauded. Father Stuart wiped tears of laughter from his eyes and clapped along with them.

The Japanese felt a touch on his arm. He looked to the side, and he discovered that Ngai Tawng had come to sit beside him. The boy was staring into the fire. His finely cut features were in profile, and it was hard to see the expression on his face. Would he pick this time to give him away? At the thought the lieutenant felt his arm tremble. The jungle boy sensed the movement, and he turned toward him. His eyes glowed in the firelight.

"I am Ngai Tawng," he said in a soft voice.

The Japanese could not understand the strange liquid words, but when the boy pointed to his chest, he knew that he was telling him his name.

"I am an uma of my people, and you have spared me."

The boy drew his longyi aside to reveal his sex.

"I am a whole person, as you can see." Tears welled up in his eyes. His voice broke as he continued. "I know terrible things, but in my heart I am thankful for what you could do. It was little compared to the big terrible thing, but it means very much to me."

The boy took the officer's wrist in his hand and squeezed it. Then he held his own wrist against the officer's wrist. He guided the officer's hand against his breast so that he could feel his beating heart.

"I hate your people for what they have done to my people," he said, his dark eyes looking deep into the officer's eyes. "I shall seek revenge until I am dead, but I do not seek revenge on you, for you are my friend in spite of it all."

There was scarcely any doubt about his meaning, although the Japanese only knew a few words of Kachin. The officer felt a lightening of the spirit. When the next song began, he listened to the boy's clear voice singing the strange melody through the nose in the Kachin way and tried to sing with him in his baritone.

The singing ended, and the fire died down.

"Father, I have sinned," he said to Father Stuart just before he left.

"You need not seek absolution," said Father Stuart, who had seen and heard everything. "You have been forgiven by an innocent child, and there is no absolution beyond that."

The very next day the Japanese major called the lieutenant and the other officers to him to discuss what to do with Father Stuart. The lieutenant argued that he was a holy man, a dreamer, a man who seeks only to look after the refugees, but at the end of the discussion the major announced that the priest must die. Within half an hour of the meeting the lieutenant appeared at Father Stuart's basha.

"It has been decided that you are to die," he said. "Men are coming to kill you."

Father Stuart hurriedly gathered up some belongings and disappeared into the jungle. When the soldiers came, he was gone. Soon the refugees dispersed to villages in the mountains and beyond. Ngai Tawng and some other hardy boys started a journey of several hundred miles far to the east to the China border and south. It seemed as if they were only going on a youth's adventure quest. The shepherd had gone, and the flock was seeking new shelter. Many refugees from the villages destroyed by the Japanese in the Hukawng Valley fled into the remote reaches of the Taung Hka where later their new villages were found by Detachment 101 officers. Villagers who had escaped the carnage at Lat Kahtawn built their new village on the east bank of the northern Tabyi Hka. The only way that the village could be reached from the outside was by wading knee-deep to hip-deep up the river for five miles. The old village sites in the Hukawng were far too vulnerable, and as recently as 1978 the Kachins still had not gone back to them. On official maps of the northern Burma wilderness the old village names still appear, but beneath them appears the legend, "deserted."

\*     \*     \*

It was at Sinlumkajee, a Kachin village on the trail that led up into the mountains from Momauk in the Irrawaddy Valley, east of Bhamo, to Sinlumkaba, that I met Ngai Tawng. I was walking the trail with Mike, a Bengali radio operator, and decided to sleep that night in the village. The duwa had made us comfortable beside the fire in his basha, and we ate a fiery curry of deer meat and gritty rice. Fatigued from the trail, we fell asleep.

During the night I shifted position on the hard bamboo slats of the floor and awakened to find a boy sitting beside the fire, his eyes on my face. As soon as he knew that I had seen him, the youngster smiled, and he held out his hand to take mine. I paid no attention and fell back to sleep. Twice more I awoke to find the boy still sitting and watching me. In the morning he was still sitting there, but now he was dozing, his arms around his legs, his head on his knees.

The headman's wife was stirring up the coals to cook breakfast.

"Your son has been here all night," I said. "Now he sleeps."

"He is not my son. He is Ngai Tawng, an orphan, and he wants you to take him with you as a soldier," she replied.

Soon Ngai Tawng awakened, and now my eyes were on him. He stretched like a cat, and his face had a confident, pleased smile. The boy was certain that I would take him with me, and, of course, he was right.

"You are too young to be a soldier," I told him as he led Mike and me along the trail to Sinlumkaba.

"Other hypenlas are no older," he said.

He was right again, for many of the hypenlas of the American-Kachin Rangers were boys in their early teens. Most of them were teenagers, in fact. When we reached Sinlumkaba, Pete Joost, Area I commander for OSS Detachment 101, agreed to take Ngai Tawng in. We found Pete, naked in an icy mountain spring, taking his morning bath. At his invitation we all immediately peeled off our sweaty clothing and plunged into the water with him. Ngai Tawng forgot his desire to be a soldier long enough to splash water at his new American friends, but when he was out on the banks of the spring, he shook the water from his head the way a dog shakes and demanded that I ask the white duwa kaba if he might be enlisted. He pointed at the bundle of his clothing disdainfully.

"I want to dress in a soldier's uniform and fight for my people with the Americans," he said.

Pete Joost laughed.

"Of course, you must be a soldier," he said.

We had a hard time finding GI fatigues and canvas jungle boots small enough to fit Ngai Tawng, but we managed, and soon he was outfitted. Over the months that followed, the boy's unflagging good nature, bright spirit, and mischievous ways made him a favorite—first with the Americans at Sinlumkaba and later with Hiram Pamplin, Stan Spector, and me in the last campaign to open the Burma Road. He quickly learned English. Somebody at Sinlumkaba—Bob Rodenberg, I think—had given him a red neckerchief, which he wore with pride. Because he seemed to embody all the hardy young masculine virtues, Pamplin labeled him "the Boy Scout." From the start, he was, above all, my young Kachin friend, and I determined that when the war was over I would bring him to America and give him a good education so that he might return to his people as a leader. This was a dream we would have for many of our young Kachin brothers.

It never occurred to me at first that there was a tragic story within Ngai Tawng, even though sometimes he would cry out in his sleep in fear and awaken from a nightmare. But soon, around campfires and in the smoky interiors of village bashas along the trails of the Loilun Range, sad and lonely in the misty mountain night, he told his story. Smokey, the cook, a Kachin who had been a headhunter in the northern Triangle, would listen in somber sympathy.

As it turned out, neither I nor any of Ngai Tawng's other American friends were to bring him to the United States to study. One night, in a show of carelessness unbefitting a Kachin boy, he was captured by Shan villagers, who in their hatred for his people tortured him and put him to death.

This story of the Americans and Kachins and their secret war behind the Japanese lines is dedicated to the Kachins and to Ngai Tawng in particular, who died like a true uma of his people.

1941-42

# The Invasion

Flying in over the mountains and the green jungles and the trim fields of emerald paddy, the Japanese bombers vectored in on one of humanity's most magnificent monuments to peace. For twenty-five hundred years the golden spire of the Schwe Dagon Pagoda has risen for 326 feet atop a spur of the Pegu Yoma. It is the largest Buddhist pagoda in the world. The city that surrounds it is at least a thousand years younger, and it did not become an important place until 1753 when the Burmese King Alaungpaya rebuilt it at the victorious conclusion of his war with the rival Mons. He named it "Yangon," the "End of Strife." Under the British Yangon, strategically situated on the Rangoon River twenty miles upstream from the Gulf of Martaban, became Rangoon, capital of Burma.

It was now December, 1941, and the bombers struck shattering blows at the docks, railroad yards, and oil refineries. Explosions erupted along the waterfront. Isolated bombs screamed down on the homes of the rich and the poor, but the poor, who lived closer to the docks, were more vulnerable. The air attack on the city honoring the end of strife marked the beginning of war.

In late December British authorities ordered that platforms be erected in the tops of giant teak and mahogany trees between the Thai border and the capital city. When Burmese air watchers climbed up to the platforms to keep an eye out for the return of the Japanese bombers, devout Buddhists took them for holy hermits. Every morning the faithful placed gifts of fruit and rice at the bottom of their trees. In the green land of Burma, with its godowns bursting with the rice harvest and great rafts of precious teak drifting down the rivers to sawmills at Moulmein and Rangoon, it was hard to believe that the war was about to extend its reach. It seemed as unlikely as the return of the days of Kipling.

In ornate Government House at the heart of Rangoon, Governor Sir Reginald Dorman-Smith pondered the latest intelligence reports from British agents in Japanese-occupied Bangkok. An Irishman who had joined the army and commanded a company of the 15th Sikhs in the border war with Afghanistan in 1919, Dorman-Smith had returned to Britain to go into politics. He had risen through the ranks of the Conservative party to become Neville Chamberlain's minister of agriculture. Winston Churchill, a fellow cabinet member, came into a meeting one day with a proposal that he said would help prepare the nation for what everybody in the room expected would be war with the Axis powers. Churchill urged that every four-footed farm animal in the country be killed so that all available wheat and corn could be used to sustain the population when the Germans inevitably began submarine warfare and cut Britain off from American and Canadian aid.

"I don't even care to comment upon such a plan," Dorman-Smith informed Chamberlain.

The idea was dropped, and Dorman-Smith had made a political enemy. When Churchill became prime minister, far-off Burma seemed remote enough from the scene of war to make it a logical place to exile the man who had opposed his plan. But now, ironically, the war seemed close at hand. With his neat moustache, his khaki walking shorts, his lean muscular legs, and his swagger stick, Dorman-Smith seemed the very model of a British governor in a tropical land halfway around the world. He studied reports that were ominous: the Japanese were readying the 33d and 55th Divisions for an invasion of Burma.

At Dorman-Smith's side during those tense hours at Government House was his military secretary, Colonel Wally G. N. Richmond, also moustached, and ramrod-straight, soft of speech, devoid of nerves. Dorman-Smith had first met his companion on the Afghan frontier when British troops were thrusting through the Khyber Pass to put down rebellious tribesmen. Wally Richmond was then a youthful pilot in the Royal Flying Corps, and he flew his Bristol fighter in support of the ground troops. As he winged low over Afghan soldiers, one of them fired at his plane. The bullet struck the magneto, the plane lost power and pancaked in a dry riverbed. Tribesmen dragged the stunned Richmond from the cockpit. Years later in his Sydney, Australia, home, he told how he was jostled and hauled before the chieftain.

"They argued whether they should turn me over to the women for the 'death of the thousand cuts' or not," he explained. "The chief decided to cut a deck of cards to see whether I should live or die. The cards let me live."

Reginald Dorman-Smith was one of the British officers who arranged to ransom Wally Richmond for several hundred thousand cartridges, valued at about $10,000. The Afghans turned the flyer over to the British on Christmas Day, 1919. The next year he left the Flying Corps to become a district forester in Burma in such districts as Pyinmana, Bhamo, Katha, Myitkyina, and Moulmein. He hired gangs of men and elephants to drag the great teak logs to the rivers down which they floated to the sawmills. He discovered a jade mine, collected Burmese art, and went on hundreds of tiger shoots. He knew the jungles and mountains through which the Japanese must invade Burma. His knowledge now served the governor of Burma as it was later to serve Detachment 101.

Dutifully, Dorman-Smith reported the situation in Southeast Asia to his old opponent Winston Churchill. There were about twenty-five thousand troops of the understrength 1st Burma Division and the 17th Indian Division who could come to Burma's defense. Though most were natives, the forces included about four thousand British and eight thousand Indian soldiers. The Japanese forces outnumbered them by at least two to one. Churchill found the report from the king's representative in Rangoon to be ominous enough, but there was little he could do. Beleaguered Britain needed troops, munitions, guns, and planes available for its own defense.

In Russia the Germans had clamped an iron siege on Leningrad and had advanced to the outskirts of Moscow from which they were slowly falling back before the counterattacking Red army and its natural ally, winter. In Libya the British were at last on the offensive against Rommel's Afrika Korps. It now seemed, for the first time in the war, that Hitler might have overreached himself and that a victory might indeed turn to ultimate defeat. The main objective of the British was to provide their North African forces with everything they needed to win a final triumph over Rommel's army. The Japanese were attacking the Philippines, sweeping southward through the Pacific, and driving the British out of Malaya. There were no available reinforcements anywhere in the world—neither British, nor for that matter American—that could be dispatched to Burma.

There was nothing for Dorman-Smith and his military commanders to do in their turn but to outfit their meager troops and move them into position to block the historic invasion routes from Thailand as best they could. Even so, there seemed no reason for panic, because mountains and jungles separated Thailand from Burma, and the Japanese army would find only a few primitive roads through them. Reports from Bangkok indicated to Dorman-Smith and Richmond that the Japanese attack would not come until April. But sooner or later, they realized, the Japanese invasion would inevitably begin, because only by conquering Burma could the Japanese cut the Burma Road and block the shipment of vital supplies and munitions to China through the port of Rangoon. On December 16, a small Japanese detachment seized Victoria Point at the southernmost extremity of Burma. They landed unopposed, and there appeared to be no reason to waste vital troops in an attempt to dislodge them. There was nothing much left to do but wait for their next move.

*     *     *

One pleasant summer day in the summer of 1941 some British army officers boarded the train at Mandalay station. Most of the other passengers were women and children, traveling as they had for generations to the cool hill station of Maymyo where strawberries and roses imported from England grew and where the bloom could be kept on pale English cheeks during the prostrating heat that was building up in the humid lowlands. The train chuffed up into the foothills of the Shan Plateau to the tidy town with its stucco bungalows. Timber bosses, traders from Rangoon, and government officials lived there. Dotting the landscape were a cricket field and English hedges, and in the English church on Sundays the boys and men who sang in the choir had real English voices. So many important government officials were in residence in Maymyo that the town was sometimes called the summer capital of Burma.

The officers went to the barracks on the outskirts of town where the Gurkha Rifles were housed. They had a fine bagpipe band that performed in the little park in the cool evenings. A Scot could grow misty-eyed out of homesickness as he listened to these dark men from the Himalayas play an old melody from his homeland.

But the officers had little interest in bagpipes, strawberries, and church on Sunday. It was their task to establish a secret camp where a special detail of one hundred volunteers enroute from North Africa were to be trained as guerrilla leaders for China. Japan was pressing China hard, and the officers knew that though their country was still at peace with Japan, everything must be done to strengthen the Chinese ability to resist.

The site for the camp was picked, and the officers let it be known around town that it was to become the Bush Warfare School. Nobody could be sure how many of the smiling Burmese and Shan servants in the stucco bungalows were covert agents of the Japanese. It could only be hoped that the true purpose of the Bush Warfare School would not be discovered. As it turned out, it was here that many of the British and Burmese personnel who were later to serve with such distinction in Detachment 101 would be trained. By August the one hundred volunteers had arrived and erected bamboo bashas.

\* \* \*

What makes a guerrilla fighter? Bob Flaherty had been born in Philadelphia in 1921 of British parents, but as a child he was taken home to England where he spent most of his boyhood. At the age of fourteen he quit school for a cabin-boy's job on the Cunard Liners. In 1936 young Bob tried to enlist in the British navy, but the examining physician discovered that he was color-blind. His disability did not keep him from the army, and he soon found himself stationed in Egypt with a tank command.

When war began, desert rats such as Bob Flaherty went on long forays into the Libyan sands, guided only by the sun, striking sudden blows out of nowhere at the Italians, who were bound to the forts and oases of the region. After fighting in the Ethiopian campaign that returned Haile Selassie to his throne Bob volunteered for commando training, although he knew that the average length of life of a commando in combat was estimated to be one minute and forty seconds. This proved to be an optimistic estimate. In late May, 1941, two thousand commandos including Flaherty had been sent to Crete to reinforce it against German paratroopers. Only fifty-two commandos survived the Battle of Crete, and Flaherty was one of them. He was captured by the Germans.

One night he slipped through the barbed wire of the camp where he was imprisoned, climbed down steep cliffs to the sea, and hid in a cave. Another British soldier, a fine mechanic who had escaped the Germans, had also found shelter there. When they came upon a wrecked LST beached nearby, the mechanic worked on the engine. As he tinkered, other British soldiers who had avoided capture also found their way to the cave until by the time the boat was ready to put to sea there were forty-eight of them. They pushed the boat off from the shore, swam beside it to shove and pull it out to a safe distance, and then started the engine. It chugged, and soon Crete was a blur of cliffs fading into the blue Mediterranean.

It took the LST ten days of intermittent drifting and puttering before the cruiser H.M.S. *Liverpool* picked up the thirsty and near-starving men and brought them to Mersa Matrûh on the Egyptian coast. That night German bombers appeared over the harbor, and in the raid half of the men who had escaped from Crete were killed. Flaherty escaped again. When he heard that volunteers were being sought to go to Burma to be trained for a hazardous mission into China, he decided that he might as well be one of them.

Once the volunteers were recruited, they were given charge of a thousand Italian prisoners of war. The Italians were happy to be out of the war, and gave the soldiers no trouble as they sailed on a British ship through the Red Sea, across the Arabian Sea, and around the southern tip of India to Colombo, Ceylon. There the soldiers left the now-jubilant Italians ensconced at a comfortable camp and went on to Calcutta and then Rangoon. From Rangoon they took the train to Maymyo.

At the Bush Warfare School the volunteers trained round the clock. They were regularly called out at 3 A.M. to do a fifty-mile trek into the jungle. North of Maymyo is an area of marshes, pools, and paddies. There they crawled on their stomachs, despite the lurking kraits and cobras, to simulate raids on bridges and culverts. Bob Flaherty became expert at judging the weak points of a bridge. He could understand at a glance exactly how much gelignite or dynamite it would take to destroy it and precisely where he should place the charge.

The guerrilla fighters were taught the Chinese language, culture, and way of life. Jackie Carter, an exuberant youth whose father had been a banker in Peking, was their teacher. They studied Japanese military methods, occupation policies, culture, and language. They practiced landings from boats, and learned to parachute from low-flying planes. When the Japanese seized Thailand, Bob Flaherty was sent to Taunggyi in the southern Shan States to prepare resistance. It was now too late to go to China. A wiry youth who had become immune to danger was waiting in Taunggyi, just as Wally Richmond and Sir Reginald Dorman-Smith were waiting in Rangoon.

\*          \*          \*

On January 20 the Japanese army invaded Burma in force from Thailand. The unbelievable news shocked Dorman-Smith in Rangoon. Quickly the 17th Indian Division deployed to meet the attack, but the two elite Japanese divisions pouring over roads and tracks traced out for them by Burmese sympathizers swept down upon Moulmein. Where the Indians and British stood and fought, the Japanese carried out brilliant enveloping movements, so that the outflanked defenders could only fall back, regroup, stand, and fall back again. It only took eleven days before the Japanese stormed into Moulmein. Within a few more weeks all of the Tenasserim Coast was in their hands, and on February 24 the Japanese army crossed the Sittang River. The British, Indians, and loyal Burmese troops fought hand to hand in bloody desperation to prevent the crossing. But even the arrival of some light tanks brought to Rangoon by ship failed to stop the Japanese. They seized Pegu and cut off the capital city from the north.

\*          \*          \*

Pat Maddox never weighed more than 120 pounds. Son of an English father and a Burmese mother, he had red hair and swarthy good looks. As a youth, he went to work in the rest house of the Tavoy Tin Company on the Tenasserim Coast as a houseboy. Other boys might gamble and play cards when they weren't sweeping out a guest room, bringing whiskey and soda with a big professional grin on their young faces, and otherwise tending to their patrons' needs, but not Pat. He read books. He studied engineering, and in time he became a prospecting engineer who scouted the jungled mountains along the Thai border for new deposits of tin. He also became an expert with explosives.

As the Japanese juggernaut rolled through the Mawchi area, the precious tin mines were captured intact. Japanese commanders flashed the good news back to Tokyo. But then one night tremendous explosions ripped through the mines, wrecking any possibility that they would produce tin for the conquerors. Pat Maddox had somehow infiltrated back through the Japanese army to Mawchi, and with his knowledge of both high explosives and the mines had set off the blasts. He then infiltrated back out of the Japanese-held territory. Later, as the Japanese invasion swept into North Burma and the Bawdwin mines at Namtu fell, he once again slipped behind the enemy's lines to use his knowledge of demolitions to destroy the rolling mills at the mines. Once he covered up his red hair with a tur-banlike gaung baung tied in a knot behind the right temple, and knotted his striped longyi in front in the correct male fashion, "Red" Maddox was indistinguishable from countless young Burmese who were drifting with the tides of war. When Red Maddox returned safely from his second exploit, Great Britain awarded him the Military Cross for valor. He, too, would become in time an agent and guerrilla leader in Detachment 101.

\*     \*     \*

When the Japanese army threatened to invade Burma, Burmese nationalists went to British officials and offered to help in the defense of the nation if Britain would guarantee independence after the war. The British refused. Since they had overthrown the half-mad King Thibaw and annexed his kingdom to Lower Burma in 1885, they had done a great deal of good in the country. Railroads and roads ran into the interior. Steamers, their paddlewheels chunking, went, as Kipling's song says, "from Rangoon to Mandalay," and for that matter, on up the Irrawaddy River to Myitkyina. Mines and oil fields were discovered and developed. Teak logs were rolled from the forests by elephants and floated down the rivers to the sawmills. Production in the fertile delta expanded so enormously that the nation became the greatest rice exporter in the world.

British Burma was wealthy and growing wealthier, but it was not all a happy country. Chettyar moneylenders came from South India and exploited the Burmese farmers with usurious interest rates. Unable to repay their loans, the farmers lost their lands to the Chettyars who then charged ruinous rents for their use. Indians and Chinese came to dominate the nation's business life, and the British kept close control of the profitable shipping, foreign trade, and mining industries. Excluded from political and economic control, the Burmese became increasingly restless. There were occasional efforts at reform, but they were insubstantial, given the enormity of the problem.

Even so, when the Japanese invasion came, most Burmese remained loyal to the British, who could at least be counted on for integrity and honesty in their dealings and whose government by law offered the possibility of a bright future. However, many chose to help the invaders in any way they could. The Japanese promised a great deal. Wouldn't it be better to trust a fellow Oriental? The Buddhist pongyis, who had been among the most determined foes of the British, provoked many of the insurrections and acts of sabotage that occurred behind British lines and provided much of the intelligence that assisted the Japanese advance. While most Burmese did their best to help British women and children in their flight before the Japanese army, some seized every opportunity for torture and rape.

\* \* \*

As the Japanese advanced upon Rangoon they were assisted by the Burma Independence Army, led by Bo Yan Naing. At most there were twenty-five thousand Burmese in the BIA. In training they carried knives and staves but few guns. They counted upon charms supplied by pongyis to bring them victory; soldiers submitted to being tattooed with extravagant tattoos on their chests and legs to make them invulnerable. Bo Yan Naing's men wore amulets with sacred relics or images suspended around their necks. The relics were tightly rolled in tinfoil and inscribed with magic spells.

Only the most gullible village youths were likely to join an army armed in the main by charms and protected by magic, but they were available in every Burmese village where Bo Yan Naing recruited. To provide the young men with proof of his own invulnerability, Yan Naing thrust an empty revolver in his mouth and pulled the trigger over and over. When it did not fire, the watching boys believed that the commander could not be killed by a gun. There was no question about it.

Commandant Than Nyun did Yan Naing one better. He tested a sacred amulet by tying it to a hen and then shooting the bird.

"I shot it ten times at close range," he explained to those who had seen the hapless bird literally blown apart before their eyes. "Amazingly, none of the bullets penetrated the bird. But it died all the same, being pulverized internally."

Each household in nearby towns was required to send rice packets for the BIA soldiers in training to eat. The packages were supposed to contain a portion of curry or some other condiment. If the curry or condiment was missing, the soldiers could be quite certain that the family who sent the package were British sympathizers. Some village girls and women put notes with their packages to show disapproval of another sort. The Burmese independence leader, Ba Maw, who became the Japanese puppet prime minister, remembered several such messages that reached his BIA unit early in the war.

"You are leaving me behind with a child, you big, black-hearted demon," read one.

"My heart's blood, how can you leave me just when our love is blossoming like a flower, our happiness is shining like the moon, and I have become pregnant?" read another.

It is not hard to imagine what the Japanese army, moving with remarkable precision on its way to victory in Burma, thought of its ally, the Burma Independence Army, and its quixotic ways.

*       *       *

The Japanese army was closing in on Rangoon. Japanese warships had swept into the Bay of Bengal, defeating a British naval detachment and sinking coastal shipping at whim. There would be no reinforcements reaching the beleaguered capital. Though Sir Reginald Dorman-Smith was reluctant to flee, by his own account of the event, "burly English pilots" forced him, an outraged Irishman, into an aircraft. The plane took off and flew to Maymyo from where he could direct the resistance.

Looting broke out in the city as police deserted their posts. Indian servants of the British who had fled to the docks hoping to board ships and return home, found themselves the target of pent-up Burmese anger. Snatching up staves and knives, the Burmese attacked them.

Just as the Japanese vanguard reached the city on March 8, the doors to the prison and lunatic asylum were thrown open, and their inmates rushed out into the city. One demented Indian strode naked into a fashionable café, sat down at a table, and ordered his dinner. To the gaping Burmese he seemed the very epitome of the fall of British Rangoon, although his performance would have been far more appropriate if he were an Englishman. Stripped by the Japanese army of the trappings of empire and their reputation as invincible rulers, the British were fleeing from the city as best they could. With them fled a terror-stricken crowd of Anglo-Burmese families and tens of thousands of Burmese as well. For many of these refugees, accustomed to the comforts and conveniences of a prosperous city, death would be waiting in manifold forms along jungle tracks far to the north.

With Rangoon's port in their hands the Japanese were able to land two more divisions to reinforce the 55th and the 33d. The 18th and 56th Divisions, fresh from the conquest of Malaya and Singapore, came ashore in fighting condition and hurried northward to where the British were still trying to halt the advance. The 18th joined the 55th before Toungoo, and the 56th came to the support of the 33d above Prome. The Japanese strategy was simple enough. One task force was to push north up the Irrawaddy River Valley, and the other was to carry out a motorized envelopment to the east toward Lashio, a key town on the strategic Burma Road.

Just four days before the fall of Rangoon, Major General Joseph W. Stilwell arrived in Chungking, the wartime capital of China. He hurried immediately to see Generalissimo Chiang Kai-shek. On March 10 he was appointed Chief of Staff of Allied forces under the generalissimo. Within a week he was in Burma, where for all practical purposes, he was to be in command of two division-sized units of the Chinese army, which had entered Burma in an eleventh-hour effort to protect the Burma Road lifeline. Shortly before, on March 5, General Sir Harold Alexander arrived to take over as British commander-in-chief in Burma.

Earlier in the invasion Chiang Kai-shek had sent General Claire Chennault's American Volunteer Group to assist the Royal Air Force in the air defense of Rangoon, the entry port for Burma Road supplies. The American and British pilots together shot down at least 250 Japanese aircraft at a loss of 50 of their own and gave strong support to the outnumbered Allied ground forces. Then in late March the Japanese Air Force struck the RAF's base at Magwe in overwhelming strength. By the time the last Japanese plane dropped the last bomb and finished its strafing run, the RAF was virtually out of action. Confronted with swarms of Japanese planes, the AVG had no choice but to withdraw from its base at Toungoo to Lashio, and not long afterward they returned to China. There was no longer any air opposition to the conquest of Burma.

The Japanese forces plunged northward in spite of determined resistance from the British and Chinese. Both the Chinese Fifth Army and the Chinese Sixth Army now moved toward Burma, but most of these forces never reached the fighting front. In total about twenty thousand Chinese soldiers did manage to engage the Japanese, but these soldiers were no match for them. In mid-April the Japanese routed the Chinese from Loikaw, and in two weeks a motorized column raced two hundred miles northward to seize Lashio. The left flank of the defending forces now was turned, and although the British, Indian, and Chinese forces to the west were to fight dogged battle after dogged battle, their ultimate defeat was ordained.

The Japanese not only had superior strength, but their ability to filter through defending lines in small parties and set up roadblocks in the rear, where their opponents thought themselves safe, created confusion and dismay. Fifth columnists were everywhere; many Burmese, now convinced that the Japanese would win, hampered the British, Indians, loyal Burmese, and Chinese however they could. One day the Japanese bombers roared over Mandalay with its red temples, white pagodas, and stupas. They took aim at the red-washed stone walls of the ancient palace of the Burmese kings. When the bombs thundered on the city, huge orange flames leaped high in the air, and clouds of acrid smoke billowed. The fifth columnists had cut the fire hoses and knocked out the waterworks. Firemen pumped water from the moat surrounding the palace in a vain attempt to save the burning city. Although it was the Japanese air force that began the tragic burning of Mandalay, fifth columnists and looters spread the flames whenever they appeared to be dying down, and for twenty-seven days and nights the city burned. The Japanese army occupied the devastated city on May 1.

*    *    *

"She'd had a vision from her Lord," explained Bob Flaherty whenever he told how the Japanese came to capture him in Taunggyi. "I'd had a vision from my CO."

He was describing Mrs. Hannah, an American Baptist missionary who refused to quit her mission as the Japanese army advanced through the Southern Shan States. Chinese units, making a last attempt to stop the Japanese, entered Taunggyi, only to retreat in disorder when the redoubtable Japanese came into view. Flaherty not only couldn't bring himself to leave Mrs. Hannah to be taken by the Japanese, but had the bad luck to be with a group of Chinese when enemy soldiers reached the town.

"They considered that I would be able to tell them something about the intentions of the Chinese, so they placed me in a box for five days a week in an effort to make me talk," Flaherty remembers.

"When I wasn't in the box, I waited on the Japanese officers, who were much amused to have British houseboys."

The Japanese were not very much amused when Flaherty seized a bayonet from a guard one night and ran it through him. Another British soldier was killed in the melee that followed and Flaherty was wounded but, taking Mrs. Hannah with them, Flaherty and some other captured British ran off into the hills. Following back roads and trails, the escaped prisoners made for the Laotian border. They crossed into Laos and found their way through the jungles along the border until far to the north they were able to cross back into Burma's Kengtung State. The Japanese army had long since captured Lashio and had reached Wanting where the Burma Road crosses into China. Flaherty and the others often had to detour around towns and villages as they moved on north to avoid being captured again.

"Sometimes we walked ten to fifteen miles a day, and sometimes only two miles," he recalls. "We suffered from amoebic and bacillic dysentery. I had a 104 degree temperature and passed only mucus and blood."

Their troubles didn't end when they crossed into China. Bandits attacked. On the road to Kunming they bargained for opium. Taking a piece of opium about half the size of a pencil eraser, Flaherty bubbled it over a hot pan. Then he swallowed it as if it were a pill to try and stop the dysentery. With incredible fortitude, the group finally reached Kunming in September. Mrs. Hannah, weighing a comfortable 180 pounds with a Red Cross patch now proudly displayed on her shoulders, and Bob Flaherty, now weighing 80 pounds, flew from Kunming to Dinjan and Calcutta on a Flying Tigers cargo plane. There Flaherty was hospitalized for a hundred days. As he lay in the hospital, he read an article that Mrs. Hannah had written about her experiences in a Calcutta religious newspaper.

"All our problems were caused because we marched on Sundays," the Baptist missionary concluded.

\*     \*     \*

The Japanese army's fighting columns punched their way ever northward until the only escape for both Allied civilians and soldiers was over jungle and mountain tracks. Wounded soldiers and 4,040 refugees were lucky enough to make it out of Burma by air. They were picked up by Pan American Airways pilots and planes, which had arrived at Dinjan in Assam on April 6, and the next day began flying into Burma to rescue refugees. Every incoming flight brought ammunition, food, and other supplies to the men still struggling to hold back the Japanese and brought out civilian refugees and wounded British and Indian troops. Flight crews roused themselves from bed at 4 A.M. every morning, and at the break of dawn they were airborne to Burma. The lumbering C-47 transports were easy prey to the far-ranging Japanese Zeros, and many crashed in flames into the jungles known to be inhabited by dangerous Naga and Kachin headhunters. The pilots, fresh from the States, became accustomed to the stench of diseased and unwashed evacuees, the reek of gangrene, and the evidences of mass nausea as the planes pitched and tossed over the mountain ridges.

By mid-April the only airport open to the British and American transport pilots was Myitkyina. Father James Stuart was there at the landing strip when Sir Reginald Dorman-Smith boarded one of the last flights out of Burma. This time the governor went aboard dejectedly, but without protest, and the plane took off in a whirlwind of dust. His departure robbed the Japanese closing in on the city of "quite a plum," as Father Stuart later noted in his journal.

It was at the airport that Colonel Stevenson approached Father Stuart and offered him three thousand rupees to help buy supplies for refugee children, who were camped nearby. Until now they had been cared for by the Church of England, but could Father Stuart take the children to a safe place? Of course, he answered, and his first flock of young refugees were taken on an overland trek northward to far-off Putao. He still had the three thousand rupees on his person more than a month later when the Japanese, advancing into the Hukawng Valley, met up with him.

The monsoons caught many of the refugees from Burma's cities who had struggled northward before the advancing Japanese over the trails that climbed over the Chin Hills for 250 miles into India's Manipur State. Men, women, and children waded in mud up to their knees and slithered down the precipitous slopes. When the trail became too steep to remain standing, the refugees crawled on their hands and knees through the mud to reach the top. Worn out by dysentery and malaria, with their life's blood sucked away by leeches that clung to them from bushes and dropped down on them from trees as they passed, many fell by the trail and died. When the streams fed by the monsoons raged and became impassable, they built crude shelters of boughs and waited for the waters to fall. They lay down in their sopping clothes and waited for death. Bluebottle flies laid their eggs on the living when they became too weak to brush them away. The maggots that hatched out fed on the bodies of the dead. Brilliant butterflies also flickered about the corpses, because in this land they, too, fed upon the dead.

The huge striped tigers devoured the refugees at will. Kraits and cobras struck at their bare feet and brought them down in agony by the trails. Even the elephants led the suffering people astray. Their wide trails, leaves and branches intertwined overhead, looked like roads to the city people who came upon them. But they led not to a village but only deeper into the jungle where no escape was possible.

Thousands died in the exodus. The exact number will never be known, but estimates range all the way from a few hundred thousand to upward of five hundred thousand. Some escaped. General Stilwell and his staff, well organized and well supplied, walked out with a minimum loss of life. They were safe in India before the monsoons began to fall, but six months after they reached Manipur, half-dead refugees were still stumbling out of the jungle.

Wally Richmond, having seen Dorman-Smith onto his plane at Myitkyina, refused to take a seat that could better by filled by a wounded man. He closed up his house, where he had lived as a district forester, gathered together 108 refugees, including a Miss Gibbs, the servants from Government House in Rangoon, and a bull terrier named Jess. He led his motley group through the Hukawng and over the Naga Hills into India. They, too, beat the monsoons and were safe in India by the end of May. Miss Gibbs died of exhaustion two days after her arrival.

An extraordinary British major, Oliver Milton, gathered together over one hundred women and children and brought them out of Burma with no loss of life. He had spent years in the jungle extracting teak and searching for mineral deposits for Steele Brothers, a mining concern. Later he was to return to Burma as an agent for Detachment 101.

But none of these men who brought refugees to safety could surpass the pluckiness of Norman Richardson, for he was only fourteen years old. Norman's mother died as the Allied retreat turned into a last rout. He led out three of his brothers and sisters, including an eleven-month-old baby, whom he carried until it died.

When Major General Joseph W. Stilwell reached New Delhi, he summed up the Allied disaster in a characteristically pithy way.

"I claim we got a hell of a beating," he said. "We got run out of Burma, and it is humiliating as hell. I think we ought to find out what caused it, go back, and retake it."

Even as he slogged over the muddy jungle trails, Stilwell had been planning for the reconquest. He committed his plan to paper soon after his arrival in New Delhi.

"My belief in the decisive strategic importance of China is so strong, that I feel certain a serious mistake is being made in not sending American combat units into this theater," he wired to the War Department on May 25.

It was Stilwell's proposal that Chinese divisions in India be trained and equipped to join with American combat forces in retaking Burma and reopening the Burma Road. Many would play a part in this great enterprise: the Indians, the British, and the Americans and Kachins of Detachment 101.

# The Recruits

Millard Preston Goodfellow had been a war correspondent in World War I and later president and publisher of the *Brooklyn Daily Eagle* and the *Pocatello* (Idaho) *Tribune*. He had always had a lively sympathy for underprivileged kids, which led him to serve as a volunteer with the Boys' Clubs of America for over forty years. He became a senior director. Then one day in mid-1941, as America's entry into the war seemed more and more imminent, this seemingly quiet and kindly man was asked by his old friend Bill Donovan to come to Washington to help him at his mysterious office in the grotesque Old State Department Building next to the White House on Pennsylvania Avenue.

The office of the Coordinator of Information had recently moved from its first cramped quarters in the Bureau of the Budget where there had been one telephone for Donovan and his seven assistants. It was on Donovan's desk, and when it rang everybody scrambled for it. In its new quarters the COI was still anything but a well-known Washington institution, although it was growing at a prodigious rate. President Roosevelt had issued an executive order to create a worldwide intelligence network. One day, in fact, a mail carrier turned up at the front desk of the Old State Building with a registered letter for Colonel Donovan.

"Donovan?" asked the guard. "I don't know of any Donovan."

He sent the letter back to the post office.

During the months and even years to come, men and women recruited by what was first the COI and then the Office of Strategic Services, the OSS, were to arrive in Washington and often spend days trying to find the organization to which they were to report.

As the shadowy COI took form, though in something of an official limbo, Preston Goodfellow played a surprising role. The kindly

Boys' Clubs director was made deputy director of special activities. The name Special Activities Goodfellow was coined to differentiate that group from Special Activities Bruce, which was headed by David K. E. Bruce, later to become one of the postwar period's most distinguished American diplomats. Bruce was concerned in the main with intelligence, whereas Goodfellow dealt with such niceties as clandestine warfare and sabotage. As it turned out, this also meant that Goodfellow would become the self-styled midwife at the birth of Detachment 101.

*　　*　　*

On Sunday, December 7, 1941, William J. Donovan, always a football fan since the days when he had played the game at Columbia University, was in a box at New York City's Polo Grounds. The Giants were playing the Dodgers. Brooklyn kicked off and had scored the first touchdown. Donovan, a Giant fan, grumbled to his companions. His blue eyes lost their good-natured twinkle and took on the icy glare that aides, either in his Wall Street law office or in two world wars, knew meant he was dissatisfied with somebody's performance. In this case, it was the eleven Giants down there on the field who were disappointing him.

Wild Bill Donovan was one of the most decorated Americans in the nation's history. Douglas MacArthur and he were the only men in the nation ever to wear the country's three top military awards: the Congressional Medal of Honor, the Distinguished Service Cross, and the Distinguished Service Medal. His exploits on the battlefields of France in World War I had made him a schoolboy's hero throughout the 1920s and 1930s. Except for his Catholic beliefs, many thought, he might have become president. In the 1930s, as Europe slid inexorably toward war, Donovan had served abroad time after time as Roosevelt's personal representative and shrewd observer. He had visited Greece and Bulgaria to try and persuade their governments to defy Hitler, and in Yugoslavia he had hatched a plot that overthrew the pro-Nazi regent's rule in favor of the youthful and pro-Allied King Peter. His fact-finding missions to besieged Great Britain had helped to persuade President Roosevelt that the British, far from being defeated beyond hope, as Nazi sympathizers were indicating, would not surrender and could not successfully be invaded. He had become an expert on how the Nazi fifth column operated and how resistance movements could be fostered. Now in late middle age, growing pudgy, but his energy and enthusiasm still as remarkable as ever, his mind at its fullest power, he was gathering together America's first coordinated intelligence service. "Wild" Bill seemed anything but "wild." His soft, measured voice actually became softer still when he was angry. He was not angry now, only a trifle disgusted.

The Dodgers had just driven again to the four-yard line, and the Brooklyn fans were screaming for another score, when the public-address loudspeaker boomed through the tumult.

"Colonel William Donovan, come to the box office at once. There is an important phone message."

When Donovan reached the box office, he learned that the president wanted to see him immediately. A military plane was warming up at La Guardia to bring Donovan, Vice President Henry Wallace, Postmaster General Frank Walker, and Presidential Adviser Judge Samuel Rosenman to Washington. Japan had attacked Pearl Harbor. Unlike Father James Stuart or Zhing Htaw Naw in the remote Hukawng Valley of North Burma, Colonel William Joseph Donovan was immediately thrust into the vortex of action.

In Washington Donovan conferred with President Roosevelt and went to work. He redoubled his efforts at recruiting and training his intelligence force. In their later writings about the period, some of his men testified to Donovan's ingenuity and persistence.

"Donovan did a fine job of recruiting able men for our operation, but he had gotten a cold shoulder from the military services. Not a single project had been approved," Preston Goodfellow wrote to Jay Niemczyk, an officer in Detachment 101, in describing the early months of war.

"The admirals and generals were not at all interested in helping Donovan to become Roosevelt's knight on a white horse," added Carl Eifler, the first commanding officer of Detachment 101.

When Preston Goodfellow learned in mid-January that that peppery curmudgeon of a general, Joseph Stilwell, had been named Chiang Kai-shek's Chief of Staff of Allied forces, he asked Donovan for permission to prepare staff studies for an intelligence and irregular warfare operation in Asia. Burma, that strategic country through which the Burma Road carried vital supplies to China, was to be given special study. The Japanese invasion was sweeping ahead, and if it were fully successful, Burma might well become the first test of Donovan's ability to organize clandestine resistance. Goodfellow submitted his COI studies through a friend in Stilwell's office in the old Munitions Building. Days passed, and there was no reply.

\* \* \*

Preston Goodfellow's phone rang. It was his friend on General Stilwell's staff, who asked him to come right over to the Munitions Building to get some favorable news. Goodfellow jumped in a cab and sped to the rambling building that was a carryover from World War I. He found his friend in a cubicle of an office, and he had a grin on his face. General Stilwell liked the project, and he was going to give the COI a go-ahead on it.

Goodfellow was jubilant. He decided that, exciting as the news was, he must not share it with anybody, even with Bill Donovan, until Stilwell's approval was down on paper.

That afternoon Donovan phoned and asked him to walk home with him. Donovan's house was on R Street, NW, in Georgetown, and Goodfellow lived only a few blocks away from him, on Q Street. Both men often walked home as a way of relaxing from the tensions of wartime Washington. Goodfellow readily accepted. Should he tell Wild Bill about Stilwell's forthcoming approval? No, he had better not. Nothing was ever certain in Washington until the proper papers had been signed and delivered, and even then things were seldom definite, particularly if an admiral or general was involved. At least so it seemed to Goodfellow, who had come to share his chief's frustration at the military brass's consummate skill at evading decisions.

The wintry dusk was settling down on the city that evening in early February as Donovan and Goodfellow walked in gloomy silence. They strode down Pennsylvania Avenue past the funeral parlor that had been in business since the Civil War, the chili joints, other tacky little businesses, and the Tower Restaurant.

The Tower was Donovan's favorite greasy spoon. He usually put in an eighteen-hour day at the office. If he could get away around dinner time, he often gathered up a few assistants and strolled over to the 1925 F Street Club. This brick building, painted cream behind its wrought-iron fence and sedate green ground cover, was an unlikely setting for the World War II intelligence chief, but many of the most significant COI and OSS decisions were made in its dining room. Donovan and Goodfellow had talked over the plans for Burma at the 1925 F Street Club. But on many days, crisis knew no dinner hour. Then, around midnight, alone and lost in his thoughts,

Donovan would walk along the deserted avenue to the Tower, where he would munch on a hamburger, sip coffee, and talk to the young quick-order chef behind the counter. The teenage youth's brash good humor helped cheer up the man who sat at the pressure center of one of the world's intelligence nets. The boy never knew who the soft-spoken and gentle man was, but he remembered that some times he was so preoccupied that he forgot to leave a tip. Often Donovan would return to his office for a few more hours to pore over the intelligence reports that arrived night and day from agents abroad. Other times he would continue on his walk home, often cutting through Rock Creek Park.

"Never did I see Donovan so low in spirits as on that walk," Preston Goodfellow wrote to Jay Niemczyk. "I had decided to await formal acceptance by General Stilwell before saying anything to Donovan about it. But when I reached his home, I weakened. On the promise by Donovan not to mention to anyone my advance information, I told him we were going to get approval of the Burma operation."

Donovan's mood shifted instantly. He himself neither drank nor smoked, but he invited Goodfellow into the house for a glass of sherry. Once within the yellow brick house, Donovan and Goodfellow settled down in French Provincial chairs beneath the high ceiling and talked for perhaps an hour. Then Goodfellow went home. He knew from experience that he had not seen the last of Donovan for the night. Donovan's wife, Ruth, stayed in their New York apartment on Sutton Place because she had no taste for Washington and her husband's night-and-day responsibilities, and he was alone except for servants. That night when Donovan went to bed he read, as was his habit, first in one book and then in another, putting the half-read volumes face down on the bedside stand and on the bed around him. He rarely slept more than five hours, and tonight, his mind teeming with excited thoughts and plans, was not likely to be an exception. Finally he telephoned Goodfellow to ask some questions he had not thought to ask.

"He phoned me three times that night," Goodfellow remembered, "the last at 3 A.M."

"You're not in bed, are you, Preston?" he asked.

"No, I'm just sitting here waiting for your call," replied the sleepy deputy director.

"Well, get your pants on and come over here. I want to talk more with you about Burma."

Goodfellow walked through the silent streets to Donovan's house where be once again extracted the promise that nothing would be said until official approval came through. Donovan once again agreed. His gloom of the evening before had vanished completely at what he saw as the first important break in the prejudice and hostility that the military had been showing toward America's new central intelligence.

The regular staff meeting attended by all of Donovan's top-level aides was held the next morning. As was the rule, Donovan called on each unit head for a report.

When all the reports had been made, he announced, "Gentlemen, I have reason to believe that our Burma show will be approved. I want all the Far East studies and operational plans speeded up—those for China, Thailand, and other fields."

Goodfellow could only shake his head.

"Of course, everyone went out of that meeting jubilant and got busy," he told Niemczyk. "Three days later the staff study came back from General Stilwell. It was disapproved."

Donovan called Goodfellow into his office, and his eyes had an icy glint in them.

"Preston, your intelligence was a little faulty," he said.

"No," Goodfellow replied, "it wasn't. Let me have that study, and I'll find out what happened."

Goodfellow returned to the Munitions Building and knocked on the door marked "General Stilwell." Stilwell's rough voice rasped, "Come in."

"General," said Goodfellow without wasting time in preliminaries, "I had something to do with the secret Burma operational study, and I came to ask you what is wrong with it."

"Not a thing," Stilwell answered.

"Then why the disapproval?"

"It's the officer you put in charge," said Stilwell. "That man, if sent out to blow up a bridge, would blow up a windmill instead and come back with an excuse."

"General," said Goodfellow, "I don't know this officer. I went to the adjutant general and asked for the name of a senior regular army officer—one who knew the Far East and, if possible, had an Oriental language. This officer's name came up. He not only had all the qualifications I requested, but had been on your staff. So, General, why don't you name the man?"

General Stilwell glared through his steel-rimmed glasses. Peremptorily, he asked Goodfellow to sit down. He picked up a pencil and began to list about a dozen names on a pad of paper. Then he started to cross them out. When there were only two names remaining on the list, he shoved it across the desk to Goodfellow.

"Get either of these two men and your project has my approval."

When Goodfellow got back to his own office at COI, he checked out the availability of the two men on General Stilwell's list. The senior officer, a lieutenant colonel, was in Texas.

"I went after him first because of his seniority," wrote Goodfellow to Niemczyk. "He died the day before I got to him."

The second man was Captain Carl Eifler, on duty in Hawaii. In 1934, Carl Eifler had been a young customs agent on the Mexican border and a reserve officer in a unit commanded by then Lieutenant Colonel Stilwell. He had turned in a report one day about Japanese military personnel rebuilding a landing strip twelve miles across the border in Baja California. The report created quite a stir, and Mexico decided to remove the Japanese. In his recent command in California, Stilwell, worried about Pacific Coast security after the Pearl Harbor attack, had asked Mexican authorities to double-check that no vestiges remained of the Japanese military activity south of Tijuana that had been discovered seven years earlier. Perhaps this is why Stilwell thought of Eifler. Or perhaps he remembered him because no one who has ever met Carl Eifler is likely to forget him.

\*     \*     \*

In his early forties Eifler was no bull of a man; he was a mastodon incarnate, a person with implacable elephantine rages, massive strengths, and unshakable loyalties and convictions, and he was always intelligent and imaginative. He added up to 250 pounds of muscle and bone, which he applied impartially to Western boxing and Japanese jujitsu. He found it impossible to speak more softly than a loud roar. On a scouting mission in Burma's Naga Hills, he once met with an equally stentorian officer with whom he struck up a ready friendship. Ray Peers, later to become 101's commanding officer, remarked, "It was said many times that these two officers provided the only instance in modern warfare wherein two persons were able to communicate with each other at a distance of about fifty yards without benefit of a radio."

After his duty on the Mexican border, Carl Eifler was transferred to the U.S. Customhouse in Honolulu where he became the deputy collector. He kept up his reserve membership, and as the international scene darkened in the summer of 1941, he was ordered to active duty as the commanding officer of Company K in the 35th Infantry. Eifler was the only reserve officer in the regiment, and the regular army officers looked upon him as a blustering and overeager nuisance whose command techniques were most likely learned in movies about Tamerlane or Attila the Hun.

"He was like a bull in a china shop, he was so anxious to succeed," recalls Colonel John Coughlin, a West Pointer, who then commanded Company L of the 35th Infantry.

Coughlin, lanky and six foot five, soft-spoken but a boxing champion at West Point, was as astounded as the other officers at Eifler's formidable excesses, but he could not help liking him. It was generally conceded that Coughlin commanded the crack regiment in the battalion, and Eifler, realizing that his own regiment needed considerable improvement, in his usual right-to-the-heart-of-the-matter way went to see the West Pointer.

"Will you help me?" he asked.

Coughlin agreed, and from then on he dropped in at Eifler's headquarters at ten o'clock almost every morning for a cup of coffee and a chance to discuss Company K's progress. By late fall Eifler's Company K was a military unit that would give a good account of itself in action. The other officers in the battalion began to respect its hulking commander. Some time that autumn a new man joined Company K. He was an athletic young sergeant with a ready grin. The newcomer's quiet charm hid a quick mind and steely courage. His name was Vincent Curl.

"Vince Curl would gladly have killed for Carl Eifler—if it were legal," said John Coughlin.

Later in Burma Vince Curl was to do exactly that.

\*     \*     \*

"The first night after the Japanese attack, we were scared to death," recalled Colonel John Coughlin in the living room of his condominium at Sun City, Arizona.

With the outbreak of war, both Captain Eifler and Captain Coughlin had been ordered to Sand Island, a bit of land in the Hawaiian Islands, where Japanese civilian nationals had been interned. Eifler and Coughlin and their men were to maintain order among the Japanese, who were reputed to be specially trained in mayhem.

"We were armed with riot guns," said Coughlin. "I ordered the soldiers to take a couple of shots at some tin cans. They'd better hit the cans or the Japanese wouldn't be afraid of us."

The soldiers hit the cans, the Japanese were in fact docile, and there were no problems at all. The problem now was to keep the internees busy. Three sergeants were directed to have the Japanese pitch their tents in a perfect row. Every peg was to be precisely in line or the Japanese would have to take the tent down and put it up again. The internees got so skilled at putting up their tents that the sergeants had to get a surveyor's instrument to find miniscule errors for them to correct. What might have caused an insurrection among American internees merely provided the Japanese with a stimulating opportunity to pursue excellence.

Captain Coughlin and Captain Eifler were living in a military duplex when, on February 17, 1942, a telegram arrived from Washington for Carl Eifler.

"Are you available for a Far East assignment?"

The wire was signed by M. P. Goodfellow, Lt. Col., General Staff, G2.

Eifler attempted to reply directly to Goodfellow by commercial telegram. He soon discovered that this was impossible. The lines from Hawaii were not open for civilian messages. General Emmons, commander of the Hawaii Department, when he understood the situation, said he would be happy to send the message to Goodfellow in Washington.

"I'll wire on your behalf," he said, "and decline the offer."

"No, sir," said Eifler.

"Why not?"

"I've never refused an assignment from the army in my life, and I'm not going to refuse this one. But I'll abide by your decision."

"Refusing assignment," wired General Emmons. "On important assignment and can't be released."

"Glad you are joining this operation," came the reply. "Will have orders issued assigning you immediately to Coordinator of Information. Leave as quickly as possible for Washington. Wire how much travel money you need. We will square travel and other expenses later."—Stimson.

Donovan and Goodfellow had obtained the permission of Secretary of War Stimson to sign his name to orders for army personnel to report to the COI for duty. "Gentlemen don't read each other's mail," Stimson had once remarked when he was Herbert Hoover's secretary of state at the very thought that American intelligence officers might want to intercept messages from one Axis official to another. But he had very likely come to the conclusion that Hitler, Mussolini, and Hirohito were not precisely gentlemen, after all. Here he was lending his name to a COI maneuver. Goodfellow had invoked the cabinet-officer's name to counter General Emmons's turndown. Carl Eifler was to go to Washington under a subterfuge, which was a fitting introduction to the COI and the OSS.

The evening the wire from Stimson arrived Eifler and Coughlin were together.

"If I need some people, would you like to come?" asked Eifler.

"I would. I'm a soldier, and I'd like to fight."

Carl Eifler left as soon as possible on a Pan American Clipper for San Francisco. As he was checking through the California State Agriculture Department's inspection point at the air terminal, a Lieutenant Colonel Harris approached and asked, "Captain, are you going into town?"

Eifler said that he was.

"Well, fine. Wait a few minutes, and I'll drive you in."

Carl Eifler hadn't been a customs agent for nothing, and he recognized that a contact had been made. Harris went off to get his car. He drove up in front of the terminal in about half an hour.

"Okay, Captain, let's go," he said.

As he drove toward downtown San Francisco, Harris asked, "Have you decided on a hotel yet?"

"No, I haven't."

"Fine. I think the Palace would be a good one for you."

Before they reached the hotel Harris wanted to know, "Have you any idea what your assignment is to be?"

"No, sir, I haven't," replied Eifler honestly enough. "I think it may be connected with General Stilwell and an assignment to China."

At the Palace Hotel, the two dined in the Garden Court. Then they walked down the street to an unmarked office. There Harris picked up a telephone. A waiting click on the other end indicated that it was a special line kept in constant readiness.

"Colonel Goodfellow, please."

Eifler could not hear what the mysterious Colonel Goodfellow in Washington was saying, but he could surmise.

"Yes, sir. He is here. Yes, he evidently does. He mentioned General Stilwell and China. Yes, he will be on the plane tomorrow morning," said Harris, his remarks interspersed with appropriate silences.

Harris hung up. He took an envelope from a desk drawer.

"Captain, this is your plane ticket and your priority. Only a member of the White House can bump you off the plane. You leave at 1300 tomorrow. Good luck."

The two men shook hands as they parted.

Harris had told Eifler that there would be a reservation for him to stay at the Army and Navy Club in Washington. When he arrived at National Airport, he took a taxi to the club and strode up to the reception desk. He gave his name, and the clerk looked blank.

"Colonel Goodfellow made the reservation."

He had mentioned the magic name, and the clerk's face was wreathed in smiles. The next day Carl Eifler was to report to the COI where he was to meet that mysterious man Goodfellow who could at will invoke the authority of the secretary of the army over the course of a soldier's career.

* * *

New additions to the COI staff turned up daily, and there was no place to put them except in the halls. An intelligence organization operates at a definite disadvantage if its headquarters staff is exposed to public view, or at least that is how Donovan looked at the matter. He walked over to the former Public Health Service buildings at 25th and E to see if suitable space for the COI could be provided there. The limestone and brick buildings were sequestered behind a wall that could provide the necessary security. They overlooked the Heirich Brewery, the Riverside Roller Skating Rink, and the Potomac River.

The COI moved in. Donovan set up his own office in the Central Building, which was imposing enough with its Greek pillars. The distinguished scientists and scholars recruited by James Phinney Baxter, president of Williams College, for the Research and Analysis Section were moved into the South Building. According to Jim Murphy, a

Donovan aide, who had been his secretary when he was the acting attorney general of the United States in the late 1920s, there was only one problem. Most of the animals used for experimental purposes by public-health researchers in the South Building remained for some months on the top floor. They were co-residents with the professors and savants.

"The question arose," said Murphy, "whether we should put the monkeys on the payroll."

Nazi propagandists came to lampoon the world's newest intelligence organization as "fifty professors, twenty monkeys, ten goats, twelve guinea pigs, and a staff of Jewish scribblers."

The public-health people would probably have never moved their animals out of the building if Donovan himself had not forced the issue. Research and Analysis badly needed the space, Donovan complained to the Health Service. An infected monkey, he claimed, had bit a secretary, and none of the girls would enter the building until the animals moved out. What if the monkey had sunk his teeth into one of the scientists, scholars, or secret agents? The Public Health people knew when they were defeated and moved the menagerie out. The animals had scarcely left when Carl Eifler arrived.

Eifler's cab climbed the hill from E Street to a steep driveway. At the entrance to the driveway uniformed guards, their automatics snug in shoulder holsters, stopped the cab. Eifler paid his driver and walked up the driveway. Guards stood at the entrance to every building. He proceeded, as he had been instructed, to Que Building, which housed a warren of temporary offices constructed by the COI for the still-expanding staff and a cafeteria that was then one of the most extraordinary eating places in the world. Renowned scholars shared tables with masters of derring-do and messengers. Everybody in the COI was caught up in an unprecedented adventure. Nobody said anything about anything much, but the atmosphere was brittle with excitement.

Carl Eifler was escorted down the long hallway past the tiny offices to a door. Stepping within, he found himself shaking hands with a quiet, smiling man, who identified himself as Pres Goodfellow. Goodfellow wasted no time. He briefed Eifler as to the nature of his mission. He walked with Eifler to the columned Administration Building so the newcomer could meet Bill Donovan and learn firsthand about the task that was being assigned to him. Donovan, flanked with maps of secret operations in the various theaters of the war, rose from his chair and held out his hand for a hearty handshake. He told Carl Eifler that he was to head the first American unit ever assembled and trained to conduct guerrilla warfare, espionage, and sabotage. Most likely the theater of operations would be in Burma, but the war was moving so fast that nobody could say for certain. The specific country would have to be determined later. Donovan believed that Eifler should have from twenty to forty men. Whom did he want to help him?

To start, Eifler asked for Vincent Curl, John Coughlin, a medical-corps doctor named Archie Chun Ming, and Lieutenant Bob Aitken, an intelligence officer, all currently in Hawaii. That afternoon Goodfellow sent out the orders: the men Eifler wanted were to be sent to Washington. When Eifler returned to the Army and Navy Club that evening, his head was swimming.

\*　　\*　　\*

John Coughlin's orders were urgent. He was to leave for Washington with a number-one priority on the next Pan American flying boat.

"The world would fall apart if I didn't get to Washington immediately," he remembered later. "But I couldn't get my wife on the plane."

John Coughlin had spent enough time in the army to know that a man had to battle the system and cut every variety of red tape if he was to keep his wife with him even part of the time, and he tried every conceivable way to get her on the plane. Finally, he could only kiss Betty good-bye and walk up the ramp into the flying boat. Right ahead of him were two attractive but coarse-faced young women. They could get on the plane without a problem, but a man's wife had to stay behind. A Chinese-American captain in the Medical Corps was already on the plane. Coughlin introduced himself and shook his hand. He was Archie Chun Ming.

"Where are you going?" Chun Ming asked.

"I bet I'm going to the same place you're going," answered Coughlin.

When he learned that the doctor also knew Carl Eifler, he was convinced that he was right. Chun Ming would be a two-in-one addition to Carl's group; he not only was a doctor, but he spoke Chinese. Chun Ming tugged on his sleeve.

"Do you see those two women over there?" he asked. "I know them. I examined them week after week. They are prostitutes."

Chun Ming's confirmation of his suspicions only annoyed Coughlin the more. Betty had to stay behind, but priorities could be arranged for a pair of whores. The sky was blue, the stewardess was attractive, and when Coughlin and Chun Ming landed at San Francisco, their Washington plane was waiting for them. In Washington they landed at National Airport and took a taxi to COI headquarters. In Que Building Coughlin listened with increasing amazement as a captain briefed him about the unorthodox organization that Carl Eifler had gotten them into. A little later he found himself together with Eifler.

"I'm with you with both feet," he said.

*     *     *

Recruiting men to carry out espionage, sabotage, guerrilla warfare, propaganda, escape, and evasion in an as-yet-undesignated country in the Far East was a baffling undertaking.

"From the start," Carl Eifler said later, "men were expected to volunteer blindly. They were advised they would likely be signing their own death warrants. Moreover, if a man indicated that he was a glory-seeker or a hell-raiser, he was turned down."

Coughlin and Eifler looked for men who had intelligence, health, courage, and a serious disposition. Preferably, a recruit should also have sophisticated knowledge of such subjects as military science and tactics, engineering, explosives, radio and other communications, precision machinery, medicine, photography, languages, or Asiatic cultures. All of the recruits were civilians, enlisted men, or low-ranking officers.

"We theoretically had the choice of the best personnel in the United States," says Coughlin wryly, "but we were so junior in rank that we had to pick only junior officers or they would have outranked us."

Sometimes a promising candidate would not even consider the assignment; more often, a commanding officer would not release him.

"Peacetime regimental commanding officers had a hard time adjusting to the facts of war," remembers John Coughlin.

"If an order comes through," threatened Coughlin and Eifler, "you'd better not try and hold them, or you'll be in big trouble."

At first no one in the military had even heard of the COI, but it soon became clear that it had formidable clout in Washington. The two recruiters went off to Georgia and to Fort Monmouth, New Jersey, to interview possible candidates. Carl Eifler had moved from the Army and Navy Club to the home of a good army friend, then Colonel Milton B. Halsey, at Fort Meade, Maryland, where he found things far more comfortable.

Mrs. Halsey, an army wife who knew soldiers, suggested so many possible candidates to Eifler that she in time became affectionately known as the "Mother of 101." One of them was Floyd Frazee, a stocky jeweler from Parkersburg, West Virginia, whose skill at working with small precision tools promised that he might be good at crafting miniature radios. Another was Don Eng, who had done wiretapping in the U.S. Customs, knew radio well, and was trustworthy. When he was interviewed by Coughlin on the West Coast, he explained that he had five children.

"Will you take care of my family?" he asked.

"You come back with me, and we'll get it all fixed up."

Don Eng's knowledge of Chinese was an important reason why Coughlin wished to recruit him, although it turned out that he could speak only Cantonese, which was not the dialect spoken by the Chinese soldiers he was to encounter in Burma. When they wrote down what they had to say, however, he was able to interpret it.

The recruits came from every walk of life. Jack Pamplin, a lanky lawyer, was singing in the choir of a Presbyterian church in suburban Washington one Sunday, when the singer seated next to him said that a man with a legal background was needed for a certain government job. He suggested to Pamplin that he phone a Carl Eifler. He made the phone call, and Eifler invited him to come to his office at the COI for an interview.

When Pamplin walked into the room, Eifler arose, a towering giant of a man with a craggy grin.

"Hit me in the stomach as hard as you can," he directed Pamplin.

"Do you mean it? In the stomach?"

"That's right. As hard as you can."

Pamplin wound up and punched as hard as he could. Eifler neither flinched nor moved. He sat down at his desk and went on with the interview. Pamplin nursed a sore wrist. Despite the odd nature of his interview and the usual warnings about the hazards of life in the COI, Pamplin decided to join. He failed his physical because of poor teeth. When he said he would get dental work done so that he could get into the outfit, Eifler knew that he really had the right spirit for the job.

Most of the recruits were army officers or enlisted men, but George Gorin, a civilian, was so new to the ways of the army that when young Sam Schreiner, also reporting for duty, saluted him, he jumped up in dismay, knocking his chair over. Detachment 101 soon had gained four infantry officers, two engineers, three radio technicians, a watchmaker, a court stenographer, a Korean patriot, and an American who had been an adviser to Chiang Hsueh-liang, a Chinese warlord. It was Coughlin who suggested Ray Peers.

\*     \*     \*

It was raining on a Sunday morning in early March. Ray Peers and his young wife, Barbara, were at their rustic lodge in the Georgia foothills. Barbara had a luminous beauty and a gentle wit that made a rainy day in the lodge a relaxing pleasure for her husband, who was attending the Infantry Officers Advanced Course at Fort Benning, about twenty-five miles away. The lodge was poorly heated and there was no telephone, but it was better than living in the bachelor officers' quarters at the fort. Peers, who had been trained in the Reserve Officers Training Corps at the University of California at Los Angeles, had entered the army in 1937 under the Thompson Act. A thousand outstanding ROTC graduates had been granted their commissions with one year's active duty. The fifty best were given regimental commissions. Peers had been one of the fifty. It was at the Presidio in San Francisco that John Coughlin, then a first lieutenant, had met the young officer. He considered Second Lieutenant Ray Peers to be one of the most promising officers he had ever met.

"By qualifying as he did under the Thompson Act, he earned a commission in the hardest of all hard ways," Coughlin said years later.

Since then Ray Peers had passed up few opportunities to sharpen his military skills, and he was on leave from his home station at Fort Leonard Wood, Missouri, for additional training.

Even as a young officer, Ray Peers had a distinguished appearance. He had an erect bearing and an appearance of great strength— not just physical or even mental but strength of character. Men somehow trusted him to do what was right. He had rugged good looks, too, but he was not a lady's man. Women often felt a little overawed by his intense dedication to the military. Barbara alone knew the soldier's gentle and affectionate side.

The farmer shook the rain from his drenched clothing and

stamped his boots dry before he stepped inside the door. The lieutenant was wanted on the telephone. It was an urgent message from Fort Benning. Peers hurried to the neighboring farm and took down the message over the phone.

"Are you interested in a combat assignment in the southwest Pacific?" asked a wire from Captain John G. Coughlin.

Peers telephoned Coughlin and asked for more details.

"I can't tell you, but it's overseas. It's a high priority job. There's a chance to get killed and a chance to be promoted," replied Coughlin.

"If you get me loose, I'll come."

"You'll get loose."

Peers went on to complete the course at Fort Benning and then returned to Fort Leonard Wood. Orders to report to the Coordinator of Information in Washington had already arrived. That afternoon Colonel Garland Williams of the COI telephoned from Washington and told him exactly how he could find the COI when he reached Washington. COI people were growing tired of new recruits wandering around the city for days looking for the still hard-to-locate headquarters.

When Peers arrived in Washington, he went to Que Building at COI headquarters to meet his new commander, Captain Carl Eifler.

"To say I was in for a rude shock would be the understatement of a lifetime," he recalled later. "After an exchange of salutes, he offered his hand. I could see it was strong, and the way he grabbed my hand was proof. He proceeded to crack every joint, smiling all the time. Back of what he was doing was a message. Danger? The next thing, as if it were entirely habitual, he took a stiletto-type dagger and drove it a good two to three inches into the top of his desk. He looked pleased."

Peers, a man not given to overstatement, was confused by the theatricality of the meeting. Eifler, still smiling pleasantly, launched into a briefing.

"The impression was of parachutes, hit-and-run fire fights, resistance movements, sabotage, of missions crisscrossed with danger," Peers concluded. He wondered why John Coughlin had mixed him up in the affair.

Peers toured the COI offices with Coughlin. Among others, he met Goodfellow, Williams, and finally Wild Bill Donovan himself. Peers had grown up in the generation of boys who had made a national hero of the heroic colonel of the Fighting 69th. He felt abashed when he entered Donovan's office, but with his quiet ways Wild Bill quickly put him at ease.

"He made us comfortable by pointing out his concern over the Japs pressing India and China. He believed good guerrillas would be invaluable in slowing up the enemy's progress, in following up every opportunity for information that could eventually mean the defeat of the Japanese," Peers said later.

Eifler may have left him wondering what he was doing in the COI, but Donovan had totally reassured him. When Peers left the interview, he took John Coughlin aside and told him how good it was to be part of the COI.

Before long, the original twenty-one members of Detachment 101 had been gathered together. Next they must be trained and transported across the world. It was already mid-March. The Japanese had occupied Rangoon on March 8, and they were now driving northward into Burma's interior.

# The Preparation

Only a few days after Ray Peers arrived at Que Building, Carl Eifler, John Coughlin, and five of the men they had recruited journeyed up to Canada. Vince Curl, Jack Wilkinson, Frank Devlin, Floyd Frazee, and Archie Chun Ming went with Coughlin and Eifler. Ray Peers stayed behind. Today motorists speeding along the postwar Mac-Donald-Cartier Freeway, highway 401, from Toronto eastward through Oshawa, have little realization that they drive past one of the most historic places in North America. Between the highway and Lake Ontario is Camp X, the first school in North America for sabotage and subversion. There, hidden from old highway 2 by an expanse of tangled brush, British, Canadian, and American experts taught courses in lockpicking, safeblowing, second-story entry, the planting of explosives and incendiaries, the use of radios and listening devices, and codes and ciphers. In the late 1940s, the secret installations at Camp X were dismantled. Today an Oshawa alderman, W. A. Dewer, is attempting to buy part of the land and reconstruct Camp X as a museum of intelligence.

It all got started when Sir William Stephenson, the Canadian industrialist who had been chosen by Winston Churchill to carry out Britain's most important intelligence missions during World War II, bought a farm on the lakeshore.

One day, after the war, in Bill Donovan's law offices at 2 Wall Street in New York City, Donovan introduced me to Sir William Stephenson. Donovan was a burly man but not particularly tall. Yet he towered over Sir William's slight figure. It was easy to see why Sir William was called "Little Bill" and Bill Donovan was called "Big Bill" by British and American intelligence people. When I met Sir William, he was one of the least-known men upon whom the fate of the Allies in World War II had depended. In recent years the man called by the code name of "Intrepid" has been given appropriate credit for his almost incredible accomplishments—and they were carried out at a time when it appeared that Great Britain was almost assuredly finished and that in all probability the fate of the United States would turn out to be equally certain and perhaps even more brutal. Sir William's manner may have been diffident, but the questions he asked me about the matter at hand were incisive, highly pertinent, and concerned highly sensitive material. I glanced at Donovan with surprise and for permission to reply.

"You can answer the questions, Dick," said Donovan. "This man is the best of friends."

Donovan's "best of friends," Little Bill, a self-made millionaire many times over, had used his own money to buy the farm so that no questions would be asked. Around the original farmhouse and barn, Stephenson's men erected an odd assortment of huts and outbuildings. Filmmakers Zoltan and Alexander Korda came from London and built accurate reproductions of the favorite retreats of Nazi bigwigs. Here agents could stage the abduction or assassination of the most hated Nazi leaders in authentic surroundings. The actual assassination of Reinhard Heydrich, the German "butcher of Prague," was rehearsed at Camp X.

Even getting to Camp X proved to be an adventure for trainees from the United States. Most went by train to Niagara Falls, from where they were driven out to Roosevelt Beach on the American side of the lake. They were taken aboard boats under cover of darkness, and in the gloom of night they were brought across the lake to Camp X. British commandos, who provided security for the camp, checked the American newcomers' credentials before allowing them to go to their quarters.

Carl Eifler's group totaled eight COI recruits. All but one were to see service in Burma. The exception was a retiring college professor, who later became well known in North Africa among OSS circles as the master of the disappearing donkey act.

"He would load a donkey with plastic explosives and hire an Arab kid to lead him to a German headquarters," explains Carl Eifler. "The boy would tie the donkey up there and slip away. Soon there'd be a blast. The donkey would disappear and with it a good part of the German headquarters."

Eifler's men took a more direct route. They put on civilian garb for the trip and got on the train at Washington's Union Station separately. They ignored one another all the way to Oshawa, Ontario. There each man had his own rendezvous with a driver from Camp X on this street corner or that. Eifler's driver kept him waiting half an hour.

"From my days in the U.S. Customs Service, I was used to setting up meets," he says, "so I became impatient. I telephoned the secret number given me for an emergency, and my transportation arrived in no time at all."

When Eifler got to Camp X he accused the British staff of "damned sloppy methods."

"What would happen if an agent whose life depended upon a split-second pickup was kept waiting?" he demanded.

The British and Canadians were not too fond of him after that. The Americans dressed in GI fatigues regardless of rank and civilian or military status. They trained apart from British and Canadian personnel. At first they were cocky. Then after a bantam British sergeant had tossed most of the heftier Americans around as if they were half-grown boys, towering John Coughlin aimed a hard kick at his groin. The sergeant seized the former West Point boxing champion by the toe and twisted his foot so that he fell to the floor with his leg bent back at the knee. The sergeant was on top of him.

"Very humiliating," remarked Coughlin later, "and I had a big swollen ankle too."

Coughlin's tumble convinced the young Americans that the staff at Camp X knew exactly what it was doing. They applied themselves to their study of what Churchill called "ungentlemanly warfare" with so much talent that one day they were able to capture the sergeant and yank his pants off him. They hauled down the Canadian flag from the top of a pole and hoisted the sergeant's pants in its place. The rise of the sergeant's pants to a place of glory happened to coincide with the visit of a British colonel from London.

"How do your boys get along with the Americans?" he asked the camp commander as they talked in the commander's office.

The commander sighed.

"Go to the window and see for yourself," he said.

The colonel gazed out the window to see the sergeant's pants flying in the breeze from off the lake.

The training was anything but serene. An instructor sneaked up behind Floyd Frazee and fired a .45 automatic close to his ears to teach him not to be startled by loud noises. The bang of the gun

broke Frazee's eardrum. Another instructor, demonstrating the ripping power of a new Magnum weapon, fired at a plowshare left over
from the days when the property was a working farm and splintered
it into bits. Fragments of steel flew into Eifler's leg. Back at his quarters, he borrowed Archie Chun Ming's knife and painstakingly dug
out the fragments. Chun Ming found him sitting on his bunk, cutting
at his bloody legs with a bloody knife.

"I don't give a damn about their camp security," he shouted.
"You've got to get into town for medical attention."

Eifler meekly submitted. A surgeon at the hospital in town completed the attempt at do-it-yourself surgery.

British Major Don Fairbairn, who had been chief of police in
Shanghai before the Japanese capture of the city, taught the Fairbairn method of assault and murder. His course was not restricted to
Camp X but was later given at OSS camps in the United States. All
of us who were taught by Major Fairbairn soon realized that he had
an honest dislike for anything that smacked of decency in fighting.

"To him, there were no rules in staying alive. He taught us to
enter a fight with one idea; to kill an opponent quickly and
efficiently," said Ray Peers.

Fairbairn had invented a stiletto as precise as a surgeon's scalpel.
He wielded it with a flashing, slashing vigor that invariably proved
fatal to an opponent.

"Why is it so long and thin?" I asked him one day in a question
period during my own course of instruction. "It doesn't have a cutting edge."

"It doesn't leave any marks on the body," he replied. "Scarcely
more than a tiny drop of blood."

Fairbairn taught his trainees to fire anything from a pistol to a
BAR at close quarters, by aiming with the body. In unarmed combat
he overcame one hulking trainee after another. With a wry smile the
wiry major would admonish his bruised and bleeding students,
"Don't let anybody lead you down the garden path."

Since the Camp X staff had been told that Carl Eifler and the COI
men were being trained for guerrilla warfare and not as agents, they
were given a graduation exercise in keeping with their intended calling. They were to simulate blowing up a train on the main-line railroad that runs through Oshawa. They must infiltrate through guards
and place a dynamite cap on the tracks so that it would be detonated
by the next passing train.

The Americans left camp and skulked through the bush country to the railroad.

"I anticipated that there would be staff people waiting at the designated place to ambush us," Eifler explained later. "So I took the men about one hundred yards away. We placed our charge, and when the next train happened along it resulted in a satisfying bang."

Having eluded the ambush, the Americans headed back toward Camp X. They were slipping along the dark beach when Eifler halted them.

"I figured that we'd most likely have to sneak back into camp to get a really decent grade on the test. Ahead of us was a concrete entrenchment, about three by twenty feet. There probably was a trip light in place."

"You hold them on the beach," Eifler instructed Coughlin. "I'll climb around back of the concrete position."

Eifler scaled the low bluff and worked his way around behind the men. Just then the trip light flashed on to indicate that the men on the beach had crossed an invisible light path. Eifler lit a piece of gun cotton and threw it blazing into the middle of the entrenchment.

"Jump, you bastards!" he shouted.

The staff men jumped. The graduation exercise was over. There was a final fraternal softball game between the Americans and a team of Canadian radio trainees. The Americans separated again for their train ride home. They met in New York City by prearrangement for a celebration.

"When we had first reached Camp X, we were told we must not reveal our identity or rank in any way whatsoever," Eifler said. "I was confident that Floyd Frazee, our only enlisted man, would be the first to blow his cover. We all agreed to pay a dollar into the kitty every time we made a miscue. We'd use the kitty to pay for a big bash after training was over. It turned out that when we held our party that night in New York, the treat was mainly on me."

\*     \*     \*

Ray Peers and the remainder of the men recruited for Burma climbed into trucks at OSS headquarters and rolled out through the greening Maryland countryside into the Catoctin Mountains, 65 miles north of Washington. There, 3 miles west of Thurmont, they found themselves in what had once been a camp for underprivileged children from the city. In late March, 1942, the camp was called

Area B. A forest of chestnut, oak, hickory, and black birch swept up and over a mountain to another group of log cabins in a valley so peaceful and tranquil that its tenant, President Franklin D. Roosevelt, called it "Shangri-La" after the enchanted valley in James Hilton's *Lost Horizon*. Here Roosevelt established his presidential retreat. Here today the president of the United States still seeks relaxation from the cares of office at Camp David, renamed by President Eisenhower for his grandson.

At one time the mountains were cut over to provide wood for charcoal burning. Then, in 1936, the federal government purchased the area as the Catoctin Recreational Demonstration Area. The forests grew back. White-tailed deer, raccoons, woodchucks, gray squirrels, and even red and gray foxes returned. Wild Bill Donovan's school of mayhem was set up right over the mountain ridge from the president's retreat.

There was some rivalry in the neighborhood. Wild Bill's boys were cocky, and the president's Shangri-La was defended by a tough contingent of U.S. Marines. On several occasions the marines and Donovan's boys fired over one another's heads in what was presumed to be good fun. This didn't exactly help Shangri-La to live up to its name.

One sunny day a group in training set up a practice ambush on the road leading into the mountains. They waited in vain for a car driven by their instructor. When at last an auto rounded a curve into view, they tensed to fire. But they recognized their targets just in time. There were the familiar figures of the president of the United States and his secretary of state, Cordell Hull. Secret Service bodyguards rode close behind. Their mock attack would have given the man who personified the very spirit of their cause a fearful scare, and what is more the Secret Service would have undoubtedly returned their blanks with live ammunition.

The training area simulated the situations they were to find in the Far Eastern theater. Trainees ran along narrow boards about fifty feet off the ground to get them used to running over housetops. If they slipped, they plummeted into a net. They walked through a darkened hall about four feet wide, when suddenly the floor dropped some six or eight inches and a papier-mâché enemy appeared. Even though they were thrown off balance, they had to fire from the hip and hit their hated adversary in the head. In the next instant the head popped up, and they had to fire again.

In Area B, Ray Peers and his friends studied demolitions, weapons, and guerrilla-warfare tactics. Don Fairbairn, who commuted between Camp X and Area B, continued to teach his brand of mayhem. The remainder of Area B's faculty was out of the ordinary too. Frank Gleason, Leo Karwaski, and Joe Lazarsky, all experts with dynamite who had learned their skills in anthracite mines around Hazleton, Pennsylvania, were called the three "Ski's." Joe Lazarsky would later tire of teaching other people to blow things up and go out to Burma to put his talents to work in Detachment 101. The three Ski's were learned in the use of dynamite, Composition C (a new plastic explosive), fuses, caps, and delaying devices which had been found satisfactory by the British commandos on their raids against occupied Europe.

When a COI recruit arrived at Area B, he changed into a pair of anonymous GI fatigues. Just as at Camp X, he lost not only his grade, rank, or civilian status, but his name and his own identity. From then on, he went by a nickname.

\* \* \*

Nicol Smith was a world traveler and adventurer with the knack of turning his exploits into best-selling books. His high-pitched voice was as well known on lecture platforms all over the English-speaking world as it was in cosmopolitan drawing rooms from Mayfair to his native San Francisco. It was not surprising that such a man would learn about Wild Bill's outfit and volunteer to serve in it. Urbane, witty, and brittle in manner, he was still warmhearted and loyal to his friends. Nicol Smith was in the same training group with Ray Peers at Area B.

"We may only have known one another's nicknames," Nicol Smith told me, "but I had no trouble in recognizing Ray Peers as an exceptional leader."

Smith was pleased when Peers and he were teamed up for Area B's graduation exercise, which compared in kind with the one at Camp X.

Dressed in disheveled private's uniforms left over from World War I, Nicol Smith and Ray Peers walked up Main Street in Hagerstown, Maryland. They had been ordered by their Area B instructor to gain entry into the Fairchild Aircraft Division plant, which was eleven miles north of town on U.S. 11. The plant made PT-19 and PT-26 primary trainers, AT-13 and AT-14 advance trainers, UC-61 utility cargo planes and C-82 cargo planes, the famous flying boxcars, later to be the workhorses of the Army Transport Command. It was closely guarded against enemy sabotage or espionage. Once within the plant Peers and Smith were to make a complete study of its layout and determine where bombs should be planted to wreak the most havoc.

Nicol Smith had friends everywhere. One was a Fairchild executive. When he heard the world traveler's unmistakable accents piping over the phone, he immediately invited him out for lunch. Yes, bring your friend.

The uniforms issued to American GIs in World War II generally fit so haphazardly and looked so peculiar that the executive thought nothing of the oddly attired young men who appeared at his office. Lunch was definitely better than Area B food, and Nicol Smith's conversation was, as usual, scintillating, so all three men had a fine time. The executive offered to take his guests on a tour of the factory.

As they walked through the plant, Smith chattered away about things half a world away while Peers made sharp mental notes about everything he saw.

"The tour lasted about an hour and a half, and we had all of the required information," Peers noted after the war. "To our amazement, the guide gave us several brochures which provided a wealth of details and statistical data."

Since they were not scheduled to be picked up and taken back to Area B until that evening, when they were finished with the tour, they drove out to the battlefield at Antietam where they spent the afternoon learning about a bloody encounter in a war fought in a far simpler time. When they returned to Area B, their instructor listened to their report and avowed that they had passed the course.

One day I asked General Donovan why it was necessary to send men out on illegal missions to test the skills they had learned. He gave me a glance of amusement.

"It's something like an internship," he said. "You wouldn't want a doctor taking out your appendix who had never had any practical experience."

It was April when Carl Eifler and John Coughlin brought their men back from Camp X and reunited them with the men who had just finished their training at Area B. General Stilwell had long since reported for duty in Burma. The Japanese were driving on Myitkyina, and the tragic refugees were fleeing through the jungle mountains to India as best they could.

\* \* \*

On April 14, 1942, Detachment 101 of the COI was activated. Carl Eifler was made the commanding officer.

Eifler sat in the office of Goodfellow's aide, Garland Williams, in Que Building.

"What shall we call the unit?" asked Williams.

"Detachment 1," replied Eifler. "It's going to be the first outfit into the field."

"No," said Williams. "We'll call it Detachment 101. We can't let the British know we only have one unit."

Actually, Williams might as well have spared his bit of ingenuity, because through the close working partnership between William Donovan and Sir William Stephenson the British knew everything worth knowing about COI. But Williams's name stuck: Detachment 101.

"A subtle kind of bravado," wrote Ray Peers after the war. "Though this was the first United States unit of its kind, a number less than 100 might not have the proper weight of age and experience; 101 seemed the very model of a unit that had been around for a long time."

Detachment 101 was scheduled to leave for India toward the end of May. A great deal had to be accomplished in the short time—less than six weeks—that remained.

\* \* \*

There was very little spare time. At that point COI had no way to outfit the new detachment, and the 101 men had to take care of the matter themselves. Weapons, sleeping bags, mosquito nets, and other personal gear for 25 men had to be ordered by telegram and telephone, mainly from mail-order catalogs. Phil Huston, who was charged with communications responsibilities, spent days listing essential radio parts and then pursuing them through both civilian and military supply sources. Archie Chun Ming bought medical supplies. Irby Moree, the field photographer, bought the photo supplies and equipment. Dave Tillquist and George Hemming purchased explosives. Everything was to be sent to the Port of Embarkation, Charleston, South Carolina, marked with task force number "TE 5405," the number assigned to Detachment 101. All supplies must be in Charleston no later than May 20.

Once the 101 men reached Asia, they would need their own transport, so they called on Colonel C. P. Townsley of the Army General Staff to use his good offices on their behalf. Colonel Townsley's good offices resulted in the delivery of fifteen hard-to-come-by Jeeps and five ton-and-a-half trucks. In two weeks the vehicles arrived at the warehouse at the Charleston docks where, week by week, the crates and boxes intended for TE 5405 were stacking up.

It was not all work. One day Carl Eifler observed that the security of vital government buildings was lax. To prove his point he had a security pass made with a picture of himself taken at the age of ten. He shoved his pass beneath the noses of guards in government building after government building and was admitted each time without a question.

Off duty, the 101 men headed for bars and nightclubs. Ray Peers, not one for such frivolity, was chagrined when one of his fellow 101'ers stopped a nightclub clock one night so it couldn't reach the hour after which drinks no longer would be served. Pulling out his newly issued automatic, he shot its face out. Time appeared, at least, to stand still, and the party went on.

\*     \*     \*

All the members of Detachment 101 had to obtain United States passports. The exact status of individuals working for the Coordinator of Information and later on for the Office of Strategic Services was equivocal. Were they civilians? Were they soldiers? Some hairsplitting legal experts decided they were members of the former group; others considered them part of the military. In any case it would be wise for them to be issued passports.

One day twenty 101 men, all in army uniform, arrived at the photographic studio at the Old State Building. The group ranged in size from 145 to 250 pounds. They had borrowed one civilian suit coat to wear before the camera. No wonder those passport photos turned out to be classics of a kind.

\*     \*     \*

A 101 man might stop a clock in a nightclub with a well-aimed shot, but there was no way to shoot the face out of the clock of war, which was ticking inexorably. Preston Goodfellow called Carl Eifler into his office.

"How well do you know Stilwell?" he asked.

"I know him damned well."

Goodfellow explained that it appeared Stilwell was beginning to · become disenchanted with the COI plans for Asia, which he had approved.

"I want you to go out by plane earlier than the group, and set things right with Stilwell," Goodfellow said. "While you are at it, you might as well take along forty pounds of these new plastic explosives."

Knowing that the U.S. Customs controlled the export of such things as explosives, Eifler asked, "Do you have customs clearance?"

"No."

"How do you expect me to get it out?"

"I thought you were expert in smuggling."

"Yes, it's my field."

"Then smuggle it."

Eifler decided to take Vincent Curl with him. He was given two sets of orders, one attaching him to Stilwell's staff and the other appointing him as assistant military attaché to the U.S. Embassy in Chungking. This would give him a second chance to stay in China in case Stilwell was indeed growing fractious.

On May 19 Carl Eifler and Vince Curl left for New York where they were to board a commercial airliner. Unknown to Curl, Eifler had packed ten thousand condoms in Curl's bag. Detonators were wrapped in condoms when explosives were to be laid under water. Before he left for the New York train, Curl's wife tried to tuck a few extra things in his bag and discovered what looked like an enormous commitment to infidelity. The more Curl explained, the more explaining he had to do. His departure for New York was a mercy under the circumstances.

When Eifler and Curl, now a lieutenant, reached New York, they bought two more matching suitcases. Curl's was packed with clothing and personal effects. The forty pounds of plastic explosives, the new Composition C, were packed in the other bag. That night Eifler and Curl stayed up all night drinking. It was an alcoholic good-bye to America, but it also had its purposes.

In the morning Eifler and Curl walked into the U.S. Customs Office at the Pan American terminal. Eifler asked with a tongue made thick by whiskey and guile where he could buy another bottle. A customs man directed him to a nearby liquor store. He looked at the burly Eifler with frank distaste. He obviously was glad to see

Eifler and Curl vanish in the direction of another bottle of whiskey. When they returned, Eifler spotted Brigadier General Melborne, whipped out a "short-snorter," those long ribbons of foreign currencies all pasted one to the other that American servicemen then collected, and began to boast of his many trips overseas. The general was annoyed but tried to be polite. The customs officer glared at Eifler with renewed contempt.

Eifler turned to a serviceman's young wife and her little baby, who were waiting to go through customs.

"Does he have a bank account?" he asked, weaving back and forth.

"No."

"Allow me to start one."

Eifler drew out a dollar. So did Curl. They handed the money to the woman. General Melborne and others in the customs line did likewise until the mother had twenty-four dollars. Grinning in drunken satisfaction, Eifler strode up to the customs counter and threw his bag down before the officer.

"Okay, what do you want to see first?" he demanded.

"Do you have any lighter fluid?"

Lighter fluid was dangerous. No explosives were to be carried aboard the plane.

"Lighter fluid? No, I don't even smoke."

He grabbed up the bag full of Composition C and walked toward the plane. The officer glared after him. He searched Vincent Curl's bag. He was relieved that the unpleasant drunks had gone on their way.

The first stop was to be Miami.

\*   \*   \*

On the night of the 21st the bulk of the group was to leave by train for Charleston. One 101 man married his girl, who had come in from West Virginia to tell him good-bye. Some celebrated their departure in a bar, and when they started across the cavernous Union Station, carrying bag and baggage toward the waiting train, their course was serpentine. Wives, sweethearts, and families were there to see the 101 men off to a destination that they were unable to disclose. There were tears, smiles, bantering humor. The newly wedded girl got on the train with her husband, and nobody had the heart to forbid her to ride as far as Charleston.

Only two men failed to turn up at the station. Jack Pamplin had come down with an angry pain in his abdomen. When it worsened hour by hour, he had checked into a hospital where a doctor took out his appendix.

Before he left for New York, Carl Eifler went to see Pamplin.

"Mr. Pamplin will be unable to leave the hospital for days," said the doctor.

"Hell, he's going to die anyway," exclaimed Eifler. "We're all going to die."

Bob Aitken stayed behind to look after Pamplin. Two days after the others left he gained his friend's release from the hospital. An ambulance brought Pamplin to Union Station, and he was carried aboard the train on a stretcher. On May 24 Pamplin and Aitken joined the other 101 men in Charleston.

\* \* \*

The Grace Lines ship S.S. *Santa Paula* was docked in Charleston, and the 101 contingent had been promised space aboard for themselves and their gear. Her peacetime beauty had been camouflaged. She was fitted out to carry troops and equipment. In April, when Carl Eifler had first requested space to take his newly formed Detachment 101 to India, he had been turned down. Only when he set about to charter his own ship did the navy suddenly discover that there would be space on the *Santa Paula*. When the 101 men arrived at shipside, they learned to their chagrin that nobody had ever heard of either the COI or of Detachment 101. Nor had anyone knowledge of any supplies and equipment stenciled "TE 5405." There was nothing to do but scout from warehouse to warehouse along the docks looking for their missing shipments. They found everything at last gathered all together in one big storage facility.

"The scene in the warehouse was most disheartening," Ray Peers wrote after the war. "There were boxes of every size, shape, and description. They had arrived by truck, train, and plane and were simply shunted into the warehouse in a big jumble and mess of boxes. Many of these boxes were unmarked or did not have tally sheets. In order to find what was in them, they had to be unpacked and then repacked."

Four days and nights remained before May 28, when the S.S. *Santa Paula* was due to sail. The 101 men worked round the clock ripping open boxes and sorting through their contents, repacking and nailing them up again. There was no time for anything more than a catnap, and no time for meals. The men lived on candy bars and bottles of soft drinks.

By four o'clock of the afternoon of May 27, almost everything had been packed and repacked, sometimes more than once, and loaded aboard the ship. Only the Jeeps and trucks were missing.

"We rummaged up and down the docks to find our damned Jeeps," remembers John Coughlin. "If a Jeep didn't have our task-force number on it, we took it anyway."

The port authorities and the ship captain informed the 101 men that their trucks and Jeeps would be loaded aboard starting at 8 P.M. There was nothing to worry about. The tired men threw themselves down on boxes and crates, wherever they could find some place to stretch out, and caught some much-needed sleep. When they awakened around 2 A.M., they discovered that not a single vehicle had been loaded aboard. The ship was due to sail at 7.

"Nobody else could take vehicles on board," said the authorities, "and there could be no exception for Detachment 101."

There was a heated argument, but finally the authorities bowed before the 101 men. They agreed that they could load five Jeeps. When they had loaded the five, they went right ahead and loaded three more. They lashed them securely on the deck. This left seven Jeeps and five trucks behind.

The ship sailed at 7 A.M. The 101 men and most of their supplies and gear were securely aboard. At the last minute Jack Pamplin had been carried aboard on his stretcher. The men collapsed into their bunks, and the ship was past Bermuda before they appeared on deck to watch the sea scudding past the rail. Even as the 101 men rubbed the sleep out of their eyes and stared out over the heaving sea to where the S.S. *Mariposa* and other ships of the convoy were plowing through the waves, the embers of Ngai Tawng's village were still smoldering, and the boy was running tirelessly down jungle paths toward his meeting with Father Stuart. The 101 men had never heard of the Kachin people.

# The Arrival

It was a blue tropical sea, but it hid German submarines. The 101 men basked on deck in the sun and looked over the waves. At a distance of about a mile, four wolfish destroyers, two on either side, protected the twenty-thousand-ton *Santa Paula,* the *Mariposa* of the Matson Line, the S.S. *Grant* of the Army Sea Transport Service, which was loaded with high explosives, and one other vessel. In the center of the convoy the veteran battleship U.S.S. *Texas* plowed through the waves, its giant guns ready in case one of the Nazi cruisers then raiding Allied shipping lanes heaved into view over the horizon. There was one submarine scare, but it turned out to be a false alarm. It was merely an episode at sea to make the adrenalin pump.

Aboard the *Santa Paula* the 101 men slept in bunks, three layers high, in a small cabin. The ship carried an enormous number of troops, and it was necessary to allow each man only one canteen of fresh water a day. Beneath decks it was hot and confining, so the 101 men spent most of their time up on deck watching the occasional dolphins, playing cards, talking, and reading paperback books provided in tidy boxes for servicemen. A British captain in the Indian army lectured from time to time on India and Southeastern Asia, and 101'ers Sukyoon Chang and John Murray taught classes in Chinese for a few hours each day. Everything went well. Only one man became ill. To soothe his raspy voice and sore throat, he ladled teaspoons of Brown's cough syrup into his mouth at regular intervals. The mixture didn't seem to cure his cold, but since it contained at least sixty-percent alcohol it put him in increasingly mellow condition. He managed to take a quart of the syrup a day.

Normally, the crossing to West Africa took less than a week, but the convoy steamed at a discouragingly slow speed, since it was not scheduled to reach Freetown for twenty-one days, when it was to rendezvous with a huge Allied convoy in the harbor. It would be unsafe to arrive on the African coast too soon.

Three days out of Freetown the troops aboard the ships awoke in the morning to find that during the night the United States Navy escort had vanished. In its place British corvettes were patrolling the sea around the convoy. They darted about like terriers, alert, searching eagerly for submarines.

The convoy arrived without incident at Freetown where the British battleships, the *Rodney* and the *Nelson,* with their immense firepower, three cruisers, several destroyers, and a flotilla of corvettes, were shepherding from sixty to eighty transports. They were waiting until 150 ships had been gathered together before they set out along the African coast to Gibraltar through the perilous Mediterranean to Egypt, and on through the Suez Canal, into the Red Sea, and across the Arabian Sea to Karachi in India.

The *Santa Paula* heaved to with the other ships of the convoy at what was called New England, a British naval base about three miles from the town. From its decks the 101 men looked ashore at the green and white buildings of Freetown perched on the steep sides of the extinct volcano which enclosed the sheltered harbor on the Sierra Leone River. Seen at such a distance, the town founded in 1787 by the British humanitarian Granville Sharp as a home for liberated slaves seemed the epitome of idyllic beauty. It lived up to its name until the 101 men were finally cleared to go ashore. Then they discovered that it was a noxious place of decrepit buildings, of filth and flies. Many of the descendants of the freed slaves had running sores on their arms and legs, and they wore sullen and downcast looks on their faces. Torrents of rain descended almost every day, and malarial mosquitoes buzzed about. The 101'ers soon learned that the town had a legitimate claim to its sobriquet of "the white man's grave."

Even before the Japanese attacked Pearl Harbor, the British had asked Pan American to establish a vital air service across Africa to supply their forces operating in the Middle East. From an African headquarters at Accra, Pan American established air bases along the West African coast and across the parched interior to Khartoum and beyond. At bases such as El Fasher in the Sudan, where the daily temperatures reached as high as 155 degrees F in the shade, the ground crews managed to operate landing fields and emergency repair facilities. In West Africa they drained stagnant water, screened windows, and munched on quinine to ward off malaria, which at one time threatened to close down the city of Accra itself.

Because of their high priorities, the 101 complement was promised space aboard a DC-3 due to depart on the morning of June 20. Floyd Frazee, Fima Haimson, and Jack Pamplin stayed aboard the *Santa Paula* to accompany the supplies on the long sea voyage to Karachi, but the others were overjoyed to go out to the airport and resume their journey by air. Captain Waters, on loan from United Airlines, was in the pilot's seat when the plane roared down the bumpy runway and bounded into the air. It soared up over the steaming jungles.

The route across Africa from Freetown led to Roberts Field, Liberia, and Accra on the Gold Coast, now in Ghana, where there was an overnight stop, to Kano and Lake Chad in Nigeria and on across the Dark Continent to torrid El Fasher in the Sudan. The hours seemed endless as the tired men leaned back against the sharp metal ribs of their seats. After the first day, they learned that veteran travelers settled down on the floor on a pile of the softest freight they could find and dozed. When the plane encountered turbulence, which was frequent in the tropics, it bucked and plunged. Even the strongest stomachs became queasy.

The plane reached Maiduguri on the morning of June 22 and Khartoum by that evening. On the following night it was at Asmara Airport, and the next night it was at Aden on the Red Sea where it blew a tire in landing. The DC-3 was undamaged, but it could not fly again until a replacement wheel was flown in.

It was several days before the wheel arrived. A light drizzle fell one day. It was the first rainfall of any sort in five years, and the Arabs walked about in it with a sensuous pleasure. Usually, the daily temperatures ranged from 110 to 120 degrees F in the shade. While they waited, the 101'ers bunked at the Royal Air Force Base, read and reread their books, talked endlessly, played poker, and wished the hot winds blowing out of the heart of Arabia would cease if only for moments. At last, with the new wheel fitted firmly in place, the DC-3 plunged down the runway and into the air. As if it had the malevolent purpose of keeping them in their grasp, the winds blew harder still until great columns of sand rose in the path of the plane. When the visibility became so poor that the pilot, flying only two to three hundred feet over the cliffs rising along the Hadhramaut Coast could not make them out, he turned around and flew back to Aden. For another eight days the 101'ers remained in Aden at the RAF Base.

"Our poker team cleaned out the pockets of the British at the Aden airport," said Bob Aitken after the war. "Then came a dog-eat-dog contest, degenerating finally into an unrestricted 'dealer's choice' affair, culminating in baseball, deuces wild, high-low, which left all but a few penniless, the others relatively affluent."

When the storm lifted on the eighth day, rich and poor 101'ers alike flew to the area of Salalah but once again had to turn back because of foul weather. The pilot discovered that he had insufficient gas to fly all the way back to Aden so he landed at Royal, an emergency strip maintained by the Royal Air Force in the middle of the Saudi Arabian desert. When their plane rolled to a stop on the desolate tarmac, an imperturbable British lieutenant emerged from a weather-beaten tin shack, the only structure in sight, and offered to share his bully beef, crackers, and jam with the newcomers. They had to fight the flies for the food, which together with gas and oil for the planes had been brought some eight hundred miles from Aden on camelback.

On the third try, on July 3, the plane made it safely to Salalah. Storms still obscured the coast so that the pilot had to fly low to make out landmarks. He was talked down to the Pan Am base, where a sign greeted them, "Welcome to the Desert Retreat." It was signed "Pan Am Pioneers Post No. 1." One arrow pointed to the "Cafe de la Paix" and another to "Cookie's Hamburger Haven." On the next day it was possible to fly across the Arabian Sea to the New Malir Airfield at Karachi. Great black monsoon clouds rose over the Arabian Sea and the coast of India. On the Fourth of July the Americans were able to toast their nation's birthday at the newly formed American officers' club in Karachi. The 101'ers sipping their warm beer were the only Americans there.

\*   \*   \*

Carl Eifler, Vincent Curl, and their suitcase containing forty pounds of plastic explosives had already reached New Delhi. When their flight from New York had set down in Miami, Eifler brazenly asked the customs supervisor to place the suitcase in his safe.

"It contains important documents," he assured him, "and I don't care to take it into the city tonight."

In the morning Eifler and Curl came to the airport to resume their flight to Brazil. The customs official took the suitcase out of the safe without a word and handed it to Eifler. There was apparently no need to declare its contents. Not when the man in charge took it out of his own safe before the eyes of the inspectors. In Brazil Eifler and Curl shuffled the bags back and forth and confused the authorities at the airport. The suitcase remained unopened. It wasn't until they landed in Cairo several days later that they ran into trouble. An Egyptian inspector demanded that they open the suitcase containing the explosives. Eifler waved a diplomatic passport under his nose.

"You have insulted me and my country," he raged. "I demand that you call the American Embassy."

Confronted with a diplomatic passport, the inspector let Eifler heft his unopened bag and stride to a line of cabs. Eifler and Curl loudly ordered a cab to take them to the U.S. Embassy. There they placed the bag in the custody of the military attaché. They checked into Shepheards Hotel, that comfortable citadel of British travelers and officials in the Middle East, and were given an airy room looking down on Cairo's main boulevard. Gazing down at the antlike crowds passing by on the sidewalk, Eifler determined to try out a new type of .22-caliber silencer-equipped pistol. He carefully aimed the pistol beyond the throng of pedestrians into a flower bed and pulled the trigger. When the shot into the flowers attracted no attention, he knew that the pistol was as silent as it was lethal.

There was only one more customs checkpoint to pass. When Eifler and Curl landed in India, Eifler dug out his short snorter and listed each bill on his currency declaration. The inspector looked over the form with disgust, waved through the pair of American officers and their baggage, and even contributed an Indian rupee note to the collection to speed them on their way.

For all practical purposes the OSS had already been born, but it was not until June 13 that a Presidential Executive Order abolished the COI and established the Office of Strategic Services. The OSS was directed by the president "to collect secret intelligence, to prepare intelligence appreciations for the Joint Chiefs of Staff, the planning and execution of secret operations, and the training of personnel for 'strategic services.'" Carl Eifler and Vince Curl were the first members of OSS Detachment 101 to reach Asia, although they had no idea that they were now OSS men instead of COI men.

At New Delhi Eifler wrapped the explosives he had smuggled into

India in plain packages marked "Personal Important," and forwarded them over the Hump by military air transport to Navy Captain Milton E. Miles, who was in charge of the embryo OSS program in China. Miles set to work training Chinese agents in their use. The agents were to be infiltrated into Anhwei Province, where they were to place Composition C in the Huilan Mines which provided coal for the Japanese-controlled industry in Shanghai and northeastern China.

\*     \*     \*

The monsoons came to Northwest India early in June, 1942. Soughing in from across the Arabian Sea, the seasonal winds, steadily blowing at their measured ten to fifteen miles per hour, pushed over the low-lying Sind Desert and the Indus River, breaking the terrible heat, which for weeks on end had stood at over 100 degrees F even at midnight. They rose against the Rajputana Upland and the high Hindu Kush. Black thunderheads formed against the mountains, and driven by the tempest, the rains fell.

Even in the desert angry clouds wallowed across the sky, and torrents of water, as much as twelve inches in twelve hours in a sere region that usually receives scarcely five inches of rain per year, gushed down on the parched earth. The Sutlej, the Beas, the Ravi, the Chenab, and the Jhelum rivers rose in flood and foamed into the mighty Indus. Whole villages and towns, hundreds and hundreds of miles of countryside, vanished beneath the flood when the Indus left its banks. The Sind Desert became one vast sea.

The 101 men, newly arrived in Karachi, found themselves marooned by the flood. Railroad embankments had crumbled into the still-rising waters. They looked up at the threatening skies, dodged the drenching storms that swept in succession down upon hapless India, where even as they gave water and life for the coming year's crops the monsoons were bringing death and devastation on a terrifying scale. The first camels that the 101 men saw were shuffling in a long single file, following a belled leader, their splayed feet, accustomed to hot desert sands, sinking forlornly into sucking mud. From the top of the minarets the muezzins called to the Islamic faithful through the storm.

For nine days the 101 men stayed at the airport terminal building waiting for the flood to subside. They slept as they could, ate what they could scrounge, and listened to British veterans, marooned just as certainly as were the newcomers to India, spin yarns that threatened to beggar those of Kipling. As the Indian night crept close and jackals yapped just beyond the landing strip, the Britishers told the listening Americans about holy men and fakirs, cobras and mongooses, dacoits and bandits. After the war Ray Peers remembered the stories of the Hurs, particularly fierce bands of bandits, who attacked camel caravans and railroad trains as they crossed the Sind Desert with impunity.

"Their specialty was Europeans," wrote Peers in his manuscript, "and their treatment was fiendish to say the least. Not much was said concerning the treatment of women captives. For men the treatment was varied, but always torturous and fatal. One method in particular struck me as highly sadistic. It involved cutting off the male organs and cutting holes in the cheeks for the testicles, goolies as they called them, to stick out after the face was sewn together. Needless to say, when it came time to make our train trip across the Sind, we stayed close together and didn't need a second urging to take our personal weapons with us."

Finally, in a break in the storms, the 101 men boarded a Trans-India Railroad train at Karachi. The train pulled out of the depot at 5:30 A.M. on July 13 and rolled up the Indus Valley. To Ray Peers, Hyderabad, high on its hill a few miles from the left bank of the river and turreted and walled by its founder, the Afghan Shah Kalhora, looked like something out of the *Arabian Nights*. Around the city the vast alluvial plain, watery after the rains, stretched to the horizon.

The travelers ordered their meals from the vendors on station platforms. Invariably, they found broiled chicken, boiled potatoes, and string beans.

"If there had been any meat between the skin and the bones of the chicken, it might have been good," observed Peers. The fly-specked food and the stench coming out of the train's toilet took away Irby Moree's appetite. He crossed the Sind sipping tea.

The winds blew up a cloud of sand that filtered into the jolting carriages and added grit to the food. The train rattled through the night. Mysterious lights flashed past the windows of the cars. Sometimes for no apparent reason the coaches ground to a halt and sat for half an hour in the middle of a village, where at any hour people seemed to be stirring about, their white dhoti-clad figures back-lit by kerosene lanterns in the open-air shops. There was the sweet smell of wood smoke from cooking fires. The Hurs might be lurking in the shadows just beyond the glimmering lights, waiting for the opportune time to attack the stalled train. Finally it was morning, and at nine o'clock the train chugged into the station at Lahore with its ancient crooked streets and city wall and its famous thirteen gates.

It was necessary to spend the night in Lahore in order to make a connection with the Delhi train, so the men went to a two-story frame hotel with a broad verandah. The 101'ers were amused to find such primitive facilities. A chamber pot awaited in each bedroom. When a guest finished using it, he rang for the room boy, who came and carried it out as if he bore royal jewels in a parade. Walking through the city to the bazaars, the Americans purchased sandal-wood fans, ivory elephants, and Kashmiri shawls to send back home. Squalor and splendor jostled one another in Lahore.

"I bought a Kashmir jacket for my wife," John Coughlin remembers. "I haggled furiously with the shopkeeper and reduced his price from $300 to $60. Later in Delhi, I learned from a merchant that I could have bought the jacket in Delhi for $40."

Coughlin gave the Delhi merchant the Lahore merchant's name. The man beamed with delight.

"The Lahore man is my son," he said. "I'm so glad you told me."

Obviously, he had good reason to be proud of his boy's acumen in dealing with naïve American soldiers turned tourist.

The 101 men left Lahore at six on the evening of July 14, and at eleven the following morning after a second all-night train ride they reached Delhi. The trip from Washington, D.C., had taken fifty-one days. They drove to the Cecil Hotel Annex in the crowded Old City and joined Carl Eifler and Vince Curl. On August 1 they moved together to the Imperial Hotel, on Janpath near Connaught Circle in New Delhi, where the American headquarters for the China-Burma-India Theater had been set up on the third floor of one wing. With its black-and-white marble lobby, its Oriental rugs and Mogul tapestries, the Imperial was a resplendent stronghold of privilege and power. Its lounges and corridors were full of high-ranking British and American officers going about the business of war. The young OSS men, fresh from the States, drew many a quizzical look as they sat together at a table in the dining room. What were these junior officers and enlisted men doing in the Imperial Hotel?

*    *    *

In their hotel rooms the 101 men could hear roosters crowing every morning. At night jackals yelped right in the heart of the city. In this land of the fiery curry, of a plain or fancy dosa for breakfast, where the sweet lemon was sweeter than an orange, and oranges tended to be flavorless, the young Americans found they had a lot of readjusting to do. Pedestrians and cows as gentle as kittens strolled in and out of the rush of bikes, rickshaws, auto-rickshaws, trucks, autos, and charcoal-burning buses spewing their showers of burning coals behind them. In the heat of the day men dragged their bedlike charpoys out onto the sidewalks and stretched out to nap with the expectation that the breeze from passing vehicles would keep them a trifle cooler. Bears danced for the entertainment of the crowds, flute-playing fakirs charmed cobras, and, incredibly, in the open place in front of the Red Fort, built long ago by the Mogul emperors, a holy man actually levitated in broad daylight. Ragged boys held out grimy little palms for baksheesh whenever the Americans appeared on the street. At first they reached into their pockets to pass out annas and rupees, but they soon learned to their dismay that to do so was to invite an avalanche of children, each begging for his small pittance.

The British had erected Connaught Circle in the center of their imperial showplace of New Delhi, but already in the heat the paint was peeling from the pillars and walls. There was unrest throughout India. Chandra Bose, the pro-Japanese Indian nationalist, inspired riots that were intended to coincide with the arrival of a Japanese invasion fleet on the long sandy Bay of Bengal beaches near Madras. Rebellious Indians tore up the railway lines, cut telephone lines, and overturned buses. They threw stones at the police, who flailed at the rioters with heavy sticks called lathis. The first weeks of August appeared to shake British rule in Delhi to its very foundations. India seemed about to crumble as a base for the reconquest of Burma. Then the desperate British, throwing all their remaining naval and air strength into action, turned back the Japanese convoy as it streamed through the Bay of Bengal toward its India landing. The rioting gradually subsided. By August 9 New Delhi was quiet.

The tumultuous first days of the month had left their mark, and at headquarters, New Delhi, a feeling of impotence and confusion sapped the resolution of senior and junior officers alike. How could Burma ever be retaken when it was not at all certain that India could be held? To the 101 men it seemed that the British had lost their nerve. They fumed at the bureaucratic delays that they met at every turn when they tried to win British cooperation for their still-obscure and mysterious mission. From the start at least, the British Director of Intelligence regularly briefed the 101 men on everything that could be learned about the Japanese occupation of Burma. They gave the OSS men maps and reports from their agents there. There were no reports from the jungles of North Burma where even as Detachment 101 was getting accustomed to the strange world of India, Zhing Htaw Naw's men, retaliating for the Japanese attack on the Kachin villages, were slipping back down out of the mountains to ambush Japanese patrols.

"They did not propose that they had a prior claim on Burma," reported Ray Peers, "but indeed welcomed a new effort in the profession of irregular warfare. It was their view that the more of us involved in it, the merrier would be the espionage accounts to be filed away in the top-secret files."

\*    \*    \*

John Coughlin insisted that the OSS men stay in good physical condition. The debilitating heat simply must be disregarded because when action finally came the men had to be ready. Even before they moved from the Cecil Hotel Coughlin led them through half an hour's calisthenics every day, followed by a run through the crowded streets. Indians had been long familiar with the adage that only mad dogs and Englishmen go out in the noonday sun, but here were still madder Americans running among the beggars, sacred cows, and sauntering crowds as if their lives depended upon it. After the run, the 101'ers played a strenuous game of one sort or another and then plunged into the hotel pool. British guests had warned the American newcomers about the impurity of the water, and they wore plugs to keep a fungus from infecting their ears. Ray Peers forgot his ear plugs one day, and as a result he suffered three months of excruciating pain from a fungus infection and came close to losing his hearing altogether.

\*    \*    \*

Carl Eifler, recalling his success as a customs agent on the Mexican border where he used criminals to gather information about smugglers and other wrongdoers, decided that 101 would do well to hire Indian criminals and dacoits. They would know what was going on at the rock bottom of Indian society and could provide critical intelligence. Since they might also be expected to help the Japanese as well, Eifler realized that he must have some means of insuring their loyalties. The British had made opium illegal in India, but Eifler knew that it was widely used by the criminal population. If he could supply opium, he could control his otherwise unreliable agents.

It proved easy for Eifler to buy opium from the responsible civilian authorities, once they learned what use he intended to make of it. The opium, he was warned, was coarse and impure, but just how impure was it? Eifler characteristically decided that he could not supply it even to a criminal without knowing its quality, so he smoked a liberal portion himself. The opium turned out to be potent enough. Eifler went into a frightening high, in which he thrashed around his bedroom, threatening to smash up the furniture. It took both Peers and Coughlin to hold him down. For Eifler the experiment ended up with a splitting headache and the realization that there must be a better way to establish an intelligence network than to work with criminals.

This was not quite the end of the episode. The same young officer who had crossed the Atlantic happily sipping Brown's syrup observed that his commanding officer had apparently been doing some exceptionally fancy celebrating. It was time for a binge of his own. He adjourned to his bedroom with two quarts of an Indian gin, later to be known by Americans throughout Burma and India as "Carew's Smooth Booze," and drank them both down.

That night Ray Peers's phone rang. It was the military police. They had just picked up the drunken young officer. He had been leaping stark naked around the roof of an Indian coffeehouse and striking heroic attitudes on the shaky parapets over the crowds.

"What shall we do with him?" asked a military policeman.

Phil Huston and Ray Peers went to the police, picked up their now nearly comatose friend, and sheepishly bundled him back to the hotel. They took him to his room and sopped him in a tub of cold water for about half an hour to sober him up. When they turned their backs just for a moment, the apparently unconscious officer sprang from the tub and raced out of the room. By the time Peers and Huston reached the hallway, he had vanished. Thirty minutes later he was found running about the corridors two floors down, to the utter disgrace of the OSS contingent.

Once again Peers and Huston ushered the now remorseful drunk back to his bedroom. He fell asleep, and they retired wearily to their own beds. The matter should have ended there, but it didn't. Their drunken friend awakened again and, feeling an overpowering need to urinate, got up from his bed and started tipsily down the hall toward the place where he imagined the lavatory to be. He opened what he thought was the correct door and walked into a bedroom where a British officer was peacefully asleep in his bed. Mistaking the round glass top of the bedstand for a toilet bowl, he stepped up and relieved himself on it. The spray splattered onto the mosquito net covering the sleeping man's bed and splashed on his bare feet and legs. The Britisher arose in such a great rage that even the drunken American's befuddled brains reacted. He sprinted from the room in terror and hid in the safety of his own bed. In the morning Ray Peers was awakened by the jingle of his telephone.

"Let me at the dirty son of a bitch," raged the British officer.

Peers did not even have to inquire as to who was in trouble again. He wondered sorrowfully what this young man was doing in OSS Detachment 101. Clearly his friend was going to have to go on the wagon, to say the very least.

\*     \*     \*

At last word reached the 101 men at the Imperial Hotel that the *Santa Paula* had reached Karachi. Peers set off by rail, although his ears were beginning to ache and his stomach was turning gyrations from a touch of what has long familiarly been known as "Delhi Belly." Retracing the route taken by the group on its first train ride across India, he reached Lahore. Beyond Lahore floods still rolled across the low country. At one point the railroad embankment was washed out, and the train could go no farther. Peers joined a hospitable Australian captain in his compartment and waited for a train to reach the other side of the break. The Australian, veteran of countless Indian train rides, brought out a wicker basket of food and several bottles of beer. The heat in the car mounted to 120 degrees F. Sick or no, Peers drank the good Aussie beer. When the rescue train arrived, he dizzily picked his way over the planks placed on the metal railroad ties across the break. Once the passengers had transferred from one train to another, the locomotive gave a long-drawn hoot and started off down the track. By the time they reached the southern port Peers's "Delhi Belly" had settled into a pernicious attack of the "Karachi Krud." Only after two days of demonic cramps and diarrhea did he begin to feel even vaguely human again.

Fima Haimson and Jack Pamplin were hard at work unloading the supplies from the *Santa Paula*. A port company made up of highly efficient American blacks transferred the 101 equipment and supplies from the ship to railroad wagons for movement to Delhi. From Delhi the shipment would be sent on to Calcutta and eventually to the OSS base, wherever that was to be. A personable young Lithuanian, who had fled from his homeland when it was invaded by the Russians, Haimson already spoke good English and had a new American's enthusiastic patriotism. During brief breaks from unloading supplies, Peers taught Haimson the fine art of driving a car. This was a particular challenge because both instructor and student had to cope with the jumble of Indian traffic, where a camel train might meander past a covey of horn-honking taxis and trucks and all the vehicles, animals, and pedestrians kept to the left side of the road in the British fashion. Peers also paid a visit to the U.S. Army dispensary at New Malir Airport, where a surgeon took one look at the noxious pimples erupting in both of his ears and lanced them. The pain was intense for the next ten weeks.

India seemed to be crawling with disease. One day Peers and Haimson were walking up a flight of stairs behind a pair of U.S. soldiers who had just arrived from America. The soldiers had observed the Indians chewing betel nut, which turns the saliva a bright red. From time to time a betel-nut chewer spits a stream of red juice, sometimes into a spittoon but usually all over the pavement.

"Boy, will I ever be glad to get out of this place," one soldier was saying to the other. "Nearly every one of these characters around here is spitting blood, and you know what that means. The last thing I want is TB, and you can bet your bottom dollar I am going to stay away from them." Ray Peers smiled at the newcomer's naïveté, but at the same time his queasy stomach and his throbbing ears urged him to agree in principle with the soldier's heartfelt desire to get out of India.

Once the supplies were all unloaded, Peers left Haimson to guard them and flew back by air to Delhi.

*       *       *

General Tai Li was stocky, with jet-black hair. His vivid eyes darted from behind his eyeglasses. He saw everything around him, and although he consumed enormous quantities of food and wine at his frequent banquets in Chungking he was never known to let his shrewd perceptions deaden. He was Chiang Kai-shek's dreaded and omnipresent intelligence chief, and his network of spies literally blanketed the world. When Carl Eifler and Vincent Curl reached India, fol-

lowed by the bulk of the OSS men, Tai Li soon knew it. He also
knew that Carl Eifler was accredited both to General Stilwell, who
despite his defeat in Burma was still Chiang Kai-shek's Chief of Staff,
and to the U.S. Embassy in Chungking. Tai Li knew as well that
General Stilwell had brought with him to the Far East a dislike and
jealousy of the British. The cataclysmic Allied defeat in Burma had
intensified Vinegar Joe's prejudices. Forestalling the OSS group who
had newly arrived in Asia was almost second nature to Tai Li, and
he lost no time in warning Stilwell that Eifler and his men were tied
in with the British. He had no desire whatsoever to have the fledgling
OSS trespassing on his intelligence preserve. The British intelligence
people were hard enough to deal with without having the Americans
also trying to decide what was really going on in the murky underside
of the war in Asia. With the Japanese consolidating their conquest of
Burma and intriguing with disloyal Chinese in China, the situation
was complicated, and the nation with superior intelligence could well
be the nation to realize the greatest advantage.

Although Stilwell did not take Tai Li's warnings seriously, as
Goodfellow at OSS headquarters in Washington had feared, he had
developed a firm prejudice against OSS clandestine warfare and intelligence operations in his theater.

It was urgent for Carl Eifler to fly to China. He had come out
from Washington with two sets of orders—one sending him to India,
and the other to China. Using the China orders he wangled space on
one of the hard-to-get Hump flights and was soon winging his way
over the lower shoulders of the Himalayas and over the North
Burma that he was to get to know so well, on his way to China's
wartime capital at Chungking. In Chungking he found Stilwell away
from his headquarters, so he made use of his accreditation as assistant military attaché at the U.S. Embassy to justify his stay in the city.

"I really intended to be accredited to General Stilwell if he would
have me," Carl Eifler explained after the war, "so I made sure that
every time I reported into the embassy the ambassador was not there.
In a month of calling on the embassy I never did deliver my accreditation. By then I had seen Stilwell."

Eifler's patience was rewarded. He strode into General Stilwell's
office at the appointed hour. He saluted, and the general returned his
salute. Rising, Stilwell shook hands. The two men exchanged friendly
pleasantries. Then Stilwell turned to business.

"Well, Eifler, what are you doing here?"

"Sir, I was under the impression you sent for me."

"No, I didn't send for you, and I don't want you."

At first he was adamant. There was no place for the OSS in Asia. Finally he relented enough to grant Eifler thirty days to find an acceptable role for his OSS Detachment 101. Then, a few days after the first interview, he reluctantly agreed to give Carl Eifler ninety days to get an intelligence and guerrilla-warfare operation started behind the Japanese lines in Burma.

"All I want to hear are booms from the Burma jungle," he concluded.

On September 28, 1942, Eifler reported to Preston Goodfellow in Washington: "Stilwell is expecting me to fail. As far as he is concerned, my failure will be the end of operations and the verification of his belief. He is testing me by assigning me Burma as a starting point and giving me the green light."

Stilwell's final directive gave Detachment 101 a multiple assignment: establish a base camp in northeast India from which operations could be conducted to deny the Japanese the use of the Myitkyina airport and the roads and railroad leading into it from the south, and closely coordinate operations with the British authorities to insure that there would be no mutual interference and that effective liaison was established.

Carl Eifler flew back to India determined to make Detachment 101 a success.

# The Secret Base

From the start the OSS men operated in India on the highest of command levels and without any written authority. The U.S. Army and the British alike found this hard to comprehend. Obviously, these were young officers with considerable ability, and since they had no evident assignment, why not give them one? When Carl Eifler returned from Chungking, one general endeavored to appoint him his provost marshal.

"The general asked me all sorts of questions," Eifler remembers. "I gave him nothing but noncommittal replies and blank looks. He couldn't believe that anybody could be so dumb and yet be a major."

The general took Vince Curl aside to ask about Eifler's assignment.

"Lieutenant, what do you know about any of this?" he asked.

"Sir, I'm his assistant," replied Curl.

Opaqueness was not limited to the top ranks. While fending off the brass's curiosity, the men were busy trying to find a place to establish a secret base. Northeast India was the most suitable base from which to put Stilwell's directive into action. It would be close as possible to the field of action, which was to be Burma, and handy to air bases at Chabua, Jaihot, and Dibrugarh, from which planes were flying over the Hump to China. Assam was the logical place, but exactly where? Carl Eifler, Bob Aitken, and John Coughlin drove a car up the winding road to Simla where Sir Reginald Dorman-Smith, after his precipitous departure from Burma, had set up a government in exile.

During the hottest five months of the year, the British rulers of India fled Delhi for Simla. Seventy-three hundred feet high in the foothills of the Himalayas rising to the north of the sweltering central plains, Simla possessed a climate enough like that of Britain to rekindle the spirit and restore health eroded by the torrid tropics and haphazard sanitation. The Tudor belfry of Christ Church Cathedral rose at the end of the Mall which was lined with teashops, banks, and stores. Any English schoolboy in India knew the story of how the bells of the church were cast from brass cannons seized from the Sikhs in the last fateful war with those redoubtable warriors. There were gardens and an eight-sided bandstand with pillars striped blue and white. Hedgerows and cottages were more reminiscent of Hampshire or Shropshire than of Uttar Pradesh or the Punjab. This was the Simla made famous by Rudyard Kipling's *Plain Tales from the Hills.*

Dorman-Smith was happy to see the OSS men at his office. He listened to their plans with approval. Yes, Assam would be the likely place to establish a base. Why not on a tea plantation? When Carl Eifler asked him if he could suggest a man who knew Burma and could speak its languages, he immediately thought of Colonel Wally Richmond, his military aide in Rangoon.

"I think that I have in Calcutta just the man who will suit you," he said. "The man, Wally Richmond, was on my personal staff all during the Japanese invasion. He knows the country and speaks the language. What date do you want him to report and where?"

Carl Eifler still was playing his personal "cloak-and-dagger" game, and as he talked to the governor of Burma, he triggered a tiny camera that peeked unobtrusively through a buttonhole in his coat. When he dropped in to see Dorman-Smith the next day, he showed him a photograph that the camera had taken of his desk. Dorman-Smith, a dutiful son, had been writing a letter to his aged mother in England. In the photo the sheet of stationery on his desk was already addressed, "Dear Mum." Carl Eifler had hardly garnered a state secret, but it was evident to the filial letter writer that these OSS men did have certain little technical tricks at their disposal.

Wally Richmond, Eifler learned, would meet him at Dinjan in Assam. He would be helpful in finding a place for the 101 forward base and in recruiting Burmese agents for the OSS. Recruiting trustworthy agents was a critical matter, because no Caucasian could move through Japanese-occupied Burma undiscovered.

The monsoons were still pelting rain down on the Assam hills when in early October Carl Eifler, Ray Peers, John Coughlin, and their new British recruit, Wally Richmond, went to Chabua to meet Colonel Henry Byroade, the commanding officer of the U.S. Service of Supply Advance Section No. 2, who was living in the home of a nearby tea planter. Byroade met the OSS party at the airport during a deluge. The temperature was over 100 degrees despite the rain.

"Why don't you get in touch with the Assam Company at Nazira?" he suggested.

Nazira was sixty miles south of Chabua on the edge of the Naga Hills, which stretched along the Burma border. The OSS men were told that they should get in touch with Allan Richardson, the general manager of the company that operated some of the finest tea gardens in Assam.

That night Ray Peers was in agony. Pus and blood drained out of his infected ears onto the pillowcase. In the morning Captain Riley of the 398th Army Hospital in Chabua drained his ears, cleaned them out, and dropped alcohol into them to stop the growth of the fungus. Peers felt better, but the pain was still intense.

There was no question about his accompanying Eifler, Richmond, and Coughlin on a jeep trip down the track that led to the Bengal and Assam Railroad towns of Ledo and Margarhita. Somewhere in the vicinity of those railroad stations the Reverend Brayton C. Case, an American Baptist missionary, who had led a band of students out of Burma during the last months of the Japanese conquest, had set up a camp. The Reverend Case was one of those rare second-generation American missionaries who had grown up more Burmese than American. Born at Myingyan in Upper Burma, he had been educated in the village schools taught by his parents. He had lived through a terrible drought with the suffering villagers at Myingyan, and when he traveled to the United States to take a university degree, he studied agriculture instead of theology in order to be of a direct economic help to his people. Upon his return to Burma he had founded the Pyinmana Agricultural School at Pyinmana in the northern part of the country. The school became famous for its poultry, pigs, and garden vegetables, all designed to enhance the Burmese diet.

Brayton Case and his agricultural school prospered until the Japanese came. Then his Burmese neighbors either sympathized with the invaders, were apathetic, or fled in terror. When Stilwell led Chinese soldiers to the defense of Toungoo, about ninety miles south of Pyinmana, rations became an immediate problem. The Chinese army could fight doggedly on a diet of rice, but they brought no rice from China and the Burmese countryside was in a turmoil. One day Case appeared at Stilwell's headquarters. Outside were a number of his students, and they had brought with them rice, vegetables, pigs, and fowl for the Chinese soldiers. The agricultural-school farm not only helped to provide the Chinese army with vital supplies, but as they retreated, the Reverend Case and his band of about forty or so students went ahead, collecting food for them. When the campaign was lost, Case and his students walked out of Burma with Stilwell. His stamina on the trail and his influence with his students impressed the defeated general. It was Stilwell who had given Eifler the agricultural missionary's name. He was certain that Case would urge his young Burmese friends to aid the OSS.

At the camp, Case readily agreed to let Eifler interview his students. Eifler asked his questions in English, and Case translated. Richmond listened in a bored way as if he could not understand the Burmese exchanges that took place between Case and the youths.

"First," Case asked Eifler, "what happens to these boys if they fail their course of training?"

Eifler gave Case a long, hard look. It was basic to OSS security that a half-trained agent could not be turned loose because he might go immediately to the enemy and tell everything he knew. Eifler's British mentors at Oshawa had explained that under these circumstances the agent must either be kept in tight security or he must be executed. In actuality, during the entire history of Detachment 101 only one OSS candidate was to prove impossible to train. He fled, was captured by the Calcutta police, turned over to the OSS office in that city, and fled again. Recaptured, he was brought to Nazira and handcuffed to a bedstead under guard until the OSS could persuade the British to jail him until after the war was over. He languished in jail, but the OSS paid his entire salary into an account which was opened for his use when he was released. Such was to be the relatively humane reality, but Eifler talked tough. Both the Reverend Case and the students must understand that this "was not going to be a Sunday School picnic."

"Any man who fails training would have to be executed. We can't have him going to the Japanese and telling them everything he's learned."

While Case gave no indication that Eifler's words were disturbing, he was deeply concerned and not a little frightened for his students. Not trusting Eifler, he remarked in Burmese to them, "Don't have anything to do with this man. He is the agent of the devil."

From all appearances he was advising the young men to assist Eifler in any way they could. The reality was far different.

"Carl, the reverend is telling the boys that you are the agent of the devil," Richmond informed Eifler.

Eifler was furious at the duplicity. He shouted at the Reverend Case, and the Reverend Case shouted back. The Burmese youths exchanged amused glances with one another at the sight of the two angry Americans. Cooperation seemed anything but likely, but in the months to come the Reverend Case and the OSS were to work together in the Burmese jungles on a mission of importance.

*        *        *

The next afternoon Peers was feeling better, and the 101 men drove together in a jeep over the rutted roads to Nazira. They splashed through muddy puddles and wallowed through quagmires, and finally arrived at Allan Richardson's comfortable bungalow. Over a cup of the celebrated Assam tea, Richardson told about the nine tea gardens that he managed, each from three to five thousand acres in size and with two to four thousand workers. From where they sat on the cool verandah sipping tea it was fifteen miles to the farthest gardens. In the compound nearby were office buildings, a dispensary, bungalows for other company officials, and a club with tennis courts. Life on the Assamese frontier was scarcely a hardship. Tigers might roar in the jungles across the Dikho River from the club and naked Naga tribesmen might come down out of the hills to sell human heads that they had taken on a raid, but an Englishman could play a set of tennis or two and relax afterward over a scotch and soda brought by a barefoot bearer.

That night the British were hospitality itself. Richmond and Eifler dined with the Richardsons at their bungalow while Howard, the company treasurer, and his wife played host to Peers and Coughlin. The Americans dined splendidly on the edge of the jungle and heard stories of how tigers, leopards, and giant cobras invaded the tea gardens at night. A herd of wild elephants had shoved into planter Peter Brooks's compound and rubbed their itchy backs on the steel beams that supported the bungalow. That was where Peers was to spend the night.

After dinner the British and their American guests met at the club for a nightcap. Monkeys chattered in the dark trees surrounding the verandah, and the river, three hundred feet wide, eddied past, making soothing sibilant sounds. Sitting back in their easy chairs, the men talked. A band of monkeys swung jabbering through the trees across the river.

"I believe I can hit one of those bastards," remarked Eifler, sipping a whiskey and soda, and he drew his .45 and fired into the gloom.

"You haven't even hit the tree," observed Richmond, sipping his own drink.

At this point the tea planters interfered. To shoot at the monkeys would offend the Hindu workers, who believed in the sanctity of all life. Eifler put away his pistol, but when the party went indoors to the barroom, he took his automatic out of its holster again.

"I believe I can knock this bottle off of your head," he told Richmond, who had been too obviously unimpressed by his shooting from the verandah.

"On one condition: if you succeed," replied Richmond, his British pride piqued, "I'll knock a bottle off of your head."

Richmond got up and stretched easily. He picked up the empty whiskey bottle and strode to the far end of the room. Placing the bottle on his head, he faced Eifler with a faint smile. Eifler aimed and fired. Glass shattered. It was Richmond's turn to shoot a bottle off Eifler's head. Glass flew again. A houseboy cried out in alarm, and servants came running to help repel what sounded like an attack by a band of dacoits. They arrived in time to see a smiling Carl Eifler shoot a cigarette off of the head of an equally smiling Wally Richmond. Richmond returned the sharpshooting compliment. Eifler handed the cork of the bottle to Richmond, who strode down to the far end of the verandah and placed it on his head. Eifler aimed. He scowled and lowered his pistol. The contest was over.

"He didn't know his risk," said Richmond years later, "for he was a crack shot, and I wasn't."

John Coughlin and Ray Peers, his infected ears aching from the shots, left the bar without a word. There were bullet holes in the walls. Their British hosts would undoubtedly have serious questions as to whether the trigger-happy members of the OSS group would make suitable guests. They walked with Peter Brooks to his bungalow. On the way they agreed, as Peers put it later, "that if either Carl or Wally had been six inches low in their aim, it would not have affected us."

Peers and Coughlin need not have been concerned over the impression their colleagues' actions, right out of a James Fenimore Cooper novel, had made on the British planters. Impeccable as their manners might be, they were a rough-and-ready frontier lot. They were interested only in helping the war effort, and in the morning they showed the Americans through the various structures that they could make available for a secret OSS base.

"You can easily see a vehicle coming across the broad tea fields at a distance," observed Allan Richardson. "You'll have privacy."

Wild elephants from the jungle had always followed a trail through the tea gardens. They rarely used the track now, but it was still called "Hatiputi," which is Hindustani for "elephant road." Hatiputi was also the name of one of the tea estates of the Assam Company, which spread along the road adjoining the main tea gardens. Richardson's assistant, who managed the Hatiputi Estate, had joined the British armed forces, and his bungalow was vacant. The OSS could have this building. The Tennis Club also could be turned over to them. With its large center hall, kitchen, and lavatories, it could house personnel, store supplies, and provide space for a photographic laboratory. From the start, Detachment 101 was determined to operate a field photo service as part of its intelligence-gathering activities. Two miles farther down the road was another bungalow which would make an ideal communications center. Campsites for agent trainees could be set up in the tea gardens and in the surrounding jungles.

The OSS men readily accepted the Assam Tea Company's offer to make its facilities available. They suggested to the planters that they let it be known that the U.S. Army was establishing the U.S. Experimental Station in the tea gardens. It was to be a center of malaria research.

In Delhi the remaining 101 men still ate at their long table in the main dining room of the Imperial Hotel next to the table set aside for General Stilwell and his personal staff. As General Stilwell, on a trip back from China, sat at dinner one evening, the detachment's one hard-drinking officer made his final dramatic entry into the room. Wearing a British military bush jacket, he strode to his seat at the table. Halfway through the meal, he leaned back in his chair and unbuttoned his jacket.

"Whee!" he shouted as a brace of pigeons flew out from their confinement within the jacket and flapped out of a window in the ceiling. General Stilwell sprang up and glared at the OSS men. The offending young officer and his colleagues alike stared morosely at their plates. It was probably just as well that the last echelon of Detachment 101 left Delhi by train only a few days later.

The party traveled to Calcutta. In Calcutta they marveled at the omnipresent bookstalls, which seemed out of place in a city where a man walking at night stepped over people sleeping on the sidewalks, or tripped on a corpse, dead of starvation or disease, awaiting the morning's cleanup gangs. They witnessed a parade of nationalists protesting the continuing British presence, and watched an agile youth climbing up an immense pile of wood, stacking it carefully around a corpse. The face of the dead man seemed to look upon the world for the last time as the flames leaped up. The travelers boarded a riverboat to steam up the Hooghly and the Brahmaputra to the port of Gauhati. There they boarded the Bengal and Assam Railroad to go to Chabua. Trucks took them south to Nazira along roads that to Irby Moree seemed more like watery canals. The monsoon rains continued to fall. The men had been traveling from Delhi for ten days.

At Nazira they found cots, blankets, and mosquito nets waiting for them. They had been drawn from the Service of Supply Advance Section No. 2 of the U.S. Army. The 101 men bought cooking utensils and food in the town bazaar. The tea planters hired cooks and bearers to look after them. Their numbers proliferated.

"The cook's caste prevented him from doing any cleaning of foods, washing pots and pans, or cleaning up," explained Ray Peers. "He had to have a helper. The bearer needed an assistant or two to wait upon tables. A sweeper was needed to clean the place, but his caste prevented him from cleaning up the bathroom. Only an untouchable could do that. We needed two chokdars as guards. In short, we needed from nine to twelve servants, whereas without the Indian caste system, we could have done with two or three."

When Peers and other Americans complained to Richardson about the sheer size of the household that threatened to engulf them, he laughed.

"This is a tea plantation," he said, "and without the proper bearers, the word would soon get out that there was something sticky about you all."

There could be nothing sticky about the U.S. Experimental Station, so the army of cooks, bearers, sweepers, and cleaners remained at Nazira in full force.

\*     \*     \*

While the OSS men were establishing a forward base at Nazira, Harry Little was dispatched to Calcutta to set up a purchasing office. Calcutta was the major business center in eastern India, and most of the things that 101 would want to purchase from the Indian economy would be available there. At the same time there were many Burmese refugee camps close to Calcutta, and Carl Eifler expected that they would be likely sources for recruits. A Calcutta office plainly could serve both functions.

Little rented a two-story bungalow in a walled compound in the Tolly Gunge District close to the outskirts of the city. To reach O house, as it came to be known, it was necessary to get into one of the taxis driven by a bearded Sikh and drive, horn tooting, out Chowringhee Road, renamed since independence to honor Jawaharlal Nehru. The road wound among the wandering sacred cows, the streetcars and buses bursting with Indians, some hanging precariously from the sides or riding on the roof, past the handsome clubs and the pastel-colored mansions behind their cast-iron fences. Turn left for a block, and there was the OSS headquarters—serene, unremarkable, and obscure. Soon all sorts of odd mail began to turn up at Box 9039 in the grandiose Victorian post office. The fledgling detachment now had both a supply and recruiting office in Calcutta and a secret base in Assam, close to the borders of Burma. It was the middle of October.

# "A" for Able

Carl Eifler called a meeting. The first team of agents must be sent into Burma by the end of the year. Late in September, General Stilwell had said he expected to hear "booms from the Burma jungle" within ninety days, and Eifler had no intention of disappointing him. He was resolute. There would be no delays.

"All things taken into account," remarked Peers, "this was utterly fantastic. We had no trainees, no radios, it was over three hundred miles away through some of the world's worst jungles, and there were less than three months to do it in. But that is what he wanted, so it became our established goal."

Peers further summed up the dilemma confronting Detachment 101.

"When we were initially recruited in the United States, each of us considered we would be going into operations behind the Japanese lines—both Carl and John had indicated that would be the case. It did not take long, however, to dispel this idea. So eager were we to get into the war that we completely overlooked the obvious. We did not take into account the problem of communication; that is, the ability to speak the language of the country and the particular dialect spoken in the locale of the operation. Nor did we consider the geography of the area, the knowledge of its peoples, its economy, its sociology, and a myriad of other details which comprise a working knowledge of the area. These things are absolutely essential to even the simplest of agent operations in order that the individual can pass himself off as a native of the area or be accepted by the people. Even this is oversimplified; an agent must have the proper appearance with respect to his physical features; he must be dressed in the proper attire down to the last detail; his documents must be in order; he must have the currency of the area and numerous other details which must be minutely planned and put into effect. If any one of these is left unattended to, the agent is immediately suspect and undoubtedly will be spotted and reported."

With a few extraordinary exceptions, all agents who were to work successfully behind the Japanese lines were to be natives of Burma. Guerrilla leaders were to be another matter. The immediate task was to recruit agents. This task was not as simple as Eifler had expected. The refugees in the camps near Calcutta had endured horrendous experiences during the Japanese attack and in their flight from Burma through the jungles and mountains, and most of them had no desire at all to return to their native land as long as the brutal Japanese military forces occupied it.

The initial assumption that British military personnel and civilians who had lived in Burma would be an enormous help in recruitment was correct. A handful of Americans also had lived in Burma, and presumably they would be more cooperative than the Reverend Case had been in their first meeting. Wally Richmond was particularly valuable in recruiting potential agents from the ranks of what remained of the Burma army. Among the first were young men with English fathers and Burmese mothers such as Lieutenants Beamish, Quinn, and Francis, and Captain Jack Barnard. Red Maddox, fresh from his last trip behind the Japanese lines to demolish the rolling mills at the Bawdwin mines, was among the first to volunteer. An Englishman, Captain Oliver Milton, later code-named "Oscar," was a descendant of the poet John Milton, and another early recruit. A young Greek, B. V. Aganoor, joined, as did Saw Judson, a Karen, who was a signaler in the miniscule Burma navy. Two candidates were also recruited at the refugee camps near Calcutta. Still others were discovered in camps along the border. Some signed up with the OSS for the pay they would earn, others because of their hatred of the Japanese, others out of patriotism, and still others simply because, marooned in India, they were homesick for Burma. All of the agents spoke English as well as at least one Burmese language and had the equivalent of American high-school studies to their credit. Three of the recruits had college degrees. British intelligence checked out their trustworthiness. The recruits journeyed to Nazira by boat up the Brahmaputra River or by rail and truck. By October 20 they were assembled at the plantation, and training was to start.

*     *     *

The first OSS man to be wounded was the doctor, Archie Chun Ming. Carl Eifler was practicing with a spear that had been carried down from the hills by a Naga tribesman, and it missed its target and impaled Archie's foot. The doctor accepted this blow from his crestfallen commanding officer with grace; he simply bound up his wound and employed his medical skills to nurse himself back to health.

Chun Ming was still limping about the Nazira base when training started for the "A" or "Able" group of twelve agents. Many of the OSS techniques learned at Camp X in Ontario and Area B in Maryland had to be discarded in the light of Burmese mountain conditions. Eifler had studied the methods employed by Lord Louis Mountbatten and his Commandos in a raid on Nazi-held Norway, and he had brought British sabotage gear with him from America. But commando methods used successfully in Europe were not likely to be successful in Burma. The basic principles promised to be valid enough, but the critical details must be refined to meet jungle conditions.

From the first day of training it became evident that the recruits could tell the Americans more about how to proceed with their mission inside Burma than the Americans could tell them. They informed their OSS mentors about the history and customs, dress and habits of Burmese, Shans, Karens, Was, Nagas, and Kachins.

Ray Peers recalls some of the questions put to A Group: "What are the trinkets an itinerant peddler sells? How much daylight filters through a rain forest? What is the name of the headman's son in the village of Wadat Ga? Is the root of the jacaranda tree used as medicine?"

"We used to sit around bamboo tables, intensely collecting such particles of information so that one day in the near future this group might sneak into Burma," he wrote later.

There was training in the use of demolitions, in weapons, and in the destruction of bridges, locomotives, trucks, and airplanes parked at airfields. The agents learned how to pick both locks and pockets with impunity, how to forge documents, read maps, kill a sentry without making a noise, send and receive Morse code, and encipher and decipher messages. At least once a day they ran an obstacle course in the nearby jungle. Carl Eifler added an inimitable touch of realism to their exercise by firing his .45 a few inches ahead of their chests, keeping a clinical eye on each recruit to see how he reacted.

The training went well, but with Eifler's deadline drawing always closer to hand, staff and trainees worked long hours. For the first three or four weeks instructors sat up every night as late as 4 A.M. to revise the training material that they had brought from the United States according to the fascinating variations in techniques that the trainees had suggested. For example, the use of explosives was hardly a novelty to men who had worked in either the teak forests or the tin mines of Burma. Red Maddox alone could come up with enough imaginative ideas on the placement of explosives to require a revision of the manual. When the newest delaying devices arrived from Washington, the Burmese had no trouble at all in mastering their use.

The late hours kept by the instructors began to tell. Since the trainees arose at 5 A.M. and started their work soon afterward, there was little time for the staff to sleep. Training for the day ended at sunset unless a night exercise was scheduled. In no time at all the Americans of Detachment 101 came to be the most haggard-looking young men in all of India. At least so it seemed to the tea planters, who watched with amazement the zeal and energy that they put into their work. No time could be lost.

\*     \*     \*

The only practical way for the agents to keep in touch with base was by radio, but as yet no long-range radio had been developed that would be light enough for an agent to carry through the jungles. To be satisfactory, the receiver-transmitter should not weigh more than twenty-five pounds, and a power pack must not weigh more than another twenty-five. The transmitter and receiver must be able to reach anywhere from two hundred fifty to five hundred miles, the estimated distances from Nazira to the North Burma wilderness areas, which were to be the sites of the first field operations. It was about four hundred miles from Nazira to Japanese-held Myitkyina, the focal point of the campaign being planned by General Stilwell and his staff. It was hoped that lightweight radios might be developed later on that would reach the entire thousand miles from Nazira to Rangoon.

Phil Huston, Allen Richter, Don Eng, and Fima Haimson were charged with building a radio that would meet the agents' needs. Huston searched the Service of Supply warehouses at Chabua. In a warehouse stacked with material to be shipped to China under the Lend-Lease program, he discovered twenty-five V-100 radios. These

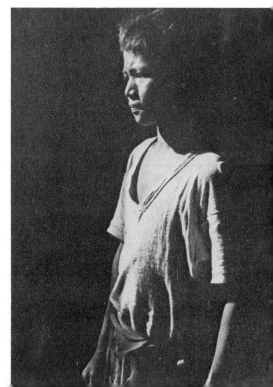

(Above) Father James Stuart of the Columban Order, pistol and Kachin knife at his belt, Aussie campaign hat cocked rakishly over an ear, was not the usual Catholic missionary in Burma. Revered by the Kachins, he dared Japanese retribution to continue his ministry to the jungle people. (Right) Father Stuart rescued scores of Kachin women, old men, and children, such as this Kachin boy, from the Japanese terror in Hukawng Valley.

(Above) The road runs through Nazira, the Assamese village close to the secret OSS base located on a nearby tea plantation. (Below) British Colonel Wally Richmond's life of adventure in prewar Burma proved invaluable when he joined Detachment 101. (Right) The first hill people that 101 men encountered were the Naga headhunters whose country reached to the banks of the Dikho River.

(Clockwise from bottom left) A 101 parachute expert suits up a Kachin for his first drop behind the Japanese lines. Over a target drop crews push supplies out of the door of a bucking and zooming plane. The parachutes break open, and the supplies waft down toward the waiting 101 men hidden by the jungle canopy. A 101 force on the hill beside their drop panels is ready to rush down the path to pick up the supply drop.

(Top left) An air drop floats down close to a Kachin village atop a mountain. (Bottom left) Parachutes descend toward a drop field marked by the recognition panels. (Below) Vincent Curl meets with Zhing Htaw Naw, Kachin duwa kaba, whose quiet, gentle manner gave little indication of his tigerish determination to avenge his people for the brutal attacks that the Japanese had made on villages in the Hukawng.

Carl Eifler, 101's first commander charms a snake.

Vincent Curl followed by agent Goldie and Zhing Htaw Naw lead Kachin hypenlas along the banks of a jungle stream.

had a range of only fifty miles, but he took them back to Nazira as a source of parts. Harry Little bought tubes on the Indian civilian market in Calcutta. Parts that couldn't be cannibalized from existing equipment or purchased were improvised. Condensers and variable tuning capacitors were fashioned out of C-ration cans, and carbon rods were drawn out of flashlight batteries to serve as resistors. Crystals for the 3500-kc frequency selected were taken from discarded Signal Corps equipment. Such a low frequency allowed the signal to carry for long distances. As it turned out, when conditions were just right, the signal bouncing off the ionosphere layers could be picked up halfway around the world. The radiomen fashioned a light chassis, resembling a metal cigar box, out of the belly skin of a C-47 that crashed in a landing. A piece of insulated wire was used as an antenna, which they soon discovered worked well when tossed over a tree or bush. The higher the aerial was placed, the longer the distance the signal would carry. The final model, power pack and all, weighed just three pounds over the projected weight. Dry cells provided the power. Each set was installed in a wooden box.

Seventy-two sets were now ready to be issued to agents, but they had to be field tested. Don Eng lugged a radio transmitter-receiver aboard a train and started out on a hegira to the south of India. As he traveled farther and farther away on the crowded Indian trains, he kept a regular schedule of transmission with the newly built radio base at Nazira. The men back at the base followed his progress with fascination. Could the makeshift equipment put together in the tea-planter's club do the job? One day there was a transmission from more than five hundred miles away. Don Eng didn't stop his journey until he reached Madras, twelve hundred miles from Nazira. The radiomen couldn't help but cheer at their success and raced one another to headquarters to let Carl Eifler know that the sets were ready for the agents to take into Burma.

OSS Detachment 101 radio at Nazira was now on the air, but it didn't use military procedures. Instead it was an odd mix of OSS enigma and ham radio, and it had no call letters. When it contacted a military unit, it never gave away its location or identity but merely sent a message and then signed off. The American and British stations in Burma and China complained to Washington about the mysterious station that was interrupting their transmissions. It sounded as if it were American, but if so, what Americans were these and where were they located?

\*          \*          \*

As supplies for the planned incursion into Burma arrived at Dinjan from the United States or Calcutta, they were stockpiled in a bamboo warehouse erected about four hundred feet from the main runway at the airfield. Bulky equipment was placed under canvas tarpaulins. The 101 men kept on guard at Chabua watched the supplies and equipment accumulate with a great deal of satisfaction.

On four days in October, without warning, the Japanese air force launched a series of raids on the airfields in the Chabua-Dinjan area from which American planes were flying the Hump. Bombers roared in and caught the defending fighters on the ground, destroying thirty U.S. transports and fighters with bombs and machine guns.

When the Japanese planes screamed down on the airport at Chabua, 101 men joined the other Americans in a mad run to the slit trenches that had been dug as air-raid shelters, only to discover that the Indian laborers at work around the airfield had been using them as latrines. Even so, they lay as close to the bottom of the trenches as they could get. The wham of the bombs only a short distance away and the clatter and whine of machine-gun fire were enough to take away their squeamishness.

The American losses were severe the first day, but after that they were able to get .30 and .50 caliber machine guns set up and fire back. One black sergeant aimed with his rifle at a Japanese Zero pulling up from a strafing run and hit it in a vulnerable spot. The plane spewed smoke and spun out of control into a nearby hill where it burst into flames. The Americans clapped their black compatriot on the back for his spectacular shot, jumped up and down, and cheered, heedless of the remaining Zeros which were spitting death down upon them. On the last day of the raids the remaining American fighter planes got off the ground and engaged the Zeros in a dogfight. They shot down several of the attackers and were able to prevent the destruction of the previous days.

"As far as Detachment 101 was concerned, the first day was the big one," Ray Peers sorrowfully noted. "In one of their first passes they hit the 101 supply warehouse and burned it to the ground. It was a good thing the dynamite, TNT, Composition C, and ammunition had been removed or there would have been an even hotter time. We lost a great amount of supplies and equipment in that raid. Some of it could be reordered from SOS or purchased on the Indian market. Other items, however, had to be ordered from the States, and it was a year to eighteen months before we were to receive them."

Detachment 101, never oversupplied, had been dealt a serious set-back by the Japanese bombers. In Calcutta Harry Little and the other supply people bought, scrounged, begged, and appropriated everything they could get their hands on in order to gather together the necessary equipment and supplies so that A Group could still get into North Burma on time.

*      *      *

"If you are bitten by one of them, better kiss your wife good-bye, because that is about all you will have time for," the planters told the Americans.

They were warning the OSS men about the krait, a tiny, wiggling shoelace of a reptile that was so deadly its venom usually brought about death within twenty minutes. If the bite was in a particularly vulnerable place a victim might die in two minutes. The krait was called the "widow snake," the "kiss of death," or the "shoe snake" because it crept into a man's shoes at night and waited, snug and happy, for him to slip his foot inside in the morning. It also was called the "door snake" because it was fond of dozing atop a door ledge. When the door was slammed, the sleeping krait tumbled down onto the shoulders of an unsuspecting person below.

"The krait is not a vicious snake," said Ray Peers, always accurate even when it came to poisonous reptiles. "He bites only in self-defense. If he is stepped on, or rolled on in a sleeping bag, he may strike. We had the most difficulty with them in our shoes. Everyone got in the habit of banging their shoes on the floor a couple of times before putting them on in the morning. There were about eight of us sleeping in one large room, and during one week, three kraits were found in our shoes."

The men had screened in an open space beneath one of the bungalows to provide more space. One night Bob Aitken and Ray Peers were working late in the enclosed space when they heard something pushing at the screen door.

"See what it is," suggested Peers, his mind on the training plans laid out on the table in front of him.

"We have a caller all right," said Aitken when he stepped to the door. "Look for yourself."

Peers joined his friend. A krait of nightmarish size was outside lunging against the screen. Instead of the pencil-like snake that they had expected a krait to be, it was an enormous, banded reptile, six feet long. In a way, the black and yellow creature was beautiful, but it also was deadly. The snake had the two men at its mercy. There was only one door leading out of the enclosure, and once a man stepped through this he had to walk down a dark passageway. In the gloom the snake could strike him at any time.

There was a screened window on the far side of the room. Peers knocked it out and climbed through the aperture. He stole up the stairs into the bungalow, returned with a shotgun, and stationed himself in a hall that crossed the one in which the snake lurked. Fortunately, Aitken had a flashlight. The snake had disappeared from the doorway, but now that Peers was in position, he carefully opened the screen door and began a wary advance. His flashlight stabbed into the gloom. There was the snake! It was coiled and ready to strike. Aitken was slow and patient. He must not goad the krait into an attack. The snake was just as slow. As it uncoiled and slid indolently along the floor away from him, Aitken kept it in the beam of his flashlight.

Peers, waiting at the cross hall, saw the patch of light advance beyond the corner of the wall. Then the snake poked its head into view. It glided forward. Peers pulled the trigger. At the shotgun's roar, 101 men sleeping in the bungalow above leaped out of their beds, snatched up their weapons, and came running. They found that the blast from Peers's weapon had blown about a foot off the front of the snake, which was still writhing in its death agony. At least, the 101 men agreed, a banded krait had the advantage of being too big to crawl into a man's shoe.

\*     \*     \*

The Naga Hills arose just across the Dikho River from Nazira and rolled away, a jumble of mountains up to ten thousand feet high, reaching across to the border of Burma to the Hukawng Valley and the Kachin villages that had been destroyed by the Japanese. Brooks rushed down the steep slopes, and waterfalls dropped from rocky ledges. The trails were shaded by the dense canopy of the jungle and festooned with giant ferns. Lianas dangled fifty feet to the ground from their hold on the great trees, which often had a diameter of four or five feet. The forest floor was strewn in places with a magnificent carpet of tiny red and yellow flowers. There were many varieties of banana trees too, some with leaves up to six feet long and three feet wide. A Naga tribesman could wrap a banana leaf around his naked body at night to keep warm and dry. During the day he could hold it over his head as an umbrella to keep off the monsoonal rain.

This was a land where tigers and leopards prowled and elephants roamed, where the bottle birds seemed to cry "one more bottle" both night and day, and brilliant green snakes slithered over the forest floor. To most OSS men fresh from the United States, the Naga Hills offered the first experience of what it was like to be in a South Asian jungle. At first they simmered in the muggy heat of the lower hills, but as they climbed ever higher on the winding trails, the sweat dried clammy on their arms. They zigged and zagged up into colder climes where at night they shivered in the chill. On the trail their legs grew heavier with the passing hours until they were barely able to stumble ahead. It was at moments such as this that a worn-out American, still unaccustomed to the tropics and high elevations, felt singularly effete and ineffective when he saw a band of Nagas come springing and leaping down the trail as if they were goats—tireless, sinewy, muscular, often with heavy loads on their heads or backs.

Once outsiders crossed what the British officials called the "Outer Line," they were in Nagaland, where the friendly villagers had become accustomed to occasional parties of white men or Indians from Assam. But just twenty miles from Nazira was the Inner Line, and the land of the Naga headhunters lay beyond. The Nagas were not known to have any particular fancy for white men's heads, but then they didn't discriminate against them either. They were known to prefer those with long hair and big ears. Given a choice, they would also prefer to sever the head of a woman or child, which would be more efficacious in the fertility rites. A young Naga warrior who wanted to bring his best girl friend a romantic offering might bring her a freshly cut-off human head. It was a very romantic thing to do, because it helped insure that she would bear him many fine children and that the crops the couple planted would grow well, too. Their reputation as headhunters made the Nagas appear to be a very romantic people. At least they usually confined their headhunting to a time when they were not busy growing their skimpy crops of rice in their mountain fields, and they usually did not take this activity too seriously unless the crops were bad or the women infertile.

It was Carl Eifler and a Burmese agent who first went into the hills to meet the Nagas. Could they be persuaded to let A Group carry out training in their jungled mountains? The base at Nazira had been chosen not only because it was close to Burma but also because the Naga Hills offered a foretaste of the terrain in which the OSS teams must operate. The jungle along the trail that Eifler and the agent at first followed lacked the high canopy that kept out life-giving light, and the forest floor was choked with vegetation. They could not see more than five feet off the trail.

As the men walked up the trail, streaming with sweat and itching with insect bites, they felt the prickly sensation that they were being observed by unseen eyes. Rounding a bend in the trail, they unexpectedly came upon three nearly naked Naga girls carrying baskets on their heads. Without a sound, the girls threw down the baskets and ran. There was the soft patter of bare feet on the path, and then silence. A slight breeze stirred the foliage by the trail, or was it a Naga spearman? The Burmese and the American were nowhere near the Inner Line, but the flight of the girls might well mean that the hard-to-understand Nagas were on the warpath.

"Call out and say we are friends," Eifler told the agent.

"I don't speak their language."

"Well, damn it, say it in any language you can, then."

The agent gave him an agonized look, but he called out in Burmese and then in Hindi. Eifler shouted friendly greetings in Japanese. The silence was more profound, except for a coppersmith, which unaccountably began its song. Usually this bird began its "tong, tong, tong, tong" chant in the night, but here it was singing in the day. Perhaps the darkness and gloom of the jungle could account for the strange behavior, or perhaps instead the bird was not a bird at all, but rather a tribesman hidden among the giant ferns, signaling to other tribesmen who waited in ambush.

The two men moved ahead up the trail until they came out into a clearing. There in the middle of the open space three Naga men, naked except for loincloths, squatted on their heels around a cook fire. They paid no attention whatsoever to the strangers and made no response or motion as Eifler and the agent spoke to them in Burmese, Japanese, Hindi, and English and then vigorously pantomimed their friendly intentions. Still without any verbal response, one man at last reached into a woven bag which was tied around his waist. He took out a tin can. The tin can contained a smaller tin can, which in turn contained still a smaller can. With deliberation he took can from within can, until from within the fifth can he drew out a piece of paper. He handed the paper to Eifler.

"The bearer of this note and his people wish to work for the U.S. Army," were the English words on the note.

Eifler laughed with relief. The three Nagas walked back down the trail with the two men.

At Nazira, Eifler installed the men from the mountains on the edge of the jungle in what he called O Camp. With elaborate sign language he let them know he wished them to make a dugout such as the Nagas were reputed to use on the rivers on the far side of their territory. Over the following weeks there was no action, but he didn't expect any, since he never did provide the tribesmen with a log. As long as the three Nagas stayed at O Camp, he believed that it would be safe enough for A Group to carry out a training mission short of the Inner Line. He could not be sure, because he never did learn who wrote the note that the Naga carried. Was it a tea planter on a tiger shoot in the hills, a British frontier officer, or perhaps for that matter, a Japanese agent? Eifler never solved the mystery, and the three Nagas lolled about their camp, undoubtedly convinced that working for the U.S. Army was every bit as enjoyable and easy an existence as a man could ask for.

At least it was not long before Eifler's confidence in the Nagas was reinforced. A Naga appeared one day at headquarters. He had run down out of the hills with the startling report that airplanes with red circles on the wings had parachuted strange men into the mountains above Nazira. Eifler indicated that he would pay a reward if they would bring in the Japanese soldiers.

Six days later, as the American staff was sitting down to lunch, several Nagas strode out of the jungle carrying a basket woven of bamboo. Unsmiling and stolid, they put it down on the table amid the serving dishes. One of the Americans took off the lid. Within were the severed heads of the Japanese. Gagging, the men dashed away from the lunch table. Carl Eifler remained seated. He calmly dug into his pocket, took out a fistful of silver rupees, and paid them to the Nagas. The Nagas clinked the rupees cheerfully in their hands, smiled at last, and slipped back into the jungle.

The OSS men were left with an unsolved question. Had the Japanese learned about their secret base at Nazira, or had the parachutists simply been dropped into the area to win friends among the Nagas in preparation for a possible military thrust?

\*     \*     \*

The Nagas were the first of the people who lived in the high mountains that tumble around the base of the Himalayas in northeastern India, northern Burma, and western China whom the members of Detachment 101 were to meet. Who were they? At a glance it could be seen that they were of Mongolian origin. They were an ancient tribe or, more accurately, the remainder of several ancient tribes who had come down into the lower mountains from the bleak Central Asiatic highlands north of Tibet. The Kachin people had driven them into the Naga Hills as they in their turn pushed into North Burma on their own migration from the inhospitable rooftop of the world.

It was time for A Group and the American 101 men to begin conditioning hikes into the hills. They forded streams and struggled through the jungle on cross-country exercises. Mosquitoes and gnats, oblivious of insect repellents, droned about their heads and arms. The insects slipped into mouths, ears, and eyes, and crept up into noses. Lungs strained for air as the men labored up the steep hills beneath their field packs. They stopped every hundred yards or so and panted for breath. It took several weeks of hard physical training before their hearts and lungs adjusted to the altitude and they learned to pace their steps. How in the devil could the Nagas, who were slighter in build than the muscular Americans at least, move so effortlessly up and down the mountains carrying such prodigious loads? Both men and women trotted along the trail beneath a heavy pack or carrying baskets of rice attached to their backs by frames made of jungle vine ropes. A tumpline reached to their forehead to give stability to the load. Both men and women were sturdy and long-waisted. They had the long tapered legs of long-distance runners.

The leeches in the hills were several inches long, and they could stretch themselves so thin that they could infiltrate through a shoelace hole. Once within a shoe, they attached themselves to the ankle, or crept up the victim's leg to find a sensitive spot, perhaps in the calf or thigh, but more often in the crotch, where they could suck blood with relative impunity. They excreted a fluid that numbed the flesh so that the animal or man suffering their attack could not feel it. At the end of a hike through the hills a man would pull off his boots or leggings and find the omnipresent leeches bloated with his blood. Just brushing them off brought the risk of leaving the leech's head affixed to the flesh. Unless it was dug out with a knife or razor blade, it would cause a nasty sore that took weeks to heal. Leeches could be taken off by several methods. One could hold a lighted cigarette up to its tail, not close enough to kill it, but close enough so that it would writhe with the heat and drop off. Or a little tobacco could be rubbed on the leech and on the skin around it to loosen its hold. A Naga had none of this trouble: when a leech slipped off a leaf onto his bare skin, he plucked it off before it could adhere. The advantages of going half naked in the jungle were evident, and later many OSS men were to do just that.

As the trainees hiked in the hills, they sometimes came upon parties of Nagas staring at them from the foliage beside the trail. Their lips were often smeared with the blood-red saliva produced by chewing betel nuts. Long tangled hair strung around the faces of both men and women. Scabs on their dirt-caked bodies were a reminder to the Americans and the Burmese trainees that any untreated sore in the jungle was likely to fill with pus within a few hours. The Americans expecting the sort of full-bosomed savage women portrayed in countless *National Geographic* articles were disappointed to see the wrinkled, dried-up breasts of most of the women they encountered on the trails. They asked one another how long they were going to have to stay in these hills before the women began to look good.

Not all the Nagas were so unsavory in appearance or smelled as bad as the villagers who resided beneath the Inner Line. As 101 men penetrated ever farther into the mountains, they began to encounter hardier, prouder men who wore red cotton blankets and a spare girdle with a flap about six inches wide that covered the genitals at least part of the time. The hair of the men was cut in neat bangs that fell to the eyebrows. The women were as bare-breasted as their sisters farther down the mountain slopes, but their skirts were well made of woven cane, and extended from the waist to about eight inches above the knees. They, too, threw red cotton blankets over their shoulders.

As a party of upland Nagas came down the trail, their naked children darting among them, they made a colorful sight. As they passed, they often sang a cheerful but eerie song. Each individual sang only one note, but they were sounded in varying orders to make up different melodies. If one of the notes was missing from a song, the group knew that one of their number was missing. Possibly enemy headhunters had got him.

Despite their dread reputation, the Nagas whom the 101 men came to know as they hiked into the mountains proved to be lighthearted and cheerful in their everyday life. During the harvest season in particular there were frequent festivals. If a festival was taking place, the people blocked the entrance to their village with piles of brush or tree branches as a warning to strangers to stay out. Nobody could enter once a dance had started, and if a dance commenced while strangers were in the village, they were not allowed to leave until it was finished. On one of their forays into the hills one OSS team entered a Naga village, where they were warmly received and where they were offered copious quantities of chang, a sour but palatable soupy home brew. "It's about time we push off down the trail," said the leader as he watched some young Naga men flourishing spears in a spear dance.

As the group arose to leave, the men aimed their spears in their direction, and it seemed wise to remain for the rest of the party. When the last food was devoured, the last bit of chang consumed, and the last dance ended, the OSS team was permitted to leave the village and go on its way.

The center of village life was the men's club. There beneath the high thatched roof, the men assembled at the thumping of a gong made by hollowing out a tree into a shape similar to that of a dugout canoe. Patient fingers carved the ends of the gong into horns and human figures. Beating the great gong with a pestle used to pound rice, the drummer called the men to meeting. During a celebration or the threat of a raid alike, the great gong beat out its message of joy or alarm.

Gathered about the gong, the men of the village made the important decisions concerning everyday life, determined where justice rested in disputes among villagers, and planned raids on hostile villages. It was indeed an easygoing, happy life in tune with the environment of jungled mountains, but let the crops be meager or the women fail to produce a sufficient number of babies, preferably boys, the mood changed, and a head raid became part of the agenda. Armed with flintlock guns, spears, and crossbows and arrows, the Naga warriors set out toward the land of their enemies. Knowing that huts built in high trees or high on bamboo stilts would provide easy lookouts with keen-eyed boys on the watch, the warriors always hid in the jungle beyond reach of discovery until it was dark. Before dawn they moved into position close to the village. Only when it was light enough to avoid the spiked bamboo stakes set up to protect the village from attack would they make their rush. Wielding their long, sharp swordlike knives with deadly precision, the attackers severed as many heads of men, women, and children as they could before the village men recovered from their surprise and fought back.

A second party was always kept in reserve, and it now attacked the village granaries, which were usually about two hundred yards away. They flung flaming torches into them, knowing that the fires would bring the villagers running to save their precious food stores before they were destroyed. Under cover of the fire, the raiding party fled into the jungle and hurried down the trails, carrying their heads dripping fresh blood, until they were at a safe distance. Among the Nagas life was made up of raid and counter-raid, death and triumph, barren fields and barren women, or fields heavy with rice and women great with child.

It was time now for A Group to undertake a practice sabotage. About twenty miles into Naga country, close to the Inner Line, was a long-abandoned coal mine that the British had opened up years earlier. Striking through the jungles, the group, by now numbering eight hardened, intensely trained men, reached the coal mine without incident. They had no idea that after they crossed the Dikho River, they had been watched each step of the way by invisible eyes. They were studying the best way to position their explosives to wreak the maximum of havoc, when a strong force of armed Nagas appeared out of the jungle and surrounded them. Behind the Nagas came a natty detail of Indian troops whom the Nagas had summoned from Assam. For a moment the hapless trainees thought of resisting, but they regained their senses.

"It would have been a foolhardy way to die," said one agent-to-be. "If I must die, I would prefer doing it in an actual operation."

Marched off to an Indian jail, they were accused of being Japanese spies. Indian authorities interrogated them to learn how they had infiltrated into the hills, and the location of their Japanese masters. The agents refused to reply. Fortunately, when the Indian authorities found they presumably had Japanese spies in their jail, they informed the Americans at the supposed U.S. Experimental Station. The Americans took a truck over to the jail and after some embarrassed explanations brought home their crestfallen agents. Infiltrating the land of the Nagas had turned out to be beyond their capacities. Would infiltrating the jungles of North Burma be any easier?

1943

# Into Burma

A silver Burma rupee bearing the face of George V, king of Great Britain, emperor of India, was considered a fair price for a day's portage, but the Shans who gathered about Carl Eifler and John Coughlin at Putao, near Fort Hertz in the far north of Burma, would not even consider it. Nor would they work for a silver rupee bearing the likeness of King Edward VII, although this antique coin contained four times the silver in the George V coins. For that matter, they would not work for a square of opium, weighing a quarter ounce, and this was the highest pay a porter could conceivably be offered.

Eifler cursed. Coughlin fumed. Just three days after Christmas Coughlin, Eifler, and Richter had boarded two DC-3s at Chabua with the eight members of A Group commanded by Jack Barnard. All wore British uniforms. The Japanese air force dominated the airspace over North Burma, and four American fighters flew along to ward off any patroling Zeros that might discover the two transports. Only a few days remained before the deadline imposed by General Stilwell, and Eifler was determined to get A Group into the field in time.

The DC-3s and their escort flew at an elevation of from ten to twelve thousand feet over the Naga Hills and the vast jungles of the Hukawng. Winston Churchill had called northern Burma "the most formidable fighting country imaginable," and there it was stretching beneath the plane. Range upon range of jungled summits reached ever higher toward the gigantic peaks of the Himalayas. The vast ocherish-brown Chomolungma, Goddess Mother of the World, the Sacred One of the Tibetans, rose to the highest eminence of ice and snow on the planet. Better known to people in the West as Mount Everest, Chomolungma was about three hundred miles away. Beyond was the enormous pyramid of 28,150-foot Kanchenjunga and

27,790-foot Makalu. It was only one hundred and fifty miles to the lower Himalayas, dominated by 25,500-foot Namsha Barwa, situated where the Naga Hills rise to meet the Master Range. The Brahmaputra River, raging at the foot of Namsha Barwa, flows through what is most likely the world's deepest canyon, but it is situated in such a tangle of mountains that it has never been explored. Only occasional wandering Kachins, Nagas, or other even less known tribesmen know how to reach the canyon.

Atop some of the mountains beneath the planes the men could make out thatched villages in the Naga Hills. These were the villages of the headhunting Nagas with whom they had already become all too familiar. Beyond the Naga country the villages must belong to the even more formidable Kachins. The OSS men had no way of knowing this, but somewhere in that wild country beneath them, in the north of the Hukawng Valley where Ngai Tawng's village now lay in desolation, Zhing Htaw Naw was already leading his men in vengeful forays against the outposts the Japanese had established in the jungled valleys.

Terrible winds from the Himalayas menaced the planes. Blowing out of the heart of Asia from the plains of Mongolia, the winds rose over the high frigid mountains north of Tibet, where the ancestors of the Kachins and the Nagas alike had their homes. They screamed over the lofty tableland of Tibet and ascended higher still over the Himalayas to sweep down on the struggling aircraft. Violent downdrafts threatened to toss them into the mountains. Motors roared defiance to the wind as the planes soared low over the forested peaks. From the air the men could make out several wrecked planes that had been plummeted to destruction by the winds.

At last the DC-3s circled the airstrip that the British had hacked out of the jungles at Fort Hertz, a military outpost named for the British soldier who had established it long ago when the first Tommies penetrated up the trails from the river valleys in order to keep an eye on the unmarked borders with China and Tibet. A single runway reached about nine hundred feet from where two trees had been felled to make a crude bridge across a stream to where four dead trees stood as markers at the far end.

Once the Detachment 101 men were on the ground they set about their business. Their plan, formulated with British liaison before leaving Chabua, was this: A Group was expected to infiltrate south through the Japanese lines which were said to be just beyond the

Kachin town of Sumprabum, fifty miles southeast, and operate against the roads and railroads that supplied Myitkyina—the main Japanese base in North Burma—from the south. They were to establish contact with the Kachin Levies, a British-led Kachin force—a remnant of the Burma army—which was opposing the Japanese south of Fort Hertz. Coughlin and Eifler intended to establish a forward base at Sumprabum. A British officer, in command of the Kachin Levies at Fort Hertz, Lieutenant Colonel Gamble, was known to be a capable officer, and the 101 men were confident that he would help them accomplish their two missions.

The only transport possible over the rough road that reached south to Sumprabum were elephants and coolies. In the nearby Shan town of Putao it proved easy enough to hire fourteen elephants to haul the gear intended for the base, but it proved impossible to hire porters. The Shans of Putao had no desire to antagonize the Japanese. The bloody attack the invaders had made on the Kachin villages to the south only seven months before may not have cowed the Kachins, but it had convinced the Shans that the Japanese had indeed come to stay. The Shans had first emigrated into the area from the Shan kingdom of Nanchao in China in the seventeenth century, and they had established seven small principalities that were grouped together in a league called Hkamti Long, with Putao as its leading town. Out in the hills and jungles, most of the people who lived in the vicinity were either Kachins or Nagas, and the Shans felt themselves to be an isolated island of civilization among savages. Shan agents had been working with the Japanese from their first arrival in North Burma, in the hopes of breaking the strength of their traditional Kachin enemies. These new men in British uniforms were not to be trusted. Let the two tall leaders curse and fume.

"It is not important," Gamble told the Americans when he learned that they had not been able to recruit Shan porters. "The Kachins will help."

Gamble sent a Kachin boy up into the mountains to ask the Kachins to provide porters, and the next morning a bevy of Kachin girls and women hiked into Fort Hertz. They laughed and giggled, and their diminutive frames seemed incapable of carrying anything at all. But on December 30, when the party set off, elephants and all, on the rutted road to Sumprabum, the Kachin women lifted loads of from thirty-five to fifty pounds onto their heads, or strapped them to their backs, and set off down the trail at a pace that left the Americans and the Anglo-Burmese agents floundering in the rear. Hour after hour the Kachin women kept to the trail.

"My God," groaned Allen Richter, as he watched the group depart. "If the women are like this, I can't imagine what the men must be like."

Richter stayed behind at Fort Hertz. Saw Judson was to be the radio operator with A Group, and Richter was to establish a radio post. He soon was on the air to base at Nazira.

"Came in loud and clear," Ray Peers noted with satisfaction.

By January 6, the 101 men had trekked the fifty miles to Sumprabum, which in the Kachin language means "jungle grass mountain." Carl Eifler established the OSS forward base at the onetime American Baptist Mission, situated about a half mile from town.

"There were three or four houses, a small church, a school building, and one other building," recalls Eifler. "There also was a broken-down Chevrolet car with the remains of a dead Chinese soldier in the front seat."

The Chinese soldier had died during the bitter withdrawal of the Chinese army through Sumprabum the previous spring. He was a grim reminder that the Japanese had won a great victory and would be very difficult to dislodge from North Burma. The formidable Japanese 18th Division was now based at Myitkyina and controlled most of northern Burma except for the Kachin-held mountains and the region north of Sumprabum, which was held by the Kachin Levies, who, Eifler noted, were armed with an odd assortment of muzzle-loading flintlocks, muzzle-loading percussion cap rifles, shotguns, British Enfield rifles, and Bren guns.

Could the Kachins hold against a determined thrust from the battle-hardened Japanese army? On January 7, four hundred Japanese started north from Myitkyina. The Kachin Levies ambushed them on the road just north of Nsopzup, some forty-five miles from their starting point. When the battle was over, only a handful of Japanese had survived, and the Kachins had disappeared into the jungle. When Carl Eifler and John Coughlin heard about the Kachin victory, they were convinced that the Kachins might well be the ally that the OSS must find in Burma if it were to form a significant guerrilla resistance to the Japanese and infiltrate behind their lines. They were elated, though they were well aware that infiltrating as many as eight men in a group was going to be extremely dangerous. Two or three men would make a much more reasonable number. It would also surely be difficult to supply agents overland, and it would be almost impossible to supply a guerrilla force later on. When it was fully realized that the group had taken about a week to move fifty miles through the jungles, and that the proposed area of operations around Myitkyina remained 150 miles away by trail, it seemed only sensible to cancel the plan.

By the time the men were in position to raid the railroad and roads leading into Myitkyina, the monsoons would return and operations would be difficult. There was an even more serious problem, as Ray Peers summed up later. The group's involvement with the Levies, troops commanded by British officers, had compromised vital security. Some of the Shans who had refused to work as porters might very likely be Japanese informers. Agents cannot be seen, known, heard, or identified. Guerrillas also require the element of surprise if they are to be successful. Detachment 101 must recruit forces who were separate from those of the British-led Levies. It was clear that A Group must return to Fort Hertz and then fly back out to Nazira.

The men plodded back up the trail to Fort Hertz. There four young boys, each the uma of a powerful Kachin duwa, came to them and asked to be taken into service. They had followed the A Group men through the jungle, their keen eyes seeing everything while remaining unseen themselves.

"We will be your eyes," said Yow Yin Naung.

"We will be your ears," said Lazum Naw.

Ah Khi and Ahdi Yaw Yin solemnly nodded their heads in agreement. When the 101 men decided that jungle boys, especially the sons of powerful Kachin leaders, would indeed make useful eyes and ears, they decided to take them in. The boys grinned with pleasure. One of them came from a village the Japanese had destroyed, and many of his friends had died. Now they could revenge themselves. The Americans were incredibly naïve and clumsy in the jungle, but they did have a certain way about them. They were cheerful and determined. Within a few days A Group flew to Nazira, and the four Kachin boys, their eyes big with excitement, flew with them. The boys idolized their new friends.

At Nazira, Carl Eifler saw one of the boys chopping a log for the fire. The boy whacked at the hardwood log some six inches in diameter with his dah. It took him six to seven strokes to cut through it. Taking the boy's dah, Eifler chopped at the log himself. He whacked at logs until he could surpass the boy's best effort by one stroke. He handed the dah back to its young owner with a pleased grin of prowess. The boy grinned back. He positioned the next log, and with two lightning strokes chopped a V in it. The third stroke cut through the wood. Eifler shook his head and admitted defeat.

"The Americans represented the highest in industrialization, modernization, education, and the like," observed Ray Peers, who had watched his commander competing with the boy, "whereas the Kachins were from the other end of the spectrum. They were backward, primitive, and most of them were illiterate. Yet with all of this difference the Americans and Kachins had a great deal in common. There seemed to be some spark that attracted them to one another. This attraction was caused to a great extent by the character of the Kachins; they were courageous, resolute, dependable, honest, and loyal. The only people who did not like them were their enemies, and they respected them."

\*     \*     \*

Refugees fleeing through the Naga Hills to escape the catastrophe in Burma during the spring of 1942 fell easy prey to the tigers, who were numerous in the jungles. Many of the enormous striped cats developed a fondness for human flesh. It was so easy to come by and was so tender, particularly if the cat was growing old and his teeth were losing their strength. Then without warning the stream of easy kills ended, and only the hard-to-catch and difficult-to-kill Nagas were left in the hills. In search of more toothsome prey, tigers invaded the Nazira tea gardens. There the lithesome girls who picked the tea proved easy to seize and just as easy on the palate. Even at their camp on the edge of the tea plantations, A Group could hear the jungle cats prowling close by each night.

There was a rash of tiger encounters as the 101 men went about their night duties. Ozzie Klein, newly arrived from the States, was driving in a jeep along the road that ran beside the tracks of the Bengal and Assam. Something huge and shadowy loped along the road ahead of him.

"That's a cow," Klein told the man at his side.

Suddenly the "cow" leaped ten feet straight up in the air, snarled, and sprang away into the dark. Cecil Crafts, a communications man who was also a new member of the group, drove a jeep along the same road with a Kachin boy. A tiger sprang into the headlights.

The Kachin pulled out his newly issued .45 and fired at the beast, which jumped over a high bank and was gone.

Ray Peers had a frightening encounter with a tiger as he drove down the road from Mackeypore to Behubier.

"The Assam Company had removed a steel bridge to smelt for war purposes," he wrote, "and had made a detour around it while being replaced by a wooden one. As I drove along in the jeep, my mind was far away on activities in Burma, and I paid scant attention to the reflections from the eyes of the small burrowing owls sitting on numerous fence posts. As I approached the bridge barrier, I could see a couple of reflections but figured them to be a couple of owls on the posts. As I came closer, the lights of the jeep outlined a large body with eyes shining. I thought it was just another water buffalo roaming the countryside. When I was about thirty feet away, he turned sideways, and there was the biggest tiger I had ever seen. I was without a gun of any kind on a built-up road where I couldn't turn around, back up, or go forward; I was completely at his mercy.

"They say tigers rarely exceed five hundred pounds, but this creature appeared ten feet high and must have weighed a ton. I could only think, 'if he makes one false move, I am going to give the jeep full throttle and head right at him.' Perhaps he was about as scared as I, because he flicked his tail a couple of times and strolled across the railroad track and into the tea garden. I waited briefly and had to follow right behind him to take the detour through the jungle.

"When I reached my destination, I obtained a rifle to carry in the jeep on the return trip, but, of course, I saw no tiger."

The next day Peers met Harold Geach, the manager of the Mackeypore Tea Garden. He told him of his experience.

"Yes, you undoubtedly saw the Mackeypore tiger," said Geach. "He is a huge brute, and do you know, that fellow has killed five Europeans in the past ten years that I know of."

A tiger might kill a human being for a snack, but it was much more worth its while to kill a water buffalo or a cow, since then there would be a good meat supply for several meals. One night a tiger jumped into the pen at the Lahksmijhan Tea Garden and stunned manager Ted Healy's prize Brahma bull with a sweep of its paw. Throwing the hapless fifteen-hundred-pound beast on its back, it seized it in its mouth and jumped over a four-foot fence, dragging the bull off into the jungle to eat the carcass at its convenience.

Tea planter Charlie Ashfield and two other men decided to kill a tiger that had brutally mauled a tea girl. They tracked it into the jungle and tethered a goat one hundred yards from a stony ledge, which was twelve feet high. Before it grew dark they climbed atop the ledge to wait for the tiger. It was well into the night when the goat suddenly bleated in terror. The tiger sprang upon it. Like typical English gentlemen given to fair play, the men at first alternated their shots. The first shot hit the tiger without killing him. He charged, and now the men fired frenzied shot after shot into him. He leaped high onto the ledge and, even as he died, his great teeth tore open the third man, who died soon afterward. There were a dozen bullets in the tiger, but he had still completed his charge, and a man was dead.

A sign was put up at 101 headquarters advising personnel not to shoot at tigers with their .45s. When word of the fate of the tea planter's companion got around, 101 men understood that if they did hit a tiger with a .45 slug, it would only serve to make him angry. As it was, even without such provocation, tigers just came naturally with a good bump of built-in anger.

Still, not all tigers were deemed bad. When a mother tiger was killed by a hunter, the 101 men adopted her cub and named her Lucy. Lucy followed the men around until one day the detachment sent her back to Washington as a present to General Donovan. Although it has been said that Donovan couldn't tolerate a six-week-old tiger cub around the office and presented her to the National Zoo, the zoo has no record of such a gift.

Ted Healy had scarcely gotten over the loss of his bull when he strolled into the drawing room of his bungalow one night to get some cigarettes that he had left on the table. The lighter was in his bedroom so he went back to get it. As he came back into the drawing room, his dog rushed past him and pawed the rug, barking furiously, about six feet in front of the table. Healy snapped on the lights. Beneath the table, coiled and ready to strike, was a king cobra, nine feet long and four inches around. It had come in through an open window.

Carl Eifler and John Coughlin discovered that Charlie Ashfield also had some cobra residents. One day Ashfield's dog circled a stack of old lumber until the men gingerly joined in pulling the pile apart. Down at the bottom, nesting securely away from prying eyes, was a family of cobras. Three of them were seven to eight feet long, and some younger ones were each two to three feet. At the sight of all the deadly, writhing snakes the men felt a cold chill in their insides.

The ones in Charlie's house were common hooded cobras, which in their maturity reach a length of nine to ten feet, but their bite was just as venomous as that of the more terrifying Hamadryad or king cobra, which can grow to be twenty feet long. One king cobra, twenty feet long or so, regularly sunned itself on the road close to 101 headquarters.

"He'd feel our jeep coming and plunge over a five-foot wire fence and disappear," said Ray Peers. "We never could get close enough for a shot."

Life at the forward OSS base at Nazira was hardly dull.

\*　　\*　　\*

Air Transport Command pilots flying DC-3s over the Hump in early 1943 knew that each flight risked both the plane and the crew. The jungled mountains ran in great craggy ridges parallel to the flight path that took them from northern Assam to Kunming in China's Yunnan Province. Furious winds roaring down from the Himalayas often flung the planes into the mountains. High cloud banks built up over the mountains and obscured the pilot's view of the peaks. Yet most of the flyers preferred a cloudy day to a clear one, when the planes were more visible to the Japanese Zeros. Once a Zero spotted a slow-moving DC-3, its destruction was almost certain.

If for any reason at all his plane were to go down, a pilot was certain to be a doomed man. Even if he survived the crash, he would be lost, probably injured, deep in a country infested by headhunters. A 4 A.M. briefing every morning, followed by a long day's flight which would not be completed until 7 or 8 P.M., added up to days of great strain. The nerves of many pilots cracked, and they did strange and irrational things. If something could only be done to rescue downed aviators, at least some of the strain could be alleviated.

Ray Peers, John Coughlin, and Carl Eifler went to see General Alexander at Air Transport Command Headquarters at Chabua to ask him for a drop plane and crew, parachutes, and an instructor to teach the men of A Group how to jump. Only by jumping could they get back into Burma and be in position near Myitkyina before the monsoons began.

As they spoke, General Alexander brought up the problem of his flight crews.

"I'd give anything to guarantee my people a chance," he said.

"That's why we're here," commented Carl Eifler.

"But what can you do?"

"We can promise that if your crews crash in North Burma, we will go in and lead them out."

"That's the sort of thing they show in the movies."

"No, sir. Those hills, those mountains are Kachin country. They are on our side, and if we could get in and show them that we mean to stay, we should be able to get your men out."

General Alexander remarked that it would be a shot in the arm to the crews' morale if they knew that, if they crashed, they had a good chance to escape the jungle. He promised to send over his chief parachute rigger to train the agents.

\*     \*     \*

Nobody knows when people began to call Master Sergeant Wayne Milligan, "Pop." He was chief parachute rigger of the Army Transport Command. Raised just across the Oklahoma border from Coffeyville, Kansas, Pop had been a ranch hand, rodeo rider, and oil-well wildcatter before he took to stunt jumping from planes at country fairs throughout the Great Plains states. While crowds held their breath, he would climb out on the wing of a rickety biplane and do unbelievable antics. At last he would go plunging toward the ground as the crowd rose to their feet in a long-drawn-out scream. He would somersault and tumble crazily as he fell to the earth. When his chute broke open with a flash of lifesaving silk, the crowd always cheered and jumped up and down with excitement. Death had been cheated. Pop made 62 parachute jumps on barnstorming trips. Then in 1929 he joined the Army Air Force. A stocky finger of a man with an incorrigible grin, he reported to duty at Detachment 101 in January, 1943. In three weeks A Group must be trained.

Detachment 101 rented another tea planter's bungalow close to Dibrugarh, only a few miles from the air base at Chabua where the drop aircraft were to be stationed. The group, which had been expanded to twelve to include the four young Kachins who had joined at Fort Hertz, jeeped over to the new quarters and met their new instructor. He immediately told them training would start the next day at 5 A.M. and would break when the sun went down, not a minute before. He meant it, and A Group was hard at work from dawn to sunset on ground training, which began with hooking up, simulated jumping from aircraft, handling shroud lines, and landing. The only time Pop could get his OSS group into an airplane was when it would

(Above) A 101 man watches his Kachin soldiers pass by on the trail. (Below) Four comrades in adventure pose before a dangerous mission.

(Clockwise from bottom left) At night man-eating tigers attacked the Assam tea plantations where 101 had its base in India, and OSS men turned hunters to protect the tea workers. Colonel John Coughlin dons a Sikh costume at 101 headquarters. 101 flew young Kachins out of the Burma jungles to be trained as radio operators. They showed remarkable talent for electronic gadgetry. At the same time Kachins were quick to learn how to care for new weapons from America.

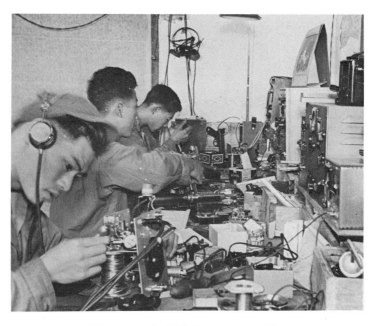

(Clockwise from bottom left) Billy Milton and his team gather for their picture before going into the field. Despite the war villagers continued to gather paddy in north Burma. A 101 commander gives terse orders to young hypenlas during a guerrilla operation. In a jungle country there were few bridges, and when a 101 group came to a stream, there was nothing else to do but wade across.

(Clockwise from bottom left) When a 101 team set up in a Kachin basha for the night, radio contact was made with base. Carl Eifler's bear treed 101 men stationed at Nazira. Kachins took rapidly to operating radios. They were even more at home with explosives used in blowing up Japanese railroad and highway transport.

(Above) Kachin villagers responding to the urgent requests of Zhing Htaw Naw and Vince Curl built a landing strip at Nawbum so that light planes could fly behind the lines. (Below) Elephants carried 101 supplies and ammunition on the march.

be on the ground between flights over the Hump. As maintenance crews worked on the engines, Pop put A Group through dry runs.

Pop's talents as a parachute-jump instructor appeared to know no limits. Somehow he managed to communicate the high points of training to the four Kachin boys, although he spoke no Kachin and they spoke no English. The youngsters had eager minds and quickly understood his demonstrations. Sometimes they stared at him in mystified amazement, and Pop couldn't help but wonder what would happen when the moment for them to jump arrived. They would be invaluable if they could ever reach the jungle again. Would they freeze in the door of the plane?

No paratroop-type parachutes were available, so Pop had to employ the primitive seat-type. The jumper had to pull the iron release handle on a chest strap to eject the pilot chute, which in turn pulled out the main chute. Pop made static lines twenty-feet long out of one-half-inch manilla rope and fastened them to tie-down rings, which he installed in the plane.

While Pop Milligan was training A Group, 101's supply officers were readying containers in which to pack equipment and supplies for the jump. Indian workers wove strips of bamboo into containers, eighteen inches on each side and forty inches deep. Each container was covered with burlap. Rice husks were packed around the equipment to protect it from the impact. Supply chutes made of broadcloth, at a cost of a little over ten dollars apiece, were rigged for the containers.

Meanwhile, the 5307th Group Photo Reconnaissance Squadron was flying over the Koukkwee Valley, which was about one hundred miles south of Myitkyina. If A Group managed to drop into the valley and set up a base camp, it would be able to carry out demolition operations against the railroad to Myitkyina, which ran something like fifty miles to the west. As soon as the field-photo men developed their day's work, the 101 men studied it for signs that the Japanese were active in the valley. The selected drop zone was isolated in the jungles, far from any villages or planted fields.

The 101 men soon made what Ray Peers felt was a bewildering discovery. Scattered about willy-nilly on the proposed drop field were scores of teak logs. Had the Japanese strewn these logs about in order to make an air drop dangerous? If so, the logs indeed might be interpreted as an indication that the tight security observed by A Group in its planning may have been penetrated or perhaps that the

Japanese had prepared a region-wide defense against possible attack from the skies. Everyone who had anything to do with the planning of the operation in the Koukkwee Valley was dismayed.

Ray Peers took the photos to A Group and showed them the mysterious logs that awaited them on the ground.

"Don't worry about the logs," said Saw Judson. "Before the war, elephants working for a teak company got them that far."

He explained that in the course of teak extraction, the logs, too heavy to float when green, would be left in the hot sun to dry out. As the sun cooked the moisture out of them, they would become lighter and lighter until finally they could float down the rivers to the sawmills at Rangoon.

When the Japanese forces came pouring into northern Burma, the teak company officials had fled. The elephants quit work, and the logs lay where the tuskers had rolled them. Photo Reconnaissance turned up no further evidence that the Japanese might be in the valley, so Carl Eifler gave the go-ahead. The jump would be made on January 26.

General Alexander had decided that the drop would be made by a B-24 bomber, which had been converted into a C-87 to carry cargo over the Hump. The plane had .50-caliber guns in its nose, top turret, waist, and tail, and if jumped by Zeros, it could fight back. Pop Milligan installed rings in the aircraft to serve as tie-downs for the static lines. Now, if the huge tail booms of the plane didn't cut the jumpers in half, everything should go all right. The exit door, Pop saw, was much too small for an ideal jump, but there was nothing to do about that.

# The First Jump

It was a misty morning at Chabua Air Field. Pop Milligan, Carl Eifler, and John Coughlin stood close to the C-87 with Jack Barnard and Saw Judson, who were to make the first jump. The two agents were suited up in the clumsy parachute harnesses supplied by the British. If the jump went well, the remainder of the team—Oscar Milton, Dennis Francis, Pat Quinn, B. V. Aganoor, and John Beamish—under the command of Red Maddox, would follow the next day. Captains Sartz and Grube, handpicked by General Alexander from his very best pilots, strode up to the aircraft. Jake Sartz was to fly the plane.

Barnard and Judson talked cheerfully enough, but it seemed to other 101 men present that their good spirits were forced. So much depended upon the success of the mission. When four P-40 fighters taxied up in readiness for takeoff, the danger of the operation seemed to be underlined. The heavily armed C-87 and the fighter planes were a reminder that the Japanese commanded the air, and that just getting to the Koukkwee Valley was going to be a chancy sort of thing. Sartz and Grube radiated the sort of confidence that men well accustomed to danger possess in its presence. There was a flurry of handshaking, jests, and laughter.

The pilots climbed into the plane. The C-87's engines sputtered, whirled, and thundered. The fighters roared as if they were ready to snap their leashes and be off in search of Zeros. Ray Peers was standing with the group of 101 men. He was not in on the day's operation, but would help the remainder of the team jump the following morning. Saw Judson was shouting something to him over the noise of the engines.

"I've lost my watch," he seemed to be saying.

It was all incomprehensible, but then it turned out to be the truth.

He somehow had lost his watch. Saw Judson was the radio operator, and he would need a watch if he were to keep the vital split-time schedules. There could be no slipup. Years before, when he was at the University of California at Los Angeles, a fraternity brother had given Peers a gold watch as collateral for a loan. The fellow student had never reclaimed his watch, and Peers had become attached to it. It kept precise time, and this was what Saw Judson needed.

"Watch?" Peers asked the question in a dazed fashion, but he peeled the watch off his wrist and handed it to Judson.

"I'll give it back when I return," Judson assured him.

A disarming smile brightened his handsome face. There was no doubt in his mind that somehow he would come back. He promised that he would take good care of the watch, turned, and climbed into the plane. The doors closed behind the last man, and the C-87 lumbered down the field for takeoff. Its motors blasted wide open. It surged down the runway, and after what seemed like a dangerously long run, it soared up into the air. The fighters followed, and then darted past the transport.

Towering cumulus clouds reached up as high as forty thousand feet. Turbulent Himalayan winds rocked the planes. Captain Sartz employed every trick he knew to try to force his plane up through the swirling clouds. Ice built up on his wings. Cramped in their bulky parachute harnesses, Saw Judson and Jack Barnard sat in the careening plane and wished that it were all over. Their stomachs tossed and heaved as the plane tossed and heaved. Around the transport, with its top speed of 175 mph, the 350-mph P-40s dodged and plunged in an effort to stay with it. This took so much gasoline that the transport was still far short of the Koukkwee Valley when it became necessary for them to turn back. They dipped their wings in a last salute and went flying homeward. The C-87 was now on its own.

The plane roared in low over the drop area, where tiny clearings appeared among the huge teak trees. Jake Sartz made two passes over the most promising of the clearings in order to get the lay of the land. There were no signs of the Japanese. All was serene. On the third pass Barnard and Judson jumped. Their chutes ripped open, and they floated down to a near-perfect landing almost exactly in the center of the target clearing. If they had dropped into the forest and hung on the high branches of a tree, they might have dangled until they either died of thirst or starvation, or were eaten alive by jungle ants, which could reach them over the tangled lines. On the fourth pass, Eifler and Coughlin shoved out the two supply containers. One parachute opened, but the other failed. The container streamed down to earth, where it would probably end up smashed beyond any use.

There was no time to waste in finding out what had happened. Zeros might arrive on the scene at any time, and they would very likely not only shoot down the transport but locate the agents. A force of Japanese and Burmese would start toward the drop zone as soon as the Japanese pilot could contact his home base. Jake Sartz made one more pass over the drop zone. The men in the plane could see Jack Barnard and Saw Judson, still yoked to their chutes but standing in the middle of the clearing, waving good-bye. On the flight back to base the C-87 hugged the treetops to avoid detection. It snaked up valleys through the ten-thousand-foot Naga Hills to Chabua, where it landed safely. It was now evening.

The scheduled time for first radio contact with the two agents on the ground in the Koukkwee Valley was 10 P.M. As the hour approached, all the 101 men at Nazira hurried to the radio shack. The night was oppressive with heat. There was no breeze. The men sweated as they waited. They shuffled about on the bamboo floor of the shack and listened to Don Eng, the radio operator, trying to raise Saw Judson. The silence was as oppressive as the night. After half an hour the operator glanced at Ray Peers. His almond eyes were without expression, but Peers knew that there was no use trying any more. There would be a second emergency scheduled time at 2 A.M. Meanwhile, the whole forward base must wait while the slow-footed minutes plodded.

Peers found himself pondering over the fate of the two men. Perhaps they had walked into an ambush. Perhaps they had been wrong about the teak logs. What had happened to his gold watch? A man thinks strange and quirky things in the middle of the jungle night when he is worried about two brave young agents. Finally it was 2 A.M., and once again the radio operator sent his signal off over the Naga Hills and into the dark night of Burma. Only silence returned.

"Everyone had his own idea as to what went wrong," Peers remembered of that sleepless night, "such as the two of them being pursued by the local inhabitants, killed by the Japs, engulfed by torrential rains, and a variety of other things, the last of which was that the radio would not work."

Red Maddox, Oscar Milton, Pop Milligan, and the operations officers at base talked all night. The four young Kachins went to their beds and slept the blithe sleep of youth, unconcerned about the dilemma that mounted in intensity with the passage of every hour. In the morning the decision must be made. Should the remaining six men and the four Kachin boys be put down into the drop zone? If the Japanese had captured the advance party, the ten would be dropping to sure death. If the Japanese had captured Barnard and Judson, they might have tortured them all night. Was there any chance that they had found out that the plan was for the plane to drop the remainder of the party the next morning? If so, Japanese Zeros would be waiting in ambush. The most prudent plan would be to send a Photo Reconnaissance plane into the area to see if there were any panels displayed to indicate that everything was all right on the ground; but if the drop were aborted, the two men would be jeopardized. Red Maddox knew Barnard and Judson well.

"If the Japanese did catch them," he said, "they never could have made them talk in one night."

Most of the men who were destined to stay at base thought it would be better to postpone the drop. Red Maddox, who was in charge of the second section of A Group, remained unperturbed.

"He never wavered, nor did he display a single emotion," Peers noted. "Without saying so, he gave the impression that he had confidence in the operation and that, if this is what we thought best, he was for it."

The final decision was to drop the second part of A Group as planned. There would be one change; Carl Eifler, the commanding officer, should not go because his capture by the Japanese would be far too damaging a blow. Under torture Eifler, redoubtable as he might be, could very well be forced to reveal top-level secrets that only he knew. Ray Peers, John Coughlin, and Pop Milligan would fly to the Koukkwee with the agents. Detachment 101 alerted the ATC to have Jake Sartz and his C-87 ready for a 2 P.M. departure. It would take that much time to get the parachutes and weapons issued and the supplies and personnel out to the Chabua strip. There were eight supply containers, including two radios, equipped with parachutes, and twelve bags of rice that were to be free-dropped. Pop Milligan had directed the supply people to pack each sack half full of rice and put it inside two outer bags so that there would be plenty of play when the free-drop impacted on the ground.

It was January 27. By mid-afternoon the morning mist had long since burned off the Naga Hills, but there were still clouds sheltering in pockets. This time there were six P-40s to escort the transport as proof that the air force took seriously the increased threat to the day's operation. The squadron of fierce fighter planes was some comfort to the men in the C-87, but just as on the day before, the escort had to turn back long before it could reach the drop zone. Near Hopin, a station town on the railroad to Myitkyina, the fighters left the transport and returned to base. At 4 P.M. the C-87 was over the drop field.

The plane roared in low on two passes. Barnard and Judson had put panels at the drop place in a prearranged pattern to indicate that their radio had been broken in the drop. The men themselves were all right. The men in the soaring plane clapped one another on the back, shouted, and jabbered with joy. The drop could be made with safety.

Pop Milligan was giving last-minute instructions to the Kachin boys. He was trying to show them once again how to pull the iron release handle on the chest strap so as to eject the pilot chute, which in turn would pull out the main chute. Peers and Coughlin stood on each side of the narrow door to try and keep the iron handle rings, which weighed at least half a pound, from hitting the men under the chin as they jumped.

The plane came in at about six hundred feet on its third pass.

"The moment of a jump is a thing of beauty," announced Pop Milligan, the old barnstormer, with such conviction that all the members of A Group laughed and pushed one another in their excitement. Body contact between friends who are about to do something dangerous together is reassuring—and at the same time a way of saying good-bye just in case things don't go right.

The first five men jumped, one after the other. As each of them leaped through the door into the rushing air, Peers and Coughlin twisted their bodies so that they fell backward into space. This kept the iron handle rings from striking them in the face. They swung free of them so they could be easily pulled.

Oscar Milton and the Kachin boys jumped on the next pass. Three of the four boys jumped as if they were veterans, although they had seen their first plane only less than a month before. The fourth froze in the doorway, his brown knuckles blanched white as he clenched the metal of the plane. Coughlin gently but firmly peeled the fingers on one hand free, and Peers as kindly as he could forced the boy's other hand loose. They both felt a great rush of sympathy and feeling for the terrified youth. Then he was flying out into space. Oscar Milton, placing a rough foot against his buttocks, had given him a shove. With a shrug and a grin, Milton jumped and went plummeting out of sight of the men at the door. They looked down after him to see his chute open. Beneath him the four Kachin boys were already drifting beneath their chutes. All of A Group were soon safe on the ground.

On the next pass the plane dropped six containers of supplies. The two radios encased in two containers were pushed out of the plane on the following drop, and on a last drop the rice was sent speeding to the earth. It was dropped about two hundred yards away from the clearing where the men had landed, because a bag of rice freedropped at two hundred or more miles per hour could easily crush any man it struck or destroy any container.

On the way back to Chabua the plane winged across the Mogaung River at dusk and past Mogaung town, where cook fires were being lit and lights glimmered in the little shops beside the dirt streets. Peers could make out Japanese fighters and bombers drawn up in neat rows at Myitkyina Airport to the right. The pilot flew east to the Irrawaddy and then on north over the Triangle to Fort Hertz before flying across the Hukawng Valley and the Naga Hills to Chabua. It was a roundabout route, but it promised a better chance of eluding Japanese attention. The C-87 was on the ground at Chabua at 8 P.M.

Leaving Milligan at Chabua, Coughlin and Peers sprang into a jeep and sped down the rutted roads to Nazira. As they braked to a halt at the radio shack, Don Eng ran out. He shouted the good news. He had contacted Saw Judson. All personnel and containers had landed safely, and A Group was in the field. Vinegar Joe should soon be hearing bangs coming out of the Burma jungle.

\*     \*     \*

The depths of the jungle mean life to a guerrilla. Beneath its forest canopy A Group's camp would be safe from discovery by Zero scouts overhead. It was almost parklike in the half-daylight of the forest floor, which could be reached only by a small portion of the sun's rays filtering through the high roof of the jungle. Wherever light did come through, strong and life-supportive, tall grasses, thickets of thorns, and tangled vines and creepers made a camp impossible.

The men watched the Kachin boys bed down that first night. They searched out places level enough to lie down and stretched out with their heads uphill. Since there was no threat of rain, they didn't bother to erect a shelter, which could be put together if necessary in

a matter of minutes. A troop of monkeys whooped hysterically overhead, and some unknown bird sounded its monotonous four-note call.
All around A Group, decaying vegetation emitted an acid smell,
which closed in around them as if it were the dank breath of some
giant and not-too-clean animal. The stench pursued the men into
their dreams. They slept well because it had been a long day, a day
very punishing to the nerves, and a day of reassurance. After the
danger of the jump into the unknown jungle, the men were exhila-
rated with the relief that is bound to follow a plunge through the sky.
They were safe and together in the jungle. Tomorrow they would
begin their operation in earnest. They felt confident.

In the morning they unpacked their equipment and supplies to
make certain that everything had indeed landed safely. No detail can
be left to chance when a group is hundreds of miles behind enemy
lines. They studied their maps. Between their camp in the jungles and
the Myitkyina rail corridor stretched the rough Hopin Hills. As a
bird flies, it was only some fifty miles from their landing place to the
railroad, but it would be at least twice as far by twisting hill trails.

Oscar Milton, Saw Judson, and the four Kachins were to stay in
camp while the remaining six men made the trek to the railroad. Milton, who wore an anklet woven of hair to ward off the evil nats, because he deemed it better than a bullet-proof vest, sat back on his
heels, the Kachin way, beside the campfire. The four boys squatted
beside him and prepared to wait. To wait in the jungle for the next
thing to happen is a hard thing to do, but Oscar was schooled in
waiting. Saw Judson busied himself with his radio set. He looped the
antenna higher in the trees so that he could send out a stronger signal
and have better reception later on when Ray Peers's gold watch told
him it was time to contact Nazira. The Kachins watched the men
who were getting ready to start on the trail, and their eyes said they
wanted to go too. Each time Jack Barnard looked in their general direction, they grinned, hoping to catch his glance, hoping he might re-
consider and let them go with him. Couldn't he see that even if they
were hundreds of miles from their home country, they would still be
able to find the trail better than any of the agents?

Each of the men in the strike party carried not only his share of
essential supplies and equipment but a load of Composition C. The
explosive was stable enough to take variations in temperature and
survive the jouncing of the trail without going off. When all was
ready, the men strode off down the trail following Jack Barnard, who
from the start set a pace that would have been killing for A Group

only a few months before. The days of conditioning in the Naga Hills and the punishing walk from Fort Hertz to Sumprabum and back had trimmed off every ounce of excess fat. Their muscles were lean and supple. As they climbed the precipitous hill trails and descended again to the next valley floor with the hip-swinging jog that they had already learned from the Kachins, they hardly broke their gait.

By the end of the first day they had hiked close to fifty miles. After a good night's sleep, slumped down by the trail, they hiked another fifty miles on the second day, so that by late evening they were setting up their camp on the last ridge overlooking the railroad. The very first 101 group to jump into the field was demonstrating the remarkable hardiness, stamina, and mobility that was to be one of the principal reasons for the detachment's success. In two days they had managed to hike through forbidding mountains for a distance which early in the month would have required almost two weeks. Jack Barnard, watching his men settle down in camp, had good reason to be proud of A Group's performance. Now, if they only proved adept with explosives . . .

Barnard gave orders that no fires were to be built. Any light glimmering from atop the ridge would alert the Japanese along the railroad that a party of some sort was camped up in the mountains. The men ate a cold supper. They ate a cold breakfast, too, and then set out down the last mountain shoulder to the railroad. By late in the afternoon they were hiding in the thickets within a few hundred yards of the tracks. They lay prone in the dense foliage and waited for the shelter of night. A train passed down the tracks, its wheels clickety-clacking, but there was nothing to do but wait with a guerrilla's patience for the dark to come.

In the dusk Jack Barnard sent one party to reconnoiter the railroad right-of-way for a few miles to the north, and led a second party along the right-of-way about the same distance to the south. They studied exactly where they could place their explosives with the most devastating effect. Whenever they heard Japanese foot patrols approaching, they slipped into the jungle. Back in their hidden camp by the tracks, Barnard posted guards against surprise. The rest of the men found a few hours of rest.

The moon rose and drenched the night with a silver beauty. The sleeping men awoke to a magic scene of mountains shouldering close to the railroad, of the twin ribbons of shining steel stretching off into the distance. It was past midnight when Barnard sent his men in pairs to do their deadly work. The men stepped swiftly along the railroad tracks in the moonlight, their eyes and ears keened for any signs of Japanese or Burmese guards. Composition C is not only stable, but because it explodes with a fierce and instant flame, it has more destructive force than either TNT or dynamite. A quarter pound of Composition C was capable of severing a steel rail or twisting it into useless junk. The three teams put their explosives into position, carefully burying each of the charges beneath rock, gravel, and cinders so that a track walker would not be able to spot them. The charges were rigged to a chemical delay fuse, about the size of a lead pencil. A wire held taut by a spring ran through the middle of each fuse, which also contained a small vial of corrosive acid. To activate the fuse the saboteurs broke the vial so that the acid could set to work dissolving the wire. Once the wire broke, the spring would snap shut and ignite the fuse. Just how long this would take depended upon the dimensions of the wire or the strength of the acid—the explosives would be set off anywhere from two to five days or even longer. Although it was possible to use chemical delays that would go off in as short a time as an hour, these scarcely fitted into the scheme of things on that moonlit night in the Hopin Hill Tract. By 4 A.M., the men had placed twenty-seven charges over a distance of five miles of track and returned to their camp. They went immediately to sleep, and all but the guards slept on through the next day, until night again provided them with concealment.

That night the men once again worked in pairs. On the north, Red Maddox and Dennis Francis were given the assignment of blowing up a span of the bridge over the Namyin Chaung, close to the town of Namhkwin, and B. V. Aganoor and Pat Quinn were delegated to bring down some smaller bridges. To the south, about three miles away, the railroad crossed the Dagwin Chaung on a one-span bridge. Barnard and John Beamish set out to destroy it. Each pair of saboteurs arrived at their destination without incident, and in the bright moonlight set about their tasks.

Red Maddox, with a fine professional eye, saw immediately where he must place the Composition C if Francis and he were to bring down the spans of the bridge. They set to work. Aganoor and Quinn also reached their first target and busied themselves planting explosives. They had almost finished the job when a patrol of Japanese and Burmese militia emerged out of the gloom beside the track and, raising their rifles, fired. Aganoor and Quinn set off their charge. It had not yet been properly placed and did little damage. They bolted

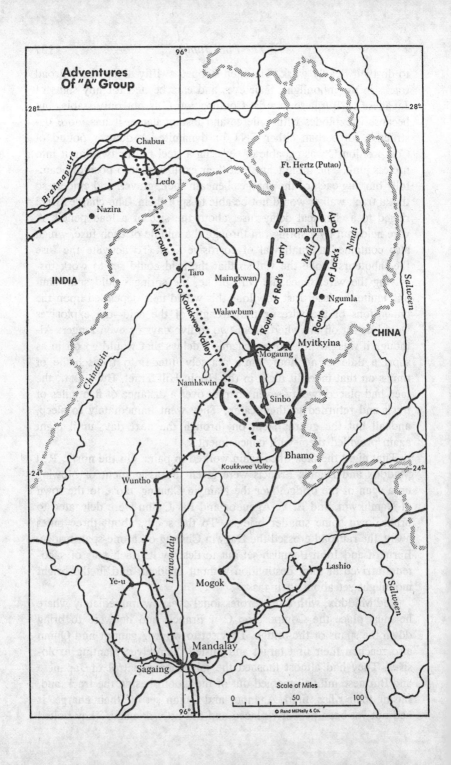

# Adventures Of "A" Group

28°

96°

Brahmaputra

Chabua

Ledo

Nazira

INDIA

Air route

Taro

Maingkwan

Walawbum

to Koukkwee Valley

Chindwin

Namhkwin

Route of Red's Party

Mogaung

Sinbo

Bhamo

Ft. Hertz (Putao)

Sumprabum

Mali

Route of Jack's Party

Ngumla

Myitkyina

CHINA

Nmai

Salween

24°

Wuntho

Koukkwee Valley

Irrawaddy

Ye-u

Mogok

Lashio

Salween

Mandalay

Sagaing

Scale of Miles

0          50          100

© Rand McNally & Co.

into the jungle while the bullets whined around them. They ran for their lives through the tangle of creepers and vines with the patrol racing after them, firing whenever they got a glimpse of the fugitives as they emerged into an unwelcome pool of moonlight. Realizing that their only hope for escape rested in holding back the pursuit, Aganoor fell back to fire at his enemies. His fire checked the Japanese for a few moments, but a single rifle is not likely to hold back a Japanese patrol. They closed in and shot him to death. When Aganoor fell, he became Detachment 101's first casualty. Quinn, given a chance for his life by his partner's heroism, sprinted through the jungle.

When they heard the sound of rifle fire and the crunch of an explosion to the south, Maddox and Francis knew immediately what it meant. Maddox fired the charge attached to the bridge. A flash and a blast, and a span of the abutment rose up in the air and crumbled in sections into the river. The water boiled and foamed around the ruins. Even as they watched, the fallen section of the bridge seemed to take on a permanent appearance in the moonlight as if it had always been lying there in the river. The two men stared for a moment and then hurried into the jungle.

Far to the south, Barnard and Beamish heard the explosions and rifle fire. They aborted their mission and started back toward the camp by the tracks, which had been agreed upon as the rendezvous point in case of trouble. When they reached the camp, they concealed themselves and waited. Only the usual jungle sounds reached them. The moonlight fell upon the nearby tracks, which still stretched pristine and apparently unbroken into the night. They had no idea that to the north the rails had been sundered by the fallen bridge. They had no idea what had happened to the other parties. They could only play the waiting game, which comes hard to men of their temperament.

Quinn fled to the north, making a large circuitous run. Somewhere behind him he knew the Japanese and Burmese still pursued, and he dared not head back to the rendezvous. Maddox and Francis also fled on a wide run of their own, deep into the jungled hills. They believed that the explosions and the rifle fire would have attracted every Japanese and Burmese within many miles. The fallen bridge would have been discovered, and somewhere behind them vengeful men must be seeking for them. They, too, feared to head toward the rendezvous point.

# Evasion

Two days passed. Barnard and Beamish waited, but nobody came. The gunfire must have meant that their friends had been ambushed and killed. To wait any longer beside the railroad tracks at the rendezvous point was unwise. They buried what was left of the explosives and, putting the remaining food into their packs, set off up the trail into the hills. Only a few days before, they had come down this trail in high spirits, hurrying toward what they knew was to be Detachment 101's first encounter with the enemy. Now it appeared that four of the team of twelve were dead, and the entire purpose of the operation was in grave jeopardy. The Japanese would be searching everywhere for the way in which agents had entered their domain. The base beyond the Hopin Hills where Oscar Milton, Saw Judson, and the four Kachins waited was not safe, and it must be warned as soon as possible. Barnard and Beamish walked faster. It was at least some comfort, as they climbed up the mountain ridges, to hear explosives detonating in the valley beneath them. The delay fuses were doing their diabolical duty, and the railroad would be of no use to the Japanese for a long time to come. Could General Stilwell hear these explosions far off at his headquarters in New Delhi or Chungking, or wherever he might be at the time? Would he be pleased or would he snort that the OSS had bungled the job?

A day after Barnard and Beamish quit the rendezvous point, Red Maddox and Dennis Francis reached it. They found no sign of the other men, although it was apparent somebody still lived and had returned to the campsite. All the provisions had been taken, and Maddox and Francis were hungry. It was three days since they had heard the rifle fire and the explosion, and they could not stay in this now dangerous place. That night they left. Their peace of mind was not helped by a report from Kachin villagers whom they met as they crossed the Hopin Hills that for some reason the Japanese had stepped up their patrol activity. For the first time they were coming up into the hills searching for something. Maddox and Francis had little difficulty in knowing what the Japanese were looking for, and their knowledge lent speed to their tired legs. Along the way, they were able to find various jungle fruits and roots to keep up their strength, but nonetheless there was always a sharp gnawing in their stomachs. It would be close to heaven if they should arrive at base camp just as a sumptuous curry dinner was ready to be served.

\* \* \*

Ray Peers, John Coughlin, and Carl Eifler studied the reports from the field, and it was clear that A Group was in trouble. Barnard and Beamish had reached the base camp without incident, and Saw Judson had come on the air at the prescribed time with a message from Jack Barnard. This report and the messages that followed were ominous: he described the operations along the railroad corridor and stated that he feared that the other members of the group had been killed or captured. He, too, had learned from the Kachins in the Hopin Hills that the Japanese had suddenly become extraordinarily active.

Barnard requested permission to move his base camp. He was convinced that, after the attack on the railroad, the Japanese were not only searching for it but would soon find it. He suggested that he break camp, cross the Irrawaddy River, and set up a new base somewhere close to the Bhamo-Myitkyina Road, where the remaining six members of A Group could attack Japanese traffic and gather intelligence. Things were going to be far too hot along the railroad corridor for any further activity in that vicinity.

What was to be done about the situation? The officers at Nazira who were guiding field operations discussed the problem at length and at times with heat. Finally a principle of command that was to become basic in future Detachment 101 operations crystallized. Jack Barnard was a highly trained and competent man, and he was in the field and on the spot. It was difficult for men three hundred miles away in Assam to tell him what to do. Nazira radio tapped out a message to Saw Judson. Operations (Opero) approved his plan and requested that he advise when and where he wanted the next airdrop.

The very next morning what appeared to be the survivors of A Group broke camp and struck out along a trail that ran to the northeast. Koukkwee Chaung, a tributary of the Irrawaddy, flowed through the heart of the valley. They might have followed the stream down to its junction with the country's greatest river, but this would have brought them closer and closer to the major Japanese strong points of Katha, to the southwest, and Bhamo, to the southeast along the Irrawaddy, which in this region flowed for the most part east to west. If they ascended the Koukkwee Chaung and crossed over the northern Hopin Hills, they would come out upon the rail corridor, and this clearly was no sensible course of action. The trail that they took climbed higher every mile it left the Koukkwee Chaung behind. The men were climbing the Koukkwee Hills.

The Kachin boys came into their own. The party had not been on the trail long when a Kachin runner caught up. He warned that Japanese soldiers had picked up their trail. The boys listened to the runner, and then led the party off onto an abandoned trail that only their jungle-bred eyes could have detected. They led the men well into the mountains before returning to lay a false trail in another direction and then carefully destroying any traces that might indicate the course the 101 group had really taken. Their ruse completely mystified the Japanese, who lost track of their quarry.

Following abandoned tracks overgrown with creepers and thickets through the jungled mountains proved hard going. It took a walk of over one hundred miles to move thirty-five airline miles into the hills. Four days had passed. It did not make the men any happier to learn from friendly Kachin villagers that the Japanese had no idea who they were or what they had been doing. They believed the 101 men to be part of the British Chindits, which at that time were operating farther south along the railroad corridor near Wuntho. This report radioed out by Saw Judson gave 101 headquarters its first information about Major General Orde Wingate's Chindits. The first Chindit expedition had been launched in early February, and on February 13 the Chindits had crossed the Chindwin River on their perilous raid into the Indaw region, further south. The British had neglected to inform 101.

That night A Group slept in a Kachin village on the summit of the last range of the Koukkwee Hills, overlooking the Irrawaddy Valley. The presence of the young Kachins in the party was proving to be a very great advantage. They not only had cheerful dispositions and ready grins, but they knew how to find edible fruits and roots, how to cross streams in freshet, and how to baffle the Japanese pursuers.

And when the party arrived at a Kachin village, they always went ahead to insure a ready welcome. This last village in the mountains was no exception, and the villagers kept guard as the worn-out men slept around the warming fire in the duwa's basha.

Saw Judson sent a message. Jack Barnard requested a supply drop in two days' time in a cleared rice paddy about eight miles northwest of the town of Sinbo on the Irrawaddy.

\* \* \*

At last Red Maddox and Dennis Francis came down out of the Hopin Hills and took the easy trail through the Koukkwee Valley to the now-abandoned base camp, but as they approached there was no smell of curry cooking. There were no friends waiting with supplies. There was no sign of the camp at all, because the Kachins had carefully eradicated every indication that A Group had ever been there. To Maddox and Francis it even seemed as if there had never been a camp on the spot. There must be a mistake. Somewhere nearby a friendly reception awaited. Still, there was the huge tree limb over which Saw Judson had thrown his radio antenna, but where were he and the others?

Although they had no supplies, Maddox and Francis decided to rest up before continuing on their way. They were dozing when birds cried in the jungle, warning of something approaching. There was a rustling sound in the saw grass along a creek. Perhaps it was a tiger, or a barking deer, but it might also be a Burmese spy or even Japanese soldiers. The two men slipped into the jungle to hide and wait. It was Pat Quinn! He stole up on the camp while his friends watched with delighted amazement. Then they stepped out into the open. The three men threw their arms around one another. Each felt an intense emotion based upon imagined loss and the surprise of reunion. Quinn told his story. He had wandered for days and had been given help at a Kachin village.

\* \* \*

Ray Peers, John Coughlin, and Carl Eifler studied the enormous map of Burma that Eifler had tacked up in what had become known as the "war room" at 101 headquarters. They had no trouble in locating Sinbo on the west bank of the Irrawaddy River, north of Bhamo. After receiving the drop near Sinbo, A Group planned to cross the Irrawaddy, and that was not a matter to be taken lightly. The Irrawaddy is the Mississippi River of Burma. Its headwater streams, the Mali and the Nmai, arise in the lofty mountains of Tibet and flow down through a forbidding country where Tibet, Burma, and China's Yunnan come together. Burma's highest mountain, Theing Wang Razi, 19,578 feet tall, is north of Putao to the east of the already mighty torrents. Within a belt of 120 miles flow not only the upper waters of the Irrawaddy, but those of the Salween, the Mekong, and the Yangtze. Separated by mountain ridges over 16,000 feet high, the rivers plunge and roar through gorges rivaled on this planet only by that of the Brahmaputra. The Salween may flow through the longest gorge in the world, but the Mali and the Nmai Hka flow through gorges which would be deemed every bit as deep and spectacular, if they only were readily accessible to sightseers or even explorers.

Twelve miles below Bhamo the Irrawaddy rushes into a lower gorge as it sweeps westward around the southern edges of the encroaching Koukkwee Hills. The gorge would be an impossible place for A Group to cross the river. The Japanese held Bhamo and its vicinity in overwhelming force. Above Bhamo the river was a vast flood, full of treacherous currents, making and destroying sandbars at its will. Perhaps it could be crossed at Sinbo, but it would take boats of some kind, and A Group had none. The supply officers suggested to operations that the drop include eight rubber air mattresses that the men could use as floats.

The morning after they received the A Group radio request for a supply drop, Peers and Coughlin jeeped over to the airfield at Chabua. They soon learned that the C-87 that had dropped the group into the field was out of commission. It had developed engine trouble on its regular shuttle over the Hump and was barely able to limp back. It would be at least three or four days before it could fly again. There was no way that A Group, endangered as it was by increased Japanese patrol activity, could wait three or four days for a drop. Fortunately, the 56th Fighter Group at nearby Dinjan airstrip had a few B-25 light bombers attached to the command. Colonel Sanders, the 56th's commander, was willing to permit one of them to make the emergency run if it could do the job satisfactorily. Dropping bombs was a lot different than dropping supplies.

Peers climbed up into the bomb bay of the B-25. The racks in the bay could hold six drop containers. In addition, six thirty-five-pound bags of rice could be supported on the bomb-bay doors so that when they were opened they would free-fall to the drop zone. Captain

Thompson was the pilot of the bomber. He watched the 101 men clambering about his plane and making their calculations.

"Will it work out?" he asked.

"We can do it," replied Coughlin.

Thompson and his crew were ready for an adventurous break in their routine. They were more than willing to go, but they must leave early the next morning so that presumably there would be less chance of being met by Zeros. Peers and Coughlin knew that an early-morning departure was impossible because they had to drive back to Nazira, pack up the drop containers, and return to Dinjan. Reluctantly, Thompson agreed that the plane would take off at high noon.

Coughlin and Peers lost no time. They sprang into the jeep and set up a rooster-tail of dust on the road as they sped back to the tea plantation. The 101 men at headquarters worked all night long to pack up the drop in woven bamboo containers, which they attached to chutes. There had been no word at all as to the fate of the four men missing from A Group, but they decided to prepare an emergency drop just in case they could be discovered from the air. It could be positioned in the rear escape hatch of the bomber. Captain Thompson could undoubtedly be persuaded to make a reconnaissance of the former A Group base camp in the Koukkwee Valley. The missing men might conceivably have found their way there.

At dawn there was time for an hour's sleep, then a hurried breakfast of a sort, and a dusty drive to Dinjan. By 11:30 A.M. the 101 men had loaded the drop into the bomb bays. Pop Milligan secured himself at the rear escape hatch to keep an eye on the emergency drop. Ray Peers eased up into the nose of the plane beside the navigator. From this vantage point he could look down on the mountains and valleys. He was to identify the drop panels that A Group was expected to display at their paddy drop field. As the plane lifted up into the air, the ground pulled away at a sickening angle and then leveled off into the by-now-familiar range after range of mountains broken by jungled valleys. It all looked close up and fascinating from the bomber's nose. In about an hour Peers found himself looking down on Indawgyi Lake. From the air it was a magnificent jewel nestled in the jungles. Then the bomber was crossing the railroad. Peers craned his neck to see what had happened to the bridge over the Namyin. A span was down in the river. The Japanese rail traffic to Myitkyina was definitely out. OSS could inform Stilwell that agents were effectively carrying out his orders to interdict Japanese traffic into Myit-kyina.

Within ten minutes the plane had flown over the Hopin Hills and was circling the clearing where, only a few weeks before, A Group had been dropped. Peers's heart skipped with joy. There were panels displayed in the clearing. Emergency supplies were needed. It was safe to drop. When they heard the plane approaching, Red Maddox, Pat Quinn, and Dennis Francis ran out into the field. They waved their arms. From his seat in the rear of the plane, Milligan dropped a streamer with a message tied to it.

"Sit tight, and we will return in a few minutes to give you an emergency drop of food," said the message.

First the plane had a rendezvous to keep with Jack Barnard's party. The plane soared off to the northeast over the route that the other members of A Group had taken, but a speed of 175 mph brought it over the drop site at Sinbo in only a few minutes. As the plane came in at a three-hundred-foot elevation, the navigator signaled Peers to open the bomb-bay doors to free-drop the bags of rice. The bags were targeted to land about 150 yards from the drop zone so as to avoid injuring the men on the ground.

Peers gripped the release for the doors, but the handle jammed. It wouldn't budge. He threw all his weight against it. Suddenly it gave way. The plane bucked when the bags all fell out at once. As the plane banked for another run, Peers, fearing the worst, could make out nothing but white from his odd angle in the sky. It looked as though all the bags had broken open, blanketing the ground with rice. The drop seemed a damnable fiasco, but then, as the bomber came in on its second run, Peers could see that all the bags and the parachute containers too had fallen within a fifty-square-foot space. By accident he had released all of the load—bags of rice, containers, and parachutes alike—in one fell swoop. The white he had seen during the bank was parachute cloth, billowing on its way to the ground.

The plane completed the drop to A Group, and with a wave of its wings then flew back over the mountains to the Koukkwee Valley. Climbing gingerly over the top of the bomb bay, Peers joined Pop Milligan in the tail. Together they scribbled out a message to Red Maddox to tell him that they would be back in two days to drop a radio operator and radio to him. They hurriedly stuffed the message in an envelope and inserted it in one of the containers. Then they were over the target. Milligan opened the hatch and dropped the containers. The men in the plane could see the parachutes open and float gently down to land at what seemed to be Red Maddox's feet.

Two days later the C-87 was flyable again, so Peers returned in it with the operator and his radio. There were no panels and no sign of the 101 men. Over the next several days photoreconnaissance planes flew missions to the clearing in the Koukkwee Valley to try and discover some clue as to what had happened. The jungle, which had opened up a few afternoons ago to reveal the three men, had closed up around them again.

\* \* \*

Jack Barnard and the others watched the six bags of rice slam into the paddy. The parachutes and their containers drifted down almost exactly on top of the rice. It was a beautiful sight to men who were almost out of supplies. The paddy had not been cultivated for years, and there was nobody around to see the drop and inform the Japanese, but the friendly Kachin villagers warned them again that the Japanese soldiers were prowling the area and would sooner or later reach the village.

The Kachins looked at the rubber mattresses which had fallen from the sky and laughed. To attempt to cross the Irrawaddy on such flimsy contraptions made no sense. Not when the Shan fishermen who lived in a village beside the river had boats. Kachin hunters had often peered out of the jungle along the riverbank to watch the Shans tie up their boats a short distance from their village. It would be easy to take what boats were needed in the middle of the night. The Shans posted no guards, but at the thought of that possibility the Kachins laughed and purposefully fingered the handles of their dahs.

The full moon that had shone down on the railroad had waned to a half moon, but there was sufficient light for A Group to pick its way down the trails to the riverbank. The boats were untended. The party got into two of them and pushed out into the current. They poled until the water was too deep; then they paddled as silently as they could. Were there Japanese patrol boats on the river? In the gloom the ghostly current swept them downstream, but finally they could see the shadowy bank on the opposite side.

A terrifying scream shook the night. A huge elephant, its tusks gleaming in the dim moonlight, rose up out of the water where it had been quietly bathing. Its enormous trunk rolled out in anger at the men and boats that had come drifting and paddling on the river.

Other huge bodies erupted into thrashing anger. For a moment it seemed that one of the herd of wild elephants would attack and crush the boats, but instead the animals, trumpeting furiously, charged out of the water and flung themselves in confused rout up the steep clay bank into the jungle. Long after they vanished from sight, the elephants could be heard crashing through the dense undergrowth.

Trembling as much with relief as fright, the men and the boys pushed the boats out into the current. They would drift away downstream and by daylight be so far away that neither the Shan villagers nor a Japanese patrol would be able to tell where they had landed in the night, or if there had been any landing at all. Once the boats had glided out of sight, A Group, the Kachins scouting the way, set off eastward into the jungle. They must find a sanctuary from which they could resume their operations.

*     *     *

The young Kachins led A Group toward one of the long-extinct volcanic cones which had been created when the uplift of the mighty Himalayas brought strains to the land east of the Irrawaddy. Lampho Buin looms eight hundred feet above the surrounding hills. The Burmese and Shan Buddhists of the region consider the peak to be sacred, and all life on its slopes is considered sacred too. Since most of the wild things living on Lampho Buin are cobras, the volcano and its vicinity are not only held in reverence but are quite deserted by mankind as well. Somewhere within the baleful influence of Lampho Buin and its dread inhabitants would be a safe place for A Group to hide out from the Japanese and the Burmese.

On the way it was necessary to cross three rivers, each a major tributary of the Irrawaddy, and it took A Group three days to reach the vicinity of the volcano. Wandering Kachin families had lived in the area. They had settled for a time, built their thatched village high on a nearby hill so as to be immune from enemy surprises, burned off a patch of the jungle, and planted their rice. For the first few years the virgin soil enriched by the ashes from the burning yielded heavy harvests, but then the crops grew sparse. The Kachins had then moved off to another area to burn off still another piece of jungle. Such itinerant rice agriculture, known as tongyaw to the Burmese, is common among the Kachins. An abandoned field was chosen as A Group's campsite.

Jack Barnard suggested that a shelter ought to be erected, and the

Kachin boys went off into the jungle. They could be heard slashing at the bamboo with their dahs. Kachin villagers traditionally divide up the labor of building a new basha. Married men cut the wood posts and the bamboo and bring it to the old men, who split the bamboo to make tie cords and slats. Men sink the posts into postholes, and men and women alike weave together the bamboo slats to form walls and flooring. The young girls gather thatch and bring it to the boys, who thatch the roof. Married women take time out to prepare the rice beer to spread good cheer, and the old women look after everybody's pigs, geese, and chickens until the work is completed. It is a happy social time with much banter and the opportunity for a lithesome girl to hand her thatch to a favorite boy, who has crawled atop the new structure with a daring display of agility. The four Kachin boys doubtless thought this houseraising was a sorry affair when they had to do it all by themselves, but they sang as they worked, and within three days had completed a sturdy four-room basha four feet off the ground on posts. It would be dry in the rain, and Lampho Buin's cobras would find it difficult to crawl in.

Supplies began to run low, so Jack Barnard asked base for a drop. But Japanese air action and malfunctions on the new C-47, making its first flights in the China-Burma-India theater, had cut down on the number of planes operating, and not a single one could be spared from the vital business of flying the Hump with supplies urgently required in hard-pressed China. For two weeks, 101 headquarters begged and agitated with the ATC to free a plane for the drop, while A Group was reduced to scrounging in the jungle for edible berries and fruit, wild rice, bamboo shoots, and what game they were able to hunt. Once again the Kachins with the group proved invaluable because they knew where to look for something to eat. Barnard, taught by American Baptist missionaries, gave his repeated pleas for supplies a biblical flavor. At headquarters men speculated as to how he could remember so many quotations from the Bible that had to do with starvation or things to eat. At last the drop came. There was antic celebration in the camp that night at the sight of such good things as C rations, K rations, and hard-as-brick chocolate bars made impervious to tropical heat, the probings of insects, and the normal appetites of mankind.

Barnard positioned his Kachin boys at lonely lookouts on hills overlooking the blacktop road that ran north from Bhamo to Myitkyina. From their vantage points, they counted the Japanese truck convoys and troop movements. Judging by the reports of the Japanese movements on the road, it became obvious at headquarters that the enemy had every intention of strengthening their hold on North Burma. Although A Group may have put the railroad to Myitkyina out of commission, the road was in fine working order, and the Japanese had simply rerouted their traffic. Barnard and his men placed explosives on key bridges one night and knocked them out. While the bridges were being rebuilt, vehicles would have to detour over temporary structures or find shallow places with firm bottoms to ford streams.

It was early May, 1943, when Opero in Nazira received a request from Barnard for permission to walk out of Burma. If A Group started the long trek northward into the Triangle at once, it could infiltrate through the Japanese positions and reach Fort Hertz in safety before the monsoons began to fall. Opero radioed permission to quit the area, and a final supply drop was arranged. A storm broke just as the plane was coming in for the drop, and the supplies scattered in the jungle. Something like one-quarter of the vital food required for a long walk was never found. There could be no time lost in looking for the missing items. Kachin villagers came to report that Shan spies had told the Japanese of A Group's presence, and soldiers were searching for them.

# Flight

Infiltrating as many as eight agents at a time had proved difficult at Sumprabum. Two, it was thought, might do better, so William Wilkinson and an Anglo-Burmese youth with the code name of George, who was trained as a radio operator, flew to Fort Hertz. Wilkinson carried with him a small leather suitcase that Carl Eifler had brought from Washington. It was the only container with a lock on it that was available at Nazira, and it held the new agent's silver rupees and opium supply. Wilkinson and George readily found Kachin porters and guides and took a trail that ran southeast into the Triangle, that vast expanse of wilderness encompassed by the Mali and the Nmai Hkas. The Japanese presence in the Triangle was limited, and Wilkie Wilkinson and George, led by their Kachin guides, had little trouble in passing their lines and arriving at the Kachin town of Ngumla.

The Mali flowed between Wilkinson's outpost among the Kachins at Ngumla and the Japanese forces. Wilkinson was situated only about twenty-eight miles southeast of the Japanese lines which remained immediately south of Sumprabum, but, protected as he was by the Kachin villagers, he was able to go about his work with impunity. He armed and trained a small force of Kachin men to protect the basha provided by the duwa in case the Japanese became aware of the 101 group and attempted an attack. He recruited other jungle-wise Kachins to observe Japanese troop movements and operations and to scout Japanese positions. Within a few weeks, George was radioing enciphered intelligence reports to Nazira. One day a Kachin duwa brought in a valuable notebook taken from a Japanese officer whom his villagers had killed. Other Kachins came with reports on Japanese movements. Everything went very well, except that somebody crept into the basha at night and stole Carl Eifler's leather suitcase. Since thievery was almost totally unknown among the Kachin people, the incident was very disquieting.

\*     \*     \*

Jack Barnard and the remnants of A Group, working northward along the Chinese border, radioed Nazira that the Japanese were in hot pursuit. Opero, Nazira, instructed Barnard that if he could elude the Japanese and proceed to Ngumla in the Triangle, Wilkinson's outpost would be able to lend his men succor. They would be taken from Ngumla to Fort Hertz. An Anglo-Burmese agent, code named Christopher, had established a supply base there where Allen Richter had set up his radio station. Christopher was a Rangoon criminal attorney, who had fled northward before the Japanese invasion. Because he had spent many holidays from his law office hunting in the jungles, he was able to survive the desperate trek through the Hukawng Valley and the Naga Hills. The Calcutta recruiting office had brought him into the OSS, with the hope that he would employ his knowledge of Burmese law to teach passive-resistance methods as well as undertake espionage. Christopher, and later Bob Aitken, presided over the Fort Hertz base, which was at the end of an air-supply line from Assam. The base was to warehouse supplies and distribute them upon demand to forward units behind the Japanese lines. Ngumla was the first such position to be set up, but other positions were to be established as soon as personnel could be infiltrated or parachuted into the field.

\*     \*     \*

Pat Quinn and Dennis Francis, sons of English fathers and Burmese mothers, had been raised in the sleepy town of Shwegugale, on the Irrawaddy River. Pat was the older of the two, and in the school that the two boys attended, he acted as ringleader in many an escapade. He was the first to enter the Burma Rifles, and it went without question that Dennis would follow him as soon as he was old enough. Each of the two young lieutenants had a ready wit and good nature, a willingness to undertake any mission, or for that matter any mischief. Together they made a devil-may-care combination, which more often than not proved trying to their peacetime superior officers. When the Japanese brought war to Burma, the two friends applied their resourcefulness to battle. Both had feared for the other's life when they had been separated by events in the rail corridor through the Hopin Hills. Now that they were together again, they could laugh at their obviously grave predicament.

Cut off as they were from the rest of their group, Quinn and Francis, with their tawny skin and dark hair and eyes, would not be immediately recognized as strangers if they were surprised by a Japanese search party. Red Maddox also had an English father and a Burmese mother, but he had inherited his father's shock of coppery-red hair and fair skin. The immediate task was to darken his face, arms, and hands with jungle dyes. Maddox then wrapped a Kachin's red-and-black plaid cotton turban or gaungpaun around his head. Not a wisp of red hair showed. All three were satisfied with his appearance, but was there still something that gave away his now-dangerous English blood? At least Maddox spoke voluble Kachin, and his ability to stay alive in the jungles had been proven by already legendary exploits.

The three hungry men broke camp one morning in January, when the mist lay upon the jungle floor like a living thing. When they started on the trail that led to the northeast up the rippling Koukkwee Chaung, they had little idea that they were beginning a thousand-mile hike. The Kachins guiding Barnard and the others had done such a thorough job of obliterating the overgrown trail that they had taken up into the Koukkwee Hills that they found no sign to follow. At several places they came upon footprints left by hobnailed shoes or the curious cloven-hoofed mark of the canvas shoes the Japanese army put on farm boys, whose big toes were irreversibly separated by the thongs that they traditionally wore back home. The footprints left by the Japanese soldiers were slender, delicate, and scarcely frightening in themselves, but they stood for military force, for Nambu machine guns and rifles, and the near certainty of capture or death if a patrol were encountered by surprise.

On the way they stopped to pick jungle fruits and dig roots to eat. Their training in jungle survival was proving to be fortuitous. At Kachin villages people pressed leaf parcels of cooked rice and sometimes tangy curried roots upon them, and once they sat down to a stew of monkey meat, made delicious by the men's hunger. They learned from the Kachins that they could turn over a log lying on the forest floor or rout about in the rotting wood of a fallen tree to find fat grubs that could be fried until nut brown to make what the jungle people considered a toothsome as well as nourishing repast.

Unlike the other men from A Group, they pressed on to the north, farther and farther from the footprints of Japanese patrols and deeper and deeper into the Kachin country. Already a 101 group had learned another principle of successful guerrilla warfare in the Burmese jungles: in times of danger, when a withdrawal must be made, the direction to go was north and preferably up into the mountains where there would be friendly Kachins and no Shans or Burmese to betray a group's presence to the Japanese.

There was one inescapable hazard that must be passed before they could escape into the security of the wilderness Triangle. Their route lay inexorably close to Myitkyina, from where the Japanese army controlled North Burma. The lay of the mountains and the rivers would have it no other way. As they drew closer, day by day, to the center of Japanese power, they could be certain that every Burmese town or village contained a detachment of enemy soldiers. What is more, there were also few Kachins in the area, and once again the three agents went hungry.

One night they stole close to a Burmese town where a bugle at dusk had betrayed a Japanese military presence. With a shrug of his shoulders, Red Maddox, his hair snug beneath his turban, walked into the town. Chewing and spitting betel nut expertly, he was quite clearly a Kachin down from the hills. He slipped close to the Japanese camp. When the Japanese were sleeping, secure in the belief that no enemy could be within hundreds of miles, he entered the camp and stole rice from their supplies. He returned to the other two men waiting at the edge of the jungle undetected. The success of the first daring theft heartened the men, and from then on they stole rice and other supplies from Japanese garrisons as they moved northward. They passed only one mile from Myitkyina itself, and in one more day they were in the Triangle. On the very next day they came again to a Kachin village where friendship, a hot curried meal, and quantities of laukhu, the violent Kachin drink concocted from fermented rice, awaited them.

\*     \*     \*

Jack Barnard and his group left their basha in the tongyaw close to the cobra-infested volcanic peak of Lampho Buin and walked eastward across the road that runs north from Bhamo to Myitkyina, which the four young Kachins had watched so faithfully. The Chinese border was only about twelve miles due east of where they crossed the road. The party turned north along the border and found themselves in the territory of the Marus, a tribe of Kachins—stocky, sturdy, and warlike—who lived in villages spaced along the border about five to ten miles apart. The Marus roved the hills in search of game, cultivated rice in tongyaws, and lived in fear of bum nats, evil spirits of the mountains, which in their Jinghpaw tongue were called "bums." They also made the first Detachment 101 contact with the Gauris, another tribe of Kachins, who are tall, aristocratic in manner, and advanced in both their social and political life and their culture. The Gauris lived mainly south of the territory through which they were moving, but a few of their villages were scattered among those of the Marus. Both tribes were equally friendly, but it was the Marus who, with their uncanny knowledge of the country and its trails, proved to be the best guides and porters. With Marus leading the way, the party made rapid progress northward. Every other night Saw Judson flung his antenna over the highest branch of a tree he could reach and contacted Nazira at exactly 10 P.M. Then one night the party crossed the Nmai Hka into the Triangle—and for some reason that nobody at base could fathom they lost contact.

\*     \*     \*

In the jungles of the Triangle a common leech is one inch long. A leech that is three inches long is called a "buffalo leech." A leech that is five inches long is called an "elephant leech." But even the common leech could stretch itself out to five inches in length to slip through the eyelet of a shoe, and the larger leeches could accomplish comparable feats in stretching in their avid thirst for blood. Whatever their length, all the leeches excreted in their saliva an anti-coagulant, similar to heparin, which kept the blood flowing smoothly and painlessly as they engorged themselves. After a leech, thoroughly sated with blood, dropped off a man or animal, the blood continued to flow. It is no wonder that stories were told around campfires about men who lay down to sleep at night and never awakened, having been drained of their blood. Let the leech leave any wound at all, and it was an open invitation to the first screw fly that happened along. Its eggs were deposited in the lesions, and in due course the hapless victim was playing host to screw worms, scarcely a circumstance to be courted.

One morning in the Triangle Red Maddox, Pat Quinn, and Dennis Francis awoke from a sound sleep and prepared to start on their way. As soon as he arose, Maddox discovered a very upsetting thing.

While he slept, a leech had crept up into his penis, and now, swelled with his blood, it had blocked the urethra. There was no way at all that he could urinate. At first Maddox cursed with annoyance, but as the blockage continued hour after hour, he groaned with pain. What was there to do? The pain turned to agony, and Maddox drew a sharp knife and prepared to cut off his own organ so that he might pass water. The others watched him as he prepared to make the cut. Should they offer to do the desperate work for him? Pat Quinn had an idea.

"Wait just a moment, Red," he said.

He cut two long thin slivers of the omnipresent bamboo. Maddox held his organ in position. His pain was by now so diabolical that he scarcely felt the two slivers of bamboo being inserted.

"It is an old Kachin trick," said Quinn, "but it's not a method used to relieve somebody's suffering."

The slivers passed on the two sides of the leech and held it fast. On the very first try Quinn drew the leech out—suckers, head, and all. The party rested by the trail for perhaps an hour. Red Maddox was ready to go on. They walked a full day's walk, stopping as usual every hour to check one another's body for leeches. Fortunately, Maddox felt no aftereffects—no infection and no ulceration.

The three men continued on northward through the Triangle, bearing to the west from time to time to avoid the Japanese.

\*     \*     \*

The Shans and Burmese had done their work well. They had tracked the progress of Barnard's A Group from day to day and reported everything to the Kempi Tai. A day's march beyond the Nmai Hka, Japanese troops closed in. The four young Kachins looked worried.

"The Japanese are on all sides of us," said Yow Yin Naung.

The others in the party did not question his omniscience, for they had learned that a Kachin has a remarkable jungle sense. He can tell the presence of enemies at several miles with an uncanny extrasensory perception.

"There must be a trail that will lead us to safety," suggested Barnard.

"I see no trail," said Yow Yin Naung, "but we must look for one."

An old wrinkled Kachin appeared as if he were a genie answering their prayers. He beckoned to them, and the Kachin boys had an urgent conversation with him. Yes, the old man knew of a trail, and he had come to lead the party of his people's friends through his people's enemies. How had he known of their danger? The Kachins know who is in the jungle besides the elephants and the tigers. The boy Yow Yin Naung was his nephew, and he had sensed that he was nearby and in trouble. The party followed the old man down a trail that was practically no trail at all. There was no way that they could carry their radio, so Saw Judson smashed it beyond repair and hid it among some creepers. They dropped extra ammunition, and went on ahead with whatever scant food supplies they still possessed, their weapons, a few rounds, and the clothes on their backs. They scrambled on hands and knees and crept through tangled thickets that appeared to be impenetrable, yet the old man knew exactly where to part the choked vegetation to reveal a narrow path. They walked for miles throughout the night and emerged at dawn on a well-traveled trail. The old man signed that they were safe now and pointed out the direction they must go. Saw Judson glanced at the gold watch Ray Peers had given to him so that he could keep radio schedules. The old man glanced at it too, and an admiring smile lit his wrinkled face.

"It is as bright as the sun," he said in Kachin.

Impulsively, Judson peeled the watch from his wrist and fastened it about the shriveled old wrist. As the party walked away down the trail away from the Japanese encirclement, Saw Judson glanced back to see the old man listening to the strange ticking thing that he had held up to his ear. The old man could not have been more bemused by Ray Peers's watch than the three Anglo-Burmese and the Englishman were with him.

"Yes, he is my uncle," affirmed Yow Yin Naung.

"But how?" asked Milton.

The boy could not explain. At least the presence of his uncle indicated that the party was getting far enough north to be nearing Ngumla. As it turned out, Ngumla was still five days' weary march ahead of them, but they were finally met by Wilkie Wilkinson's agents, who at last brought them to the basha where the OSS men lived. They climbed up the ladder and found Wilkinson and George awaiting them unconcernedly. The same Kachins who had guided them had kept Ngumla informed about their progress.

Jack Barnard and his group rested at Ngumla for a week. They gorged themselves on Kachin food and army rations and regained their strength. Wilkinson provided them with guides and porters, and they infiltrated through the Japanese lines in the vicinity of Sumprabum and continued on to Fort Hertz. From there they flew to Nazira and a tumultuous reunion.

Only two days after the arrival of Barnard and his men, a jubilant message arrived from Bob Aitken at Fort Hertz. Kachin runners had come to Captain DeSilva of the Kachin Levies to say that Maddox, Quinn, and Francis had encountered the Kachin duwa kaba Zhing Htaw Naw in the mountains. Zhing Htaw Naw's men had watched over their progress for several days and had at last guided them to the camp from which the chieftain was leading his increasingly bloody attacks upon the Japanese beyond Sumprabum. Zhing Htaw Naw had fed the wanderers. Even in their worn-out condition they observed the astute military defenses that the duwa kaba had erected around his base. He clearly was a leader to be reckoned with, and, judging from the scores of Japanese heads displayed in the village, his men already represented a formidable striking force.

Zhing Htaw Naw's men guided Maddox, Quinn, and Francis to the Kachin Levies' headquarters. They then appeared at Bob Aitken's post. Ray Peers and Pop Milligan, who had dropped them into the field, flew to Fort Hertz to bring them back to Nazira.

"You Yanks certainly make good shoes," remarked Red Maddox when Peers shook his hand at the airstrip. "We have been wearing these shoes since we dropped in almost five months ago, and they are still in good shape."

*       *       *

The celebrations, the debriefings, and the critiques went on at Nazira for days. Ray Peers summed it up:

"We knew that we were neophytes in this type of business, but we were determined to take advantage of our mistakes and not commit the same error twice if we could possibly avoid it. We set up a procedure of trial and error. As this operation and succeeding operations progressed, an account was maintained in minute detail. Each message was analyzed. When the personnel returned from the field, they were debriefed, and also required to write an inclusive account of their activities, good and bad. By this means, we were able to isolate the sound practices and use them to develop effective operating procedures. Those practices which were not so sound were either discarded or modified. The working procedures which had been established were continually stressed in the training program so that, by the time we were ready for large-scale operations, there was a hard core of highly skilled agents and operational personnel."

There were specific faults to remedy. The parachutes had been cumbersome. Eifler had already radioed OSS Washington for back-pack personnel chutes. These arrived by the Air Transport Command's speedy Red Ball Express, together with some U.S. Army cargo parachutes. Pop Milligan had performed a miracle in training A Group to jump in three weeks, but if Detachment 101 were to jump most of its personnel into the field, there would have to be a crew of drop masters to train each individual. Because of the necessity of recruiting and training these men before they could be sent to India, a year was to go by before the first of them reached Nazira.

The critiques of A Group continued. A unit of twelve men was too large to operate behind the lines; it was not mobile enough, it attracted too much hostile attention. Since no field group was any stronger than its weakest link, there was twice as much opportunity for a group of twelve to be weakened than, say, a group of six. Six, in fact, seemed the ideal number. It was large enough to contain all the essential skills a group must have.

Also, the failure of A Group to rendezvous after the night of violence on the railroad to Myitkyina underlined the necessity of working out better rally-point procedures. There should be alternate and fixed meeting schedules, and alternate operational plans had to be ready in case of disaster. Strikingly, the failure of A Group that night was the first and also the last time that a group of 101 agents failed to reach its rendezvous point during or after an action. At least one individual in each group should have medical training. Red Maddox argued persuasively for this improvement. All the men of A Group agreed, including Oscar Milton, whose skill for living in the jungle was so marked that he had come out of the experience in better health than when he jumped in.

There were also too many times when the agents of A Group had not kept in touch by radio. More powerful radios must be developed, and there must be a better way to provide energy for the transmissions than dry-cell battery packs, which had only thirty hours of life under the best of conditions. The men in communications set to work on a hand generator, which would be lighter and more powerful.

As for A Group, the first OSS team to be sent into Burma and one of the very first OSS teams to go into the field anywhere, it was broken up. Each member had proved himself in the jungles. Each was to be invaluable as a leader of a group of his own.

# Disaster

While A Group was finding its way out of Burma, Peers and Eifler had not been standing idly by. Detachment 101 was busy recruiting prospective agents in Calcutta and in the refugee camps and bringing them to Nazira for training. By the end of 1942 there were six separate training camps made up of thatched bashas constructed by the planters at 101's request. Each was tucked away on high land that would not flood in an isolated location somewhere among the tea gardens. In time there were to be twenty-six such camps, in which each group of agents slept, ate, and trained by themselves so that they knew nothing about the training and missions of the other units. Each camp even had its own cook. Instructors made their rounds of camps, and the groups of agents were scheduled separately into such common facilities as weapons ranges, obstacle courses, and recreational areas so that they never encountered the personnel of another group.

"This was necessary," explains Ray Peers, "because no matter how courageous a person may be, if the enemy wants him to talk badly enough, he will talk. It may take time, torture, drugs, etc., but there is a limit to human endurance, and when the individual reaches his limit, he will talk, even against his will."

Thus A Group had trained in its own area, and its members knew nothing about what was first called B Group, but which generally became known as O Group, for British Colonel Ottaway, who before the war was the manager of the tin mines at Tavoy on the Tenasserim Strip. Harry, Cyril, Lionel, Ken, Billy, and John were Anglo-Burmese, who had all worked in the tin mines. Colonel Ottaway had recruited them into Detachment 101, and it was their idea that their group should be named for the man who had taken them out of the depressing refugee camps. Their camp was in the Lahksmijhan tea garden named for the Queen of the River, and it was on the banks of the Dikho. It was at this tea garden that manager Ted Healey's prize Brahma bull had been killed by a tiger. The jungle was just across the river. When heavy rains fell, the river swirled around the camp. The men deemed the flood good training for the group. If crocodiles had invaded the camp, they would have had an added learning experience.

When O Group's training had progressed far enough that they could be sent out on a test mission, they were assigned the problem of penetrating a British air base to photograph and sketch the facilities and the disposition of the planes. They were to learn the hours the airport was in operation and when it was closed to traffic. They would determine how the base might be sabotaged.

After a railroad journey to the vicinity of the base, the Anglo-Burmese penetrated the guard lines without difficulty. They walked all over the airport without being questioned, took photos, and drew sketches. Their leader was a young mining engineer, and he made some particularly pertinent observations in respect to sabotage.

When their work was done O Group started home by rail. At a railroad station they got off on the platform to buy refreshments from a vendor. A local security patrol approached and without a moment's hesitation arrested them on suspicion and marched them off to jail for questioning. Realizing that if he were caught with the camera and sketches he would have to admit that he was an OSS trainee, the leader worked a brick of the cell wall loose and hid the incriminating objects behind it.

One by one the men were taken into a guard room, stripped, searched, and interrogated by a British officer. The officer found nothing on their persons, but he sent them to a detention camp anyway. Before they left the jail, the leader was able to take the camera and sketches from their hiding place. Once they were at the camp, he removed the film from the camera and concealed it in a bottle of pills they were carrying with them. If the camera were discovered, O Group might yet be able to save the negatives. He rolled the camera up in the tent flap. At the camp the British questioned O Group for several days and then, satisfied that they were not Japanese agents or Indian nationalist *provocateurs,* released them. They returned to Nazira triumphantly with their camera, films, and sketches. It was now March 1, 1943, and O Group was ready to be sent into the field.

The men were transported by jeep over to the camp at Chabua, where Pop Milligan gave them their parachute jump training.

*     *     *

The Lawksawk Valley was two hundred miles south of where A Group had jumped into the field and seventy-five miles southeast of Mandalay. If O Group could be dropped into this valley, they could obtain vital intelligence and perhaps rescue Allied aviators who had gone down in the area. One problem seemed insurmountable. The distance from Chabua and Dinjan to the Lawksawk Valley was so far that any drop would have to be carried out without fighter escort, and there were Japanese fighter bases in the vicinity at Namsang, Laihka, Heho, and Meiktila. ATC was happy enough to let Captains Sartz and Grube pilot one of their C-87s on the operation, but only if the flight originated in China, which was nearer to the drop zone.

Would General Claire Chennault's 14th Air Force be willing to provide fighters to accompany the drop? The only way to find out was to ask Chennault. An exchange of radio messages indicated that 14th Air Force Headquarters was interested, so O Group, accompanied by John Coughlin, Floyd Frazee, Ray Peers, and Pop Milligan, got aboard the C-87 and flew over the Hump to Kunming, China, where the 14th Air Force was based. Once they were on the ground in China, O Group fretted. Their morale was high, and they were anxious to get back into Burma. Negotiations dragged along until Coughlin and Peers went to see Generals Morgan and Vincent. They listened to the arguments that the two 101 men made, reported the conversation to Chennault, and won his approval for the project, providing that on the return flight the C-87 bombed Lashio, an important rail and road center on the Burma Road. Peers and Coughlin had no choice but to agree, but exactly how this was to be done from a plane that had no bomb bays was a matter of conjecture.

At 11 A.M. the next day, the C-87 took off as scheduled with four of Chennault's P-40s dashing into the air after it. Before the plane left the ground, the door on the side of the fuselage behind the wings had been taken off so that it would not impede the jump. The jumpers sat well back from the open door in the order in which they were to leave the plane. Now that the moment they had been training for was drawing close, the prospect of jumping into enemy-held country was losing its attraction. The planes flew over the Yunnanese mountains cut by the deep slash of the Salween Gorge and back into

Burma. One of Chennault's top pilots, Johnnie Alison, led the P-40s in brilliant precision flying. He wedged his plane between the wing and the tail of the C-87 so close that the 101'ers could see the mischievous grin on his face. None of this superb airmanship was wasted on Pop Milligan. About one hundred miles beyond Lashio the fighters peeled off and started back to Kunming, and the C-87 was on its own.

As the plane approached the drop zone, Pop Milligan was busy taping the ankles of the men who were about to jump. This would help prevent crippling sprains when the men's feet hit the ground. Twenty minutes to go, and the jumpers were given cups of coffee laced with brandy. As they circled in over the target area, both Peers and Coughlin noticed with alarm that it was only a few miles from a pair of villages.

"The villages are too close for safety," said Coughlin.

The leader, a quiet-spoken man, was unruffled.

"I know the country," he said. "There is nothing to worry about."

Both Peers and Coughlin argued that the mission should be aborted, but the O Group leader was adamant. They must jump. There was absolutely nothing to worry about. After all, he did know the country.

Captain Sartz brought the C-87 in low at three hundred feet so that it was hidden from the villages by a low range of hills. Perhaps the villagers might not discover the drop was being made. The plane made three passes, the first one for the men, and the next two for equipment and supplies. It made the final run over the drop area. The leader waved jauntily from the ground. All was in good shape as far as he was concerned, but as the plane pulled up over the hills, the 101 men in it could see villagers running along the trails toward where O Group was gathering up their supplies and gear.

The C-87 climbed to about six thousand feet and flew northward over the hills. As it passed over the highway that ran from Mandalay to Hsipaw, the pilots spotted a Japanese convoy of thirty trucks. They dropped to treetop level and charged down on the convoy, firing bursts from the plane's .50-caliber machine guns. The trucks skidded and plunged off the road in every direction to make their escape. Some overturned and burst into flames. The 101 men who had caused the destruction cheered and clapped one another on the back at their success.

The plane was drawing close to Lashio. Since there was no bomb bay, the thirty-pound bombs had to be tossed out the open door when the target was right. Peers and Coughlin sat sideways in the open door with the wind rushing around them. Every lurch of the plane in the turbulent air threatened to tumble them into space.

They practiced with a pair of bombs as they passed over the Bawdin mines at Namtu. First they had to pull the pin and then shove the bomb out. The first bomb exploded harmlessly in the jungle, but the second bomb threw up a fiery column close to one of the mine buildings. Then they were over Lashio airport, with the green light flashing beside them to let them know that they should push the bombs out the door in dead earnest. The bombs tumbled down crazily, one after the other. Down on the ground the Japanese troops soon had their anti-aircraft and machine guns in action, and white puffs, curiously benign in appearance and disarmingly pretty, exploded just off the tips of the wings. Bullets rattled into the fuselage.

"I'm hit," cried an airman standing right behind Peers and Coughlin. "I'm dying."

Peers and Coughlin hurriedly shoved out the remaining bombs, and Jake Sartz skillfully guided the plane over a nearby mountain crest that blocked off the ground fire. He flew low through the valleys as far as the Salween Gorge in order to avoid Japanese pursuit planes. Milligan and Frazee had taken care of the airman who had been hit. There was a small flesh wound in his leg, and they bound it up to stop the flow of blood. No bones were broken.

Two hours after the attack on Lashio, the plane landed at the Kunming base. Even as it raced down the runway, its motors stopped. It was out of gasoline. The Japanese anti-aircraft fire had punctured the gas-transfer system so that fuel in the reserve tanks could not be piped to the main tanks. The plane had to be towed off the runway. The 101 men stared at it in dismay. There were over 250 holes ranging up to three inches in size. It took a day to repair the C-87 so that it could fly back to Chabua.

Not a single radio contact was ever made by O Group. John Coughlin flew back to China and scouted over the drop area in a borrowed B-25 bomber, but there were no panels, no sign whatsoever of the agents. On March 4, 101 men gathered around the radio in Nazira and listened to the regular news broadcast in English from Tokyo. There was the usual mix of propaganda and half truths. Then the men froze at what was broadcast next.

"A recent report revealed that a group of six British spies landed by parachute at a certain point in northwestern Burma. Entertaining the idea that any place where there were no Japanese troops was safe, they were greatly shocked when a group of alert Burmese villagers immediately rushed at them. In the struggle that followed, the brave villagers killed three of the spies and captured the rest and subsequently delivered them to the Japanese troops stationed near by."

Perhaps Ray Peers was beginning to have something of the Kachins' sixth sense, but he had felt uneasy about the entire Lawksawk Valley venture from the moment the plane left the ground in Kunming.

"I have yet to see an operation that was not without a sense of good or evil omen," he remarked later, after several such experiences. "The dismal sense of warning, of disaster, is stronger with some than others. It may get you nowhere to listen too carefully, but when it pounds, then another place, another day is wise."

Peers determined that in the future no agent leader was ever going to argue him into making a drop when he believed it was unsafe.

"In such a situation, an agent going into operation becomes so physically and emotionally keyed up that he cannot exercise prudent judgement, and somebody with an objective viewpoint should make the decision," he declared.

\* \* \*

Most 101 men thought he was Scottish, but Father Dennis MacAlindon was born at Lurgan in County Derry, Northern Ireland. Like his friend Jim Stuart, he was educated at Navan, the world headquarters of the Columban Fathers, near Dublin, and he too came to Burma to work among the Kachin people. When Father Stuart escaped the Japanese soldiers coming to kill him at Napa, he fled to the mission at Kajihtu. There he was met by Father MacAlindon. The two priests lost no time in taking to the trail. If the Japanese army was looking for Father Stuart, they might well be looking for Father MacAlindon as well.

They had not gone far when they were stopped on the trail by Japanese soldiers, who apparently had not heard of the search being made for Father Stuart. They let the two men go when they protested emphatically that they were Irish citizens and neutral. Their only concern, they insisted, was being good shepherds to Christian Kachins. Some of the soldiers, convinced that the priests were lying, followed them to the Kachin village where they slept that night. Before they went to sleep, the duwa in whose house they were to rest showed the two priests a box of hand grenades and two shotguns left behind by the British.

"Japanese soldiers have followed you to our village," he said.

They lay down with the shotguns at hand. In a few hours the Japanese soldiers entered the village and started to surround the house. The two priests, roused by their Kachin host, fired off blasts of shotguns through the roof and tossed grenades out the windows to keep the Japanese back. They vaulted through a back window and dashed into the jungle. Both were accustomed to the terrain and made several miles' progress before dawn. They hiked ever northward, day after day, until they reached the safety of Fort Hertz. From there they flew out to India.

Once they were in India, the priests took the long train ride up to Simla in the hill country for what they believed would be a well-earned rest. They had hardly arrived when Captain Allan Richardson, aide-de-camp to the governor of Burma, called on them. The message he brought was vague, but it had something to do with being of further service to the Kachin people, and involved going to Nazira in Assam to see a certain Carl Eifler. Simla, with its year-round spring, its unhurried pace, and its remoteness from the events they had witnessed in the Hukawng Valley, was beginning to grate upon them both, and they readily accepted the invitation. Back they went to Nazira, where they talked to Carl Eifler, who offered to reward them handsomely indeed if they would assist Detachment 101 in its efforts to train and place agents among the Kachin people. They agreed, but from the start they devoted all their pay to the purchase of clothing and school things for the Kachins.

"We want to reopen the mission at Kajihtu as soon as we can," said Father Stuart.

He had no idea that both he and Father MacAlindon were to perform signal service in the field for the OSS, and that he in particular would in time command an entire operational area. He was to become the very irregular chaplain of the very irregular combat group that he had joined out of his affection for the Kachins.

Father Mac was the first to go back into Burma. Wilkie Wilkinson reported from Ngumla that he was having interpreter problems. Not only George but the three other agents by then assigned to Ngumla, code-named Forward, were all Anglo-Burmese, who knew little or no Kachin. Yet Kachins throughout the Triangle were sending information about the Japanese in to Wilkinson via what he called the "bamboo grapevine." When he heard of the language gap, Father Mac volunteered to trek back into Burma. He flew to Fort Hertz and then walked two hundred miles in a circuitous journey that brought him around the Japanese lines. At first he stayed at Ngumla, but as soon as interpretational procedures were set up, he moved ten miles away to Kajihtu village, from which he had fled with Father Stuart only a short time before. If the Japanese attempted to return to Kajihtu, he was confident that the Kachins would know of their approach in plenty of time to make a second escape.

At Kajihtu Father Mac was content. He taught a school of village children and tended to the mission church until he was summoned by runner to Ngumla. Then he hurried down the jungle paths to Forward base to interpret for the Kachin informants who had come in out of the jungle with fresh reports.

\* \* \*

General Donovan had instructed Carl Eifler to cooperate with the British high command as well as with General Stilwell's headquarters. When Lieutenant General N.M.S. Irwin, British commander of the Eastern Army, sent Eifler a message asking him to come and see him in New Delhi, he flew to the Indian capital as soon as he could. General Irwin received the OSS commander in his office at the Imperial Hotel. He pointed to a map of South Burma hanging on the wall. He located Akyab on the map. The Japanese had a strong fighting force there, which could move in any direction with impunity. It posed a threat to India. If Detachment 101 could impede the flow of supplies over the road along the coast from Sandoway and the port of Rangoon in the same way it was obstructing roads in North Burma, it would be a boon to Allied arms.

Eifler's strategic eye seized upon Taungup Pass north along the coast from Sandoway as the place to block the road. Under cover of darkness a submarine or fast boat could put a group of agents ashore on Ramree Island, from where they could cross the strait by boat and then proceed to the pass not far away on the mainland. General Irwin nodded in understanding, and he promised to supply boats to put the OSS team ashore.

Upon Eifler's return to Nazira, he handpicked the men of what was to be called W Group from Burmese and Anglo-Burmese agents training in several camps and brought them all to a camp of their own, where training was to be intensive and specialized for the task assigned to it. When all was ready, Eifler, Wally Richmond, and Vince Curl went by plane with W Group to Chittagong, an Indian port on the Bay of Bengal, which was to be the jump-off point for the operation.

The Royal Indian Navy proved helpful in providing essential information on the tides and currents and weather on the coast of Burma. The navy was to provide launches from which the men would go ashore in rubber reconnaissance boats. These could be buried in order to keep from attracting the attention of the Japanese. The agents packed forty pounds of gear and supplies in each of their packs. They planned to bring another fifteen hundred pounds of supplies ashore and hide this in the jungle away from prying eyes.

W Group set out from Chittagong in three Indian navy launches. The squadron expected to arrive off Ramree Island in the middle of the night when Japanese air, naval, and shore patrols would be least likely to discover it. As the boats furrowed the Bay of Bengal waters, Eifler did his best to show W Group how to use the rubber boats for a landing. They had just been issued at Chittagong, and there had been no time for training.

It was a foggy night, but even through the mist the men could make out Burmese farmers burning off last year's paddy. The smell of burning rice stalks struck the returning Burmese with nostalgic force. It was going to be good to be in their own country again, even if danger plainly must be waiting on that darkened coast where from time to time lights blinked. At 1:30 A.M. the launches arrived at the destination. Their motors stopped, and the boats rocked lazily in the swells of the sea. When the rubber boats were lowered, they swamped in the same gentle swells and had to be righted and baled out.

Agent Slim went over the side and climbed into a boat. He paddled silently off into the mist to see that the coast was indeed clear. There was a puttering sound out in the dark.

"It was a Japanese patrol boat," Slim said when he returned. "There are shacks along the beach. It is not just jungle. There are barking dogs and Japanese patrols."

The rubber boats were retrieved, and the launches moved at about twelve knots farther south along the coast. There were only a few hours of darkness left when the boat stopped once more. Again the rubber boats swamped in the waves and had to be baled out. Slim climbed into a boat and went off into the dark once more. He returned to say that the way was blocked by huge rocks.

"No boat can get through," he said.

There was no time to explore farther along the coast for another landing place. The party must go ashore now or not at all, and Carl Eifler ordered Slim to swim in through the rocks with a rope around his waist to show the way he had gone. The others could then follow him in the rubber boats. Slim, having seen in the dim light how the waves dashed against the rocks, refused to go. At the same time, a British officer warned Eifler that the launches would leave before dawn, come what may—whether the men were aboard, ashore, or in between.

Eifler cursed. He unbuckled his gun belt and unloosed the rope from around Slim's waist so he could tie it around his own. He slipped overboard into the sea and soon swam to the rocky reef, trailing the rubber dinghy. He found his way over the reef and into deep water, then hit another reef and more deep water before he could reach the shore. He pulled on his small rope. It was attached to a large rope which, when it in turn came to his hands, he then could use to pull the rubber boats ashore. W Group and three British officers came ashore in the boats, splashed up on the beach, and in fifteen minutes had the supplies unloaded.

When they were finished, Eifler solemnly shook each agent by the hand and warned him not to be taken alive. He climbed into a dinghy with the British officers and started back toward the launch, towing the two rubber boats behind him. Somehow they got loose and went bobbing off into the surf, now pounding on the first reef. They could scarcely be left on the reef to attract the attention of the Japanese at dawn, which was drawing painfully close, so Eifler jumped into the sea again to recapture them. The surf seized him and smashed him hard against the sharp rocks. Stunned from a heavy blow in the head and bleeding, he yet managed to seize the line to the boats and hoist himself back into the dinghy.

Rowing furiously toward the sound of anchor chains being lifted, the party arrived at the launches just in time to depart. The dawn was only half an hour away, and if the captain delayed even a moment, he risked having the boats trapped by the tide. Exhausted, his head pounding, deaf in one ear from a blow from the rock, Eifler lay on the deck. Richmond gave him pain-relief pills, but there was nothing else to do until the launches reached Maungdaw and safe harbor on the morning of the ninth.

The OSS radio stations at Chittagong, Calcutta, and Nazira all were tuned to the frequency of W Group, but the agents who had gone ashore in the night on Ramree Island never made contact. Many months later OSS put ashore another group of agents on Ramree Island, and they learned the tragic story. W Group had landed safely and had hidden in the jungle without being seen, but unfortunately they had dropped a dry-cell battery, which was to be used as a spare for the radio. A fisherman strolling the beach found it in the morning and took it to his village. The battery was brought to the attention of the Kempi Tai, and the Japanese and Burmese combed the island in search of suspected agents. W Group avoided their pursuers for several days, but finally they were surrounded, captured, and to a man tortured and put to death. Despite Carl Eifler's parting admonitions, they had been taken alive.

# Knothead

"Vince Curl could charm a snake," Wally Richmond claimed, "and I've never known him to go into a Kachin village without instantly attracting a retinue of Kachin kids, all crowding around him, all talking and laughing. This was always a sure way to the hearts of their elders. Vince Curl was America's secret weapon in Burma."

Many of the OSS men who served in Burma had something of Curl's feckless good spirit and were as outgoing and friendly toward the Kachins as the Kachins were in their attitude toward one another. The Kachins had always treated the British as friends who were much too austere but at least were dependable.

"They found the Americans a much friendlier type of Englishman," Wally Richmond further admitted. "Before we were done, even we Britishers who worked in the OSS learned to unbend. It seemed incredible at first, but we discovered that the so-called sour people of North Burma only wanted to be loved!"

Vincent Curl was ordered into the field among the Kachins in late spring, 1943, to establish a base somewhere north of Mogaung and Myitkyina comparable to Wilkinson's at Ngumla. He had already had the experience of leading a group of agents out the route of a proposed military road to run through the Naga Hills and the Hukawng Valley from Ledo. Curl, Fima Haimson, the radio man, Jack Pamplin, the Washington lawyer who had by now mastered the mysteries of cryptography, and the Anglo-Burmese agents Hefty, Goldie, and Coco, were to leave for Fort Hertz by plane in a few days, and the men who composed Opero were sitting about trying to invent a code name. Once during a staff baseball game on a fallow field in the tea gardens, Vince Curl had dropped an easy pop fly.

"You damned knothead," growled a fellow team member.

"You need a code name for that damned knothead?" somebody now demanded.

Opero immediately named Vincent Curl's group, "Knothead." Knothead was destined to become one of the most outstanding of all the 101 field units in Burma. Fima Haimson was a man of quiet, dependable good nature, a characteristic that came to typify the most successful OSS men in the jungles. More irascible or temperamental men often developed emotional problems under the strain of the wilderness and the tension of being behind Japanese lines. Jack Pamplin was soft-spoken, cerebral, but with a steely determination that surfaced as a quiet courage in the face of danger.

Bob Aitken welcomed Knothead at the Fort Hertz airstrip. He took them three miles up the valley to a two-story frame house with a corrugated iron roof, which was his headquarters. Knothead bunked in a neighboring basha. Bob Aitken had made friends with the Kachins, and several were working for him at his Fort Hertz supply base. Before the group bedded down that night, he dispatched a runner up into the hills, and by the end of the following day more than a dozen sturdy young men had come down to the corrugated-roof house, ready to shoulder Knothead's burden and to find the way through the jungles. They squatted back on their haunches in the shade of the bashas and laughed and talked and waited for the morning when the small expedition was due to leave for an unknown destination. Where was Knothead going? Carl Eifler had given Vince Curl the general directive of setting up a base north of Mogaung and Myitkyina, from which he and his group could gather intelligence about Japanese troop and supply movements along the railroad and roads leading to Myitkyina from the south. They would also attempt to ambush train and truck traffic and to blow up bridges and track. Vince Curl had some specific ideas as to how this might be done.

"Where can I find Zhing Htaw Naw?" he asked Bob Aitken.

Curl had talked to Red Maddox, and he had learned of the Kachin duwa kaba, who was leading a resistance of his own from a hidden lair deep in the jungles and mountains. Bob Aitken and his Kachins could not say, although the listening Kachins seemed to look at Vince Curl with a new respect. There was scarcely a Kachin in North Burma who had not heard by now of Zhing Htaw Naw's vengeance upon the Japanese for their cruel attacks on his people's villages.

In the morning Knothead set off along the trails that wound through the Triangle to Pasi Ga on a western tributary of the Mali

Hka, about half the trail mileage to Sumprabum where the Japanese advance had halted. The British-led Kachin Levies were head-quartered at Pasi Ga, and from them Vince Curl and his men learned that if they were to set up a base north of Mogaung and Myitkyina, it would be best to try and infiltrate the Japanese lines by heading due west.

"Where can I find Zhing Htaw Naw?" asked Vince Curl again.

Captain DeSilva of the Kachin Levies did not know, but one of his Kachin officers replied, "Beyond the mountains to the west. Beyond the Kumon Mountains."

The lofty Kumon Range separated the Triangle headwaters of the Irrawaddy from the Hukawng Valley and its swirling Chindwin River. Knothead, the guides leading the way, set out on the trail that ran westward to Shakyu Ga, a Kachin village at the foot of the Kumon Mountains. They arrived there that evening. In the morning they would set out southward around the western flank of the Japa-nese positions. West of Sumprabum was a wilderness, and the Japa-nese had no knowledge whatsoever of the progress of enemy parties that might be moving through the country. Knothead walked south-ward for about seventy-five miles, each day passing much like the one before, as the party climbed one foothill of the Kumons after an-other, each ascent followed by a drop down again into the next valley.

From the Kachins Vince Curl learned, as would American 101 men after him, how to place each foot solidly on the hill as he climbed. By pushing with the thighs, and never pressing down with the toes, a Kachin can climb effortlessly hour after hour, carrying a burden on his back without straining the tendons attached to the heel, a painful affliction that incapacitates many mountain hikers. Coming down the precipitous slopes, Vince Curl learned that a Ka-chin leans backward so as to balance against the pull of gravity and absorbs the shock of each plunging step with the full strength of his thighs and sturdy knees. In this fashion the Kachins kept up a brisk pace, more akin to a trot than a walk.

Knothead halted at a Kachin village in which the leading duwa of the region east of the Kumons had his basha.

"We will help you fight the Japanese," the duwa said.

Coco had been picked for the team because he presumably spoke Jinghpaw, but his knowledge of the language of the Kachins proved very sketchy. Between Vince Curl's rudimentary Jinghpaw and

Coco's linguistic efforts, it was possible to determine in general what the duwa was saying, but fine understandings were impossible.

"Where can I find Zhing Htaw Naw?" asked Vince Curl.

The duwa pursed his lips in Kachin style toward the mountains looming to the west. Vince Curl decided on the spot that he would lead Knothead over the Kumons in search of Zhing Htaw Naw. He could fulfill his orders by remaining on this side of the mountains and working with the duwa who sat with him on the platform of his basha, but he had set out on a personal quest to find the Kachin resistance leader. Every Kachin to whom he mentioned the name of Zhing Htaw Naw had reacted. What kind of man could this Kachin be?

Every evening, on schedule, Fima Haimson contacted Nazira with his radio transmitter. He not only carried batteries, but he also had packed a portable hand-cranked generator, which Phil Huston at Nazira had developed as a more dependable source of power. At first Huston and the other communications men working on the generator had doubted that it would be satisfactory. When it was turned, the machine made a high-pitched whine, which could be heard at least four hundred yards away. Fearing that the sound would give away the location of any operator who used it, Huston next housed the generator in an insulated box in order to dampen it. This also markedly increased the weight. Then one day, after taking the generator out into the jungles near Nazira, Huston discovered that the normal level of sound in the jungle—the drone of the insects and the calls of the birds—drowned out the whir. It could not be heard more than twenty-five feet away. Whenever Fima Haimson set up his radio to contact base, the Kachins lined up to take turns at rotating the generator. Such was the routine in Detachment 101 camps over the next two years. The radio fascinated them. As Ozzie Klein, another 101 operator, was to discover, when the wires connecting the generator to his radio set came loose, the Kachins also competed with one another for the chance to hold them together. Let the blue spark jump across the loose connection and perhaps prickle his fingers, and the Kachin holding the wires would laugh with the thrill of it all.

Opero concurred with Knothead that it would be advisable to cross the Kumon Range and search for Zhing Htaw Naw. From high hills on the fringes of the valley the Kumon Mountains had appeared to Knothead as a misty blue range rising beyond the bright green of the foliage. They had promised cool air to men who came sweating up a steep hill to a summit from which they could look far away and up to their misty eminences. Now that Knothead was climbing the Kumons themselves, they soon discovered the truth in the old Kachin saying, quoted by the political anthropologist, Edmund R. Leach, of Cambridge University: "In the valleys farming and the roads are easy; in the mountains farming and roads are difficult." The men climbed beyond the jungles onto high slopes where stands of tall pines alternated with patches of meadows. At night the chill winds from the Himalayas swept down on their camp, and, accustomed as they were to the steamy Triangle, they shivered in their bedrolls.

From time to time Knothead met Kachins on the trail. Usually they were on their way from their village or kahtaung to another village where a lweje or market was to be held. They carried handicrafts or fruits or vegetables to barter at the lweje. Sometimes they were on a hunting trip; other times they were just on a social visit. They were friendly and confident in their approach to the strangers, whose arrival never seemed to surprise them.

"Where can I find Zhing Htaw Naw?" Curl asked.

The parties of Kachins smiled and pointed on up the trail toward the summit of the mountains. Knothead struggled on higher and higher. Then they met men sent by Zhing Htaw Naw himself to greet the party. But though they guided Curl and his men on through the mountains toward the Hukawng Valley, they explained that the party could not in fact see the duwa kaba.

"Why can't we see him?" demanded Curl. "We are friends."

"You are friends, but you cannot see the duwa," replied a young Kachin, whose bold eyes and erect bearing indicated that he was a person of some consequence.

At first there was no more explanation than that, but then the young Kachin warrior added, "The duwa is sick."

"I can cure him," said Curl.

It was a rash promise, but Curl, whose pack contained a veritable apothecary of Western medicines and nostrums, had taken the gamble. Not long afterward, the party emerged on the highest mountain ridge where they could look down on the green sea of the Hukawng Valley, far below. Cane brakes, vast stands of bamboo, and swamps alternated in a haphazard pattern with stretches of jungle and occasional low hills. The Hukawng, shaped long ago in another geological time by the Tsanpo, a Tibetan river that changed its course to become today a tributary of the Brahmaputra, is the only major break in the great mountains. In the valley swamps, malaria is endemic, and it was malaria that had felled Zhing Htaw Naw.

"I can cure the duwa kaba," Curl told the young Kachin.

Finally the Kachin said that he would lead him to the duwa, but only he would be permitted to enter the village where the duwa lay ill in the village duwa's basha. The rest of the group must camp nearby and wait. Vince Curl agreed, and he set out with the Kachin along the trails that led within a matter of hours to a village erected by refugees from the southern Hukawng on a mountain shoulder. Zhing Htaw Naw had shifted his headquarters several times since he had met Red Maddox and helped him on his way to Fort Hertz, but Curl could see the same meticulous preparations against enemy attack that Maddox had noticed. The Kachin guide brought Curl to the duwa's basha where he found Zhing Htaw Naw curled up beside the cook fire half asleep.

"Kaja-ee, duwa," Curl greeted the sick man, who looked at him with glazed eyes.

"Kaja-lo," replied the duwa politely despite his illness.

"I can help you," said Curl in English.

Zhing Htaw Naw's keen mind groped through the malaria fever to grapple with the strange presence. He understood only a little English, but he understood the sympathy and confidence in Curl's voice. Curl took a bottle of quinine out of his pack and administered a strong dose to the sick man. He wrapped him in his own bedroll, holding it tight around his shoulders, which were shaking with the malaria ague. Beckoning a Kachin boy to him, he had the youngster hold the bedroll tight around the duwa. If he could only make him sweat enough it would help break the grip of the fever.

While the boy kept the duwa covered, Curl added some powdered soup mix to a pot of water boiling over the fire. He spooned the soup into the duwa. The warmth and nourishment of the soup, the heat from the fire, and the bedroll around him caused Zhing Htaw Naw to break into a furious sweat. Then the fever was broken. Zhing Htaw Naw fell asleep, his brow cool, his handsome face untroubled.

Vince Curl sat by the duwa's side. The Kachin leader was a man in his late thirties, strongly built, with an aristocratic high-cheekboned face. His breath was easy now. Vince Curl, too, fell asleep. In the morning both he and the duwa awoke. Now they could talk. They already were fast friends. The remainder of Knothead was sent for, and Coco, the interpreter, was pressed into service. With his halting efforts, Curl's smattering of Kachin, Zhing Htaw Naw's smattering of English, and many sketches drawn in the dust before the village duwa's basha, the American and the Kachin agreed to make common cause against the Japanese.

"Zhing tried to tell me about the fate of his villages in the south and why he hated the Japanese as he did," Vincent Curl said after the war, "but I couldn't understand him. I knew that the cause of his anger was sufficient, and I knew that he and his people were fighting for their own freedom. He would welcome our help. It wasn't until later on when Father Stuart joined me as an interpreter that I heard the entire story of what the Japanese had done. By that time I had come to love the Kachin people myself, and I was as horrified and as angry as he was."

Fima Haimson contacted Nazira from Zhing Htaw Naw's village headquarters. Knothead requested an arms drop for 250 men. He gave the coordinates, and on the day set for the drop the familiar C-87 came roaring over the Hukawng to drop case after case of rifles, shotguns, tommy guns, and ammunition. The parachutes fluttering down from the sky attracted the Kachin women just as much as the arms did the men. Curl gladly let them gather up the chutes as they lay in the drop field close to the village, for he knew how starved they were for cloth. Let them make new skirts and blouses. As for the men, they broke open the crates and snatched up the weapons. With only a few hours instruction, every Kachin had mastered the use of the most advanced weapons the Americans could drop to them. There was only one problem; Vince Curl had asked for arms for 250 men, and already Zhing Htaw Naw had 300 clambering for arms to fight the Japanese. Within a matter of a few months, he had over 1,000 Kachin boys and men armed with American weapons ready to attack the Japanese wherever they were to be found. Ngai Tawng's father, a duwa, became one of the officers of this first unit of what was to become known as the American-Kachin Rangers. It was now June, and a year had gone by since his village had been destroyed by the Japanese.

Ray Peers was intrigued by the story of Zhing Htaw Naw, which Red Maddox had brought out of the jungle. He studied the daily reports that were radioed to Nazira from Knothead in the Hukawng Valley.

"The legend of Zhing Htaw Naw proved true in every respect. He was a small, quiet, uneducated, and innocuous-appearing person, but was filled with innate intelligence, had the courage and cunning of a tiger, was highly respected by his people and hated the Japs with a passion.

"It was quite obvious that the joining together of these forces would work to the mutual benefit of both parties. Zhing would provide the people to be trained, the knowledge of the area, and the leadership while, on the other hand, Lieutenant Curl would provide contact with the Allies, and arms, ammunition and other forms of support."

This was to be the classic partnership between the Americans and the Kachins that was to make the American-Kachin Rangers of OSS Detachment 101 one of the most formidable guerrilla groups ever to operate.

Vincent Curl and Zhing Htaw Naw moved their field bases to the villages of Taikri and Nawbum, close to one another at the headwaters of the Chindwin. The guerrillas fanned out in units of fifty or sixty men to begin their operations against the Japanese. Zhing Htaw Naw had an intelligence network reaching throughout the Hukawng Valley and its approaches to the south and east. In only a few weeks his agents were bringing in such a vast amount of intelligence about the Japanese every day that it was impossible for Fima Haimson to radio all of it to base. OSS sent more personnel in to join Knothead at Nawbum. One of these newcomers, Father Stuart, infiltrated in over the trails much as the original party had done. Other men jumped in. Then Carl Eifler gave orders that both Knothead and Forward were to build thousand-foot-long airstrips so that men could be taken in and out with greater ease and safety. The most practical way to remove wounded or sick men was in a light plane. The Japanese air force controlled the air, but a light plane, winging along close to the treetops, could usually slip in unobserved.

It was the Kachins who put the finishing touches on the two landing fields. They erected thatched huts on the strips so that they looked like villages from the air. When a plane was expected, the huts could literally be picked up and carried to the side of the airstrip so that the plane could land.

\* \* \*

John Raiss was a scion of an old San Francisco family and a leading member of the New York Stock Exchange. Stu Power, a fellow

101'er, remarks that "he carried himself with an elegance that enabled him to deal with coolies or Lord Louis Mountbatten."

He arrived in India in the summer of 1943 and checked in with Harry Little at O House in Calcutta. There he fell in with Nicol Smith, the ebullient scion of another old San Francisco family. After finishing up his training at OSS Area B, Smith had been Ray Peers's partner in the graduation exercises at the aircraft factory near Hagerstown. Then he had gone on an OSS mission to Vichy. With the successful conclusion of his work in France, he had been given the task of coordinating the Thai underground and was on his way to China, from where he was to infiltrate into Japanese-occupied Thailand. Raiss was awaiting his first 101 assignment from Carl Eifler.

The two San Franciscans strolled out the garden gate of O House and met a thin Bengali wearing a loincloth and carrying a wicker basket. He spoke to them with a fine Oxford accent and held out his hand.

"Baksheesh, gentlemen, baksheesh."

"Baksheesh, hell!" exclaimed Raiss, preparing to deal with a snake charmer with the same aplomb he would employ in dealing with a coolie or Lord Louis. "He's probably a Jap agent."

The head of a cobra perked out of the basket and craned to look at the two Americans.

"Give one rupee, gentlemen, and I will command a cobra to appear at your feet."

"Where?" asked Raiss.

He shifted his feet from where he imagined the cobra might appear.

"Anywhere you wish."

Raiss flipped a silver rupee to the snake charmer, who closed the lid of his basket and shuffled across the road. He picked up a stick lying beside the road and snapped it in two. Throwing the two pieces down in the road a few feet in front of the Americans, he made a graceful pass with his hands. Instantly two cobras appeared at Raiss's feet, lifting their heads to glare at him, darting their tongues in and out. Raiss and Smith stood transfixed.

"One more rupee, one more cobra!" suggested the thin Bengali in his incongruous Oxford accent.

"Can you make them come out of that garden in there behind the gate?" asked Raiss, indicating the garden of O House.

"For one rupee, one cobra anywhere."

"Here's five rupees. Fill 'er up."

He handed a bill to the Bengali, who picked up a handful of sticks and tossed them past the Gurkha guard at the gate. Cobras came writhing out of the bushes and appeared mysteriously among the flowers.

"I thought you gave him only five rupees," observed the pragmatic Smith. "He's on his ninth snake now."

Raiss dug his hands into his pocket and took out a roll of notes.

"My God," he said, as he observed a hundred-rupee note was missing. "I gave him the wrong bill. Let's get out of here."

The two Americans walked quickly off down the street toward Chowringhee, leaving a very disconcerted Gurkha guard. At least this is the story as told by Nicol Smith. There rarely is a shortage of yarns to spin when 101 men get together, and it seems sometimes that at least half of them are about John Raiss.

\*      \*      \*

When John Raiss arrived at Nazira, Carl Eifler called him into his office and gave him his first 101 orders.

"There is an airplane for sale down south," he told Raiss. "You go down and buy it for me. I understand they are asking $90,000."

He explained that even as they talked, Kachins were leveling rice paddies at both Knothead and Forward to make landing strips for light planes, but 101 had no light planes. Neither did 101 have much money at the time—certainly not $90,000—but the detachment did need a light plane and needed it right away. Raiss soon discovered that there was no way to purchase the plane down south. He also soon learned that the United States Air Corps did not have any light liaison aircraft available in India, so he must either obtain a plane from an Indian civilian or from the Royal Air Force. The RAF was by far the better bet.

Tucking two cartons of hard-to-get Camel cigarettes beneath his arm, Raiss went to New Delhi to see Air Marshal Sir Richard Peirse, chief of the RAF in India. Nobody would ever accuse the air marshal of trading a plane to the smooth-talking OSS man for two cartons of American cigarettes, but the fact remains that Raiss returned without the cigarettes and had been told that he should go to Dum Dum Airport near Calcutta on a certain day and at a certain hour, where he would meet a young British officer with a clipboard in his hand. He would be studying numbers on planes at the field and matching them up to papers on his clipboard.

Raiss turned up at Dum Dum as he had been instructed, and there indeed was the young Britisher, studying a plane. Raiss sauntered up to him.

"That's my airplane," he said with confidence, as he had been told to do.

"Oh, thank God," said the officer. "I'm glad of that, because I have no record of the plane and was wondering what to do with it."

The plane was a two-seat biplane De Havilland Moth, 1925 vintage, which was in excellent shape and ready to fly. Detachment 101 now had an airplane, antique as it might be, and Carl Eifler lost no time in hurrying to Calcutta to pick it up. He had learned to fly when he was in the U.S. Customs Service on the Mexican border, and he got into the plane and revved the motor. Raiss sat behind him as the plane, which was to be known affectionately by 101 men as the "Gypsy Moth," raced down the runway and bounced up into the air. Making refueling stops along the way, Eifler flew the Gypsy Moth to Nazira, where he landed on the newly finished two-thousand-foot landing strip in the tea gardens. Because this and other light planes that 101 was to fly had red rudder tips, it was inevitable that they became known throughout the detachment as "The Red Ass Squadron."

\*   \*   \*

Forward's bamboo grapevine reached farther and farther through the jungles as the summer months of 1943 passed. Kachin agents brought in the names of Shans, Burmese, and even a few apostate Kachins who were working for the Japanese. They kept check on Japanese military movements and even penetrated into Myitkyina. Other Kachins volunteered to serve as hypenlas in a force of about three hundred guerrillas whom Wilkinson recruited and trained. Still other Kachins worked on the construction of the landing strip.

One duwa in particular led in recruiting, directing agents, and providing workers for building the airstrip, and Wilkinson radioed to Nazira with the proposal that the duwa and Kachins like him be rewarded with "rice, salt, tobacco, medals." The cryptographer who enciphered the message followed usual military procedure by spelling out the commas it contained as "CMA," and when Carl Eifler received the message, which had been partly garbled in transmission, he pondered for a moment as to what a "CMA medal" might be. No matter, he would refer the problem to Harry Little in Calcutta. From Calcutta, Harry Little checked the availability of "CMA medals" with OSS in Washington, and when he received word back that the U.S. Army knew of no such award, he immediately set about having one made. What operations in Nazira wanted, operations got.

"CMA" was made to stand for "Citation for Military Assistance." On one side an artist designed a medallion of silver about the size of a half-dollar with the letters "CMA" appearing above the American eagle, as on the great seal of the United States. The other side showed a peacock to represent Burma. A green silk ribbon with six Burmese peacocks embroidered in white silk was also created so that the medal could be suspended around the neck of the meritorious Kachin. Since each of the medals cost the OSS fifty dollars, they were no mean award, and as the months went by they became the most sought-after honor to which a Kachin could aspire.

# The Prisoner

The jaunty Japanese pilot climbed into the cockpit of his Zero and waved his hand in friendly farewell to his ground crew. He was soon in the air, holding his position in a tight formation of pursuit planes. They sped northward from their home field at Meiktila, near Mandalay, toward the giant mountain ridges over which American transports were lumbering on their way to China. His mouth was dry, and he licked his lips, which were dry too. It was always a stomach-churning thing to go hunting through the cloud banks that hovered over the mountains for the American planes which, heavy with their cargoes, were as ponderous as flying whales. Several times before he had come up on the transports, and ignoring their feeble gunfire and clumsy efforts at evasion, he had streaked in to make his kill. The huge planes had burst into flames and careened out of control into the mountains.

When it came to configuration, a B-24 bomber converted into a C-87 transport and a conventional B-24 looked alike. General Chennault, realizing that the almost daily attrition of the transports bringing supplies over the Hump was becoming a critical factor in the defense of China, determined to send a flight of B-24s, armed from propellers to tail. Some of the best gunners in the air force would be at the guns. The crews were instructed to fly the planes in a tight formation so that they would be able to cover any approach with a withering fire.

The Japanese planes came out of the sun in a classical attack on what appeared to be a flight of transports. The Zeros from Meiktila dove in to cut the American formation apart so that each of the big planes could be gunned down with impunity, but something was terribly wrong. When the Zeros closed in for the kill, the formation did not break and scatter for safety; it held tightly together. Suddenly .50

gunfire erupted from dorsal and tail turrets, and Zero after Zero, struck by deadly gunners, fell in flames. At least twenty Japanese fighters, and perhaps as many as thirty, were shot down on that day. The pilot from Meiktila's plane screamed out of control. He snapped back his hatch cover and pulled his escape lever. Then he was out in the cold air, drifting helplessly toward a mountain shoulder, shaggy with great trees. There was no time to be frightened. At least he was alive. Far away to the left he saw his plane strike the ground, burning furiously. Myitkyina and a friendly air base were only a few miles away, to the right.

\*       \*       \*

From Nazira, Pat Quinn and Dennis Francis had returned to Burma together again, as was their wish. They had established a base camp at Arang, code named Pat, only twenty-five miles north of Myit-kyina, and already had mustered a guerrilla force of about fifty Kachins. Their men were attacking Japanese truck and rail traffic in and out of Myitkyina. One day Kachin runners came to report that a Japanese airplane had fallen in flames in the mountains.

That same day Kachin villagers, not far to the south, saw the Japanese pilot come floating down to the earth. They waited for him to land. He smiled when he saw the villagers, but at the same time he loosened a pistol in its holster at his belt. He unstrapped his para-chute, and in his impossible-to-understand language asked for an easy-to-understand thing. He wanted to be led through the jungles to the nearest Japanese position. The Kachins smiled, and several young men pointed the right way to go. They would lead the Japanese up into the mountains. Their faces indicated that it was the right way to go, but they led the pilot farther and farther away from Myitkyina at every step. It began to rain.

The Japanese scowled, pulled out his pistol, and brandished it at the Kachins. He should have reached Myitkyina long ago. These brown natives were playing some sort of desperate game with him. Two Kachins hit him from behind, and others jerked up his gun arm so that his shots went wild. The Kachins trussed their captive up with vines and brought him deeper into the mountains to Pat.

Pat's evening radio schedule with Nazira contained surprising news. We have captured a Japanese pilot. Should we try and smuggle him out through the Japanese lines or should we kill him? When the message was deciphered at Nazira's message center, a whoop of triumph went up. The air force had been searching for months to locate the hidden fighter-plane bases from which the Japanese Zeros rose in such a deadly swarm. The Japanese had done a masterful job of secreting the planes. American bombers had attacked and attacked again the known bases, but the attacks had not affected the Zeros in any significant way. Now perhaps this captured Japanese pilot could be made to tell where his base at least was situated.

"Hold him. We'll get him out," was the return message from Opero.

Another message went out to Knothead at Nawbum. Jack Pamplin was to proceed immediately to Arang, seventy miles away, over the mountains. Vincent Curl was to finish any necessary work on his landing strip. To make certain that he completed the job in time, a drop of tools was to be made. If the Japanese prisoner could be brought overland to Knothead, Carl Eifler had every intention of flying in to bring him out. Within two days Pamplin had reached Pat at Arang, where he found the Japanese pilot still tied up and under heavy Kachin guard.

When the American entered the basha where he was held prisoner, the pilot glared at him in contempt. So, indeed, there were scheming Americans behind these natives. Kachin soldiers ignored his anger and tied him down onto a bamboo stretcher. He must be kept totally immobile on the trail, or he might perhaps fling himself over a cliff to his death rather than be taken to what he must surely know would be interrogation.

Pamplin and sixteen Kachins set out on the trail back to Nawbum. The trail climbed up over Chinglaptu Pass through a wild and dangerous region. The Kachins reported that there were no Japanese to be found, but the country contained many tigers. Pamplin hardly needed to be told this because, even at Nawbum, a huge tiger stalked men going from the village to the landing strip. In the pass the trail led along the lip of deep gorges. The Kachins carrying the prisoner tilted the stretcher toward the cliff wall so that he would not be able to shift his weight suddenly and tumble himself and bearers over the edge. Pamplin and his sullen prisoner arrived safely at Nawbum.

The next move was up to Carl Eifler. Knothead was not only 140 miles behind the Japanese lines but 275 miles from Nazira, which was beyond the round-trip capacity of the Gypsy Moth. Before Eifler could begin his flight, it was necessary to air-drop fuel to Knothead so that the plane could be refueled for the return flight. Eifler was confident of his ability to fly the biplane through the wilderness to Nawbum, but when word came in to Nazira that Forward had captured a Japanese infantry officer, he decided to fly to Ngumla and bring the man out for interrogation as a rehearsal for the flight to Knothead. The flight to Forward and back went without any problems.

The strip at Nawbum was ready. Nazira radioed to Knothead that Eifler was on his way. The Gypsy Moth took off at Chabua, the Assam airfield closest to Knothead, and flew low over the Naga Hills and the Hukawng Valley to the Kumon Mountains and Nawbum on a steep mountain shoulder. When the plane zoomed in low, the Kachins cleared the bamboo huts off the field. Eifler looked down on the airstrip, which twisted and dipped in a serpentine fashion. He shook his head at the prospect of landing on it, but there was nothing to do but try, and he was successful. As soon as his plane rolled to a stop, Kachin soldiers seized it and wheeled it into the shelter of the forest. They put the huts back on the strip so that no passing Japanese plane could spot it.

The Japanese pilot was in excellent physical condition, knew how to incapacitate the airplane, and at a glance could be seen to possess the true samurai spirit. He was capable of any action at all that was necessary to balk his captors. Vince Curl and Carl Eifler had no choice but to bind him fast to the second seat of the plane, tie his arms and legs securely, and as a final precaution inject him with a syringe that Archie Chun Ming had provided. The prisoner lost consciousness as soon as the powerful shot hit him. Just to be certain, Eifler tied a noose around his neck with the end of the rope dangling in his lap. If he revived and began to cause trouble, Eifler had every intention of throttling him into submission.

On the takeoff Eifler barely lifted the Gypsy Moth over the trees at the end of the runway. He winged over the mountains, taking advantage of mountain passes, since he could not gain enough altitude to surmount the higher peaks. A rainstorm struck, but he used his compass, altimeter, and tachometer to make his way through to Chabua. On the ground Archie Chun Ming waited with an ambulance to take the still-comatose prisoner to a secure place where he could revive in safety.

Interrogation proved useless. The Japanese stared without a glimmer of interest or emotion as an OSS interpreter, Sukyoon Chang, questioned him over and over in his own language. Some of the

Americans wished out loud that Eifler had left the prisoner at Naw-bum where the Kachins might have interrogated him in their own fashion. In Zhing Htaw Naw's care he would have lost that contemptuous look on his face in a hurry, but nobody at Nazira was willing to resort to torture.

"For all practical purposes we had about given up hope," Ray Peers noted. "He was not providing any information, and he appeared to have no documents of any value. He had a diary with him. It was good reading but did not say anything. He also had some pictures of the ordinary variety, with his Burmese girl friend, standing by the airplane, and the like."

The 101 men had all looked at the pictures over and over, but there was nothing valuable to be seen. Then somebody noticed that the tall grass in the rear of the picture appeared to be uneven and had holes cut into it. Phototechnician Irby Moree blew up the picture in the laboratory, and the mystery of the hidden Zeros was solved. The Japanese had dug pits for the planes and sodded them over. They had also sodded the approaches so that from the air the entire area looked like a meadow. Strange-appearing shadows on the photo were all there were to betray the hiding places. Then Sukyoon Chang learned something of importance from the pilot. He was based at Meiktila.

When OSS men showed the photos taken from the Japanese to Captain Burman, A-2 of the 10th Air Force, he went to a file and took out other pictures of the Meiktila airfield which had been photographed by air reconnaissance, and there he noticed the same shadows around the edge. In a few days B-25s took off from an airport in Lower Assam and bombed and strafed Meiktila airport, concentrating their attention on the shadows that revealed where the Zeros lay hidden. The Japanese had many other such air bases, all of them cleverly concealed, but the attack on Meiktila helped immeasurably to cut down on Zero attacks on United States transports over the Hump.

*     *     *

Early in October Carl Eifler was on another flying mission behind the lines in Burma. Lieutenant General Stratemeyer, commander of the Eastern Air Command, had provided 101 with a new L-5 light plane in Calcutta which was then ferried up to Nazira. Eifler also recruited pilot Lee Majors from the Flying Tigers, and the two of them flew from Nazira to Fort Hertz and on the following day to Forward. The landing strip at Ngumla sloped downward and then slanted up to a stand of tall trees. Eifler and Majors managed to land. Their plane was rolled into the jungle and covered with vines and leaves to hide it from the Japanese.

Eifler conferred with Wilkinson. The Kachins poured liberal libations of their potent laukhu from the bamboo tubes in which they kept it in honor of the visiting American duwa kaba. Perhaps it was the laukhu—more likely it was the tricky landing strip—but when Eifler and Majors took off, their plane failed to gain flying speed and crashed into a bamboo thicket about a half mile beyond the field. Eifler was in the passenger's seat, and the impact threw him against the back of the pilot's seat. He cut his leg and his mouth. Majors was uninjured, but the plane was wrecked beyond any possibility of repair. The Kachins hid the wreckage in the jungle. To Fort Hertz and the nearest airstrip that would take a big plane was a long hike indeed, and the pilot had only a pair of Oxfords to wear.

Wilkie Wilkinson's feet were the same size as Majors's, and he loaned him a pair of his GI shoes. Wilkinson and Father Mac decided to join their visitors on the hundred-mile trek to Fort Hertz. The four men wrapped their heads in silk maps, shoved their hands in their pockets to keep off the mosquitoes, and set off down the trail. Ten days later they walked into Fort Hertz, footsore and in bad temper. They flew on to Chabua. Unshaven, ragged, the shoe soles flapping loose on his feet, Eifler walked into a dinner being given by General Stilwell for some British and American civilian VIPs, including Wong, then a well-known newsreel photographer. The general gave Eifler a cursory look.

"Have you eaten?" he asked. "Sit down."

"I've just walked out from behind the lines in Burma."

"You look it."

As the dinner progressed, Stilwell would ask a question. Then when Eifler began to answer, he invariably interrupted.

"Shut up and eat your dinner."

"He reminded me of my father," Eifler recalled ruefully after the war.

When it came time for Eifler to leave, Stilwell, very much a commanding general, ushered him out of the room; but once the door had closed behind them, he put his arm around the OSS man's shoulders.

"Carl, I wish you'd quit taking these damned fool chances," he said.

Years later, when Stilwell lay dying in a hospital in the United States, Carl Eifler stood outside on the hospital lawn, his eyes on the light burning in the general's window, and he wept bitterly.

*          *          *

"During the colonel's long walk out of the jungle we were enjoying a respite from having our asses chewed out for failing to behave like supermen," recollects Sam Schreiner. "But at the same time we were trying to estimate the level of rage that the accident and loss of time might have produced in the colonel's breast. It was sure that there would be hell to pay when he got back."

Eifler reached Nazira in the middle of the night and went directly to bed. In the morning Schreiner, at work in the message center, deciphered a message from Washington. It said that Eifler had been promoted to a full colonel. Schreiner took the message to Floyd Frazee and wanted to know if they should wake him up.

"Hell, yes!" announced Frazee, and the two men shook Eifler awake. Eifler sat up in bed and blinked the sleep out of his eyes. When he heard the news, his angry glare turned to a broad grin.

"We had the first toast of the day right there on the porch outside his bedroom," recalled Schreiner. "It was a tradition then to honor promotions by dunking the recipient in the pond in front of the headquarters. Despite his new chickens and formidable bulk, several brave people suggested that we accord Eifler the same honor."

"Well, I'm not going alone," growled Eifler. "As of now, Sam, you are a staff sergeant."

The 101 celebrants tossed first Eifler, then Schreiner, and for good measure Father Stuart, who was still at base, into the pond. Father Stuart landed on his feet with the Scotch intact in his glass. Standing face to face with Schreiner, he dipped his fingers in the glass of whiskey and baptized him.

*          *          *

"To the president of the United States!"

The British tea planters and their wives lifted their glasses and clinked them with the glasses of the 101 men.

"To the king!"

The glasses clinked again. Back and forth went the toasts, and the conviviality deepened and broadened and ran in a joyous freshet. It was the Fourth of July, 1943, and the Americans of Detachment 101 at Nazira were giving a party in honor of their nation's birthday. They had invited their British friends out of appreciation for the camps and roads they had built, the food and labor they had supplied.

The party started in the middle of the afternoon, and it broke up at 3 A.M. on the fifth. The 101 men pushed and shoved the six Britishers still on hand into the rear end of a truck. Eifler and planter Charlie Ashfield set off in the cab of the truck to take them home. In a few miles they ran into a ditch and had to walk to Ashfield's tea garden, about two miles away.

"It had a fine, sobering effect," said Ray Peers.

*　　*　　*

An OSS man reporting for duty to Detachment 101 found that part of the challenge of his new assignment was getting there.

"You will report to a Colonel Eifler at 101 Detachment in northern Assam," Pete Joost was informed at OSS headquarters in Washington.

"Yes, sir," answered Joost, "but where is northern Assam?"

In April, 1943, when Pete Joost arrived at Karachi, after a 65-day trip from the United States, he learned that none of the port authorities or anybody else had ever heard of either Colonel Eifler or Detachment 101. It took three weeks for Joost to reach the obscure headquarters on a tea plantation at Nazira.

Cecil Crafts, after a long journey by ship to India, was given instruction to take the narrow-gauge Bengal and Assam Railroad to Mozenge Siding.

"I overshot it by a hundred miles," he admitted later. "I got back on the train and retraced my route, keeping careful track of the stations. When I finally got off at Mozenge Siding, there was nothing but piles of lumber and an Indian who could speak no English except to say, 'Get out of the sun.'"

Crafts rode with a pile of logs on a cart into the jungle where he took another narrow-gauge plantation rail to still another point, where at last 101-man Floyd Frazee, driving a jeep, met him. When the jeep pulled up in front of the 101 headquarters basha at Nazira, some of the men were having dinner on the verandah.

"Look what I got here," said Frazee as he swung out of the driver's seat.

"Take it back," said one of the diners between forkfuls of fiery curry. "Anything that gets lost as easily as that, we don't want."

"He wasn't jesting," said Crafts, who nevertheless was soon put to work teaching radio and cryptography to agents and building radio sets.

Some OSS men flew, as I did, in an ATC transport from Dum Dum airport at Calcutta to Chabua. We passed over the tawny flood of the Brahmaputra toward the great snowy summits of the Himalayas. Chabua turned out to be a dusty landing strip and a collection of ramshackle warehouses. There would be a phone call to a mysterious number that we had been given in Calcutta, and in about four hours a truck or jeep would pull up at the strip. A grinning Indian or Kachin driver would jump out and toss our gear in back.

The truck bounced and jerked over dusty washboard roads into the tea plantations. As dusk settled down, the newcomer entered a wilder country of dense jungles broken by turbulent rivers flowing down out of the mountains. There were occasional villages, a glimpse of cooking fires and brown faces illuminated in the flickering light. It was instant adventure, to be driving alone with an uncommunicative native driver through the dark night, heading toward an unknown destination.

Other OSS men went by train and sometimes part of the way by riverboat on the Brahmaputra. They got acquainted with the Bengal and Assam Railroad on which locomotive engineers often stopped the train so that they could make a cup of hot tea with water drawn from the engine boiler. Sometimes they ate C rations on the trip; sometimes they scrounged on station platforms for what they could buy. They got acquainted with cockroaches up to three and a half inches long and a half inch wide. Bill Martin, later to be one of 101's top field commanders, was kept awake at night by the cockroaches trying to chew their way into the K rations his group carried.

Ozzie Klein, Bill McLaughlin, and some nineteen other eighteen- and nineteen-year-old radiomen, all recruited from the Illinois Institute of Technology in Chicago, started out on the morning train from Calcutta. Klein, a private first class, was nominally in charge. They were given one box of C rations for the trip, but by that afternoon, their rations were eaten up. At 3 P.M. the train stopped with a jerk.

British troops got off and filed aboard a steamboat waiting at a dock on the broad Brahmaputra River.

"Where's Nazira?" asked Klein.

"Get on the boat, buddy," said a British soldier. "We're on our way to the front at Imphal."

The Americans got aboard. Nazira must be somewhere near Imphal. The British officers were on the top deck, and Gurkha and Tommies were down below.

"Where are your rations?" a British officer asked Klein.

"We don't have any."

The officers were so disconcerted by a group so terribly inept that it had no rations, no mattresses to sleep on, and apparently was commanded by an eighteen-year-old PFC, seemingly retarded at that, that they brought mattresses and installed them on the officers' deck. They supplied the Americans with meals for the three-day boat ride. When the British got off the boat, so did the radiomen. Their experience with the Bengal and Assam Railroad began at this point. They rode on the narrow-gauge line for two days and one night into Assam at a speed that suggested that there was no emergency, no war, and the Japanese were not poised in Burma just beyond the shaggy hills to the east.

Later arrivals riding the Bengal and Assam discovered that the speed of its trains had increased in an astounding fashion. An entire cadre of railroad men from the Burlington Railroad had volunteered to make up the 745th Railroad Battalion. They had been trained on two divisions of the Pennsylvania Railroad between Fort Wayne, Indiana, and Montpelier, Ohio, and Fort Wayne and Peru, Indiana. Then they sailed to India where they took over the Bengal and Assam, determined to rush supplies such as aviation gas and engines to the air bases in Assam. They plotted the increased speed of the trains against the proposed increase in derailments and doubled the speed.

"It didn't help our relations with the British when two of the trains we were operating piled head-on into one another," said Oliver Grutzmacher, who served on the line between Mariani and Tinsukia. Soon cars were lying upside down in the gorges and wrecked rolling stock lay along the tracks, but the trains moved with great dispatch. Supplies were rushed to Assam and to Ledo, from where a new road was being hacked through the Naga Hills toward the Hukawng jungles. OSS men on their way to Nazira at least arrived faster than before, even if a bit more shaken.

When an OSS man finally did reach Detachment 101, he received a welcome surprise. Commander Jim Luce, a naval doctor, who was directed to report for duty at 101, arrived at 2 A.M. at the train station at Nazira. A jeep came and picked him up. In the morning he sat down to an excellent American breakfast. He found the company congenial and the conversation stimulating.

"One had the impression that no matter what India might be like or what type of war was being fought, here was a well-ordered outfit which had a big job to do and in which there were a good number of solid, intelligent American officers," Luce noted in a manuscript written at the end of the war.

An OSS man's first night at Nazira long remained in his memory. What Mickey Kaliff remembered most was a blue velvet cushion hanging on a wall. Kachins had rescued it from the Japanese plane that crashed in the hills near Pat at Arang. Carl Eifler had hung the cushion on the wall to remind his men of 101's success in bringing out the pilot and learning how the Japanese hid their planes at Meiktila.

"When the headquarters later moved forward to Myitkyina, I took the cushion because nobody else wanted it. I carried it through the rest of the war and took it home with me," said Kaliff.

The last time Kaliff, a successful insurance man, noticed the cushion it was years later and his chauffeur was using it to sit on as he drove him around San Antonio, Texas.

# Beyond the Ledo Road

British engineers had started work on the Ledo Truck Road through the Naga Hills in February of 1942. They intended to construct the road through the wilderness to Fort Hertz, but the conditions they met in the mountains brought the work to a standstill. Vinegar Joe Stilwell had described the country as, "Rain, rain, rain, mud, mud, mud, typhus, malaria, dysentery, exhaustion, rotting feet, body sores," and the British experience confirmed his statement. Up to two hundred inches of rain fell in a year, mostly during the monsoons, when a river might rise thirty feet in a day and wash out bridges and embankments as fast as the crews put them in.

In October of 1943—with the British having made little progress in the preceding year and a half—Colonel Lewis A. Pick, a soft-spoken Virginian who was a specialist in flood control, took over the task of building what his men called "Pick's Pike." Major General Raymond Wheeler, who commanded the supply corps, established his headquarters at Ledo, as did Stilwell's Northern Combat Area Command (NCAC). The jungles around Ledo turned overnight into sprawling camps and barracks, mess halls, hospitals, motor pools, and supply dumps. Dibrugarh, where supplies and equipment for road construction were unloaded from Brahmaputra River boats, became Ledo's sin city. Whorehouses blossomed among the homes of river traders and tea planters on the back streets leading down to the docks. All night long Hindi music shrieked from the houses. Clouds of incense swirled through the dimlit rooms to cover up the pungent smells. Any soldier who went to Dibrugarh, no matter on what business, was likely to be given prophylaxis by zealous medics who roamed the streets like a medical press gang.

One day John Coughlin and Carl Eifler went to see General Wheeler at NCAC headquarters at Ledo. The general and the two

OSS men decided to walk through the Naga Hills into Burma to get a better idea of the problems that Colonel Pick's black engineer battalions were going to meet once construction got under way. Three OSS agent groups of Anglo-Burmese were to range ahead of the party. Friendly Nagas had reported renewed Japanese probes into the Naga Hills. The agents were to act as a screen against Japanese attack.

Robby was chosen to lead M Group and operate about fifty miles south of the projected route of the Ledo Road. Skittles was picked to lead L Group on a scouting expedition through the upper Naga Hills toward the Hukawng Valley. Jocko's J Group of five men was sent farther north into the valley of the Tarung River to forestall a Japanese intrusion down that tributary of the Brahmaputra. J Group ascended the Tarung Hka for about seventy-five miles and established an outpost at Miao village. They patrolled the far side of the hills so constantly that the small Japanese party reconnoitering the area became convinced that a large Allied force opposed them and gave up their attempt to reach the Brahmaputra Valley by descending the Tarung. In January, their mission accomplished, Jocko and his agents were withdrawn.

M Group did not do so well. Robby hired Naga porters to carry their packs up into the mountains. They had not gone far when the porters stopped and gabbled fearfully. Their jungle instincts told them that enemy Naga headhunters were drawing near. Throwing down their packs, they ran away. M Group had no great desire to encounter the headhunters either, so they, too, took to their heels. M Group returned to Ledo thoroughly demoralized.

L Group's expedition was a different story altogether. Its leader, Skittles, was to be one of the most remarkable OSS agents in Burma. Whether it was a question of developing a new method of directing air attacks on hidden jungle targets, delivering a Shan baby, or performing a marriage ceremony to unite an American 101 man with a Chinese muleteer's daughter in something less than holy matrimony, Skittles was never at a loss as to what to do. Stocky of build, with a perpetual smile wreathing his round face, he was unflappable. He had been born of Chinese parents in Burma and raised as a Burmese citizen.

Skittles was not his real name. Henry Hengshoon, a very successful mining engineer, was given the code name because of his inordinate affection for the British game of ninepins, which became well known through the expression "It's not all beer and skittles." Before the war his job had taken him all over Burma; he spoke not only English, Burmese, and Chinese, but also Hindi, Urdu, Siamese, Kachin, and five other hill-tribe languages.

Skittles and his L Group were assigned the task of guiding General Wheeler and his party over the route of the proposed road. They trekked up the twisting trail that led through what American GIs building the road were later to call "Hell's Fire Pass." This was the route of the "Road of Death" taken by refugees fleeing the Burmese holocaust of the spring of 1942, and L Group came upon frequent skeletons, some with the remains of garments rotting in the muggy jungle.

Skittles led as General Wheeler's party moved along the trail toward Tagap Ga. They came up over a swell and were confronted by a patrol of Japanese soldiers. The leading Japanese aimed and fired just as Skittles aimed and fired. Both men then leaped behind fallen teak logs close beside the trail. When L Group edged forward to flank the Japanese positions in the logs, they discovered that the enemy had fled. Work could go ahead on the Ledo Road.

The Japanese probes into the Naga Hills ceased altogether. Groups L, M, and J were disbanded. Skittles set out to join Knothead at Nawbum, Robby was sent to Forward at Ngumla, and Jocko was assigned to instruct other agents in the camps at Nazira.

*　　　*　　　*

George Drown was the sort of Englishman who might be expected to dress in evening clothes for dinner served with all the proper flourishes by a barefooted bearer at his base camp at Htawgaw in the mountains along the Chinese border. In practice, he had to content himself with crisp shorts and a well-laundered shirt, knee-length socks and jungle boots, but he never traveled away from his base without his personal valet. Twice a day this Kachin gentleman's gentleman would lather his face and hand him first his razor, then his towel, and finally his toothbrush and toothpaste so that he could perform his toilet.

I later met George Drown at Momaukkajee, south of Htawgaw. I had arrived, trail-weary, at the basha where he was living as comfortably as if he were at his London club.

"Drown here," he announced as he arose from a camp chair and held out his hand. "What about a nice hot bath?"

It was late November, and a chill was settling down on the high jungle.

"If you can offer one," I replied.

"You'll have to walk for it. Here, take a towel."

Towels over our arms, we strolled up a trail that led into a box canyon in the hills. A stream wound through the canyon, and there were isolated pools which steamed in the twilight. Water from thermal springs boiled to the surface of the pools. A pair of Kachin boys helped us scoop out two holes in the sand of the canyon floor about the size of bathtubs.

"The trick is to mix the water to your preference," explained Drown.

He showed me how to dig a channel from a hot-water spring to admit steaming water and a channel from the stream to bring in cool water. When we had the right mix, we blocked up the channels and slipped into our tubs for as fully appreciated a soak as I've ever had. Lolling in our jungle tubs, we talked of London and music, for Drown was a talented musician.

More than that, Drown was a consummate intelligence officer, who had come to 101 from the Kachin Levies. He usually covered about forty miles a day on the rounds of his advance posts. His reports from the field were incisive, detailed, and often colorful. It was he who captured the Japanese whom Eifler had flown out from Forward. He had also surprised a Japanese officer on the trail and shot him to death to seize his pouch with precious maps. When he captured a Shan spy, he tied him down on a hill while the Kachins looked on with grinning anticipation. He deposited twenty pounds of explosives beneath his victim, attached a long fuse, and lit it. He quietly questioned the captive about his activities as the fuse burned closer and closer.

"You'll have to excuse me," he said as if he were leaving a dinner party. "I will have to do without the pleasure of your company, but there is no way out of it."

He barely had time to saunter out of range. The Shan cried out. He babbled the names of other Japanese informants. As if he were grinding out a cigarette butt, Drown put out the fuse. He smiled.

"Let's just talk a bit more about the subject at hand. It's quite fascinating, you know," he said.

\* \* \*

Oliver Milton, code name Oscar, had emerged in June from his jungle experiences with A Group in better physical shape than he had gone in. Opero soon dispatched him on a second mission. Before he set out for Fort Hertz and his new assignment, he walked into British headquarters and created quite a fuss. The high command was not prepared for a not-so-elegant British officer, to stroll into headquarters wearing a longyi, a floppy Gurkha hat, and a British army shirt bearing his major's pips. Behind him walked one of the Kachin boys from A Group, ready to act upon his slightest whim, his jungle eyes taking in every detail of the headquarters.

Oscar had been born in Penzance in Cornwall, the only place in England, as he was proud to say, where palm trees grew. A poor boy with nothing much to look forward to in Penzance, "except at the most a clerkship," as he put it, he left when very young. In Germany he studied German and proved that he had a remarkable knack for learning languages. In time he was to read and write twenty-eight languages and master six scripts. Roger Wolbarst, an equally extraordinary American 101 man, and Oscar's closest friend in the detachment, claims that he could learn to read and write a new language in about six weeks.

Oscar traveled to Burma to work for Steele Brothers in the jungle where he easily learned to read and write Kachin. He married a Lisu woman, who was a nurse; but when the war came, she fled for safety with another man. Oscar, a handsome man with a way with the ladies, shrugged the whole matter off. He led a group of over one hundred women and children out of Burma before the advancing Japanese without losing a single one, and was recruited into the OSS. His son Eric soon joined 101 to be trained as an agent. An amateur botanist (for whom a Burmese plant which he discovered was named), ornithologist, photographer and painter of talent, who spent odd hours on his mission sketching the Kachins around him, Oscar could live indefinitely on edible plants. He carried only a knife, since he felt that firearms made it impossible for him to make friends with jungle people. His lack of deadly weapons was not to be interpreted to mean that he was not deadly in his own quiet way. Oscar picked two of the original Kachin boys from A Group to go back into Burma with him. One of the best Anglo-Burmese radio operators also went along.

What would happen if the Japanese were to throw a strong force against the Kachin Levies defending Sumprabum and drive northward to capture Fort Hertz? Oscar was given the task of setting up a secret field station deep in the Triangle near the remote Himalayan headwaters of the Nmai Hka to serve as an alternate 101 outpost in Burma in case Fort Hertz were lost. From Fort Hertz Oscar and his team trekked for weeks deep into the wilderness until they had reached the mysterious land of the headhunting 'Nungs, a Kachin people who had been visited by only one other white man, in the 1850s. The odd name of the tribe was almost impossible to pronounce in English, but it sounded something like "knung."

When Oscar reached the first 'Nung village, the people, who had never seen a white man before, fled into the jungles. One of Oscar's Kachin boys unpacked a tiny portable stool that he always carried for his leader, and Oscar sat down upon it with his back to the village. He held a steel mirror in his hand so that he could look over his shoulder. He sat patiently for several hours, unmoving, letting the jungle people become acquainted with his back turned so indifferently and nonchalantly upon their hiding places on the fringe of the jungle.

At last Oscar caught a glimpse of a 'Nung boy peeking from the bushes, bright-eyed, curious. He remained still. Then there were two more small heads. A boy slipped out of the jungle and watched him, ready to spring back to safety in case Oscar made any movement. He sat still and watched through his mirror. Other boys emerged, and a bold one stole toward him. Now the bold boy was peeking over his shoulder. Oscar smiled into the mirror, and the boy looking in the mirror smiled back. He turned and handed the mirror to the boy, who took it and laughed aloud at seeing his own face looking back at him. In a short time other boys came close. One of Oscar's Kachins handed out some other mirrors, and when small girls joined their brothers, he handed them beads.

A bee buzzed close. Oscar plucked it out of the air, and held it in his hand. The children noticed it did not sting him. He let it fly away. He stood up and executed a deep backbend, touching his hands to his heels, and the children laughed. He sat down and put his feet behind his head. He folded his feet in his lap and walked about on his hands. The children were enraptured. When the 'Nung adults saw that the fascinating, strange man did not harm the children, they too came out of the jungle. At their head was their duwa, Law Kaw, who from that day until Oscar's departure from Burma, was scarcely ever to leave his side. He became what the British call a "batman." He mixed Oscar's drinks, with which he began every dinner in camp, cooked, and served him his meals. Smokey, as we called the cook with our guerrilla group in the Loilun Range, also was a headhunter from the far northern Triangle. It was a matter of conjecture at dinner as to exactly what men like Law Kaw and Smokey put into the curry. Ngai Tawng, always mischievous, would mention a few unsavory possibilities with a straight face.

"Oscar always ate by himself," said Larry Grimm, later to be one of 101's area commanders. "He wouldn't mess with others, whether he was in the field or back at base."

Squatting on his heels in the Kachin way, Oscar would set out food for the nats before he ate. After dinner he might talk quietly with other Kachins or Americans, but sooner or later he would fill up his pipe with opium, sit back, and look upon the world about him with measured calm.

For nine months Oscar stayed in the wilderness of the northern Triangle. During this time he kept regular contact with Nazira, but he never saw another Caucasian. He was an adventurous Englishman in the tradition of Lawrence of Arabia, who could make an almost complete cultural adjustment. He became a white 'Nung, giving himself wholeheartedly to their way of life, though it is unlikely that he ever took a head. He explored the wilderness so that if he were called upon to establish a new Burma base for the OSS, he would know where to locate it. Then when it was certain beyond doubt that the Japanese were no longer able to threaten Fort Hertz, he was ordered to withdraw. He hid his spare radio and came south down the Nmai Hka and through the hills toward Bhamo. As might be expected, he had learned the 'Nung language. When he fell in with other OSS groups, he talked with Law Kaw in his almost unknown Kachin tongue, and nobody around them could tell what they were saying. It did not make his fellow 101 men feel entirely comfortable to listen to the cryptic conversation and to observe at the same time that Law Kaw was not only completely devoted to Oscar but was reputed to be a headhunter of consummate skill.

"None of us ever wanted to pick a fight with a man like Oscar," observed Roger Wolbarst.

\*     \*     \*

Len Coffey was an Australian officer who first met 101 men when Carl Eifler and John Coughlin hiked into Sumprabum, where he was on duty with the Kachin Levies. He was a sprightly man with a devil-may-care demeanor, but his manner hid a terrible anger. He had been in command of a detachment of troops during the bitter retreat down the Malayan Peninsula to Singapore. His beautiful niece was a nurse in Singapore, and when it came time to evacuate the crumbling bastion of British imperial power in Asia, she joined other nurses on the docks waiting for lighters to take them off to the ships in the harbor.

"There they stood, pretty and crisp in their white uniforms, obviously nurses dedicated to saving lives, certainly not combatants," Coffey told Roger Wolbarst in a quiet moment at Nazira. "The Japanese planes came over. They ignored every military target in sight and roared down on the docks. They strafed and strafed again the defenseless girls. I saw my niece dying there on the dock with her right arm blasted off. I went berserk."

How berserk did Len Coffey go? In the field in Burma whenever his Kachin Levies captured a Japanese prisoner, they knew that they must bring the man to him. He looked over the prisoner, put aside his own weapons and then sprang on him like a tiger.

"He literally tore him apart with his own bare hands," said Wolbarst. "When he'd finish, he'd be bathed with Japanese blood."

Opero was not at all sure that Len Coffey would make an ideal 101 officer in the field, so he was assigned to operational planning in Nazira and later recruited agents at Calcutta. He could help even the score with the hated Japanese through a less brutal, if not as emotionally satisfying, method.

*     *     *

OSS in Washington instructed Navy Lieutenant Commander James C. Luce to go to China and establish a hospital. When he reached Calcutta, he discovered that the Japanese had made his mission impossible. They had captured the area where the hospital was to be located. Jim Luce was not discomfited. He gladly accepted the job of improving the medical services of Detachment 101. Archie Chun Ming at Nazira was the only doctor for a hundred miles, and he also was serving as an interpreter and instructing Burmese and Kachin agents in the use of demolitions, small arms, and rudimentary first aid. He plainly could use all the help Luce could give him.

Luce arrived at Nazira on November 3. He soon met Carl Eifler, who though suffering from the blow on the head he had received that summer at Ramree Island, was still as Luce put it, "the driving power of the outfit."

"He is a tremendous man with a florid countenance and a voice that would dwarf a circus barker into insignificance," noted Luce. "I never heard him talk in any other than maximum volume."

Eifler lost no time in telling Luce "that six months' to a year's medical supplies had to be gathered together and prepared for air drop." Luce was either to walk 125 miles from the airstrip in Burma at Fort Hertz to Forward's headquarters at Ngumla or be parachuted in. It was too dangerous to fly him into the airstrip.

"No one knew when I could get out. The entire time would be spent behind Japanese lines and if I didn't like the idea, I could 'get the hell out,'" Luce remembers.

Archie Chun Ming was indeed happy to see a fellow doctor, and he offered to help him get ready for his mission to Forward. The two doctors climbed into a jeep and drove to Chabua. They took a day to collect the drugs, instruments, and other medical equipment that Luce would need in Burma. The medical supplies had to be packed with great care so that later on they could be dropped to Ngumla. There could be no time lost, because Luce was expected to make the trip into Burma with an officer, two radiomen—Eddie Scharf and Homer Summers—and eighteen Burmese who were being sent to augment Forward. Departure date was set for November 8.

It was decided that they would walk in, because Japanese control of the air made any jump too hazardous. Luce anticipated the entire experience with considerable trepidation; it was scarcely what he had expected his assignment in Asia to be when he left Washington. Navy men as a rule are not sent on 125-mile jungle hikes through the enemy lines. Just before departure time he learned that the officer who had been designated as the leader of the party had been taken ill and would not be able to go.

"You'll have to lead the party," Eifler told Luce.

This development was hardly calculated to give a navy doctor peace of mind. The departure was postponed for two days. On the afternoon of November 10, the group got into trucks and drove to Chabua. In the morning they flew in a C-47 to Fort Hertz.

"We flew over the lower end of the Himalayas," remembers Luce. "The pilot got lost, and the copilot and radioman also."

The OSS men got out their maps and tried to find the way. The plane flew for an hour over the jungles until it came in sight of a cluster of white buildings with red tin roofs. Perhaps this was Fort Hertz. A few seconds later flak bursting around the plane suggested that perhaps it was not Fort Hertz, after all. The C-47 swung northward from the anti-aircraft fire and in ten minutes passed over a large river. By checking the turns in the river and the contour lines on the map with the river and the hills around it, Luce was able to determine their location. They were just south of their objective. In fifteen minutes they arrived at last at Fort Hertz.

The landing was scarcely a run-of-the-mill affair. The pilot was new to Burma and Fort Hertz. He twice attempted to land the plane, but each time the wheels jolted on the strip, he realized that he could never manage to brake it before he would be out of runway. He gunned the motor and swooped up into the air again. On the third try the plane hit the runway with a jolt that jarred the men and tossed the cargo around. The plane rolled to a stop just short of the river.

Bob Aitken, informed by radio that the party was coming, was at the airport. He took the party to his headquarters. With the help of Len Coffey, still with the Kachin Levies, bullock carts and coolies were rounded up. The coolies were Burmese prisoners of war taken by the British. Luce and Bob Aitken went by jeep into the mountains to talk to the Kachins about the carts and bullocks. A Kachin driver was at the wheel. On the return trip the jeep came upon an elephant train, eight huge animals led by a bull. At first the elephants politely backed off the trail to let the jeep go snorting past. But as they passed the bull, he let out a ferocious snort and charged after them.

The driver jammed down the accelerator, and for two hundred yards the jeep gained on the elephant. Then he slowed, out of respect for the sheer five-hundred-foot drop on his side of the road. He skidded close to the brink.

"Look out!" shouted Bob Aitken.

He swung his submachine gun around to fire at the elephant. The angry beast was lumbering along with amazing speed only ten yards behind the jeep. The driver plunged down the accelerator, and the jeep spun wheels and leaped away down the trail, plunging from one side of the road to the other. This time the driver kept up his speed for a mile, and by that time the elephant had given up the whole business.

It was taking time to gather up the transportation. Luce now had five elephants, three bullock carts, and forty coolies. He was still at Fort Hertz in the morning when Carl Eifler arrived at the airstrip. He exploded in rage. Taking a long drink of whiskey to deaden the pain in his head, Eifler angrily criticized the doctor.

"I wouldn't still be here if you hadn't bungled the advance preparations," Luce dryly responded.

Luce also told Eifler that his "aberrations of behavior were due to his own excesses and were not medical."

Eifler glared, but had nothing more to say.

The next morning about 11 A.M. the group finally got under way. By 6 P.M. they had covered ten miles. The men found it easier to walk along the overgrown trail by stepping in the giant footsteps of the elephants that led them. Luce spent a sleepless night. On the next day the group made eight miles. Two carts broke down; three elephants ran bawling into the jungle and couldn't be recaptured. The coolies, who had been held prisoner for a year, were in poor physical condition and could barely stagger along under the loads.

Luce conferred with Eddie Scharf and Homer Summers. At the rate they were going, they would never reach Ngumla. They decided to send a Kachin runner back to Len Coffey at Fort Hertz to ask for Kachins to carry the loads. The prisoners of war simply were not able to hike the 125 miles and were sent back under guard. The runner ran thirty miles during the night and brought the message to Coffey in the morning. By mid-afternoon of the next day forty-four Kachins trotted into camp. They picked up the loads that the prisoners of war had set down. Luce also decided that he had seen enough of elephants on this journey and sent them on ahead with the elephant boys. The party set out on the trail, and by that evening they had covered sixteen miles. The next day they hiked the fourteen miles to La Aung Ga by early afternoon. Navy man Luce ached all over, but he was beginning to find his land legs.

The group was now to infiltrate around Japanese lines. Luce put Summers in charge of the radio section, and deployed some of his scouts ahead to screen the point of advance. Others took on the job of rearguard protection. Three Kachins assigned themselves to Luce as his bodyguards. In most American-Kachin Ranger units the Kachins usually performed some such function. They invariably became deeply attached to their American comrades and had no intention of letting them be shot. Though they followed most orders with alacrity, they were always stubborn in their refusal to leave *their* American. Try to slip off into the jungle for personal reasons, and, even then, smiling young Kachins would glide unobtrusively behind.

"It makes me feel like royalty or something to be guarded so closely," I once remarked to Hiram Pamplin as I walked sheepishly back into our camp with Ngai Tawng and one of his friends tagging along behind me.

"Or a goddamned idiot, who can't be expected to look out for himself," growled Pamplin.

"The Japanese or their sympathizers find white officers to be prime targets," a Kachin informed Luce.

At six A.M. on November 23 the group commenced the infiltration. Scouts ranged ahead. On November 28 Luce and his men arrived at Htingnan Gatawng, where the doctor was stricken with malaria. He shook with the violence of his ague, which mounted in intensity even though he had prescribed both Atabrine and quinine for himself. For the next few days the party commenced its daily march at 4:30 A.M. so that they could get off the trail before Luce's temperature mounted to its afternoon peak. On November 30, they were on the last lap of the journey. They had managed to pass the Japanese lines. Luce felt sharp pains stabbing in his chest. Hiking on the trail with malaria had given him a severe chill, and he now realized that he had contracted pneumonia. To come all this distance and die of pneumonia in the jungles of the Triangle would very likely be the doctor's fate.

Luce took sulfadiazine to combat the infection. He had two Kachin boys sit up with him all through the night. Whenever he dozed off, they were instructed to awaken him. He must be awake so as to take sulfadiazine at the right times. In the morning Luce swallowed 150 grains of sulpha and he felt good enough to insist upon going on. The Kachins made a litter out of bamboo and vines, eased him onto it, and carried him on to Ngumla. Sick as he was, Jim Luce had reached his position in the Triangle.

\*     \*     \*

Three months had passed since Carl Eifler was thrown against a rock in the surf off Ramree Island. His head still pounded with pain. An officer at Chabua had given Eifler a seventy-five-pound bear cub, and he wrestled with it, as 101 men came to think, whenever his head was hurting so much that he could not think straight. During the contest nobody could figure out who growled the loudest, the bear or Eifler. One day he seized a hapless officer who had angered him. He lifted him up by the front of his shirt and shook him like a rat. The man turned green with terror. His rages at new men were terrifying.

"What do you do?" he demanded of a recruit. "I can walk seventy-two hours without sleep or drink."

Roger Wolbarst remembers working in the message center beneath the verandah off Eifler's quarters. Furious arguments would break out between Eifler and the other top commanders of the detachment.

"Eifler would split the table with one mighty blow of his hand to make a point," Wolbarst says. "All of us below would shake with terror for fear table and all would come through the floor."

One day Eifler met up with a snake charmer. He took a cobra from the man and wound it around his own neck. He wound another cobra around his neck, and then he kissed one of the snakes on the head.

"It broke up the snake charmer's act," he told me later.

"I kept a car in New Delhi," he recalled one recent day in a saddened mood. "I had an Indian license plate on it. I was driving into town with Richards, Vinegar Joe's pilot, passing lorries and meeting them, when a boy ran ahead of us. I missed him with the front end, but my back fender hit him. He had compound fractures of the leg.

"I put him in the car and rushed him to the hospital. The general staff stared when I carried this Indian kid into the hospital. When we took his clothing off, we discovered that the child was not a boy at all but a little girl. I'd always wanted a daughter. She was a village waif, all raggedy, but I had her transferred to a British hospital. Later I was told she died. I pushed her case although a friend told me to forget it. He said that if word gets out, all the kids in India will jump in front of you. For fifteen hundred dollars, I could have taken care of her."

After this incident Carl Eifler, the redoubtable commander of Detachment 101, would sometimes sit with his craggy head cupped in his hands and stare at the ground. His men saw his huge shoulders shake, and he would be racked by a huge sob—or was he only clearing his throat? They did not dare to interfere, and their affection for the "old man" of the outfit and his monumental tempers and equally monumental affections and concerns could not find expression.

One day in early November a crisp young officer from OSS headquarters, Washington, flew into Chabua. It was Duncan Lee, sometime junior partner in General Donovan's Wall Street law firm, and an aide to the general.

There was a furious outburst from Carl Eifler that night when Lee attempted to question him about his command of Detachment 101.

"When you come from the general with low rank on your shoulders and try to tell a full colonel what to do, you're in trouble!" raged Eifler. "If Donovan has something to say to me, let him come and say it."

A few days later Carl Eifler checked into the 20th General Hospital in Ledo. He brought Sam Schreiner with him to act as liaison with Detachment 101 headquarters. The doctors were mystified as to what was the matter with the big man. He had received a savage blow on the head, but tests had to be made. It would take time. They shook their heads and drew long faces at his gigantic rages. The events of the war pressed on, and Eifler, despite the agony in his head, decided that he must see General H. L. Boatner, chief of staff for the Chinese army at Ramgarh. He stormed out of the hospital and drove over there.

After the war Boatner recalled Eifler's visit. "They've got me in the hospital for being nuts," Eifler complained. "You know I'm nuts, but I'm not the kind of nuts they think I am." Then, without further explanation, he returned to Ledo.

Finally, he left the hospital for good and returned to the command of Detachment 101 at Nazira. Everything went on as before. The reports from the field still came in to Opero. Agents trained, and guerrilla forces continued their operations. But Eifler was changed. Never a man to spare himself any hardship or danger, he now took risks that appalled the men around him. One day deciding to fly off on a liaison mission, he strode into the hangar where the Gypsy Moth awaited. A mechanic turned the propeller, and without warming up the engine or waiting to taxi to the runway, Eifler gave the motor full power and roared out of the hangar, sped across the strip and into the air.

\* \* \*

After his angry meeting with Carl Eifler a chastened Duncan Lee flew on to China, where he also had a critical message to carry from General Donovan to the commander of OSS Detachment 202, 101's counterpart there. Most members of 101 were convinced that Lee had come to Asia mainly to make a situation report to General Donovan on the command of their detachment. In actuality his trip was made to check the readiness of OSS detachments in both China and India-Burma to play a greater role in the Allied campaign to retake

Burma, a plan which had been drafted at the Quebec Conference in August, 1943.

Franklin Roosevelt and Winston Churchill listened to many advisers at their meeting in the walled Citadel in the old French-Canadian city before making the historic decisions that were to change the conduct of the war in Asia. None was more colorful than Orde Wingate, a somber man in his early forties with a wicked wit, a man who spoke with a rasp ever since he had attempted to slash his throat in a fit of melancholy while he was a patient in a Cairo hospital. He was a man who could live on mule and python meat in a campaign in the Burma jungles, who wore a tropical helmet and jungle fatigues into the conference room. Lord Louis Mountbatten, who was present in his usual impeccable attire, remarked that the helmet was of pre-1914 vintage and must have been obtained from a museum or from an ancestor.

The chiefs of state and their top military advisers listened carefully to what the man in the battered tropical helmet had to say: it was Wingate who had originated the Long Range Penetration Group. Eccentric, emotional, brought up on the Old Testament by a widowed mother who poured all her loneliness into her brilliant son, he had managed to serve both British intelligence and the Zionist cause in Palestine in 1936. He had taught guerrilla warfare to the Jewish settlers.

General Moshe Dayan attributes a good deal of Israeli military know-how to him: "He taught me and many another Israeli soldier everything we know."

In the liberation of Ethiopia from Italian rule, Wingate had led a force of seventy British officers and men and a thousand Ethiopians and Sudanese on a six-hundred-mile march through the desert. It is said that the march took the lives of twenty-five-thousand camels used for transport. When the camels became so fatigued that they sank down and would not move, Wingate ordered fires built under them to force them to go on. The stench of burned camel flesh marked the passing of his army. The last of the sorry beasts died on a hill that looked down on Addis Ababa. Addis Ababa fell, and Wingate escorted Haile Selassie back to his throne. It was when the British high command did not show what he felt was appropriate appreciation for this accomplishment that Wingate attempted to slit his throat in Cairo.

Wingate had arrived in India when General Sir Archibald Wavell took over command in April, 1942. The disaster in Burma had then entered its last phase. His task was to form the 77th Brigade, the Chindits, as a Long Range Penetration Group to be employed in a return to Burma. On February 2, 1943, Wingate and his Chindits, a force of three thousand British and Gurkhas, had pushed two hundred miles into Burma, blowing up bridges and cutting the railroad to Myitkyina. The results of the two-month raid were controversial. It was startling to realize that A Group of Detachment 101, with only a dozen men, had accomplished as much as Wingate's entire force.

"As a military operation, the raid had been an expensive failure," said the commander of the British 14th Army, Lieutenant General William Slim. "It gave little tangible return for the losses it had suffered and the resources it had absorbed. The damage it did to Japanese communications was repaired in a few days, the casualties it inflicted were negligible, and it had no immediate effect on Japanese dispositions or plans."

Winston Churchill disagreed with Slim. He said of Wingate, "He is a man of genius and audacity, and has rightly been discerned by all eyes as a figure quite above the ordinary level. There is no doubt that in the welter of inefficiency and lassitude which has characterized our operations on the Indian front, his force and achievements stand out."

Churchill brought Wingate to Quebec. He commanded attention as soon as he strode into the conference room. General H. H. Arnold, commander of the U.S. Army Air Corps, remembered Wingate's entrance. "You took one look at that face, like the face of a pale Indian chieftain, topping the uniform still smelling of jungle and sweat and war and you thought, 'Hell, this man is serious.' When he began to talk, you found out just how serious."

When Wingate talked, he spoke not only for a new and larger Chindit expedition but for an increased role for Detachment 101 in the reconquest of Burma. There would be 101 liaison officers with the Chindits, and both organizations would cooperate to cripple the Japanese from behind their lines.

When Lord Louis Mountbatten was chosen at Quebec to be the Supreme Allied Commander, Southeast Asia, the Chindits and Detachment 101 were assured an important place in Allied planning. His experience as the head of the Commandos made it easy for him to realize the importance of guerrilla warfare in determining the outcome of the campaign to be waged in Burma. The Americans at Quebec agreed to form a military unit which was to strike deep into North Burma and take Myitkyina as a first critical step in the reopening of the Burma Road to Allied supply convoys and ultimately the reconquest of Burma. The Chinese army, which had retreated to India in the debacle of 1942, was training at Ramgarh and, under General Stilwell, would join in the attack.

Duncan Lee was charged with a preliminary assessment of the OSS potential in Asia. Donovan himself planned to make a trip later on. The young officer, having finished his meetings with OSS people in China, boarded an Air Transport Command C-46 in Kunming for the flight back over the Hump to Chabua. He chatted easily with two other VIP passengers, Jack Service, attached to the United States Embassy in Chungking, and Eric Severeid, a young war correspondent.

The flight went without incident until the plane was fighting to gain altitude over the Naga Hills, the last range before India. Without warning one engine sputtered and backfired. There was no time to be lost. If a Himalayan downdraft caught the crippled plane as it struggled over the Naga Hills, it would certainly be smashed into a mountain. The pilot ordered his passengers to bail out. Severeid, Service, and Lee struggled into parachutes and jumped out the door toward the shaggy, jungled mountains. No sooner had the three men baled out when the motor roared healthily again, and the pilot was able to fly on to Chabua, where he landed safely.

Where were the three passengers? They put out emergency panels as soon as they landed, and an air search discovered them. Pop Milligan was immediately pressed into service to supervise an emergency air drop of supplies, together with maps and directions through the Naga country to Mokachuang, about seventy miles away on the Indian side of the hills. As they plodded through the hills, Naga tribesmen kept a close eye upon them and reported their progress to Detachment 101 at Nazira. Ten days later they walked into Mokachuang. There 101 jeeps were waiting for them and drove them to Nazira, where they arrived as Ray Peers observed, "not too much the worse for wear." For men who previously had been a desk-bound Washington OSS officer, a correspondent, and a state department official, the incident proved to be an inkling of what the campaign being planned for North Burma was going to be like.

# Donovan

Two years to a day after Pearl Harbor was attacked, William J. Donovan, code number 109, landed at Chabua. When the stocky director of the Office of Strategic Services appeared in the transport's doorway, Carl Eifler, who had come to meet his chief, could see that he was not in the best of moods. He was soft-spoken and courteous as usual, but there was an icy glint in his blue eyes. Eifler greeted Donovan and carried his bag over to the Gypsy Moth, waiting nearby. The two men got in the plane and flew to Nazira where they landed on the strip.

Donovan toured the 101 facilities and expressed his satisfaction at how much the detachment was doing with such slender resources. He immediately sent off messages to Washington directing that more personnel, equipment, and funds be made available to Detachment 101. Carl Eifler took him into the 101 war room at headquarters, and the general fixed a cold eye on the seven maps hanging on the wall, each depicting a different plan for the location of OSS teams in the field. Donovan sat down on a bamboo chair.

"Well, Eifler," he asked, "what are you doing?"

"General Stilwell told me he might want to approach Burma in seven different ways," replied Eifler. "I was supposed to organize each one of them, and I did."

For a moment Donovan did not comment. He studied the maps. When he spoke, his voice was as soft as ever.

"That's what I mean about you, Carl," he needled. "You are too goddamned ambiguous about organizing. What do you mean by organizing seven different eventualities?"

Eifler suppressed his anger.

"Sir," he said throwing down the challenge, "would you like to go behind Jap lines and find out for yourself?"

Donovan smiled as if he were accepting a friend's invitation to go for a drive through the Virginia countryside.

"When do we leave?"

"First thing in the morning, sir."

Eifler had challenged Donovan to undertake a daring trip. Normally, even 101 men would not fly into the forward bases, and yet Eifler was proposing that the director of the OSS do just that. The trip might well be called foolhardy. But could Donovan, whose heroism had made him one of the most decorated men in the nation's history, disregard a direct challenge to his bravery? Eifler thought not. The prospect pleased him. In the field behind the Japanese lines his chief would soon discover how much indeed had been accomplished. He was an experienced military commander, and he would recognize and appreciate merit when he saw it.

Eifler decided to fly General Donovan to Knothead. But since the camp was about 150 miles behind the Japanese lines and some 275 miles southeast of Nazira, it was impossible for the Gypsy Moth to fly there and back on a tank of gasoline. It was first necessary to arrange for a fuel drop. Ray Peers and John Coughlin got in touch with the ATC the following day and asked for the gasoline as well as other supplies and ammunition that Vincent Curl had requested. Eifler informed Knothead that he was bringing in 109 the next day. He arranged a radio signal with Curl that would be flashed to base when Donovan and Eifler had landed safely.

Nicol Smith was still at Nazira training his Thai officers for the infiltration of their homeland. He was Donovan's roommate that night. As the two men got ready for bed in the basha in the middle of the tea gardens, Smith found himself puzzling over why the head of the OSS was risking not only his life but all the critically important secrets he carried around with him in his head. There was little that he did not know about Allied plans all over the world. Smith could restrain himself no longer.

"General, aren't you risking your life?" Smith asked.

"Everything is a risk," replied Donovan. "My boys are risking their lives every day."

Once after the war I asked the general a similar question about the trip behind the lines.

"I was risking my life," he replied with a twinkle, "but I was not risking any secrets. I carried an L pill ready to put in my mouth."

Since I, too, once carried an L pill as a necessary precaution, I knew what he meant. The capsule is filled with deadly potassium cyanide. The skin of the capsule is insoluble. Swallow it, and it will go through the digestive system without causing even the slightest inconvenience. Chew it, and it means death. We were taught to secrete the capsule beneath the tongue so that it could be taken in an emergency to bring almost instant death, which was unquestionably preferable to torture.

Smith and other OSS men at Nazira stayed awake worrying for fear that somehow word of the next day's event might have leaked to the Japanese, but Donovan, in Smith's words, "slept like a babe." In the morning the general gave Nicol Smith his wallet and identification papers for safekeeping.

"If anything goes wrong, it'll be just as well if I'm incognito," he said.

"That's an understatement, General."

After breakfast, 109 refused the parchute offered to him by Eifler as they prepared to go to the airstrip.

"I'll ride the plane down if we crash," he said. "I can't afford to be captured."

Donovan's grandstanding was in character.

"General, if we land within fifteen feet of the enemy, I will bring you back," said Eifler. "Please put on your chute."

Donovan strapped on his chute. Before they got into the plane, the two men posed for a picture to be taken by Field Photo. With goggles pulled up on their foreheads and aviator caps on their heads, they looked, as an irreverent 101 man, Vince Trifletti, put it, "like a couple of well-fed pilots out of *Wings*." John Ford, the motion-picture director, who was in charge of OSS Field Photo, had come out from Washington, and he directed the photography. The situation had a Hollywood theatricality to it. It almost seemed that if Ford had shouted, "Cut," the principals waiting by the plane would look to him for directions on how they could improve the scene.

Then the theatricality was at an end. The two men were in the plane and bouncing down the strip cut among the neat rows of tea bushes. Eifler hugged the treetops as he flew over the Naga Hills to avoid Japanese fighters. When the plane reached Knothead, Eifler circled while Kachins raced to pull the simulated bashas off the airstrip.

"The strip ran up the side of a hill," Eifler told me afterward. "It was short, but gravity helped us to slow down before we reached the far end."

"On that day I lived about five lives," Vince Curl says today. "The plane rolled to a halt, and Donovan and Eifler got out. I'd met the general in Washington, and he strode right up to me and gave me a real hug. It seemed just as natural seeing him in the middle of the Burmese jungle as it had to see him behind his desk."

Donovan was a field man at heart. He watched with approval as the Kachins hurried the mock-up bashas back into place and rolled the plane into a jungle hideout. His quick eye for critical detail observed the defenses of the camp, the smiling young Kachin soldiers who, as Eifler remarked to him, "were scarcely as tall as their rifles were long." Back in Washington he had followed the regular situation reports from Eifler on the field operations in Burma, and he looked about him for the first glimpse of Zhing Htaw Naw, who was the Burmese equivalent of a top French marquis. Donovan planned to go to China as soon as he returned to Nazira in order to confer with General Stilwell. Galahad, the American task force that Roosevelt had promised to Churchill at Quebec, would require all the guerrilla and intelligence support that the OSS could give to it. From his desk in Washington it appeared that only the Kachin people could provide the British, Americans, and Chinese who were to fight for Burma with the irregular warfare operations that were so essential. Were they truly as remarkable a people as Carl Eifler and his people seemed to think?

Father Stuart, a broad smile on his bearded face, approached the general. Beside him walked a slight brown man, his bearing erect, an equally broad smile on his face.

"His eyes alone gave away his penetrating intellect," Donovan told me later.

Zhing Htaw Naw bowed his head slightly to the general out of respect and courtesy. Then he looked him square in the eye as a Kachin is taught from boyhood. Vincent Curl had told him that the worldwide head of the OSS was flying into the jungle to visit Knothead. Zhing Htaw Naw was impressed, but he met Donovan as an equal. Over the next several hours Donovan questioned and questioned again every man at Nawbum, but, above all, he conversed with Zhing Htaw Naw. Father Stuart acted as the interpreter as the duwa kaba and the director of the Office of Strategic Services talked about the Kachin people and their resistance. Zhing Htaw Naw told the story of the Hukawng villages and how his people were resisting the Japanese everywhere. He expressed his gratitude to Vincent Curl for the American weapons, and he asked for more so that he and his fellow duwas all through the hills could arm increasing numbers of Kachins. He put his arm around Vincent Curl's waist in the Kachin way.

"He is the lifeblood of our people," he said.

"Zhing Htaw Naw is my buddy from the inside out," said Curl.

As the American and the Kachin stood, their arms around each other's waist, Donovan had a strong visual impression of the American and Kachin partnership. It was soon time for Donovan and Eifler to go. Donovan was exultant at his meeting with Zhing Htaw Naw, and he clapped Eifler on the back. The big man grinned at the success of the day. Donovan was seeing for himself what 101 had accomplished—at least at Knothead. He was plainly impressed.

The Kachins wheeled the refueled Gypsy Moth out on the strip, which had been cleared for the takeoff. Donovan and Eifler got into it.

"Rev it up all you can and then take off," Curl urged Eifler.

The Kachins took hold of the plane and held it back as Eifler revved the engine. At his signal they gave it a push, and the Gypsy Moth went rolling down the field, as Eifler put it later, "like a tumblebug. We were taking off downhill, and we gathered speed slowly because of Donovan's weight."

Eifler failed to mention his own considerable bulk. At the end of the strip the lofty trees of the jungle loomed, and there was little chance that the struggling Gypsy Moth could climb over them. At the last minute Eifler swerved ninety degrees to the left to plunge through a gap in the forest rooftop. The plane cleared the trees by a few feet and then roared down over the river, passing about five feet over the surface. Donovan grinned.

"We haven't got the power on the nose of these planes that we should have," he shouted over the roar of the engine as the plane at last gained air speed.

"I told Carl to give the plane all it got when he took off," says Curl, "but he started off easy. When he banked between those trees, I shut my eyes. I waited for the crash. When the roar of the engine over the river came, I shouted with joy."

Eifler buzzed the strip to say good-bye to Knothead and started back on a tree-hopping journey to Nazira. Ray Peers was waiting for the return of the Gypsy Moth. He summed up what the trip had accomplished:

"Using Father Stuart as an interpreter, Donovan conferred at great length with Zhing Htaw Naw and some of the lesser head men. The world of General Donovan's global war, his travels and activities were beyond the imagination and comprehension of these nomadic hill people, but he made a great impression upon them. Similarly, these people through their integrity, enthusiasm, and guerrilla ability made an equally effective impression upon him. This was one of the great capabilities which General Donovan possessed, and it did much toward the creation of trust and mutual understanding with all people with whom he came in contact."

John Coughlin was less impressed than Ray Peers about the strategic value of the flight behind the lines. He returned to Nazira from a trip of his own to discover that Eifler and Donovan had gone to Knothead. He never expected to see either of the two men alive again. That night he took the jubilant Donovan aside.

"General, what were you thinking about to go in there with Carl?" he demanded.

One of Donovan's great strengths as a commander was his accessibility to men of all ranks who served under him, and he did not bristle at Coughlin's question.

"I had to," he replied.

"You should have considered more things than your damned honor. If I'd been here, I would have reminded you of every one of them."

From the start of the adventure, Donovan had understood all the consequences, but in a cool-headed way he had balanced them off against the overriding need to assess the potential of the Kachins in the forthcoming campaigns in Burma. Yet he understood that the outspoken John Coughlin was acting only as a concerned friend. Not knowing Donovan's true motivation, he had assumed that his superior had acted out of honor alone. Donovan was never loath to let men presume his motives to be no more complicated than the obvious ones. He looked crestfallen, but he was buoyed by the recollection of a bold and resourceful Kachin leader whose people were determined to fight the Japanese in every way they could. He knew that no guerrilla group can ever succeed unless it has the full support of the people among whom it must live and fight. The Kachins alone met this test. The Americans needed only to arm, equip, and train them where necessary, and then tie their activities into the grand design of Allied strategy. In the morning Donovan was scheduled to fly to China to see Stilwell. He now knew what he could promise Vinegar Joe on behalf of the OSS in Burma.

It was clear that he must obtain better liaison planes for Detachment 101 than the venerable Gypsy Moth. He handed a message for Washington headquarters to the cryptographer on duty. Ten L-5 planes were to be sent to Nazira as soon as possible. They were in fact delivered in Assam in time for the 1944–1945 campaign.

In China, Donovan reviewed the readiness of OSS Detachment 202 to play its intended role in the months ahead, and he met with Stilwell. Stilwell, who had observed firsthand the decisive role played by the Burmese fifth column in the fall of Burma to the Japanese, had no difficulty in comprehending what the director of the OSS hoped to be able to do. Vinegar Joe willingly gave Donovan his wholehearted approval.

\*     \*     \*

When Donovan returned from China, he found that Carl Eifler had become seriously ill. The big man could not sleep at night, would not take the medication prescribed by doctors at the 20th General Hospital at Ledo, and disregarded their advice in other respects as well. The pain in his head had become furious.

"OSS and General Donovan had much at stake in the success of 101 and in the development of strategic operations in the CBI Theater," said Ray Peers. "Carl had done a magnificent job, but was simply not up to it. General Donovan had to face the issue and make a decision, which he did by relieving Carl for physical and medical reasons."

On December 11, 1943, John Coughlin was placed in charge of all OSS operations in the CBI Theater with Donovan's orders to pay particular attention to the situation in China. On the same day Carl Eifler left for the United States. On December 17, Coughlin in turn asked Ray Peers to take over the command of Detachment 101.

"The departure of Carl was like the end of an era," noted Ray Peers. "He was a show within himself, and an excellent job he did. I know of nobody who had the drive, imagination, and courage to get an operation like this started. It was the first unit of its kind, and there was no precedent upon which to work, and it took a lot of everything to get it going. For all of his effort and heroic acts, Carl left the theater without an award of any kind; all he received was a pain in the head."

Lieutenant Commander Hal Williams, who was working on 101's radio problem when Carl Eifler was relieved of his command, expressed the feelings of many men in the detachment. He told the OSS commander in China, Naval Captain Milton E. Miles, "He was doing too well and not taking any crap off any of them."

The man that General Stilwell had once introduced to his staff as "the army's number-one thug," was flying home, and Ray Peers was in command.

1944

# The Hukawng

The clouds surged heavy and ominous through the skies over North Burma that winter of 1943–1944. It was the season that usually is sunny, a welcome interval between the monsoons, when the land can begin to dry out before the next torrential rains fall. In February the unseasonable rains lashed the jungled mountains week after week, and the trails turned to sinks of mud. Up in the mountains the chill air of mid-winter, combined with the drenching rain, was enough to make a man's teeth chatter. The rain was still falling when General Stilwell called a meeting at his new combat headquarters, near the Kachin village of Shadazup in the far north of the Hukawng Valley. He asked 101's new commander, Ray Peers, to bring Chet Chartrand, who was to be the OSS intelligence liaison officer at his headquarters. His son, Colonel Joseph Stilwell, Jr., the intelligence officer for the Northern Combat Area Command, was also to be present. The four men sat down on field chairs in a half-tent, half-bamboo basha that Ray Peers remarks was "barely large enough to hold the general's field cot, a small table, and a couple of chairs."

Stilwell, in his khaki-colored sweater, turned-up collar, ill-fitting canvas leggings, and battered campaign hat from World War I, its brim streaked with the sweat of the previous summer, sat at the table. At 61, he was a bony man with tightly cropped gray-black hair and a deceptively fragile appearance. Stilwell, according to the China-Burma-India GI newspaper, *The CBI Roundup,* showed an unflagging sense of humor which "only fails him in case of monsoon and stuffed shirts."

The near monsoonal rains making a morass out of the campaign, which he was planning in North Burma to implement the decisions of the Quebec Conference, undoubtedly tried his sense of humor, but at least he would not find Ray Peers or Chet Chartrand stuffy, although

Chartrand spoke with a clipped British accent, a characteristic which Stilwell usually found obnoxious since he was anything but an Anglophile. Chartrand had been a tutor to the children of a sawbwa—a Shan prince—and he had lived for years in Burma. Stilwell peered through steel-rimmed glasses at a map of North Burma spread out on the table before him. During World War I an ammunition dump had exploded at Belrupt in France and injured his left eye. A subsequent cataract of the lens and deformity of the pupil made it difficult for him to make out his fingers at three feet. The strain of studying reports and maps by candle or kerosene lantern in the field had further weakened his vision.

He commenced the meeting by outlining the first Burma campaign and the decisive Japanese victory.

"They beat the hell out of us," he admitted.

He went on to explain how the best part of two Chinese divisions had escaped to India where they had been trained at Ramgarh, north of Calcutta, under American officers. In the autumn they had come up to Ledo ready to play their role in the reconquest of North Burma. The 38th Division was commanded by General Sun Li Jen, who had studied in America at Virginia Military Institute, and the 22d by General Liao, a formidable fighter from the hills of southern China. Sun Li Jen's advance units had pushed through the Naga Hills in advance of the mainly black American engineers building the Ledo Road and had entered the Hukawng Valley where they were halted by the outposts of General Tanaka's 18th Division, the same elite forces who had led the invasion of Singapore and the drive north from Rangoon in the first Burma campaign. All told, the Japanese in Burma had six divisions plus several battalions of combat troops— some 150,000 men altogether, with another 100,000 in Combat Support Forces and the Imperial Air Force.

A Chinese battalion of about 1,000 men had come up against three companies of about 500 men at Yupbang Ga. As they had been taught by their American mentors, the Chinese tried to bypass the Japanese in order to force them to withdraw, but instead of falling back, the Japanese dug in and commenced an encirclement of the Chinese flanks.

"Here for the first time the Chinese ran into a type of Japanese fortification which was to delay them time and time again in the Hukawng Valley," Peers remembers Stilwell explaining. "It was the simplest form of fortification, but as strong as concrete. The Japanese would locate a clump of bamboo ten to fifteen feet in diameter, burrow under it, chop out the center, and build their fortification with the thick bamboo surrounding it. The bamboo was not the fishing-pole type familiar to us; rather it was what was known as bullaca bamboo, from four to eight inches in diameter and capable of withstanding light artillery fire."

The Japanese turned back the Chinese attack, but when General Sun deployed a second regiment on their flank, they withdrew. Both sides had lost heavily, and the 38th Division was now probing farther into the Hukawng. The 22d Division, not to be outdone, had been sent to capture Taro, fifty miles to the south.

"As General Stilwell told of the progress, it was quite apparent that he was well pleased with what had been done," says Peers.

"This shows you what can be done with these Chinese outfits if they are properly fed, armed, and trained," said Stilwell. "All you have to do is give them a little combat experience and they are as good as any combat units you will find anywhere, including our American forces. They are accustomed to deprivation and can get along on a few handfuls of rice, peanuts, and fish. In this sense they can make out with far less than American troops, except for ammunition. They are a little jittery and will shoot at the crack of a twig, but this too is being reduced as they get confidence in themselves."

When Stilwell had finished outlining the campaign in the Hukawng to date, he asked that Peers and Chartrand brief him on the espionage, sabotage, and, above all, the guerrilla operations that Detachment 101 was carrying out. He wanted to know where the teams were located and what were their strength and capabilities. Peers briefed him about the OSS groups in the field, and Stilwell asked questions. He asked about terrain, rivers, bridges, the health of various Burmese, British, and American 101 men. He studied the map in front of him. When Peers and Chartrand were finished, he sat back and thought over what he had heard.

He looked at the two OSS men through his steel-rimmed glasses.

"This may come as a shock to you, and I am sure it will surprise a lot of other people," he finally said, "but I fully intend to be in Myitkyina by this summer, and that means before the monsoon rains set in."

The monsoons begin in early June in the jungles of the Hukawng and the Triangle. There would be less than four months to advance over two hundred miles through some of the most difficult country in

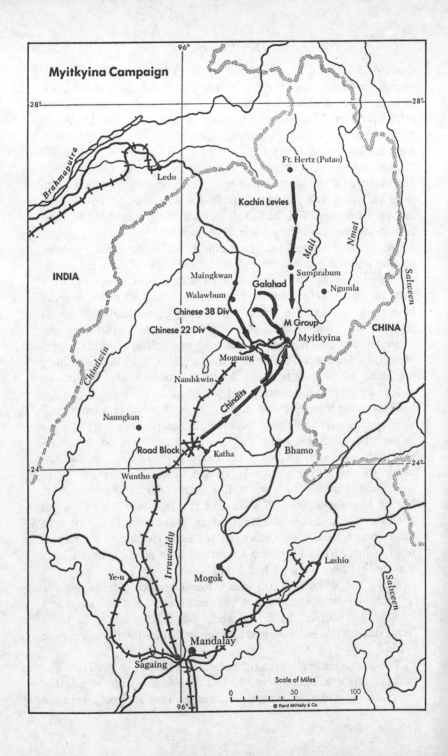

# Myitkyina Campaign

*Brahmaputra*

Ledo

INDIA

*Chindwin*

**Kachin Levies**

Ft. Hertz (Putao)

*Mali*

*N'mai*

*Salween*

Sumprabum

Ngumla

Maingkwan

Galahad

Walawbum

**Chinese 38 Div**

M Group

**Chinese 22 Div**

Myitkyina

CHINA

Mogaung

Namhkwin

*Chindits*

Naungkan

Road Block

Katha

Bhamo

Wuntho

*Irrawaddy*

Lashio

Ye-u

Mogok

*Salween*

Mandalay

Sagaing

Scale of Miles

0          50          100

© Rand McNally & Co.

the world, against the best efforts of the Japanese 18th Division, which was headquartered at the very city that Stilwell proposed to capture. To accomplish his purpose he would also be able to draw upon the 5307th Composite Group, an American unit. Even as the men talked in the basha-tent, the Americans, to be known later as Merrill's Marauders, were traveling across India by train on their way to Ledo, the jumping-off point for Burma. They were to make a foray around the Japanese northern flank. Wingate's Chindits were to strike south of Myitkyina to try and disrupt Japanese communications and supply lines. The Levies were to pin down the Japanese at Sumprabum.

"It is going to be touch and go, and we will have to utilize every resource at our command," the general summed up. "I am convinced that these Kachins can be made into good soldiers, and we want them on our side. Certainly the last thing we want to have happen is for them to go over to the Japanese. The other thing we are going to need is intelligence and lots of it. In this respect, we can't expect too much assistance from the Chinese because of their tendency to not only exaggerate, but overestimate at the rate of about ten to one.

"Here, now, is where you and 101 come into the picture. This is what I want you to do, and, if you think you can do it, tell me what you need in terms of resources to get it moving immediately. I want you to expand your guerrilla force to a strength of about three thousand as quickly as you can. The bulk of the guerrilla forces should be located around Myitkyina so that when the combat forces get ready to put on their final push you will be prepared to give them maximum assistance. The other thing I want you to do is to extend your espionage activities; extend them south of Myitkyina and Mogaung and farther if you would like, but above all, make certain we can depend upon their information. Now that is about it. Can you do it? I am not going to try to tell you how to do it. That is your job."

"Yes, we can do it," replied Peers, "but we need some things to get it moving on the time schedule you desire. Specifically, we need some qualified personnel, some arms and ammunition, a priority for aircraft to parachute in personnel, supplies, and equipment; and finally, we need approval for shipment of some of the backlog of critical personnel and equipment, particularly signal equipment that we have waiting in the United States."

"All of this seems reasonable," said Stilwell.

The four men checked over every item on Peers's checklist in diligent detail.

"I hope you realize how much we are depending upon your outfit to get the show on the road," Stilwell concluded. "If you fellows can do the job that I expect for the Myitkyina campaign, you can automatically plan on increasing the size of your force to ten thousand, or whatever it takes to do the job and to extend your espionage networks well to the south."

The meeting ended. At Nazira, General Donovan had told Ray Peers, "Remember you are working for General Stilwell and you are taking your orders from him." Detachment 101 now had a mission that was to help determine the outcome of the war in Burma. It was indeed going to be a touch-and-go affair at best. The Japanese had plans of their own. While the meeting was being held in General Stilwell's field headquarters, they were moving still larger forces into Burma to prepare for the invasion of India. Lieutenant General Mutaguchi's 15th Army was preparing to attack across the Chindwin toward Imphal and Kohima. Tokyo radio broadcasts boasted that the Japanese attack would be a "March to Delhi," but in reality the offensive was an effort to cut the Bengal and Assam Railroad and the Brahmaputra River supply lines upon which Stilwell's men depended. On January 7 Japanese army headquarters in Burma received an order from Tokyo's high command: "In order to defend Burma you may occupy and secure the vital areas of northeastern India at the opportune time." The Japanese had no intention of giving up North Burma.

If China was to remain in the war, North Burma must be recaptured. Only then could the Burma Road, with its proposed Ledo Road connection, be reopened to truck convoys to the beleaguered Chinese nation. The Burma Road was scarcely a new artery of the world's commerce. It followed the ancient overland trade route between the Roman Empire and India and China. Chinese records show that the region of Burma through which it passed was then inhabited by a people who wore rings in both their noses and their ears. Much later, Marco Polo journeyed over the Burma Road as an emissary of Kublai Khan to the king of Burma at Pagan. When the Japanese attacked China in 1937, the invaders overran the coastal cities and closed the country to foreign trade and assistance. The Chinese government of Chiang Kai-shek fled to remote Chungking in Szechuan Province and vowed to carry on the war.

In 1938, one million coolies went to work with pick and shovel to make the ancient Burma Road passable by trucks so that China would have a new supply route through Burma. From fifty- to a hundred-thousand coolies died in the construction of a new lifeline for China. With the completion of the Burma Road, Kunming, at its China terminus, grew from the sleepy provincial capital of Yunnan to a busy entrepôt of three hundred thousand.

Driving the Burma Road was never conducive to relaxation. Chinese drivers kept neither to the right nor the left side of the road, but invariably took the side farthest from the yawning precipices along which it ran. To save gasoline, they switched off their engines at the top of a long grade and coasted down to the bottom, navigating the labyrinthine turns in a cloud of ocher dust. When brakes failed, they plunged off the road and fell to the bottom of the omnipresent gorges. At least by the time I drove over the road at the successful conclusion of the Allied campaign to reconquer Burma, Japanese air attacks had ceased. During the early days, trucks navigating the undulating suspension bridge over the Salween Gorge were a particularly attractive target, and to this day the bottom of the gorge is strewn with rusting vehicles.

The road was lost when the Japanese overran Burma, and China was once again isolated from the outside world except for the American planes flying the Hump carrying a bare minimum of supplies.

As the Chinese 38th and 22d divisions advanced into the Hukawng, the roadbuilders were right behind them. They were constructing a gravel road three lanes wide for 112 miles through the Naga Hills to Shingbwiyang at the head of the Hukawng Valley. The country was so little known that the roadbuilders underestimated the distance from Ledo to Shingbwiyang by 42 miles. From Shingbwiyang the road was to run south down the valley through Maingkwan, where the Japanese had slaughtered all the Kachin boys in their reign of terror in the Hukawng, to Walawbum and across the towering Jambu Bum to Shaduzup. From there it would go to Inkangahtawng, Kamaing, and Mogaung and then east to Myitkyina, from where an existing road led to a juncture with the Burma Road. To complete the road the engineers were required to move 13,500,000 cubic yards of earth, build bridges that were destined to be swamped after the next monsoonal floods, and over the last approach to Myitkyina construct a two-mile causeway of logs through a swamp. From Ledo to Myitkyina was 260 miles. When Japanese agents reported to the Kempi Tai that roadbuilders were hard at work only a few-score miles behind the Chinese enemy, they realized that the attacking troops were not carrying out a feint but were embarked on a major Allied campaign that must be halted north of Myitkyina.

\* \* \*

Even before Peers and Chartrand went to Shadazup to meet with Stilwell and his son, Opero at Nazira determined that a third field team, the equivalent of Knothead and Forward, should be established near Taro, then still held in force by the Japanese. This group, code-named Tramp, would gather intelligence about the Japanese movements in the Hukawng Valley. It would not disturb the Japanese and would fight only if attacked. Red Maddox, formerly of A Group, had by early December completed a series of search flights over the Malay Peninsula, and was assigned an Anglo-Burmese second-in-command, a Burmese radio operator, and three Kachins. They were to train for six weeks at Nazira and then walk about 150 miles through the Naga Hills to the vicinity of Taro.

Shortly before the men were to start into the hills, Opero changed the plan. The headhunting proclivities of the Nagas were not to be ignored, and most of the route led through their country. Tramp was scheduled to jump into Burma on January 15, 1944. A few days before the jump, a reconnaissance plane flew over the area and located a level place, about two hundred yards long and fifty yards wide. At each end the small plateau dropped off from fifteen hundred to two thousand feet into overgrown ravines. On the southern rim of the plateau there was a Kachin village with about ten bashas. The village was only about ten miles west of Taro, but it was in an almost impregnable position.

On the fifteenth, Tramp was suited up in air-corps escape chutes with metal release handles. A fighter escort accompanied the drop plane, and Pop Milligan and Ray Peers flew along with the team. There was a high wind blowing when the drop plane approached the target. Red Maddox and the radio operator jumped first, and they landed in the middle of the drop zone. The next stick of two jumpers landed some fifty yards downwind, but the third stick of two Kachins were caught by the wind and blown toward the deep ravine. Peers and Milligan held their breath. Then they could breathe again. The men drifted down on top of the bashas. Villagers came running and climbed up on the roofs to rescue them. The plane dropped three thousand pounds of gear and rice and then a streamer attached to a message asking about the fate of the men who had landed on the bashas.

After Peers and Milligan reached Nazira, they received a radio message from Tramp. When it was decoded, they learned that the two Kachins who had fallen on the roofs claimed that it was like landing on a feather bed. All three Kachins had relatives in villages nearby, and they were delighted to report that the girls in the neighborhood were very much impressed by their exploit. Tramp fell to work recruiting agents and about fifty guerrillas to protect the base from the Japanese at Taro. Agents were soon active throughout the Chindwin River Valley and as far east as the Lonkin jade mines and the distant railroad corridor to the south.

\* \* \*

The following is an excerpt from a representative report from Wilkinson at Forward to Opero at Nazira, dated December 31, 1943. It was once classified as secret, but it is of value now only because it suggests the enormously complicated and detailed nature of 101's field operations. The period covered is a brief one. Other Detachment 101 groups were carrying on equally involved activities, and the complications grew as 101 expanded from a few field operations to hundreds scattered all over Burma.

"During this period our men were based at two places forward of Ngumla. One group was based at Sagribum and the other at Sumpawng Mata. The group at Sagribum has had four fights with the Japs during this period. The first already mentioned was at Gwiwang. The second was at Lakawng where a party of seven of my men ambushed twenty Japs and killed five and wounded ten. Of these latter, three died later as a result of their wounds. Third scrap was near Mara. This occurred when the Japs were on their way to Sapu on the 28th of December. No casualties were claimed. At this time our men are following the Japs who have gone to Sapu. Last reported at Sumka-Uma. The group which was based at Sumpawng Mata had no contact with the Japs and all but seven of them were turned over to the Levies on the first of December. The remainder under the leadership of Kiwi assisted by Don were sent to the Nmai Hka across from Chipwi and Lakawng for the purpose of harassing the Japs by destroying dumps and bridges if possible and sending back information. Their exact location is not known as they don't have a radio with them. However Chuck with his radio is to join them in the next few days.

"A group of five Kachins were trained to use the light machine gun. This group has been with the men based at Sagribum. I have not had a report as yet as to the effectiveness of their fire. I have, however, received complaints, and quite agree, that the gun is too heavy to carry through the jungle. It takes four men to carry the gun and 1000 rounds of ammunition for it. Even broken down the gun is much heavier than a BAR which is the weapon which I believe is suitable to our needs in ambushing. You get the fire power from it, it is easier to set up, and is much lighter to carry. I have ordered BARs to be dropped and when I get them I will retire the light machine gun.

"A group of five Kachins have also been trained to use the mortar. Due to the scarcity of the ammunition they have been able to fire only eight live rounds. They are not the fastest crew in the world, but they are fair at setting up a gun and leveling. The hardest thing to teach them was to estimate ranges, which I'm afraid as yet is not so good. Neither is their correction for windage. However, I believe that they will do all right when the time comes. They went with a Levy platoon to the motor road the latter part of November but returned without having fired a shot as there were no targets.

"I have had a man trained to use the telescopic sight you sent me. He is to join Kiwi near Chipwi as a lot of long-range sniping can be done in this area. He is due to leave as soon as the Jap situation is clarified in the Sumpawng Mata area.

"When Commander Luce arrived on the third of December, he brought with him a group of eight Kachins. These men were given explosives, money, and other supplies and were sent to the area between Kwitu and Ningchangyang. They were to attack Jap supplies coming up this road. Further they were to attack targets on the motor road from Myitkyina to Sumprabum as far north as Nsop. To date nothing has been heard of this group.

"As mentioned in my last report Mac had been sent to the Myitkyina area. He was instructed to gather information and that as soon as I could I would send an operator down to join him. This has been done. The operator that Colonel Eifler flew in, Tawng, has been sent down and has arrived safely. He is living in the jungle and works through a contact man. He does not contact Mac personally but has a man pick up messages from him. He also has his own information net. The information that has been coming from these two men seems to me to be excellent. However, you can judge better from where you are. Mac has done an excellent job and has gotten himself a job with the Japs as a general contractor. He should be able to travel rather freely. His one fault is that he wants to have arms and ammo, explosives, etc., sent to him. I radio that when the time comes we will send the items requested but at the present it is not feasible and will spoil all our plans for that area.

"With the arrival of a base operator—Summers—I was able to fulfill George's ambition and send him out on his own. He was sent to Wachon. He was accompanied by a headman from a nearby village who stated that George could be hidden quite easily in the jungle near there and that he would gather information for George. This man is an old soldier and is very reliable in his figures and valuation of Kachin reports. George also took three Kachins with him to turn his generator and to help gather info. He has arrived successfully and has sent in information but is handicapped by the fact that he does not have any maps, none being available at time he left. These will be sent to him as soon as the courier arrives.

"Another radio operator, Eric, was also sent south. He is located near Tumpang in the jungle. He is to gather information on movements along the road to Htawgaw and along the Nmai Hka. He also will send agents to the area around Myitkyina. He arrived safely and has been sending back what I consider excellent information.

"All of these men who were sent out with radios took the bare minimum with them. This included money, opium, pistol, and a radio. All wore native clothing and had native accessories for the rest of their personal belongings. Unfortunately neither George nor Eric could speak Kachin but had with them a Kachin who could speak Burmese fluently.

"Although the above report of operations is not in detail, it covers generally the operations carried out during this period."

Having concluded his assessment of Forward's operation, Bill Wilkinson then went on to cover intelligence assessments of a political, economical, strategic, and military nature. He discussed Japanese air action.

"From the twenty-first of December the Japs have had an air patrol every morning between the hours of 7:30 and 8:30. They approach from the south, circle just north of Ngumla, and depart toward Myitkyina."

Wilkinson finished with a report on personnel at Forward:

"I lost two of the India-trained men during this period. The first to go was Dopey. He had had an infected toe, and it did not seem to get better so I sent him back to Htingnan for treatment by the doctor. He died on the ninth of November due to tuberculosis of the lower bowel.

"On the tenth of December Big Stiff died when a booby trap he was experimenting with went off. The details are not known of just what caused the accident. A Kachin found him lying on a trail. The medical report of Commander Luce has already been sent in. He was buried just outside our camp."

Bill Wilkinson had been ordered by General Donovan to relinquish his Forward command and report to China where he was to train Chinese guerrillas. At midnight of December 31, 1943, he turned over command of Forward to Navy Doctor Jim Luce.

"Although he is a doctor, he acts more like an infantry officer," he commented. "Since he has been here he has quickly grasped the situation, and is completely familiar with my plans and operations."

Wilkinson proved entirely right about this extraordinary navy doctor, who now found himself hundreds of miles from the nearest body of saltwater in command of Forward.

\*       \*       \*

On what 101 men still talk about as Black Friday, January 18, 1944, Harry Martin of OSS Field Photo and a column of Kachins were walking the trail from Fort Hertz to Ngumla. Up ahead a few miles were Gerry Larsen, newly arrived from the States, with another small detachment of Kachins. The two Americans had flown from Nazira to Fort Hertz and were on their way to Jim Luce's base with reinforcements. They were only about three hours' walk from Forward when they heard the firing in the sky.

At first it was hard to make out anything through the gap in the jungle roof over the trail, but then two Japanese fighters streaking around a C-47 came into view. As they watched, the transport broke into flames and began to fall. Even after the C-47 plunged out of sight, the firing in the sky continued, and Martin knew more American planes were being attacked. In time he was to learn that eighteen Japanese fighters had jumped three American C-47s on their way to make a drop to Forward. All three of the planes were shot down. On two planes all the air-force and 101 personnel aboard died; on the third, two men of the aircrew survived.

Only a few weeks before that fateful day the 1st Combat Cargo Unit of the 2d Troop Carrier Squadron had arrived from the United States. Since they were trained in aerial supply drops, the responsibility for resupplying 101 field units from the air was transferred from the ATC to them. Successful drops were made to Forward and Knothead without untoward incident. Opero was busy building up the two key field operations, and Jim Luce now radioed in a list of arms, ammunition, and supplies so that he could increase his effective guerrilla force to five hundred men. It would take three transports to carry the requested drop. On January 18, accompanied by an escort of six fighters, the transports set off on their mission.

Bernard Bauman and Tom Riley, 101's air-drop officer, were in the first plane. Riley was to supervise the drop, and Bauman, a navy pharmacist's mate, was to jump. Now that Luce was the commanding officer at Forward, he needed a man to help provide medical attention to the sick and wounded. William Krautwald and Elmer Gallovitch, close friends, had both been professional football players back home, and they were aboard the lead plane in order to help muscle the heavy containers out of the doors. Art Meehan, a Field Photo cameraman, was on board to photograph the drop. Aboard the other two planes, air-force men made up the drop crews. Harry Gibbons of 101 was aboard one of the other planes to help as a kicker.

The planes soared among the huge cumulus clouds. As they crossed the Kumon Range, the cloud formations grew dense, and the pursuit planes flying at an altitude of some ten thousand feet lost sight of the transports. Unable to find the C-47s in the clouds and running short of gasoline, the fighters turned back to Chabua. The tragedy occurred as the transports went into their drop patterns over Ngumla. Japanese Zeros appeared from the south. As they dove on the transports, the big planes scattered and tried to run for cloud cover. Splitting up their own formation, the Zeros went after each of the planes. They shot down the first two in such rapid order that none of the OSS men or the crew had the slightest chance to parachute.

The third plane was also struck, and it turned north in a vain attempt to reach the airstrip at Fort Hertz. As the plane began to lose altitude despite every maneuver the pilot tried, he ordered the crew to bail out. When the others jumped, he too leaped from the plane. Only the pilot's and the copilot's chutes opened at all. The pilot's chute burst open only a few feet above the ground, and he jolted against the surface. He was unhurt. The copilot's chute was just opening when he fell into a thicket of bamboo. The stiff stems slashed him to ribbons. Seventeen air-force men and six 101 men were dead.

On the ground Harry Martin and his Kachins pressed on to Ngumla. When he reached base, he told Jim Luce about what had happened to the drop planes.

"I think I can locate one of them," he said.

Jim Luce ordered him to set out at once to search for it. Martin took with him a Kachin radio operator named Aung, the Anglo-Burmese agent named Kiwi, two other agents, and some Kachin soldiers. They hurried through the jungles until in three or four hours they came upon the crash site. The wreckage of the plane still smoked. Nine badly burned bodies were scattered about. There was nothing to do but dig graves. Martin took one of each man's dog tags with him and buried the other with his body. He returned to Ngumla, sad and shocked at the experience and with a renewed realization of how formidable an opponent the Allies faced in North Burma.

At Ngumla Kachin runners had come in to report that villagers from Marau Zup had found the second plane. Again, Martin and his group set off at once for the second crash site, which turned out to be on the banks of a small river. The villagers had already buried the dead in a row, and their dog tags with them. Martin saw no point in disturbing the bodies, so he took photos and returned to Ngumla. Father MacAlindon, Gerry Larsen, and another group of Kachins set off to find the third plane, which was at last discovered much farther to the north.

Ray Peers was stunned by the news from the field, but he knew he still had a job to do. He had to get the supplies to Forward. He placed John Raiss in charge of the drop and ordered him to plan for a daylight flight when the weather was so bad that the Zeros could not fly. Unfortunately, on the first attempt to get supplies to Forward, the weather was so very bad that the C-47s could scarcely fly either, and they had to return to base without making the drop.

For several weeks the weather was either so good that the Zeros would be waiting in what the air force now called "Suicide Alley," or so bad that when the drop planes flew they could not find Ngumla in the gloom. For twenty-seven days Forward went without supplies. The men on the ground grew hungrier and hungrier, living only on what they could discover in the jungle. One night Father Mac walked over from his village leading a goat. He killed the goat and brewed up a stew, necessarily thin enough to serve so many half-starved men.

With the situation at Forward growing desperate, Opero decided that an attempt must be made to drop at night. It was dangerous enough to dare the sheer cliffs and mountains around Ngumla in the daylight. A night drop was doubly dangerous, but one moonlit night Pop Milligan and John Raiss flew with a courageous 2d Troop Carrier Command crew.

As the drop planes approached Ngumla they saw a ring of fires that Jim Luce's Kachins had built along the high ridges surrounding a natural bowl in the mountains. A drop zone about half a mile in diameter was clearly marked off from the night. The parachutes went drifting down toward the dark within the circle of fire. It was a near perfect drop. The next day Forward recovered almost all the supplies dropped in the night.

\*      \*      \*

Richard Walsh, a navy lieutenant, arrived from Washington to join Detachment 101, and Ray Peers immediately ordered him to make an inventory of the effects of the 101 men killed in the ill-fated supply drop to Forward. He undertook his first assignment in 101 with what Ray Peers observed was "dispatch and efficiency." He inventoried the effects, shipped the belongings home, and prepared affidavits. He worked with a heavy heart. Hank Gibbons and he had been friends since boyhood. Later, as he worked in 101's supply operations, he told Ray Peers how hard it had been to close out the record on the life of one of his dearest friends.

"Even if I had known this at the time, I would still probably have designated him to do the job for the simple reason that there was no one else present to do it," Peers remarked after the war.

# Weretigers

The Japanese were past masters at camouflage. They hid their gasoline and ammunition storage areas, their vehicle parks, and quarters for their troops in the jungle so that they could not be seen from the air. There was no way that their installations could be observed by United States reconnaissance flights. Intelligence reports on Japanese targets were radioed in by 101 from the field and brought to 10th Air Force headquarters, but even then fighter-bombers could not find them. Skittles had an idea.

Skittles and Hefty reported to Knothead. They had infiltrated into the Mogaung area along the road that led into the Hukawng Valley. It was their task to spy out Japanese installations and to inform on Japanese supply and troop movements into the Hukawng. The Japanese, feeling themselves threatened by the advancing Chinese, were moving reinforcements toward Maingkwan and other garrisoned towns farther north and west. When the air force could not find the targets reported by Skittles and Hefty, Skittles realized that a more precise way of locating them must be worked out.

The method Skittles came up with was simple. He would select a prominent landmark, a big tree, a trail junction, a bridge, or something of the sort that could be picked out easily enough on an air photo and by the pilot of the fighter bomber. He would then give the polar coordinates, the distance along a given azimuth, from the landmark to the target. If this method would not work, he supplied a series of reference points to lead the pilot from the landmark to the target. In this way the pilot need not even see the ammunition dump or vehicle park. The plan seemed to work. Time and again, when a plane dropped its bombs on or strafed an apparently innocent patch of jungle, violent explosions resulted. The attack had been successful.

The Japanese realized that Allied intelligence must be discovering the precise location of the targets. They immediately suspected the Kachins, and orders were given to shoot on sight any Kachin seen in the vicinity of their installations. Then one day a report reached the Japanese that two American spies were hiding out in a Kachin village and masterminding an entire network of Kachin informants. At night a detachment of soldiers was sent to the village to capture the agents.

Skittles and Hefty were sleeping in the village duwa's basha when the Japanese burst in the door. As usual, the basha was on pilings six feet or so off the ground, but the two 101 agents plunged through a window to the rear and landed on their feet. They sped into the jungle. The intelligence reports so damaging to the Japanese continued to flow from the Mogaung area. Not only did Skittles and Hefty designate the targets, but they reported accurately on the results. In Knothead's situation report to Opero, Curl remarked of the reports that "the best one we have had thus far is one target designated southeast of Kamaign in which thirty cartloads of dead Japs were hauled away." The Japanese redoubled their search for Skittles and Hefty.

*     *     *

Ray Peers had a problem. Detachment 101 had been operational in Burma for slightly over a year, and its rapidly expanding organization in the field was confronting him with such an increased volume of command decisions that he could no longer cope. Once three thousand guerrillas were operating behind the Japanese lines to support the Chinese and Merrill's Marauders on their advance on Myitkyina, his task would become even more burdensome. What would happen if the American-Kachin Rangers grew to be a guerrilla force of ten thousand men? Headquarters, Nazira, was adding more supply men to take care of the increasing demand for air drops. More communications men were coming out from Washington to make certain that critical intelligence and operations reports from the field were not delayed in transmission and were quickly deciphered and put in the hands of the necessary people. All of this helped, but the problems continued to balloon.

There was only one solution for the command problem. Ray Peers decided to decentralize operational control to the four area commanders, Vince Curl, Jim Luce, who had replaced Wilkinson, Red Maddox, and Pat Quinn. Each was closer to the tactical scene than

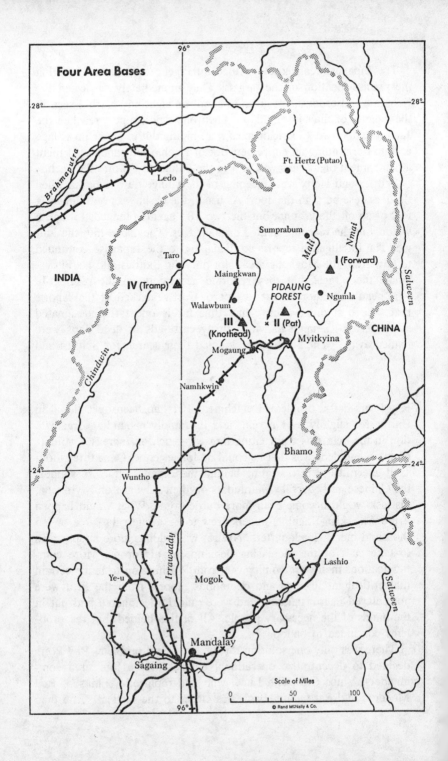

**Four Area Bases**

28°

*Brahmaputra*

Ledo

28°

Ft. Hertz (Putao)

Sumprabum

*Mali*

*N'mai*

INDIA

Taro

IV (Tramp) ▲

Maingkwan

*PIDAUNG FOREST*

I (Forward) ▲

Ngumla

Walawbum

III ▲
(Knothead)

× II (Pat) ▲

Mogaung

Myitkyina

CHINA

*Salween*

Namhkwin

*Chindwin*

Bhamo

24°

Wuntho

24°

*Irrawaddy*

Ye-u

Mogok

Lashio

*Salween*

Mandalay

Sagaing

Scale of Miles

0        50        100

© Rand McNally & Co.

96°

96°

he was, and each was now a veteran jungle fighter. They would work within a directive from Opero. Peers outlined the role each group was to play as follows:

"Forward (at Ngumla, Luce)—expand to a force of approximately fifteen hundred guerrillas; harass the Japanese along the watershed of the Irrawaddy; extend guerrilla operations to the south in order to oppose Japanese reinforcement of Myitkyina, and expand espionage operations southward into the Bhamo area.

"Pat (at Arang, Quinn)—raise a force of about four hundred guerrillas; harass the Japanese along the road and railroad from Myitkyina to Mogaung; and expand intelligence activities south in the Koukkwee Valley.

"Knothead (at Nawbum, Curl)—raise a force of one thousand guerrillas to operate behind the Japanese lines in the Hukawng Valley; and extend espionage operations into the railway corridor and into the Lonkin Jade Mines area.

"Tramp (at Taro, Maddox)—move the base camp out of the Naga Hills into the Chindwin River Valley; raise a force of about three hundred guerrillas; and extend intelligence operations eastward toward the rail corridor and southward to rear of the Japanese force on the Imphal Front."

Ray Peers issued his directives by radio, but he also decided that he must fly into the field to confer with the commanders who had airstrips in order to make certain that everything was fully understood. The Chinese were already moving into the Hukawng Valley, so it was of primary importance for Peers to visit Vincent Curl and Zhing Htaw Naw as soon as possible.

* * *

Ray Peers flew to Fort Hertz in a C-47 with a load of gasoline and other supplies. There he met a young ATC pilot, Lieutenant Cahan, who had been clocking some air hours in the Gypsy Moth just to get the feel of the 101 plane. From Fort Hertz Cahan was to fly Peers to Knothead and then on to Forward. The Gypsy Moth landed at Knothead without any trouble.

All was going very well at Nawbum except that the huge tiger still patrolled the paths from the village to the airstrip. So far he had not attacked anyone, but his presence scarcely contributed to a sense of security. While Peers was meeting with Curl and Zhing Htaw Naw, a report came in from Skittles and Hefty concerning their close escape from the Japanese soldiers. Between the tiger and the Japanese army, 101's commander was getting a firsthand impression of what life was like in the field.

It was time to fly to Forward, and Peers and the pilot got into the Gypsy Moth. Cahan surveyed the narrow strip in the jungle. From the end of the strip where he revved up the engine, he could see only about one-third of the runway. The first part of it was level, but the rest ran downhill at an alarming angle. He gripped the stick with such intensity his knuckles whitened. The Kachins had removed the camouflage huts from the field and waited to the side to carry them back into place as soon as the plane took off. The motor roared, and the Gypsy Moth rocked down the strip, rice stalks from the old paddy blowing in the wind after it.

"As we were taking off we almost had flying speed when we reached the edge of the plateau, but not quite," recalls Peers. "We bounced two or three times and were just airborne when we flew into one of the camouflage houses sitting alongside the runway.

"I was sitting in the front seat and was well strapped in. Aside from a few superficial scratches, I was unhurt. However, as we were flying into the house, I had looked back and the wings of the biplane were being folded back so that the upper wing had clamped onto Lieutenant Cahan's head like a nutcracker. At the last fraction of a second his head popped out of the vice, and the wing crumbled into a thousand pieces."

Peers was unhurt, and Cahan suffered nothing more than severe headaches. The Gypsy Moth was not so fortunate. It was wrecked beyond repair. The Kachins dismantled it. They hid the parts in the jungle so that they would not draw unwelcome Japanese attention. Now Ray Peers, 101's CO, was stranded two hundred miles behind Japanese lines. To walk out would mean a three weeks' journey through difficult country, which would make it impossible for him to carry out his day-by-day command responsibilities, to say nothing of continuing his vital visits to the other 101 field bases. Harry Little took the initiative. He contacted NCAC Headquarters, and they sent two L-4 liaison airplanes to Shingbwiyang. From there the planes flew to Nawbum to bring Peers and Cahan out.

Lieutenant General Stratemeyer at the Strategic Air Command in Calcutta came to 101's rescue and provided an obsolete L-1, an expression of his great appreciation for the 101 rescue of pilots downed in Burma. The L-1's cruising speed was only sixty-five mph, but it could take off and land at about thirty mph over short and rough strips. There were few strips shorter and rougher than those that the Kachins had hacked out of the jungle at Nawbum and Ngumla and were likely to build in the future at other 101 field bases behind the Japanese lines. As soon as the plane arrived at Nazira, Peers continued his command trips and flew to Ngumla to meet with Jim Luce. Neither Pat nor Tramp as yet could accommodate the landing of a plane, so Peers had to be content with radio communications with those two bases.

\* \* \*

Until early 1944, Detachment 101 was charged with deep penetration operations, while V Force, a special Recon group formed by Stilwell with British and American personnel, was responsible for the close-in scouting ahead of the advancing Galahad forces. At the February conference with Stilwell, the general had decided to transfer the V Force of four officers and thirty-five enlisted men to the OSS. Now they had gathered at Taro, recently taken by the Chinese, to meet with 101 officers to learn their new duties. Red Maddox had already set up a new base nearly one hundred miles deeper into enemy territory at Tamanthi, but at Peers's request he returned to Taro. Maddox and the V Force men looked askance at one another. Both 101 and the V Force had developed a strong *esprit de corps,* and the prospect of a merger had little appeal to either group. But together they turned a paddy field into a small airfield. Then Ray Peers flew in, and with tact and a clearheaded presentation of what their combined role would be, he skillfully submerged the differences.

"Ray made us forget the petty animosities that threatened to divide us," remembers Pete Lutken, one of the four V Force officers.

At Taro it was determined that Red Maddox would remain the area commander, despite his repeated pleas that he be allowed to recruit and lead one of the planned guerrilla units. Pete Lutken and another V Force man, Dow Grones, were to establish small American-Kachin Ranger units and make their way southward into the valleys west of the railroad line to Myitkyina. To reach their designated areas both groups would have to cross one of the most uninhabited places in the world, more than ten thousand square miles of wilderness almost totally devoid of any human inhabitants. For the next fortnight Lutken and Grones remained at Taro with Maddox as he indoctrinated them into 101 operating procedures, air drops, communications, and ciphers and codes. They recruited Kachins for their hazardous missions.

*　　*　　*

Pete Lutken, a soft-spoken Mississippian, was destined to be one of the most remarkable of all the 101 field commanders. A tall, lean, long-legged man, he was able to hold the trail as long as the most rugged of the Kachins, and the mobility of his unit was to appall the Japanese. Since I had once walked with a small party of Kachins from Namhpakka, close to the Burma Road, over the Loilun Range to Mongwi, a hiking distance of perhaps ninety miles, in a little less than two days, Ray Peers decided that I might possibly be able to keep up with Lutken and prepared to have me jump in to his assistance. The difficulty was that Lutken didn't stop long enough for a drop to be made. The war was changing rapidly, he had little time to waste, so he ended up living off the land more than any other commander. When Opero made an unrequested food drop and slowed down his movement, he heatedly radioed back, "Don't send food. Send more ammo." At base it was said that Lutken had become more of a Kachin than the Kachins; he preferred their food, could hike for days on monkey meat and roasted grubs, and preferred the company of the hypenlas to that of the Americans who were unlucky enough to serve under such a rugged commander.

Lutken had joined the ROTC at Mississippi State College, had been called up in December, 1941, and by the following spring was at Karachi as a member of an airborne anti-aircraft machine-gun outfit. He had helped to train the Chinese divisions at Ramgarh and had gone to Ledo with the Chinese. As the 38th and 22d divisions prepared to cross the Naga Hills in October, 1943, on their way to attack the Japanese in the Hukawng Valley, Colonel McNally at Stilwell's headquarters called in Lutken and another officer. He spread a map out on the ground at his feet. He pointed to the Naga Hills.

"We have to move the Chinese through the mountains," he said. "Can we get horses through?"

Lutken took a closer look at the map.

"I want you to go and find out if horses can be used as transport out there," said the colonel.

Lutken, a Boy Scout when he was a youth and now one of the most rugged scoutmasters in Texas, knew all about trails and compass bearings, and he realized that the contour lines that looked so innocent on the map indicated some treacherous country.

"It'll take about eight days," he said, "to make the trip in and out."

Lutken and the other American took two Chinese soldiers with them. They did not bother to ask anyone about the trail but started up a two-foot-gauge railroad.

It was also the last time Lutken saw India for a year and a half. When they reached the end of the railroad, they struck off into the mountains to Rang Lun where they found a company of Punjabis in a strong defensive position. British Captain J. R. Wilson of the V Force was in command. Lutken pushed on for a few more days to satisfy himself that with difficulty the Chinese could get their horses through. He returned to Rang Lun to send his report back to Colonel McNally.

Lutken was still at Rang Lun when a Japanese force struck at the Kalat Ga air-warning station farther into the hills. Other groups retreated through Lutken's camp in their haste to get out of the way of the Japanese who, it appeared, were attacking in force. Nobody had any idea of what was out in the mountains in front of their positions.

"The Chinese would not patrol," Lutken explained. "They'd dig holes and stay there."

At Rang Lun, Lutken had met a Naga chief named "Two Hats" because he wore both Naga and Gurkha headpieces. From him he had learned a little of the Naga language. Through him he recruited a few Nagas to help him scout the region toward Kalat Ga where the Japanese had wiped out the defenders. In this casual way Pete Lutken became a member of V Force serving under J. R. Wilson who, scouting ahead of Chinese forces, had moved his group farther forward to Togap. Bill Cummings, an agricultural missionary from one of Burma's pioneer American Baptist Mission families was number-two man under Wilson. As Lutken probed deeper into the mountains looking for the Japanese, he sent Naga runners back to Togap with reports for Wilson which included the information that the Japanese had faded back into the jungles toward their own positions in the Hukawng.

When he completed his first assignment for the V Force, Wilson gave him the task of trekking into the Hukawng Valley to spy out possible locations for liaison airstrips to be built when the Chinese army had conquered the region. Lutken was also to see if any of the crude roads opened into parts of the valley before the war by the British could still take vehicles and what transportation might be possible on the rivers. To act as guides for Lutken, Wilson sent two teenage Kachins from villages isolated among the Nagas on the Indian side of the border.

It was at Pebu in the Naga Hills that Lutken first met 101 agents. Two Kachins who were followers of Zhing Htaw Naw asked his own Kachins pointed questions about their business in the hills. Apparently satisfied with their replies, Zhing Htaw Naw's men went on their way, and Lutken walked through the deluge of rain to the Loglai Hka, which might afford possible boat transportation on its way down to its juncture with the Tanai Hka. The Loglai Hka was a raging torrent, one hundred yards wide. Since he could not cross it, Lutken determined that he would see if it could at least be navigated by a raft.

Six Nagas from a village on the riverbank offered to help Lutken and his two Kachins build a raft, but on their side of the river there were only huge trees with wood so heavy that it would not float. For a day Lutken and his men scouted up and down the river looking for a copse of bamboo from which a raft could be constructed. Then on the opposite bank he spied a raft tucked into some thickets on the riverbank.

Lutken, a strong swimmer since boyhood, waded into the river until the current threatened to sweep him off his feet. Then he swam until at last he was able to grab hold of vines on the opposite bank and pull himself out of the water. He cut a long pole and fashioned a hook on it so that he could grab hold of shrubbery on the bank and pull the raft upstream. He reasoned that if he got far enough upstream, he would have some chance at least of paddling the raft across the river before he would be swept downstream past the remainder of his party. The strategy worked. As he sped down the river past the men on the bank, they rushed into the water, grabbed hold of the raft, and hauled it ashore.

Everybody fell to work to enlarge the raft so that it could carry all nine men and their supplies. Tying the gear and supplies onto the raft, the men got aboard and, poles in their hands, set off. Within moments, the river had broken the poles and swept the raft out of control. The raft rushed downstream into the Taung Hka.

"In an effort to stop the runaway raft, I grabbed hold of a vine dangling down from a huge tree," Lutken remembers. "I tied it around my waist, hoping to stop the raft, but it snapped tight and almost cut me in half before it broke. We hit a submerged tree and everybody was thrown off the raft. The supplies raced away down stream, and we were separated from one another. I almost drowned, and I expected that some of my men had drowned."

Lutken walked down the riverbank trying to find either people or supplies. Every now and then he shouted, but there was no response. He had no gun and no knife. It was night now, and the rain began to fall. He must try to find other survivors. At midnight he heard the first shouted response to his own cry. Throughout the night, he was joined by others, one by one, until seven of the eight missing men were accounted for.

"One fellow still had his knife," Lutken remembers. "With the aid of his knife we built a shelter out of plantain leaves. By 2:30 we were out of the rain. I had my trusty waterproof matchboxes in my pocket, and I was able to get a warming fire going. One of the Kachins had recovered a rifle from the lost raft, and by dawn's early light he dropped a monkey out of a tree with a shot."

The Kachin tossed the monkey onto the coals. The animal's hair burned off as the flesh roasted, guts and all.

"We had roast monkey," Lutken says. "It tasted good but was stringy and tough. Later on I got used to eating it disguised in a stew or curry. Monkey meat is dry and, like venison, has no fat."

The jungle was so tangled that it was a three-day walk back to the confluence of the two rivers. There was no trail along the riverbank, and the men had to hack and tear their way through the undergrowth as best they could. Then it was another five miles up the Taung Hka to the Hku, or the headwaters of the river, where a village appropriately called Taung Hku was situated. Lutken found that it was crowded with refugees from the Japanese attacks on the Hukawng villages. Their duwa had taken the title of "Sharaw," meaning tiger, as evidence of his implacable thirst to avenge the Japanese brutality against the Kachin people.

The Kachins fed the party and helped them build a new raft of bamboo, thirty feet long and five feet wide. A platform was erected in the middle of the raft to hold what belongings the men still had left. They constructed a sweep and installed a rudder in the back. In a week the raft was ready to navigate the river.

"It was a great ride," says Lutken. "Rushing rapids sometimes rolled the raft completely over, but we'd right the raft when we got on the other side."

After trying water travel in the Upper Hukawng Valley, Lutken returned to Togap. The rivers did not look good for navigation, and he had learned that the roads were controlled by the Japanese. Perhaps it would still be possible to scout out some good locations for airstrips. Lutken and his Kachins took to the trail again. At Ninh Bien, they found a Kachin village within a few hundred yards of a Shan village in which there was a Japanese garrison. The proximity of the Japanese did not keep the Kachins from welcoming Lutken. They invited him to the headman's basha, where he sat nervously with his rifle pointing at the door. All the men and the boys of the village came to gaze at the tall American who had come with the two young Kachins and the strange Nagas. Lutken, who had been learning the Jinghpaw tongue from the boys, spoke a few halting words.

"I am the first of many to come," he said.

The Kachins helped him find an open place a few miles away which was two miles long by half a mile wide. They led Lutken to the field at night, and he paced out its dimensions by moonlight. It would make a fine airfield. Before he left the area that night, Lutken sneaked into the Shan village where the Japanese were asleep. They had not even posted a sentry. He carved a scurrilous invitation to the Japanese in English on a tree, smiled with satisfaction, and by morning was well on the way back to Togap. Lutken made several more trips into the northern Hukawng Valley searching for possible airport sites. He crossed the valley to explore the eastern side close to the high Kumon Range.

*     *     *

Pete Lutken's experiences with the Kachins were to make him one of 101's most effective guerrilla leaders. After he returned to Togap, he led a party of American engineers to the possible airport locations that he had discovered. The Kachin scouts pointed out the footprints of Japanese soldiers in the soft earth of the trails.

"Duwa, the Japanese have sent men out on the trails to look for the Americans. They are going that way," said a scout, and he pointed down the trail with his lips in the direction the party was traveling. "We must not walk on the trail."

The Americans grumbled when Lutken explained that they could no longer follow the trail. It was much easier going that way, and

Major General William J. Donovan, director of the OSS (right), confers with 101 commander, Ray Peers, at Chabua. Donovan flew behind the Japanese lines to meet with Vince Curl and Zhing Htaw Naw and judge the Kachins for himself.

(Clockwise from bottom left) A 101 pilot with a Red Ass Squadron plane. At Nawbum Father Stuart told General Donovan of the tragic Japanese attack on Kachin villages and why the Kachins would never give in to the invaders. Only wreckage remained of the drop planes shot down by the Japanese near Ngumla.

(Clockwise from bottom left) Vince Curl never failed to delight and charm Kachin villagers. General Joseph Stilwell and 101's commander, Ray Peers, discussed 101's future operations at Shadazup. Two of Bill Martin's agents pose in a Kachin village. Kachin boys carry a wounded hypenla on a jungle stretcher.

(Clockwise from bottom left) A Kachin youth wears much of his wealth about his neck. Later his bride will wear the necklaces. 101 men often lived in comfortable Kachin bashas. They followed the trails that linked together the Kachin villages. Stalwart Kachin porters carry their burdens from a landing place on the Mali Hka.

(Above) Packs had to be gathered up for each day's trek. (Below) A Kachin ferry crosses the Mali Hka.

they could make good time. Only when he insisted did they take his advice and follow the Kachins. Within a few miles they balked at the sweaty labor of forcing their way through the vegetation, the insects, and an occasional snake, and headed back to the trail. Soon there were more Japanese footprints, which once more inspired them to follow the Kachins through the tangled jungle for a few miles. Then, weary and torn by the thorny foliage, they insisted on returning to the trail.

The Kachins were in the lead as they neared Ninh Bien, their eyes searching the jungle for sign of the Japanese.

"The enemy are very close," a Kachin told Lutken.

The enemy was indeed close. In only a few moments, Burmese and Japanese soldiers fired from ambush. The Kachins in the lead hit the dirt and lay sprawled on the trail. A furious fire fight blazed. One American engineer, Roland Brown, was shot dead with the first burst of fire. His body lay in the trail. The others had disappeared into the bush. From his place of concealment, Lutken could see neither friends nor foe, but bullets whined about him from all directions. Then the firing stopped. The Japanese emerged from cover and searched the Kachins and the American lying in the trail as Lutken watched. Then they moved off down the trail, their guns ready for any survivors of the ambush. When the Japanese were safely out of sight, the two Kachins got up, dusted themselves off, and grinned at Lutken when he emerged from the jungle. They had not even been hit and had been "playing possum," as Lutken put it later.

The remaining Americans lost no time in following Lutken and the Kachins deeper into the jungle. There they camped. The trail lost its appeal. They had scarcely quit the site of the ambush when a group of Burmese and Japanese returned. The Burmese cut off Brown's head, hands, and feet. They cut a bamboo pole and hoisted Brown's bloody head on top of it. With the head held aloft in triumph, they paraded through the Kachin village at Ninh Bien.

"This is what happens to Americans or British who come back here," they shouted to the villagers.

The Kachins watched impassively until the Japanese and Burmese soldiers, carrying their grim trophy, had returned to the Shan village. Then they packed up what they could easily carry and fled into the jungles. Their scouts quickly discovered Lutken's camp. The villagers, covering their trail behind them, had come to Lutken to make common cause. When it was safe to do so, Lutken slipped the engineers out of the jungle to the safety of the Chinese lines. In the guerrilla warfare that was to follow, the duwa of Ninh Bien was to be Lutken's trusted lieutenant.

\* \* \*

During that winter of 1944 the Chinese divisions were reluctant participants in Stilwell's plans to advance against the Japanese from the northwest and take Myitkyina. Whenever they were finally coaxed or forced into attacking, their bugler would blow the command to charge and they would rush forward with fixed bayonets. The Japanese Nambus slaughtered them.

"If there were ever another war, we'd want the Japanese and not the Chinese on our side," remarked Pete Lutken.

In one of the encounters Lutken was hit in his rear by a burst of Japanese machine-gun fire. He kept his command despite the pain, because there was no better place than his Kachin camp to go to anyway. For two months the Chinese advance stopped cold. Lutken continued to learn the Kachin tongue and nursed his wound. In early March he met with Peers and Maddox at Taro where he was briefed on his 101 mission and lost no time in recruiting more Kachins. Many of the first eighty Kachins who joined were villagers from Ninh Bien, who wished to follow their duwa and the tall American, whose feet, they decided, were the largest ever given to man. In reality, Lutken's feet were indeed size fourteens, and supply back at Chabua had a great deal of trouble finding shoes to fit him. Once during the thousands of miles of trekking to come, Lutken's boots were completely worn out, and he was reduced to wrapping his feet in gunnysacks. These left extraordinary tracks on the trails, and the Shans reported to the Japanese that the Kachins were led by some sort of giant, most likely a cannibal who drank human blood and copulated with tigers.

The village jaiwa joined his force too, and over the months to come went into frequent trances to foretell the future.

"I never made a move without checking with him," Lutken says.

When he reached a Kachin village, Lutken always conferred with the council of elders as well.

From Taro, Grones and Lutken led their Kachins south through Singaling Hkamti and into the almost uninhabited wilderness for two hundred miles to the Uyu River. At the Uyu, Grones went on down the river, and Lutken struck east into the mountains. He and his men ran out of food and were reduced to making meals of the jungle roots.

*   *   *

Once a thousand people had lived in the valley to which Lutken now came. He stood on a high ridge and looked across the green jungles to the mountains on the far side. Where had all the people gone? Why had they gone away? The Kachins had a strange answer.

"It is because of the weretigers, duwa," said the jaiwa.

The other Kachins nodded their heads. They refused to enter the valley. It was one thing to fight the Japanese, but it was another thing to enter the domain of the magic tigers. No bullet or spear could wound them.

"A Kachin hunting party went in the valley," the jaiwa said. "It was only a week ago, and the men sat around their fire in the night. Suddenly several tigers attacked out of the jungle. One jumped over the fire, seized a hunter by his waist, and escaped. The hunters fired at him, but their bullets could not harm him."

"A Japanese patrol passed through the valley only ten days ago," continued the jaiwa. "In the middle of the valley they camped on a river bank. That night the tigers attacked the camp and ate all of the Japanese."

Lutken's Kachins built their campfires on the high ridge overlooking the valley, but they would not agree to cross the valley in the morning. Other 101 men have thought that perhaps they were haunted by ancestral fears of the giant tigers of the Burma jungles and imagined that weretigers existed. After Peter Lutken entered the valley, and after I too had an experience with a tiger at Sinlumkaba that same year, neither of us will ever be certain.

My tiger came in the night. I was sleeping in a stone rest house built by the British at Sinlumkaba, high in the mountains close to the Chinese border. The heavy wooden door of the house was closed, but the catch had long since been broken off, and it would not fasten. Sometimes in the night a gust of wind blowing through the valley would push the door open. We slept with our feet to the door. On my right was Mike, the Hindu radio operator who had walked into Sinlumkaba with me, and on my left was Ngai Tawng. We'd been playing cards late by candlelight, and I had won, which was not the rule. It was surprising how rapidly Kachins, even a youngster like Ngai Tawng, could learn to play winning cards. I slept soundly.

"Dick!"

Mike was shaking me awake.

"What's the matter with you?" I growled.

"Dick! Wake up, there's a tiger outside the door!"

I listened. Something was scratching at the door.

"You're crazy. It's just a dog."

"No, it's a tiger. That's his claws."

Ngai Tawng slept peacefully. I sleepily reasoned that if there was indeed a tiger outside, a Kachin boy was more likely to know it than a pudgy Indian who had been born and raised in Calcutta. Mike insisted.

"Get your carbine," he said. "It is a tiger!"

"Mike, damn it all, go back to sleep. Last night you had an attack of malaria and kept us awake most of the night, and now you've got an attack of the tigers."

Despite Mike, I went back to sleep. In the morning we went to the door and opened it. There were enormous pugs to show where a tiger had indeed come up the house, encircled it, paused at the door, and scratched his claws against it. With the slightest pressure, he could easily have opened the door and in one or two bounds been upon us. Even in the morning light I felt an involuntary shiver, but I was not nearly so frightened as Ngai Tawng. He stared at the tracks, his eyes round.

"Duwa Dick," he said in a shaking voice. "The tiger has five toes."

"Does it matter how many toes a tiger has?" I said. "I know people who have cats with five and even six toes."

"Duwa Dick," he said. "Only a weretiger has five toes, same as a man has five fingers."

I could see that the boy was very frightened for the first time since he had joined us. I put my arm around his shoulders.

"Don't worry," I assured him. "The tiger won't be back tonight."

"That is so," he said. "If he wanted one of us, he could have had us last night. He won't bother us again."

Nothing more was said about weretigers until one night when our company of American-Kachin Rangers camped in the Loilun Mountains. Hiram Pamplin was sick with dysentery, which had so weakened him he could scarcely keep to the trail. He managed to move ahead only by supporting himself with the stock of his rifle. We stopped by the trail, and Stan Spector, our radio operator, and I saw to it that he was made as comfortable in his sleeping bag as possible. We set up the camp, and a chill mist came swirling down around us. A few days before, the jaiwa of a village through which we passed had joined us. Unlike most jaiwas I met among the Kachins, he was a very supercilious and overbearing man, who took to bossing the hypenlas, which immediately antagonized their officers. They were afraid to talk back to him because they believed that he was able to play magical tricks. The night before, he had placed a C-ration can in the coals of a fire just as he had seen the soldiers do. He had not punched holes in the can to let the steam escape, as the others had done. He stood warming his backside at the fire, waiting for the C rations to warm up to his liking. A loud pop, and the can flew up and struck him in the seat. He howled with surprise and felt himself ruefully. Everybody laughed but Ngai Tawng, who punched holes in another can, placed it among the coals, and when it was ready, brought it to the jaiwa with the respect that a Kachin boy properly owes to a village elder. The jaiwa, who had been sulking at the side of the camp, accepted the tin of food. From then on he not only favored Ngai Tawng, but he quit making a nuisance of himself.

Tonight, as I sat by the fire warming myself, Ngai Tawng came up with the jaiwa at his side. Stan Spector had gone off with some Kachins to keep his regular radio schedule with Area I headquarters. Ngai Tawng squatted on his heels beside the fire, and the jaiwa squatted beside him.

"The jaiwa wishes to be our friend," said Ngai Tawng.

"That is good, for we are his friends," I said.

We sat for a while, and the mists whirled closer.

"Do you remember the time at Sinlumkaba when the weretiger came, and you doubted that it was a weretiger?" Ngai Tawng asked me.

"I remember, and I still doubt."

The jaiwa listened.

"Some villages are well known for their weretigers," he said. "There is said to be one near Sinlumkaba, to the east and closer to the Chinese border. You have to know the right spells to turn into a weretiger, and those people know the spells. My village also has men who know the spells."

"How do you turn into a weretiger?" I asked.

Whenever a jaiwa tells a legend of his people, sings one of the old ballads, or speaks of magic lore, he sucks in air through a puckered mouth as if he is fanning his imagination with his own breath. He alters his voice to speak in a reedy whisper. The jaiwa spoke in this soothsayer's voice.

"You must take off all your clothing so that you are naked before the night spirit. The clothing should be rolled into a neat bundle. Then you must throw yourself naked on the ground. You roll from side to side as a tiger rolls in its ecstasy, and you say the incantations. As you roll, your body lengthens, and your head flattens and changes its place in relation to your shoulders so that it is as a tiger's head. A tail appears from your tailbone, and your legs and arms turn to paws. Your nails grow into claws, and your body grows stronger and furrier and striped until you are a tiger. When you speak, you growl, and when you shout, you roar."

The strange voice and the strange words filled me with dread, for the thought came to me that perhaps this very jaiwa could turn himself into a tiger. The thought had occurred to Ngai Tawng too, and he spoke to the jaiwa in a very respectful, almost pleading voice.

"How can a weretiger become a man again?"

"The tiger goes about his business of killing and devouring his prey. He may seek vengeance on a villager who has become his enemy. He may seek the flesh of a woman. He may devour his own wife or his daughter, but he often prefers to enjoy instead the firm flesh of a young boy."

The jaiwa stopped to look almost hungrily at Ngai Tawng, who hunkered down farther on his heels with a stricken look on his face.

"A tiger may roam for many miles, and he may be away from his village for weeks, but at last he comes back to where he has left his clothing. When he sees the clothing lying on the ground, he may then turn back into a man. He rolls and stretches and grows smaller and once again takes on his human form. He puts his clothing back on and returns to his village."

Lutken, sitting in his camp with the Kachins and looking down on the valley that the Kachins said was infested with weretigers, knew that there was something down there in the dark that had frightened his brave Kachins. He called the duwa to him. According to his maps, the valley was forty-two miles across.

"Will you cross the valley if we make the entire trip between dawn and sunset?" he asked. "I promise you that we will not camp in the valley or be in it when the night comes."

Even with Lutken's reassurances the duwa was not at all happy about telling the men that they must cross the valley. The fires were kept high all that night. The men jammed close together about the fire to sleep.

"I slept in a hammock," Lutken recalls. "Usually I slept by myself, but that night the Kachins jostled one another to sleep beneath me."

At first light, the company ate breakfast in haste.

"I've never eaten so fast," Lutken says. "I've never walked so fast or so far as when crossing that valley either. There was not a sound or a single clank of equipment as we went down the trail that led down into the valley. I got a foreboding feeling. The valley was dark with a canopy of giant trees, and the cover along the trail was, nevertheless, thick. It was muddy."

At noon the hurrying Kachins reached the river that flowed through the heart of the valley. It was clear that there, beneath a large banyan tree, the Japanese patrol had camped. The supplies and equipment of the patrol were scattered about as if a violent storm had struck. There were struggle marks, but no signs of the soldiers. Everywhere were enormous tiger pugs. Somebody had carved "TIGER" in English on the trunk of the trees. "Run, don't camp here" was carved beneath it in smaller letters. Nearby on the trunk a similar warning was cut into the bark in Burmese script.

"I guess the Japanese couldn't read either English or Burmese," Lutken told me.

The Kachins glanced at the havoc about them and forded the stream without a moment's pause. They ran on up the trail with Lutken, for once, puffing along behind them. They did not even pause when they passed by a half-eaten Japanese soldier decomposing by the trail. Lutken didn't pause either. Terror chased after the fleeing men. They did not stop running until they were well up on the mountain on the far side of the valley. They kept moving, glancing fearfully behind them. Finally at midnight, when they were well out of the valley, the hypenlas stopped their flight and collapsed in exhaustion. Even then they started up from their sleep to look in terror back down the trail toward the valley of the weretigers.

Pete Lutken and his Kachins climbed up the trails into the high mountains in search of a prosperous village where they could establish a base from which to attack the Japanese. When they did find such a place, they discovered that it was suffering from smallpox.

Forty-two of the villagers, mostly children, had died of the disease. Lutken pressed on until he came to Unding Bum, which was only five miles southwest of a Japanese regimental headquarters. It was now April, 1944.

# Galahad

At Quebec Roosevelt and Churchill had given the name Galahad to the combined operations of the Chinese army in North Burma and the American 5307th Composite Group against Japanese-held Myit-kyina. Brigadier General Frank Merrill, who commanded the 5307th, took a jeep ride in late January, 1944, with James Shepley of *Time* and *Life* to watch his men practice crossing a river near Ledo. In only a few days the American force was to start over the partially built Ledo Road to Shingbwiyang in the Hukawng Valley of Burma. The Chinese army was stalled in the northern Hukawng, and the Americans were expected to make a wide flanking movement from Shingbwiyang around the contending Chinese and Japanese and establish roadblocks in the rear of the enemy. It was an adventurous and dangerous prospect. Certainly, Shepley maintained, there must be a more colorful name than the 5307th Composite Group.

"It has no appeal," he told General Merrill. "I'm going to call your outfit 'Merrill's Marauders.' "

Ray Peers was returning to Nazira, and he flew into Ledo to pick up a jeep and drive to the area where the Marauders were camped. There he talked to General Merrill and Colonel Charles Hunter. They explained to the 101 commander what they were going to do.

"Their first job was to get the unit assembled at or near Shing-bwiyang," wrote Peers after the war. "General Merrill said that in order to condition the troops and to serve as a shakedown he was going to move the unit from Ledo to Shingbwiyang by foot over the Naga Hills portion of the Ledo Road which was then under con-struction. I advised him against it, and suggested he fly or truck them over. An individual has only so much stamina in the jungle, and after periods of exertion must be rested. . . ."

Peers explained that Detachment 101 had discovered this the hard way in its behind-the-lines operations.

"We believed in going full out when we had to, but our personnel were taught to conserve their strength, rest, and eat whenever they could."

Merrill and Hunter listened to Peers, but they were adamant. Their men were ordered to march the 125 miles over the muddy road through Hell's Fire Pass to Shingbwiyang. From Shingbwiyang they struck on through the jungles for another one hundred miles or so before fighting their first engagement at Walawbum on the proposed route of the Ledo Road south of Maingkwan, which the Chinese were now approaching. Before they were to arrive at Myitkyina, the Marauders were fated to march some 750 miles through the jungle.

"This took a lot of reserve stamina out of them," remarks Peers, "and it was only a question of time before the remainder ran out."

The intention of military planners at the Quebec Conference was that the 5307th Composite Group should be trained by Orde Wingate as part of his Long Range Penetration Groups and directed by him in the field, but Stilwell, seeking a more clearly defined role for American arms, had succeeded in detaching the unit for service under his own direction. Stilwell's choice of General Merrill to serve as the 5307th commander was controversial when he made it, and it became more controversial as the Marauders played their role in the campaign to take Myitkyina. The men of 101 and the Marauders alike still speculate as to what might have happened if an officer with the instincts and experience of Wingate or 101's own Carl Eifler or Ray Peers had commanded the Marauders instead of Frank Merrill, who was inexperienced in jungle warfare. Certainly, critical errors in judgment led to subsequent command difficulties that, before the campaign was concluded, came to reflect upon American arms. If Wingate had been present at Peers's side when he tried to dissuade Merrill from marching his men to Shingbwiyang, he would have given him strong support. The British general, the greatest exponent of Long Range Penetration Groups in this century, believed that in jungle warfare a group such as the Marauders could not keep up its effectiveness for more than three months without being pulled out of the field for a recuperation period.

*        *        *

At Shingbwiyang General Merrill was rightfully uneasy about the map. There was Walawbum, but could his men ever find it? Their route led through poorly mapped country. Pete Lutken had not yet gone south with Dow Grones, and Merrill asked him to provide a Kachin guide. Lutken talked to his Kachins, and they all recommended a famous rhinoceros hunter who knew every part of the jungle. Chinese traders were willing to buy all the rhino horn that he could bring out of the jungle, because in their country aging men prized a concoction made from powdered horn as a means of restoring their virility. The hunter's pursuit of the beasts had brought him far and wide. Unfortunately, he was already far off in the jungles through which the Marauders must make their way.

Ndigu Ga, the hunter's twelve-year-old son, came to Lutken's camp in place of his father. Lutken looked at the slight boy. He had learned that many Kachin boys of twelve already had a substantial claim on man's estate, but it was still hard to take the youngster seriously.

"I will go in the place of my father," Ndigu Ga said.

"Do you know this country?"

"Yes, I do."

"Do you think you can get them across?"

"I went with my father."

Pete Lutken took Ndigu Ga to General Merrill, who stared at him with amazement.

"He is the best guide we have," said Lutken. "He will take you to Walawbum."

Merrill grimaced, but he had little alternative. Unerringly, Ndigu Ga led the American fighting men of the 2d and 3d battalions with their 360 American mules and 340 Australian horses over the trails to Walawbum. Just before the village of Lagang Ga the second battalion turned off the trail and circled westward through Wesu Ga and across the Numpyek River to intercept the Walawbum Road three miles the other side of the town. The third battalion continued on to Walawbum itself, and the first battalion remained in the rear as a reserve. Before the campaign was concluded, all of the horses were to die in the jungle, but the mules in the main were sturdy enough to survive.

\* \* \*

Jim Tilly had reached Detachment 101 in August, 1943. He had been recruited into OSS from the ski troops training in Colorado, so according to military lights, it was only logical that he should be sent to tropical Assam on his first assignment. When he reported to Carl

Eifler, the tall, pink-cheeked young man snapped off a regulation salute.

"Cut that crap," snarled Eifler. "Just tell me the story of your life."

Taken aback, Tilly muttered something about flying.

"Eifler immediately appointed me as pilot for the organization," Tilly remembers, "notwithstanding the fact I was color-blind and not qualified by the army to fly."

Fortunately, there were as yet no planes in the detachment. As Tilly puts it, "I started as messenger, pilot, mess officer, instructor, and censor. In December, 1943, I drew the short straw, was issued an old ragged parachute, and was pushed out the door into the Knothead area by Tom Riley."

Tilly was put to work extending the runway at Nawbum to fifteen hundred feet. He had no engineering background, no mechanized equipment, but hundreds of willing Kachins.

"I can do it in three weeks," he told Eifler.

"You can do it in three days," roared Eifler.

Tilly had the job done in a little over three days. In the jungles he took to wearing a wraparound, blue Kachin longyi that reached halfway down his calf, topped by a GI khaki shirt. By the time Merrill's Marauders were following young Ndigu Ga through the jungles to Walawbum, Tilly was already a veteran guerrilla leader. He commanded a unit of fifty of Zhing Htaw Naw's men. Now, as the Americans advanced, Tilly and the Kachins attacked the Japanese positions that lay ahead of them. In four days, according to 101 reports, they killed an estimated 150 Japanese, blew up supply dumps, and burned Japanese trucks without suffering a single casualty. They slipped into the jungle, leaving the Japanese demoralized.

The Marauders came out of the jungle from the northeast guided by the Kachin boy, and set up a roadblock on the road over which the Japanese army moved supplies from Moang to Walawbum and Maingkwan. Before the war Maingkwan, the most important Kachin town in the Hukawng Valley domain of Zhing Htaw Naw, had been the place where teak rafts were made up on the Uyu River. They were floated down the Uyu to Homalin on the Chindwin and on down that turbulent river to the Irrawaddy. The fall of Maingkwan would be both a tactical and psychological blow to the Japanese—it was here that they had massacred all the boys of the town. With the Chinese approaching from the northwest, and the Marauders' roadblock cutting off supplies, the Japanese found themselves in difficulty. Things might have been worse for them had they not discovered an alternate trail that bypassed the roadblock. They widened the track so that their motor transport could move over it. The new lifeline was critical, and in order to protect it the Japanese threw a strong force against the Marauders. They attacked across a stream and were mowed down by the hundreds as they made charge after charge. It was heroism, but it was futile. About 850 Japanese were killed, and only seven Americans wounded.

The Japanese began to withdraw from Maingkwan to escape being cut off by the Marauders, but the Chinese caught the rear guard still in the town. The fighting raged through the jungles nearby with both sides losing from two to three thousand men. When the battle was over, the Chinese had gained the town. The Allies had won a signal victory over General Tanaka's army, and the way was now open for the advance south through the Hukawng Valley toward Myitkyina.

Behind the Japanese, now withdrawing before the combined Americans and Chinese, the American-Kachin Rangers struck with fury. Zhing Htaw Naw and his people were fighting for the freedom of the Hukawng and seeking a bloody vengeance for the destruction of their villages. Reinforcements hurrying to the front were ambushed and slaughtered. The psychological effect of a Kachin ambush was a terrifying thing to the once-confident Japanese. They employed jungle materials in what seemed to their enemy to be the most fiendish of ways. When hunting wild pigs in the jungle, the Kachins planted pungyis, bamboo stakes, sharpened and hardened in the fire. They hammered the rounded ends into the ground for a depth of about two feet so that the stakes were rigid. About two feet of the stake stuck out of the ground. Then they drove the pigs into the pungyis so that they were impaled and easily slaughtered. If a pig could be hunted in this fashion, why not a Japanese?

They concealed the pungyis behind fallen logs and in tall grass or jungle shrubbery beside the trail. Some pungyis were ankle-high, some knee- or hip-high, and some just the right height to stab a man in the throat or the chest. Shorter pungyis tripped a soldier trying to take cover from gunfire so that he fell on the longer ones. The Kachins, who were familiar with dozens of jungle poisons, wanted to poison the stakes as well, but 101 men drew the line at this. Once the Kachins had learned the use of hand grenades, they also strung twenty-five to fifty of these at intervals of five yards or so, connected by an electric wire to a detonator so as to make the ambush even more deadly. An OSS report on Kachin warfare states that, "Every operation was planned to effect maximum surprise, to have a short period of violent shock action, and then disperse before the enemy could react."

The Kachins were masterful in setting up the ambush. They positioned themselves so as to enfilade the trail with gunfire. Ray Peers describes the Kachin methods:

"The first requisite was a proper ambush site along a well-used Japanese trail. A site overgrown with heavy jungle foliage was the most desirable, and the Kachins would take particular pains to insure that it appeared natural, no broken branches, no disturbance of any kind. There were numerous plants along the jungle trails which could forecast the ambush; if touched, they wilted immediately. The guerrillas knew everything there was to know not only about the enemy's movements, but about rocks, plants, trees, weather. Their efficiency was based on knowledge of all things. They undertook an ambush with the same preoccupation one finds in an architect planning a building."

Kachin scouts peering out at the Japanese from the jungle were responsible for tracking Japanese movements with exaction. The Kachin architects of Japanese disaster sometimes would fall to work at a certain point unless they had received a report on their adversaries' positions. I once asked a Kachin hypenla why he considered a certain spot suitable for entrapping the Japanese.

"The jaiwa has said it will be," he said.

Not only the jaiwas but even the youngest hypenlas seemed to be able to fathom the Japanese movements through some sixth sense, and their hunches as to what the Japanese were doing usually proved right. If the Japanese were following a native guide along the trail, the Kachin fire spared him. This was not because of humane feelings but simply because almost all the guides the Japanese were able to find were, in fact, 101 agents, who were doing their best to make sure the Japanese either went astray or fell into an ambush.

Nor was a Kachin ambush a simple one-stage affair. It was a sophisticated enterprise when arranged by a man such as Zhing Htaw Naw. The Kachins likened their system of ambushes to the two hands of a man. They conveniently overlooked the thumb and said that the four fingers of the hand stood for four ambush points. This meant that a company of American-Kachin Rangers could ambush four trail points at once. After a Japanese force struck the ambush points, the four fingers of each hand pulled back to two additional ambush points, represented by two clenched fists. When the Japanese in turn struck these two points, the Kachins would fall back to a pre-arranged rendezvous point a safe number of miles away from where they could move off into the jungles to look for another place to trap the Japanese.

The veteran Japanese troops holding the front were appalled to find themselves fighting a two-front war. Nothing like this had happened during their conquest of Malaya or their victorious drive through Burma. The Kachins were the devil's breed. As they retreated before the Americans and Chinese, fighting every inch of the way, they had to combat a cruel and cunning enemy who were attacking behind their lines, fading into the jungle only to attack again in some unexpected place scores of miles away. The guerrillas' amazing mobility dismayed the Japanese commanders.

*   *   *

At Tingkrung Hka, about halfway to Shadazup, a force of Japanese held the village on the riverbank against the Marauders who, after the Allied victories at Maingkwan and Walawbum, were coming down through the Hukawng. The Chinese were moving up to support the advance. Tilly and his Kachins from the Knothead group came up on the other side of the village and attacked the Japanese, who imagined that the Marauders and the Kachins were acting in concert against them. The Japanese withdrew. In reality the Marauders had no idea that the Kachins were even there and were mystified as to why the Japanese suddenly broke off the engagement. The Marauders pushed on. They learned in their turn about the way in which bamboo can slash a man, how ugly leeches can be to both man and beast. They set up camp in the dusk.

"Hey, Yank, don't shoot!" somebody was shouting from the trail.

Undoubtedly, it was a Japanese trick, and the Marauders on perimeter duty released the safety catches on their M-1s.

"We are friends! Hey Yank, don't shoot!" came the voice again.

Jim Tilly of Detachment 101 came into view in his blue longyi at the head of a small column of Kachins. Charlton Ogburn, Jr., in his book *The Marauders* describes the appearance of the first detachment of American-Kachin Rangers that they were to encounter.

"His innocent-looking young cutthroats under their Aussie hats with the broad brims turned up rakishly on the side appeared both businesslike and touching, especially when he brought them to attention before Colonel Osborne, himself doing about-face and saluting with parade-ground formality."

The Marauders stayed overnight at the Kachins' hideout at Jaiwa Ga. They camped among paddy fields on a ridge, and with the jungle people guarding the perimeter they could sleep with a welcome feeling of security.

Some of the officers sat with Tilly and the Kachin leaders in the village duwa's basha. Tilly and the Kachins smoked a pipe of opium. Phil Weld and Sam Wilson, young Marauder officers, were there, and as they watched the firelight flickering on the matted walls and listened to the tales of ambushes and escapades behind the Japanese lines, they both determined that when the campaign was over, they would volunteer to join Detachment 101. Tilly's Kachins had captured both the imagination and the heart of the Marauders. Ogburn later wrote, "Waylaying the soldiery of the Japanese invader as they did in their artful ambushes, they made us think of a Robin Hood version of the Boy Scouts, clad, when in uniform at all, in green shirts and shorts. Some of the warriors could not have been above twelve years old, and while some had highly lethal burp guns slung around their necks, others carried ancient muzzle-loading fowling pieces."

It was obvious to the Marauders that the Kachins had a better knowledge of where the Japanese soldiers were than the Japanese commanders did. The good-natured youngsters had an air of competence that won a fighting man's respect. Both the young soldiers and the adults at Jaiwa Ga impressed them with their friendly, open-faced ways, their fine aristocratic features, and their charm. The men could not help but admire the bare-breasted Kachin women and noted that when they gave biscuits or a piece of chocolate to a Kachin child, he thanked them courteously. The Americans who had grown accustomed to the begging children of India noted with approval that a Kachin child never begged. On the other hand, if he could discover any way in which he could be helpful, he immediately did what was necessary. All he expected in return was a smile, a word of approval, or an affectionate hug.

When dawn came, Tilly watched the Marauders saddle up for the next day's march.

"Here goes the front," he remarked rather sadly. "I won't be behind the Japanese lines any more."

\* \* \*

Jim Tilly did not long remain on the safe side of the lines. His American-Kachin Rangers infiltrated over back trails past the Japanese positions. As the Marauders advanced on Shaduzup, northwest of Myitkyina, Tilly and his Kachins broke up every Japanese effort to organize a counterattack. Detachment 101 units under Knothead's direction struck the Japanese from the Mogaung area northward.

From their base at Arang, Pat's units struck at the railroad line that ran between Myitkyina and Mogaung. They blew up nine bridges and wrecked three trains full of essential supplies. They also attacked trucks and staff cars on the roads out of Myitkyina. Their intelligence reports concerning the Japanese efforts to supply and reinforce the crumbling Hukawng front proved extremely timely.

The Japanese, once confident of their skill in the jungle, grew fearful as the jungle people hunted them. A Kachin attack during the day was frightening enough, but the Kachins operated with equal effectiveness at night. On the other hand, the Marauders, knowing that the jungle and its people were on their side, had discovered a new confidence. In early March they captured Shaduzup after a brisk battle.

Inkangahtawng was the next important Japanese-held town. The Marauders struck out along the deep valley of the Tanai River through the jungled foothills of the Kumon Range. Zhing Htaw Naw's men not only scouted the way for the Marauders, but they kept Vince Curl fully informed as to their movements. On March 17, an advance party of the Marauders swung around a bend in the trail and were confronted by a white man in a partly Australian, partly British, and partly American uniform.

"I'll be damned. A goddamned white man way down here in Jap territory," said the man at the point.

The apparition held out his hand.

"Glad you got here, boys. We've been waiting eighteen months for you to arrive."

"Curl supported the finest beard I have ever seen on any human being," wrote Colonel Hunter. "Deep auburn in color, it was carefully brushed back from a precise part in the center of his chin, in two luxuriously flowing waves."

The Marauders had come upon the outer perimeter of Knothead's defenses at Nawbum. The 101 field base was surrounded by trail blocks and trail watchers for twenty miles in each direction so that no Japanese would be able to approach it by surprise. Trip wires had been stretched across trails and attached to sections of dry bamboo strung in the jungle nearby so that anybody approaching would rattle it and give warning. If enemies were expected, the Kachins attached the trip wires to artfully conceal hand grenades. In all directions from Nawbum pungyis were laid to stab a prowler who might try to sneak up on the outpost in the night.

The Kachin villagers welcomed the Marauders to Nawbum. They swapped chickens and fresh eggs, rice and jungle vegetables for American canned goods. Father Stuart presided over a Sunday religious service for the Americans. It was an ecumenical affair from the start. The bearded Catholic priest performed a mass, but the Kachins, who had been taught hymns by the American Baptists, sang *Rock of Ages* in their own language while the Americans sang along in English.

When it came time for the Marauders to push on, the "Myiahprap Hpung," which is Jinghpaw for the "Lightning Force," made up of two hundred Kachins and such 101 men as Jack Pamplin, Vince Curl, Robert Rhea, and Father Stuart, pushed on ahead of them. Before they left, Curl and Kachin elephant boys brought seven elephants in single file, each holding the tail of the one ahead with its trunk. A baby elephant frisked along at the side of his mother. The column halted in front of General Merrill.

"The elephants are at the disposal of Galahad," said Curl.

Merrill gladly accepted the huge animals. He had already lost many of his horses and needed transport. The Missouri mules looked with suspicion at their new partners in military transportation, and the elephants looked back at them with apparent disbelief that any animal with as dubious a parentage as a mule could truly exist. With the American-Kachin Rangers in the lead, the Marauders started on their way. When they crossed the Tanai Hka, the elephants waded into the deep water as if it were a mere puddle. When the water rose over his head the calf used his trunk as a snorkel and trotted across at his mother's side.

Not only were Zhing Htaw Naw's men leading the Marauder advance, but other 101 units were ranging behind the Japanese lines springing ambushes and sabotaging installations. At one point the

Japanese surrounded a battalion of Marauders, but OSS agents Skittles and Hefty, learning of their plight, brought friendly Kachins to the rescue. The Kachins broke the Japanese lines so that the Americans could escape. The Japanese fought fierce delaying actions, but they fell back time and again.

Ahead of the advancing Marauders loomed the Kumon Range and Jambu Bum, the shaggy mountain that separates the Hukawng from the Mogaung valleys. The way to Myitkyina lay through the Mogaung Valley. The Japanese held the key pass in force, and they were convinced that at last the Marauders had advanced as far as they could go. There was no way for them to surmount the lofty, forbidding Kumons.

\* \* \*

General Stilwell followed the advance of his troops with satisfaction. There was no question at all that the dramatic sweep of the Marauders had been made possible by the Kachins of Zhing Htaw Naw, and he determined that he would fly to Nawbum to see the guerrillas at firsthand and meet Vincent Curl and Zhing Htaw Naw himself. General Merrill had already presented the Kachin duwa at Nawbum with one of the first two sniper's rifles with telescopic sights that had been air-dropped into the field. It was known that Zhing Htaw Naw had personally killed something like 150 Japanese since that cruel day in Ngai Tawng's village, and Merrill thought that the rifle might facilitate the Kachin's revenge. Stilwell intended to present the Kachin with the CMA Medal.

An American-Kachin Ranger platoon was drawn up at attention, their young faces solemn. General Stilwell reviewed the Kachins. The duwa kaba stood to the side smiling with approval at the hypenlas' military bearing and precision in the manual of arms. Father Stuart interpreted as the general spoke of the American appreciation for the extraordinary Kachin contribution to the victories in the Hukawng. Then he pinned the medal on Zhing Htaw Naw's chest.

"To the Kachins General Stilwell was the biggest of the duwas," said Ray Peers, who had flown in along with the general. "No greater honor could be paid."

\* \* \*

General Stilwell continued to be fascinated by the American-Kachin Rangers of Detachment 101 and their unorthodox jungle warfare.

For instance he was intrigued by an OSS operational report that Danny Danielewitz and his Kachins had wiped out several hundred Japanese soldiers in an ambush near Indawgyi Lake. This was far behind the Japanese lines. When he learned from Ray Peers that it would be possible for Danielewitz and the Kachin sergeant-major to be flown out, he asked that they be brought to his NCAC headquarters.

Danielewitz was another quixotic 101 man. Only a few months ago Peers had gone to the airstrip outside NCAC headquarters to meet two OSS men, who were arriving from the United States.

"I was not prepared for what I saw," he wrote. "One of them was about five feet five inches tall and about two hundred pounds with a thick beard. The other, about six feet and well put together, had what looked like a violin case under his arm. It couldn't be a violin. I was sure it was a tommy gun and that somebody was pulling my leg, so I made him unpack it. It was a violin all right, and its owner, Lieutenant 'Danny' Danielewitz, assured me it gave him a great deal of pleasure. I was sorely tempted to send both of them back to Nazira to get straightened out, but they were needed so badly in the field that I decided to send them on."

The fat man crashed when he was flown in to Forward. The plane ground-looped when its wheels sank into the mud of the strip under his weight. He proved to be of no service whatsoever. Danielewitz and his violin landed safely at Knothead, and soon Vince Curl sent him south with some of Zhing Htaw Naw's new recruits. Whether or not his violin playing around the campfires at night was the magic ingredient is not known, but Danielewitz developed a remarkable rapport with the Kachins. American rapport with the Kachins was the first step in making an effective guerrilla unit, and reports began to come in from Danielewitz detailing particularly heavy Japanese kills. Such success stories engendered Stilwell's interest.

A 101 liaison plane flew Danielewitz and his top Kachin officer out from a jungle strip in the hills southwest of Myitkyina. Harry Little met them at the strip outside Stilwell's headquarters because Ray Peers was away. Danielewitz was now bearded and had not brought his violin with him, but he was wearing a turban wrapped around his head and a longyi. The Kachin was dressed in shorts, tropical shirt, and military boots, with all his brass and leather "shined like a new silver dollar," as Ray Peers put it. Little took one look at Danielewitz and marched him off to get him cleaned up, shaved, and into a uniform that would not shock General Stilwell. Then, with a 101 interpreter, he ushered the field men in to the general.

Stilwell asked all sorts if questions, and everything went very well until the general asked, "How do I know how many you actually killed?"

The Kachin unfastened a bamboo tube tied to his belt and shook out what looked like dried apricots onto a table before the general.

"What are those?" asked Stilwell.

"Japanese ears," replied the Kachin. "Divide by two and you will know how many Japs were killed."

Stilwell was convinced, but he also summoned Ray Peers immediately upon his return to Nazira.

"When I arrived," recalls Peers, "he asked me if I had heard of the Kachin practice of removing the ears of their victims. I could only admit that I had heard of it, but had never seen the results of any such practice. He then quoted to me chapter and verse of pertinent sections of the Rules of Land Warfare, which said the bodies of the dead were not to be mutilated. Moreover, he directed that I take whatever action was necessary to have it stopped immediately."

Peers discovered that this was easier said than done. The Kachins had been taking heads for hundreds of years, and it had been a substantial accomplishment on the part of 101 men serving with them to get them to be content with the ears only. To a Kachin the procedure was simply a convenient way to tally the dead—far more efficient than counting on fingers and toes and a very convincing way of reporting to a Kachin superior.

"Under strict direction and supervision the area commanders were able to bring it gradually under control, but it was nearly six months before we had it entirely eradicated from all of the Kachin Ranger forces," states Peers.

Several months after General Stilwell had ordered Ray Peers to end the Kachins' penchant for cutting off Japanese ears I had my first experience with their method of tallying. One night as I traveled through the Loilun Range with a small party of Kachins, we stopped in a village inhabited by Chinese, whose ancestors had crossed over the border several centuries ago. We put our sleeping bags down that night atop brick sleeping hearths, beneath which a fire could be kindled to ward off the night's chill. The fleas chewed on us unmercifully. In the morning a wizened old Kachin came into the village.

"Who is this?" I asked Ngai Tawng.

"He is a 101 agent who is in the employ of Lazum Tang."

In the Sinlumkaba Hills, Lazum Tang was every bit as illustrious a duwa kaba and American-Kachin Ranger leader as was Zhing Htaw Naw in the Hukawng, and some who knew him well considered him even more important. Ngai Tawng helped me find out what the man wanted. He had learned we were in the area, and he had come to report.

"Kachins from my village have killed many Japanese," he claimed, scratching his gnarled calf with a horny left foot.

"Tell him that this is very fine, but how many did he kill?" I asked, being just as naive as General Stilwell had been.

The old man carefully took a package of bamboo leaves from out of his longyi and unwrapped it. Out tumbled some two-score human ears, all quite recently severed. Their hapless owners had been Japanese stragglers from the forces falling back toward the Burma Road to the east. My stomach jumped.

"He wants you to buy them," said Ngai Tawng, who never failed to be amused at what he considered to be my odd American sensitivities.

I felt thorough disgust.

"You expect me to behave like the hair-buyer of Detroit!"

Later on, Ngai Tawng insisted upon knowing all about the British commander at Detroit who had paid American Indians for the scalps of settlers on the American frontier, but now he merely stated, "You will have to buy them, duwa Dick."

I protested, but I finally turned over a stack of silver rupees for the ears. Lazum Tang had made a promise that must be honored. I took them to Mongwi where I gave them to Pete Joost.

"You, of all people to be bringing me something like this," he said with his jovial grin. "Go give them a decent burial."

I dug a hole and buried the ears. It was not always an easy thing to be an American in the American-Kachin Rangers. The Kachins had a habit of getting their own way more often than not, and only a man with the character and determination of Ray Peers would have even tried to stop the Kachins' ear-taking, let alone have succeeded in making his ruling stick.

*     *     *

The major Japanese offensive to break through into India began in February when a force of 125,000 men swept toward Imphal and

Kohima. Their advance units reached within three miles of the Bengal and Assam Railroad, over which all the Allied supplies for the entire North Burma campaign were moving. It was a rugged hilly area with almost impenetrable copses of bamboo, but though the Japanese found the terrain anything but favorable to their offensive, the veteran divisions did not falter.

Badly mauled by the advancing Japanese, the British 14th Army withdrew but fought back with a tenacity that began to tell on their enemies. At one point, as the Japanese threatened Kohima, the British brought back every soldier and weapon they had all the way to the Ledo terminus of the Ledo Road. In all, 20,000 British were stripped from other less vulnerable points to help meet the attack.

Even as the Japanese advanced, American-Kachin Ranger units were threatening their rear and harassing their transport bringing supplies to the front. One Kachin force burned eleven warehouses full of supplies and badly needed equipment. They infiltrated a motor park and destroyed at least forty trucks and ten artillery pieces. Ten especially trained Kachin demolitionists and an American roamed up and down the railroad supply line at will. They blew up five bridges and derailed and shot up three trains. The Japanese, it appeared, were about to sever the Allies' supply jugular leading through Assam, but at the same time their own supply jugular through Burma was bleeding their offensive to death. As the Japanese strength was spent, their offensive was first blunted and then turned back on itself. The powerful Japanese force that had invaded India now retreated toward Mandalay. Kachins led by Dow Grones and Pete Lutken continued their guerrilla attacks on the Japanese as they withdrew.

# Chindits

When General Donovan was at Nazira in December, he called Pete Joost to him. In his college days Sherman B. Joost had been the captain of the Princeton boxing team. He was a well-muscled, urbane, cheerful man, who out of boredom with the diplomatic cocktail circuit in Washington had joined the OSS in the hope of undertaking a mission to Afghanistan. When Joost reached India, he was instead directed to join Detachment 101. Over the months that followed, he had proved himself extraordinarily competent in the planning and execution of training and supply missions.

"I want you to report to Flip Cochran as the OSS liaison officer," Donovan told Joost.

At Quebec General Arnold had promised Wingate that the first Air Commando Force would be formed as an elite glider unit to carry his Chindits on their second long-range penetration into Burma. Named for the chinthe, stone lion-headed dragons that guard the entrance to Burmese pagodas from evil, the Chindits were dedicated to rescuing Burma itself from evil—that is, from the Japanese invaders. The commanding officer of the 1st Air Command was as legendary a person as Wingate himself. Colonel Philip Cochran had, incredibly enough, been given fame as Flip Cochran in cartoonist Milton Caniff's strip, "Terry and the Pirates." After participating in the invasion of North Africa, Cochran had undertaken his assignment in India with characteristic elan. Pete Joost reported to him at Lalaghat in January, 1944, and immediately pitched in to help shape the supply and glider training for the two divisions of polyglot troops that Wingate had assembled. At the same time, he kept Ray Peers informed as to the Chindits' progress. He also passed on 101 intelligence reports concerning the Koukkwee Valley into which the Chindits were to swoop, not far from where Detachment 101's A Group

(Above) On the trail through the lowlands the Kachins seemed out of their element. (Below) Coffy, Wilkinson and Larsen relax over coffee and cigarettes at La-awn-Ga, a Kachin village deep in the the wilderness Triangle.

(Clockwise from bottom left) Kachin villagers knew the paths that led over the mountains. The Mali Hka ripples past a 101 party. The Kachins hiked as much as 50 miles in a single day. Dick Dunlop (left) and Pierce Ellis trained together in Washington. Ellis went with Roger Hillsman on a key mission to the British army.

(Clockwise from bottom left) Hiram Pamplin, one of the most outstanding field commanders, always had time for Kachin villagers. Dick Dunlop and Ngai Tawng stayed at this Buddhist temple at Mongwi before crossing the Loilun Range to the Hosi Valley fight. Ah Tha, a typical good-natured Kachin boy, was badly hurt in a grenade explosion. He was nursed back to health only to lose his life in a second blast. 101 men had room in their hearts for Kachin kids, stray pups, and for Lucy, the orphaned tiger cub.

(Clockwise from bottom left) Kachin hypenlas were fond of gambling. Americans and Kachins listen as a Kachin jaiwa narrates a new ballad of the American-Kachin Rangers. The coveted CMA Medal is presented to Kachin heroes. A hypenla displays his CMA medal with the pride of a warrior race that once again had won the victory against a formidable foe.

(Above) Kachin emblems of victory rise from a throng of Kachin soldiers who have come to Sinlumkaba to be mustered out of the American-Kachin Rangers. (Below) The Kachins, in festive costumes, celebrated the end of the Burma campaign.

had established its temporary base over a year before. The Chindits were to disrupt the Japanese rear and divert forces away from the fighting in the Hukawng Valley as the Americans and Chinese continued their drive on Myitkyina from the northwest. They were to cut off communications and supplies by interdicting the railroad and roads that connected South Burma with Myitkyina.

The Chindits were indeed a polyglot outfit. The unit included Scots of the Black Watch, Gurkhas, Sikhs, twelve 101 Kachins under agent Saw Judson, West Africans, Nigerians, and some hefty black soldiers of the King's East African Rifles, in which Idi Amin, of dubious future fame and uncertain tenure as the president of Uganda, served as a sergeant. Training these men for the glider operation tried the patience and teaching talents of both Cochran and Joost. The training doubtless tried the Chindits as well. One doughty black came to his British commanding officer to warn him about the Americans and their flying machines.

"Sir, I am not afraid to fly," he said, "but I must tell you that those airplanes have no motors!"

This soldier's apprehensions were no doubt cleared up during the first practice exercises. C-47s lofted the gliders into the air. There were fifteen of them, each containing a dozen armed men. When the training was completed, a dress rehearsal of the landing in the Koukkwee Valley was held in India. Lord Louis Mountbatten and his staff were on hand for the demonstration.

"The most impressive sight I have ever seen," said Mountbatten.

On March 8, 1944, in the late afternoon, the Chindits boarded the gliders at Hailakandi. Each C-47 was prepared to pull two gliders aloft. The entire flotilla made an impressive sight, covering about a mile and a half of the airfield. Their destination was Burma. Some of the men were to be landed at a paddy named Broadway, to please the Americans, and the others at a paddy named Piccadilly, to please the British.

"The C-47s were roaring their motors," Joost told me, "when a Photo Recon plane came flying in and landed. There were fresh pictures of the landing zones. Huge teak logs were scattered all over Piccadilly. The big question then was, did the Japanese know of the Chindits' plans? Had they scattered the logs around on purpose? Were they going to be waiting? If so, the whole project was suicide. What about Broadway? Well, there were no logs on Broadway.

"We all wondered what Wingate would do. He stood there pulling at his beard while he studied the pictures. Flip Cochran and the rest of us argued either for a postponement or for a go-ahead. Wingate made his decision. 'We'll land both divisions at Broadway,' he said."

Joost ran to the lead glider on the third plane, to which he had been assigned, together with some Africans and Kachins. He checked his pack, his ammunition, his loaded-for-action tommy gun, a carbine, a .45, and an assortment of grenades.

"I was more than ready to take on a regiment of Japanese all by myself," he recalled with amusement. Once in the field, he traveled light, as did all successful guerrillas, and this meant toting along only the essential military hardware.

Joost strapped himself into his narrow seat. There was a tense moment. Nobody talked or even seemed to breathe. The takeoff was smooth, and the C-47 roared ahead toward the Naga Hills, pulling the gliders behind it. When the planes and their gliders reached the Koukkwee Valley, the moon had risen. The paddy was below. The C-47 dropped down, circled, and returned to make a final pass over the field which, to Joost craning his neck out the window, looked as small as a postage stamp. The American pilot of the glider cut loose from the C-47, and the glider drifted gently and serenely down toward the landing.

As soon as the glider plowed across the field to a stop, Joost and the others jumped out and pulled it out of the way of the gliders yet to come. They had scarcely made it to the edge of the field before the next glider came streaking in to its landing. The first six gliders landed safely, but the seventh split wide open on the remains of a dike in the middle of the field. Before the wreck could be gotten out of the way, the eighth glider plowed into it, and after that, glider after glider followed until there was a mass of wreckage. Dying and injured men moaned in their anguish. Ninety men were killed, and as many injured, but 125 gliders managed to ferry 1500 Chindits 100 miles behind the Japanese lines.

Perimeters were posted. Saw Judson knew the valley well from his experience there with A Group, and he quickly moved his Kachins out into Kachin villages and covered strategic points on the trails that surrounded Broadway. The agents made so many lasting friendships in the villages that when the Chindits were withdrawn, they were able to stay on and gather additional intelligence for 101 and organize still more guerrilla units among the Kachins of the Koukkwee Valley. The Kachin agents brought in reassuring reports. Apparently the

Japanese, who were only about fifteen miles away, had no idea that the Chindits had landed. They were making no countermoves.

The next day's activities ended the secrecy. C-47s flew into the paddy field to disgorge bulldozers, other equipment, and engineers to construct an air base. The Chindits formed into strike columns and hurried through the jungle to attack the Japanese. Soon Japanese bombers arrived and dropped their bombs on the field, but the Chindits withstood the attack. When a Japanese force of five hundred men at last moved against Broadway a few days later, three hundred Gurkhas surprised their camp at dawn and wiped them out. Now the Chindits set about their business of disrupting Japanese communications and supply routes and drawing off Japanese troops not only from the Hukawng campaign but also from the Japanese attack on India itself, which had already begun with an attack on the British forces defending Akyab in the south of Burma. Since November, 1943, the Japanese had increased their divisions in Burma from five to eighteen in preparation for the invasion of India.

When Franklin Roosevelt was given a report on the successful landing of the Chindits, he wrote to Winston Churchill, "I am thrilled by the news of our success under Wingate. If you wire him, please give him my hearty good wishes. May the good work go on. This marks an epic achievement for the airborne troops, not forgetting the mules."

The mules had gotten into the gliders with the men, and now that the Chindits were on the ground, their sturdy backs were carrying the heavy equipment and supplies down the jungle trails as the Chindits pressed home their attacks on railroads and highways.

Pete Joost joined the Dah Force—seventy Kachins with British officers, who were to slash across Burma (with the speed of a flashing dah) into the Sinlumkaba Hills to contact the Kachins of that region. It was two hundred miles from the Koukkwee Valley to Sinlumkaba, the Kachin capital in the hills. On the way, the Dah Force was to harass Japanese transport, but it was to make sure its main mission was not jeopardized by knocking out a few trucks. Six days after the Chindits landed at Broadway, the Dah Force moved out on the trail. They followed the route taken by A Group on its way out of the valley, and just as A Group had been, they were pursued by the Japanese. Some two hundred Japanese soldiers brushed time and again with the Dah Force's rear guard to which Joost had been assigned. In its flight from the Koukkwee Valley A Group had eluded the Japanese because of the jungle craft of their young Kachin guides and because they were smaller in number. The Dah Force's British commanders did not give the Kachins any say in the route they were taking, and, in any case, it would have been difficult for such a large number of men to conceal the direction it had gone. At night the men slept in villages after the Kachins set up perimeter defenses against surprise.

"We were able to outrun the Japanese," Joost told me, "but we couldn't outrun the tigers. They were thick in the country and would attack our mules at night. In the morning we'd find a half-eaten mule, dragged several hundred yards from the camp."

Franklin Roosevelt might well comment from Washington on the achievement of the mules, but he had no idea at all how heroic the poor beasts actually were required to be. The men crossed the Bhamo-Myitkyina Road, where A Group's four Kachin boys had once spied on Japanese traffic. By early May they were safely in Kachin territory where the pursuing Japanese did not dare to go. About fifty additional Kachins joined up as they moved from village to village. By the middle of May they were approaching the Chinese border in an area dominated by the Japanese. One evening about nine o'clock they were attacked by a strong force of the enemy. Fighting a rearguard action, they decided to march all night to try and contact a Chinese guerrilla group that the Kachins had told them had crossed from Yunnan. The Chinese were said to be based at the old deserted British fort at Nahpaw, on the border. By six in the morning the Dah Force was at Nahpaw.

The fort seemed right out of "Gunga Din." It was a decrepit structure of brick and wood built by the British during their early days in North Burma, surrounded by a fifteen-foot-high stockade with an enormous door at each end. It was perched high on a hill looking down on twin villages, a Kachin village and a Chinese village, in the Simpapa Valley. Joost could see at a glance that the fort was very vulnerable to attack. It was far too exposed to mortar fire, and the Japanese, the Dah Force had learned to its discomfiture, possessed light and highly mobile mortars that they seemed to be able to haul almost anywhere.

There were indeed Chinese guerrillas at the fort. Their leader listened to the Dah Group's plans and agreed to join with them in fighting the Japanese. Dah Group unpacked, since the Chinese leader assured them he had considerable strength in the vicinity of Nahpaw.

"I'll be away just a short time," he assured Joost. "I have some arrangements to check on in the village."

He set out for the Chinese village at the foot of the hill. It was now mid-morning. The Dah Force posted guards and was about to get some much needed rest after the all-night march, when a Kachin called Joost's attention to columns of men approaching on trails that climbed the Burma side of the hill.

"We counted twelve hundred of them. They were dressed in Chinese clothes, but the Kachins told us that they were Japanese," Joost said. "They were still an hour or two away from us, but we sent the Chinese leader an urgent request for reinforcements."

The leader informed the Dah Force that it should hold the fort. He would bring reinforcements. Joost would much rather have left what obviously was turning into an untenable position, but there was nothing to do but set up gun positions in and around the fort and wait for the enemy to come up. At dusk the Chinese returned.

"The reinforcements turned out to be three very young Kachin boys!" Joost said.

A British captain had fallen ill earlier in the day with an attack of malaria, and Joost went to his cabin within the shelter of the stockade to see how he was feeling. He was helping to ease the sick man when a fusillade of rifle and machine-gun fire broke out. Joost shook the British captain out of his feverish lethargy, and they peered out the cabin door. Bullets whined past. A stockade door about fifteen yards away suddenly broke open, and a knot of Japanese rushed in. Joost and the Englishman opened up on the men with tommy guns and piled them up dead in the doorway.

They were checking the corpses when the gate at the other end of the stockade burst open in turn. Captain Railton, another British officer with Dah Force, flung himself through the door and dashed through the yard. Behind him raced a shouting horde of Japanese, bent on taking him alive. The Englishman sprang over the piled-up corpses and dashed out through the other door into the dark. The Japanese leaped the corpses and ran after him. Joost and the sick captain stood transfixed.

In only a minute and a half, Railton raced through the far door a second time and sped across the enclosure with the Japanese still in furious pursuit. The hare in this mad race was so intent upon escape that he had not seen his fellow officers standing in the shadow of the stockade. The hounds in the race were so intent on the quarry that they didn't see the other white men either, although hare and hounds both passed within five yards of them.

"Bet he does it again," said the captain to Joost.

He was right. In another minute and a half, Railton made still a third wild dash through the door. He flashed across the enclosure, leaped the bodies, and disappeared into the night. This time Joost and his companion brought the chase to an end. They fired a burst out of their tommy guns, and before the Japanese could fire back, they sprang out the far gate into the sheltering night themselves. They ran down the trail away from the fort.

Some twenty-five Kachins had survived the debacle, and they joined the officers. The Kachins had waited in the stockade, laughing softly and talking among themselves, even though they knew that to do so was to court almost certain death. It was against every one of their jungle-warfare instincts to remain in such a vulnerable place. Before they could reach the safety of Kachin and Chinese villages, the men fleeing the fort were twice ambushed in the confusion, first by the Chinese and then by the Kachin villagers.

"The Kachin ambush was the terror of the two," said Joost. "They had set out pungyis and several of our men were caught on them and badly wounded."

The prospect of Kachin pungyis spearing Kachins had not been anticipated, but the entire affair had been hopelessly scrambled by the British officers and the Chinese commander. The Japanese made no effort to advance on the Kachin village, where the remnants of Dah Force had taken refuge. To Joost's amazement, Captain Railton strolled into the village three days later.

"As I leaped through the door that third time," he told Joost, "I tripped and fell down a hill. Your burst of fire distracted the Japanese so that they did not see me fall."

When Railton hit the ground, an arm pulled him down to the ground, and a hand clamped over his mouth to keep him quiet.

"Keep still, Sahib," a voice whispered in his ear.

Railton and his unseen friend lay in the dark and listened to the Japanese in the fort celebrating their victory with good British rum. Before the night was over the two men managed to crawl away. Railton's benefactor turned out to be a fugitive from the Indian army, who had fled into the area at the end of the first Burma campaign. When he heard that British soldiers had returned to the Sinlumkaba

Hills, he came out of hiding and was on his way to join them when the gunfight broke out. He too had seen Railton's epochal run.

Dah Force was scarcely a capable military unit in its present condition. When the men wounded in the villagers' ambushes were well, the British officers led the Anglo-Kachin group away toward Myitkyina, where it might be helpful in the expected attack on the town that was the site of General Tanaka's headquarters. Pete Joost stayed behind. The Chinese leader had been killed in the fighting. The new leader was a Colonel Jhao, and he welcomed Joost to his command. He always rode a white mule fitted out with a brightly colored saddle. A porkpie felt hat perched on his head.

Jhao, who had about eight hundred Chinese guerrillas under his command, was under constant pressure from the Japanese. The month that Joost spent with the Chinese was a month of alarms both night and day. Joost could not speak Chinese, and Jhao could not speak English, so he never knew what was about to happen.

"Then the colonel's secretary came up to me," Joost recalled. "He was a Mr. Hsee, and he had been well educated at a French mission in China. He spoke to me in Latin. I'd learned Latin in college, and from then on we communicated with one another that way. That is the advantage of having a Princeton education."

Realizing that the Chinese guerrillas could accomplish a great deal more against the Japanese if they had logistical support from Detachment 101, Joost decided to strike out for Myitkyina where the Kachin jungle grapevine rumored that an American force was now laying siege to the town.

\*     \*     \*

A paper prepared jointly by Detachment 101 and G-2, NCAC, summarized 101's services with the Chindits:

"Detachment liaison officers, radio teams, and guerrilla scouts served with the Wingate Expedition. These units provided intelligence cover and combat patrols for both flanks during the memorable march northwards from the Henu railway block to Mogaung. Detachment special agents also accompanied the British forces which cut the road south to Bhamo.

"The exchange of daily situation summaries between General Lentaigne's and General Stilwell's headquarters was effected through the Detachment's liaison officers and its radio net."

The Chindits made a real impact on the outcome of the war in

North Burma, but Orde Wingate did not live to see it. Flying to Delhi in March to make a report on the initial success of his men, his plane encountered misty weather. Visibility dropped to zero, and the plane smashed into a hillside. His loss was felt by both British and American forces, and particularly by members of Detachment 101, who recognized in this strange, iconoclastic man a kindred spirit.

Upon Wingate's death, General W.D.A. Lentaigne had taken command of the Chindits. His forces operated along the railroad corridor to the east of where Lutken and his Kachins were carrying out their own war of attack and withdrawal.

"They established a block on the railroad at what they called White City, after a sports stadium in London where the popular football team, the Queen's Park Rangers, then played," Lutken says, "and another block at what they called Blackpool, named after an English seaside resort. Ironically, the African troops held Blackpool. Idi Amin was among them."

The Chindits scouted up and down the railroad and halted Japanese traffic at a time when it was critical that they get trains through to supply their forces defending Myitkyina. The Blackpool block was about forty miles away from where Lutken and his Kachins were camped in the mountains looking down on the valley through which the railroad to Myitkyina ran.

"We could hear a battle raging around what we later learned was the Blackpool block," says Lutken. "From time to time there'd be a great growling roar that sounded loud even as far away as we were. We discovered in time that the Japanese had run up an enormous spigot mortar, which shoots a shell about the size of a boxcar. In an ordinary mortar the shell is dropped down a tube. Instead of a tube, the spigot has a huge solid post, which is fixed to a plate that sits on the ground. The shell, which has a hollow center, fits over the post. It is simply enormous and contains a huge charge.

"When these huge shells began to come down on them, it was too much for the blacks. They abandoned the block and fled into the mountains to the west side of the railroad. It grew silent down in the valley, and we knew that the battle was over, for better or for worse.

"A few days later we got a super-urgent message from Opero. It stated, 'We have lost contact with Blackpool. Broken off. Find out.'

"Our Kachins fanned out over the trails to find out what had happened to Blackpool. They hunted for two days before they finally found most of the King's East African Rifles on the far side of Indawgyi Lake. When we located them, I couldn't get over these huge, blue-black fellows who spoke the king's English with such precise Oxonian accents. The Kachins guided the blacks out of the jungle so that they could rejoin their command."

At the other extreme were the Nigerian soldiers fighting with the 16th Chindit Brigade under British Brigadier Ferguson. They spoke no English at all. Together with West African troops they moved north toward Lake Indawgyi and the railroad corridor. They cut their way through elephant grass, fifteen feet high, southwest of the lake, making less than a mile a day, and reached their destination exhausted. They, too, were given aid by 101. When Ferguson's brigade reached the railway corridor later in the campaign, they drove the Japanese away and secured the railroad for Allied use. American black engineers were brought in to repair the railroad. They found the Nigerians mystifying.

"Who are these guys?" one American demanded. "Boy, they must really be illiterate. They don't even speak English."

Long after the Chindits had left the Hopin Hills, Saw Judson and his Kachin agents remained in the area. They gathered intelligence and radioed it back to base. Even more important, they lived in the Kachin villages and recruited men to augment the American-Kachin Rangers who would inevitably play a momentous role in days to come.

# The Airport

The Japanese army retreating from the Hukawng in May was in a vengeful mood. The soldiers knew only too well that the Kachin people had played a critical role in their defeat. General Tanaka's vaunted 18th Division had lost heavily in killed and wounded. Much of its equipment had been captured or destroyed. Because supplies could not reach the front, the men were hungry. Now the monsoons were falling, and defeat turned to anger and hatred. Several Kachin villages in the valley which had escaped destruction the previous year were still under Japanese control. Sadistic soldiers rounded up the hapless villagers. They shot men, women, and children and sliced them with sabers. Along the Mogaung River they slit the Kachins open and pushed their dead bodies into the current. In village after village they seized victims and submitted them to the water treatment.

"They were brutal and sadistic," noted Ray Peers. "The victim was tied and spread on the ground and water was continually dripped in his mouth until his system could no longer handle it, and he swelled like a balloon. Then repeated thumps or jumps on the abdomen caused untold pain."

In villages close to Bhamo, Japanese soldiers crowded men, women, and children into bashas and drenched the structures with gasoline. Then they torched the bashas. As the people tried to escape the flames, they shot them and congratulated one another on the accuracy of their aim. The trick was to shoot a person who was burning so that he died in mid-scream.

All of this cruel behavior on the part of the Japanese military is scarcely typical of the Japanese in Burma. For the most part the Japanese army behaved with at least indifference toward the native population, but the soldiers had developed a great fear of the Kachins.

Japanese officers had come to believe one Kachin hypenla in his jungle was worth ten Japanese soldiers. Actually, the mortality ratio of Japanese to Kachins showed the Kachins to be a much more formidable enemy than that. Fear breeds hatred, particularly on the part of a proud army such as that commanded by General Tanaka, which after a long series of glorious victories now found itself falling back in defeat, hungry and tattered, not so much because of operations of the Chinese and Merrill's Marauders but because of the devastating behind-the-lines attacks of the Kachins. The jungle had always been dangerous, but now the outskirts of even large-sized towns and garrisons became deadly.

The Japanese also found the Kachins incomprehensible, and this made them even more vindictive. They could not forget the occasion when a Japanese captain went to a Kachin village, intending to try and win friendship. He was admitted to the basha of the duwa. Kachin honor requires that a householder extend every hospitality to a stranger who is a guest in his home, and the duwa entertained the captain according to tradition. Then the moment the officer stepped out the door, the duwa pulled his dah from its scabbard and sliced off his head. He had discharged his duty as a host, and now he was free to discharge his duty as a Kachin who hated the Japanese. The Japanese saw this turnabout as just plain treachery.

Ironically, many Kachins who had volunteered to follow Zhing Htaw Naw into the American-Kachin Rangers had believed that once the Japanese were driven out of the Hukawng and the Mogaung valleys, there would be no reason to pursue the retreating armies into Burmese territory. Others argued that since the Americans had helped them fight the Japanese and free their people, they should help the Americans fight until the Japanese were driven completely out of Burma. The new cruelties of the Japanese army decided the issue.

"Word of the atrocities spread like wildfire through the Kachin bamboo grapevine," says Ray Peers.

The Kachins' anger and resentment flared up with renewed fury. Zhing Htaw Naw vowed that his people would not cease their war until the enemy had been driven out of Burma.

*       *       *

Maung was trained as a radio operator and agent. When the air corps asked Detachment 101 to provide periodic reports on the Japanese landings and takeoffs at Myitkyina airport, he was given the assignment. He jumped into Pat at Arang. Pat led him over the hills to a mountain, which was only ten miles from the airport.

There Maung settled down by himself. He watched every Japanese movement through binoculars. In this way he kept a minute-by-minute, running account of exactly what the Japanese were doing. As soon as a Japanese plane taxied out to the runway, Maung was on the air directly to base at Nazira. A few minutes after the Japanese plane was in the air, Maung's report arrived at the 10th Air Force. In his spare moments he searched the surrounding countryside from his aerie and discovered a secondary airfield that the Japanese had hoped to keep secret.

Once a week a Kachin came from Arang to bring Maung food and water so that he need never stray away from the lonely vigil on his mountain top. What he observed just sitting and watching made Maung one of the most valuable agents that Detachment 101 had sent into the field in Burma.

\*     \*     \*

It was General Stilwell's idea. Colonel Kinnison's 3d Battalion of the Marauders and the Chinese 88th Regiment of the 30th Division—designated as K Force—and Colonel Hunter's 1st Battalion of Marauders and the Chinese 150th Regiment of the 50th Division—designated as H Force—were to form one unit which would employ the code name of Galahad. General Merrill, now partially recovered from a heart attack that had struck him during the Hukawng campaign, was to be in command. As Galahad advanced on Myitkyina, the Chinese 22d and 58th Divisions were to take Kamaing. The Chindits were to throw a block over the rail corridor and prevent the Japanese at Myitkyina from receiving reinforcements from the south. Colonel Kinnison's K Force, followed by Colonel Hunter's H Force, led off from Nawbum on April 28. Ahead of them Bill Martin's Kachins scouted the jungles. Shortly after his arrival from the States in February, 1944, Martin had jumped into Knothead at Nawbum. Within a week he had been sent out with seventy Kachins to assist Jim Tilly in attacking Japanese transport and communications. He was now given the task of guiding the Marauders to Pat at Arang and then on to Myitkyina.

The Kumon Range reaches heights of 9,000 feet, and Maura Hkyet, the pass through which the Kachins proposed to lead the

Marauders, was 6,100 feet in altitude. The same early monsoonal rains that were harassing the Japanese withdrawal handicapped the Americans and their Kachin scouts as they attempted to find a way through the high mountains. Many of the mules had been killed when the Japanese surrounded a Marauder battalion in the Hukawng, and now the remainder were having a miserable time. The rains slicked the clay of the trails so that men and mules alike slipped and fell. Mules tumbled over cliffs head over heels and broke their necks or stabbed themselves to death on the copses of bamboo growing at the foot of the precipices. The 3d Battalion lost twenty mules in one short stretch, and since each mule carried valued equipment, this took a severe toll on the effectiveness of the fighting force. One day the Marauders advanced only a few miles because of the difficulties that beset them at every turn in the twisting trail.

Hearts pounding and gasping for breath, the Americans climbed up the trail behind the agile Kachins, who stopped from time to time to wait for them. Sometimes the GIs had to scramble on all fours, their heavy packs making them look like they were displacing the mules in the military order of things. They camped for the night halfway up the mountain and pressed on in the morning toward the top, where the scrub trees were covered with moss and lichen. In contrast to the humid and hot Hukawng, it was cold at the summit of the pass, and the men shivered. So many Marauders, as well as the two Chinese regiments who were to follow them over the pass, threw down their equipment in their fatigue that when Vincent Curl sent a party of Kachins over the trail in the wake of the soldiers, they were able to collect enough booty to fill two warehouses. They picked up two thousand blankets alone.

At Ritpong, on the east side of the range, the Americans had a costly fight with the Japanese. The enemy withdrew, but they left after them the question of whether they had guessed the intention of Galahad to strike directly at Myitkyina. They also left behind mites, which chewed upon the tired and hungry men. Typhus carried by the mites soon sickened 149 men, many of whom had to be evacuated. Some died in the jungle beside the trail, and many more died in the hospitals in Assam. Nor was typhus the only disease the men encountered. Malaria (transmitted by the fierce mosquitoes of the area), blackwater fever (a form of malaria marked by chills, remittent fever, vomiting, jaundice, and hematuria), and dysentery were common. Some of the men, made particularly wretched by dysentery, cut the seats out of their pants to make it handier when their bowels ran. Leeches and bloodsucking flies paid indiscriminate attention to both men and mules. Ticks put in an appearance and infuriated the men by showing a singular faculty for affixing themselves to their genitals. The Marauders, their stamina sapped by the jungle and enemy action, were approaching the limits of their strength.

Kinnison's K Force feinted to the east toward Nsopzup, where the Japanese had a garrison. They met the enemy at Tingkrukawng and fought a holding action to keep them from attacking Hunter's H Force which, with Bill Martin and his Kachins in the lead, was able to push on toward Arang on the way to Myitkyina. Pat had constructed a landing strip at Arang, and the Marauders' sick and wounded could be flown out from there to Assam. Bill Hazelwood of Pat's group and a contingent of Kachins joined Galahad at Arang, and they were to be of signal service in the advance on Myitkyina. Far more important, another remarkable young Kachin boy reported for duty.

"Nau Yang Nau did his quest in the jungles through which the Americans and Chinese must go," a duwa at Arang explained to Pat, who had asked the Kachins to provide a guide who knew the approaches to the Myitkyina airport well.

Nau Yang Nau was fourteen years old, slight of build, but with a Kachin's wiry strength. When Galahad had advanced to only a day's march out of Myitkyina, he was brought to the head of the H Force column. Walking directly ahead of Bill Martin, he led over long-deserted trails that he had discovered in his life in the jungle. If the boy could bring the Marauders to the airport by night, they might surprise the Japanese defenders at dawn.

The night of May 15 was dark. At about ten o'clock, as they followed the trail, Bill Martin was immediately behind Nau Yang Nau.

"I bumped into him when he stopped short," he remembers.

"Duwa, I've been bitten by a snake," the boy softly told Martin.

Martin took out his flashlight and shined its beam on Nau's bare foot. He could see the fang marks behind the center toe of the left foot. By word of mouth a report of the accident moved from man to man back along the halted column. Four thousand men waited to see what would happen. Their fate hung on the fate of a Kachin boy. The Kachin's sharp eyes had seen the snake squirming off into the undergrowth after the bite. It was a krait, and he knew that unless something was done immediately he would die in about twenty minutes. He must keep himself alive or he could not lead the Marauders to the Myitkyina airport. Martin tightly tied a piece of cloth around the boy's calf to slow the flow of blood from the wound to his heart.

Martin's Kachins were already digging a small pit. Now they dumped some silver rupees into the pit. The boy thrust his bitten foot into it.

"Probably the cool, wet earth felt good on the poor kid's foot," Martin recalled. "It was beginning to swell."

Dr. McLaughlin came running from Phil Weld's I and R platoon, which followed Martin's Kachins, and lanced the wound. He applied suction cups to it, and two Marauder officers, Laffin and Dunlap, took turns sucking the poisoned blood from the now badly swollen foot. Martin got in radio contact with Colonel Hunter at H Force headquarters, which was stalled on the trail about halfway back in the column, and explained the situation. Doc McLaughlin asked for permission to use a flashlight. Light security was in force, but Hunter readily replied, "Affirmative." Everybody waited to see whether Nau Yang Nau would live or die. The youngster had placed his foot back in the hole in the ground. His leg was swelling fast. His eyes were on Bill Martin as if in apology for making such a mess of things. Colonel Hunter now radioed that the column must move on.

"It will kill him," Doc McLaughlin radioed back. "We will have to give him at least two hours rest and attention."

"Doc," Hunter replied, "he has got to go on until he collapses. Too much depends on this man. I'll send up my horse. Put him on it, and let's get going."

Colonel Hunter himself brought his horse forward, and helped the boy mount.

"He was a very sick kid," Martin recalls. "But he was a real Boy Scout, the sort of kid that is all heart and courage."

At about 2:30 in the morning the long column of men moved forward through the dark with Nau searching out the trail from horseback. Apparently the krait's bite had not impaired either his keen jungle eyes or his Kachin's sixth sense at divining which way to go. It was only a few hours before the advance party came upon the Mogaung-Myitkyina motor road, and soon after that they reached the railroad. At dawn they surprised a Kachin on the trail. Seeing the column of men emerging from the jungle, he tried to hide. Nau called to him in Kachin, and he emerged from hiding and told Nau that they were close to the Shan village of Namkwi. No, there were no

Japanese in the village. Some had been there a day or so before, but now they had all gone away.

The Kachins and the Marauders surrounded the village and then sent men in to awaken the sleeping villagers. The Kachins explained to the Shans that they would not be injured, but they were not to leave their village, because it was too well known that their people helped the Japanese in every way they could. All that day and the following night the Marauders waited in hiding around Namkwi. Nau Yang Nau rested in a basha, his lips parted as he struggled for breath. Bill Martin took time from his preparations for the next morning's dawn attack on the airport to stop in from time to time to see how the boy was doing. Nau had led the column to within three miles of the airport. Martin's hypenlas could lead the Marauders into position for the attack.

Before dawn H Force and the Kachins moved into position in dense jungle at the edge of the airport. When they saw the lights of cooking fires spring up at the Japanese strong points surrounding the strip, they attacked. Surprised and shocked by the appearance of their enemies out of the woods when they should have been at least seventy-five miles away, the Japanese snatched up their weapons to defend themselves, but they had no chance. The Marauders seized the airport and drove on to the railroad station in Myitkyina against only light resistance.

"At this stage everybody was exuberant, congratulating one another, and looking forward to a speedy end to the campaign. General Merrill flew in from Arang and assumed local command. K Force, two to three days' march away, were notified and told to expedite their movement," wrote Ray Peers.

The 101 commander received a message from General Merrill saying, "Thanks for your assistance. We could not have succeeded without the help of 101."

Bill Martin and his Kachins were already at work removing fifty-five-gallon steel oil drums from where the Japanese had left them on the runway of the airport and were preparing to blow up a railroad bridge over an Irrawaddy tributary. A train passed before Martin could get the TNT into place, so it escaped. Soon afterward a violent blast demolished the bridge. Meanwhile, at the airport, the Kachins rolled the drums off the runways into the revetments. The airport was now open so that General Merrill could land and take over command. British light anti-aircraft units also came wafting down out of the sky in some of Flip Cochran's gliders.

Father Stuart had arrived at the Myitkyina airstrip, and he noted in his journal that the brave Kachin boy, Nau Yang Nau, had been evacuated by air to Chabua, where he was placed in the military hospital. It was reported that he was doing very well and would make a full recovery. Father Stuart also noted that a Kachin boy who had served with the Lightning Force had been captured by the Japanese. They had tied him to a tree and stabbed him to death with bayonets.

But the Kachins who had fought side by side with the Marauders in taking the airport were now "on strike." They had not been issued clothing or proper equipment, water bottles, entrenching tools, helmets, or weapons.

"They said," reported the Father, "rightly too, that they were willing to fight in their own fashion but that if they had to fight with Americans, they wanted the same chances, as their heads were just as vulnerable and their lives as precious to their friends."

Ray Peers had sent the things the Kachins needed, but General Merrill, who had flown in by light plane from Arang to take command, had "short-stopped" the equipment for his own men. The Kachins, who shared every hardship and danger as brothers in arms with their American officers in the American-Kachin Rangers, had been disturbed by their treatment at the hands of the Marauder officers. The matter was quickly righted, but the Kachins had learned that not all Americans were as easy to understand and like as their OSS friends.

Father Stuart now set off on an assignment more to his liking. He was to travel back over the trails through the Mogaung and Hukawng valleys taken by the Chinese army. The Chinese had lived off the land as they advanced, and Father Stuart now paid out 22,000 silver rupees to Kachin villagers who had given them rice, chickens, pigs, and other supplies. He also vaccinated villagers against smallpox, a plague that follows in the wake of armies, whether they are defeated or victorious.

\*     \*     \*

War has its interludes. The men of 101 celebrated the victories to the south at a manau—a Kachin festival—at Sumprabum. They drank copious drafts of Kachin laukhu. Afterward Father Stuart and Father MacAlindon set off in a jeep down the rutted road. Their course was uncertain.

"Father Mac," said Father Stuart, "aren't you driving a bit erratically?"

Father Mac considered the situation before he answered.

"Ah, but Father Stuart, 'tis you who's drivin'."

Father Stuart, who tells of the incident in his papers, admitted, "I looked down, and sure enough, I was!"

\*    \*    \*

Elsewhere there was no interlude in the war. When a charge he was placing went off prematurely, Bob Henning, the Area I demolitions expert at Ngumla, lost an arm. Jim Luce, his commander and doctor, did everything he could for Henning, but he had to be flown out to save his life. Gerry Larsen, also of Area I, became so ill on the trail that he could go no farther. A contingent of one hundred Japanese soldiers was in close pursuit of Larsen's Kachins, and he ordered them to leave him behind so that they could avoid capture. Instead, the Kachins made a stretcher and placed him on it. They carried him up and down the mountains until they were safe from the Japanese. Two of Forward's best agents died of blackwater fever within a few days of one another. It was a bitter thing for Jim Luce, a doctor, to see these valued friends sicken and die and be helpless to assist them.

Then one day the Kachins brought a young Kachin to Luce. He had been manning an outpost during a Japanese attack. A bullet wound in the forehead had pressed his skull against his brain so that he had lost consciousness. His fellows lashed him to a stretcher and carried him for four days back to Ngumla. Jim Luce took one look at the youth's head and knew he would have to operate. It was incredible that the boy was still alive. He ordered the Kachins to sweep out and thoroughly scrub a basha to be used as an operating room. When everything was ready, the Kachins gathered around to watch the doctor cut into the skull. Ed Damen held up a lantern and a flashlight to provide light, and Luce went about his business with as much care and precision as if he were in surgery back at his hospital at Ashland, Oregon. The operation was a ticklish affair at best, especially with the boy's friends all looking over the doctor's shoulder, but it was successful. The young Kachin fully recovered. He did have a bad scar to remind him how close he had come to death.

A B-25 returning from a bombing mission crashed into a swamp about twenty miles north of Myitkyina, and Dennis Francis and a party of Kachins hurried to the scene from Arang. They found the crew of five alive but in terrible condition. There was no possibility that they could survive a trip by surface over the Mogaung Valley's precipitous trails, so Francis and the Kachins hastily leveled a meager three-hundred-foot-long airfield in the paddies. Francis notified Opero at Nazira, and a liaison pilot named Anderson flew his two-seater L-1 in from Myitkyina to pick up the injured flyers. He made five trips, a trip for each man, bringing them all out to Myitkyina from where they could be flown to the hospital at Ledo.

In Area II, Vincent Curl's leg steadily worsened. He had twisted it badly in a fall over a tree stump during a supply drop. For three months he had been hobbling about on crutches. Now he had to be evacuated. An L-1 flew Curl out from Knothead, and when it became obvious that his leg could not be mended at a field hospital in India, he was invalided to the United States. After twenty-eight months overseas and fifteen months behind the lines, Vincent Curl, Zhing Htaw Naw's closest 101 friend, had gone home. Jack Pamplin took his place at Knothead as well as any other man ever could hope to do.

\* \* \*

There was no interlude in the war at Myitkyina either. The day before the dawn attack on the airport, 101 agents went into Myitkyina town while the Marauders rested at Namkwi. They reported to the Northern Combat Area Command and the Galahad Force that only about three hundred Japanese soldiers held the town. Two Chinese battalions were given the task of taking Myitkyina. One battalion, bugles blowing, entered Myitkyina moving northward along the Irrawaddy River, and the other attacked from the west.

"All went well until the two converged on the railway station in the center of town about dusk," Ray Peers noted. "It has been reported that Japanese snipers between them started picking them off. Whatever the reason, they soon became heavily engaged with each other and inflicted such severe mutual casualties that they had to be withdrawn."

The chance to capture Myitkyina itself had been lost, along with the element of surprise. Two days passed before the Chinese regrouped for a second attack. Their blunder had turned to nought all the heroism and suffering of Kachins, Chinese, and Americans on the jungle march on Myitkyina. With communications to the town still open, General Tanaka rushed troops from garrisons at Mogaung to the west, from Maingna and Seniku across the Irrawaddy from Myitkyina, and from scattered posts elsewhere. Within two days Tanaka succeeded in bringing about twelve hundred additional soldiers into Myitkyina, and within a week the garrison would swell to three thousand men; within three weeks there would be five thousand Japanese holding the city. Kachin road watchers reported the movement of Japanese forces into Myitkyina, and 101 guerrillas were striking at the outlying towns that were being stripped of their garrisons in General Tanaka's determination to hold Myitkyina at all costs.

When the Chinese finally attacked, the Japanese threw them back with great losses. Digging defenses with their usual skill in rice paddies, elephant grass, and in the surrounding jungles, the Japanese prepared to make the capture of Myitkyina a very costly affair.

"The terrain and the defense favored the Japanese, but the strength and freedom of action favored the Allies," summed up Ray Peers. "The Japanese were battle-wise and had effective leadership throughout. On the Allied side, the Marauders were spent. Their ranks had been depleted by battle casualties, diseases had taken a heavy toll, and their morale was sagging. The Chinese, with but few exceptions, were untried troops, and their leadership left much to be desired."

The Marauders had discovered just how inexorable a campaign in the jungle can be. Wingate's three-month limitation rule was proving to be tragically realistic, and the Marauders had ceased to exist as a first-rate fighting unit. General Merrill himself, incapacitated by his third heart attack, finally had to give up command.

The monsoons swept down on the besieged and the besiegers. The rains afflicted the Allies more than they did the Japanese. Malarial mosquitoes rose in swarms, and it did not matter to them what side the man they bit was on. Soldiers on both sides died of a fearful cerebral malaria which killed in only a few hours. Attack and counterattack became a way of life for the opposing forces. The Japanese, surrounded, their supplies cut off, fought valiantly and efficiently against the Chinese and the now-dispirited Marauders. The inept leadership of the Chinese won nobody's enthusiasm but General Stilwell's, and Vinegar Joe was probably steadfast in his support of their action at Myitkyina mainly because, with the Marauders weaving and bobbing like punch-drunk fighters, there was little alternative. The brilliant Allied campaign in the Hukawng had turned into a fiasco.

\* \* \*

In June, 101 American-Kachin Rangers continued to make successful attacks on the towns from which the Japanese had withdrawn most of their men for the defense of Myitkyina, though raids on Seniku, Woshawng, and Sadon made it necessary for the Japanese to keep at least a battalion in each of those locations. The Kachins had taken over the entire Allied left flank from the Irrawaddy River east to the Chinese border. Three hundred of Forward's Kachins took Kwitu airport from the Japanese in a sudden attack after a sixty-mile march.

Ray Peers and a pilot, Sergeant Dale, flew an L-1 to the newly captured Kwitu airstrip, only eight miles northeast of Myitkyina. Peers conferred with 101 men Dan Mudrinich and Jake Esterline, and then flew back to Myitkyina, where Dale and he intended to land. They had passed over the Irrawaddy about ten miles north of the field when Peers, listening in on radio earphones to Dale's conversation with the control tower at Myitkyina, heard the operator shout, "Get that goddamned transport out of the middle of the runway so we can get these fighters off."

This was discouraging comment for two men flying in an unarmed L-1 to hear. Peers suggested that they ought to make a 180-degree maneuver and fly back to Kwitu. He knew that his Kachins had control of that airstrip, and after everything that had already happened at Myitkyina, no prudent man could be certain just what might be going on there now. Dale disagreed. There would be no problem. He could land. He headed his small silver-colored plane toward Myitkyina.

Ray Peers was the first to spot the ten Zeros in smart formation. They were busy escorting a Japanese bomber, which was dropping supplies to the besieged garrison. Before they could alter their course, Dale and Peers found themselves right in the thick of things. Fortunately, the L-1 was among the first Allied planes in the theater to be painted silver, and in the confusion, the Japanese fighter pilots took it for one of their own planes, even though a closer look would have discovered the U.S. insignia on the wings and fuselage. By the time the Japanese had discovered their initial mistake, the Americans had finally got the transport off the runway, and P-40s were screaming up for the attack. The L-1 fled the scene without being molested, tree-hopping to safety.

Not long afterward, Ray Peers and pilot Sergeant McCullough flew down to the Bhamo area on a mission. Their return flight to Myitkyina proved to be just as exciting as Peers's previous one, except that this time there were no Zeros. As they came in low about half a mile west of the airfield, Peers looked down to the ground and made out men firing their weapons.

"We could see people firing on the ground, but didn't think they were firing at us until holes started appearing through the wings," he said afterward.

When the plane landed at the airport, there were over one hundred holes in the wings, tail, and fuselage. It turned out that the 275th combat engineers, newly arrived from the States, were doing a little simulated battle training, not far from where the actual battle for Myitkyina was raging at the very moment. The engineers had taken the L-1 for a Zero, and they opened up on the plane with everything they had.

\* \* \*

Colonel Gordon Seagraves, the famed Burma surgeon, had set up his field hospital at the Myitkyina airfield. His staff had rigged tents out of brightly colored rayon parachutes so that operating rooms, dispensaries, and the quarters of doctors, nurses, and aides were all a cheerful red, blue, green, purple, yellow, and white. That is about as far as the cheer went, because Seagraves and the other doctors were operating on about seventy-five wounded every day. When Ray Peers stopped by the hospital unit to discuss a matter with Seagraves, the doctor was in surgery attending to a Chinese victim. Peers went to find him.

"I figured I had a pretty stable stomach," he recalls today, "but after about twenty to thirty minutes of watching Colonel Seagraves use an ordinary butcher knife to cut away gangrenous flesh from a Chinese without benefit of anesthesia, I simply could not take it and had to retire until he had finished and could talk for a while."

Allied casualties from sickness and wounds mounted as the siege of Myitkyina continued its bloody course.

\* \* \*

Pete Joost made his way through the jungle from the Chinese border with a few Kachins to show him the way. He slipped past the Japanese lines to the Myitkyina airport. General Stilwell, anxious to know what was going on in the field, asked that the 101 man, who had been four months in the jungle, be brought to him at his headquarters, then at Shaduzup. At Shaduzup tents and bashas made of bamboo and tarpaulins clustered on the steep hillsides on both sides of the road. Just beyond Shaduzup was the airstrip, and on it Joost, after a flight from Myitkyina, landed in an L-1.

General Stilwell stared at him. With his loss of at least thirty-five pounds, and his ragged clothes and shaggy beard he was an amazing sight. Stilwell listened to his request for assistance for the Chinese guerrillas on the border. He said he would like to help but that he was having enough trouble supplying the two Chinese divisions now in action.

"Do you know Colonel Peers of the OSS?" he asked.

"I know him very well," replied Joost, somewhat amused that the general did not realize that he, too, was an OSS man.

"Peers will be here tonight," replied Stilwell. "Talk to him about organizing some Kachins behind the Japanese lines in the Bhamo area."

That night Ray Peers arrived at Shaduzup and, in his usual way, expressed concern at his fellow 101 man's sorry appearance and condition. At the same time he was anxious to put Joost back in the field. First Joost must go to the hospital in Calcutta for medical attention. In Calcutta, Joost learned that he was not only suffering from dysentery and malaria, but his intestines crawled with worms.

Once he was cured, Joost returned to see Peers. He was to command an area of 101 operations from a base somewhere near Bhamo. He was to secure intelligence, ambush and hurt the Japanese in every way he could, and spearhead the advance of the Allied troops once Myitkyina had fallen. As for Myitkyina, Peers asked Joost to supply intelligence about Japanese activities, set up roadblocks to deny the enemy reinforcements and supplies, and to cut off all retreat to the east and south of the city once the inevitable Japanese withdrawal began.

Joost's initial headquarters were to be at Kwitu. One day he flew with Peers to the Kwitu airstrip where Mudrinich and Esterline were waiting for them. The Kachins had set up ambushes in every direction, and their patrols were striking out at the enemy on all the approaches to Myitkyina.

From Kwitu Joost was soon able to dispatch additional agents into Myitkyina itself. It was not practical to try and send a Kachin there, for the Japanese now were shooting Kachins on sight, but Joost was able to enlist the assistance of Burmese, Shans, and Indians, some of whom worked at Japanese headquarters, which had been set up in 101 man Wally Richmond's former house. Couriers brought regular reports to Joost from the agents who radioed the intelligence to base. Richmond, who had lived in his house as a forester in North Burma, obligingly gave the air force detailed instructions on how to hit it. It was ironic that in every raid made on Myitkyina from that point on Richmond's house was the target.

# The Fall of Myitkyina

The 16th Brigade of the Chindits approached Mogaung from the south, and the 114th Regiment of General Sun's 38th Division, having taken Kamaing, approached from the north. Agent Skittles and his operatives worked out of General Sun's headquarters, and 101 American-Kachin Ranger groups served as an intelligence and combat screen around both the advancing British and Chinese forces.

Brigadier Mike Calvert, the commander of the 16th Chindits, contacted Skittles when his force was still about a day's march away from Mogaung. He wanted to know the situation in the town. Skittles responded that there were "only twelve Japs with two machine guns in Mogaung." It appeared that there would be no difficulty in taking the town.

"Brigadier Calvert ordered his men to make a bayonet charge on the town, and the Japanese machine guns mowed the attackers down," Skittles recalls, learning once again the sorry lesson that intelligence men are forever learning: commanders may get accurate information about the forces confronting them, and yet make disastrous moves for peculiar reasons of their own. But the British force broke off the attack, and the Chinese, who had come up, took the city. It was June 26.

Four days later, the Allied officers held a dinner in Mogaung to celebrate their victory. At the end of the dinner, the Chinese, Americans, and British signed a captured Japanese battle flag and presented it to Skittles, who still keeps the flag with him to this day. The fall of Mogaung was indeed a significant blow to the Japanese. Until it fell, they had been operating trains every night from the south through Mogaung to Myitkyina. The capture of the town also cut the highway between the two towns. Now Myitkyina was isolated. Heroic as the Japanese defense might be, it was clear they were doomed.

Pete Lutken offers some observations on the last days of the Japanese rail traffic into Myitkyina. His Kachins were attacking the rail line farther south, where it passes among the Hopin Hills. Blackpool, where the King's East African Rifles set up their ineffective block, was at Hopin in the corridor. Now Lutken saw that at Kadu, not far from Hopin, the railroad crossed a bridge over a deep valley. Blow that bridge, and the Japanese could never manage to get the line back into operation. It would be an even more devastating stroke if Lutken could demolish the bridge when a train was crossing it. Lutken and his Kachins did blow the bridge, but they failed to take a train with it. The Japanese soldiers entrusted with defending the rail corridor swarmed after the Kachins, but after a brief fire fight the guerrillas escaped into the jungle.

"The trains that the Japanese were operating by this time were a far cry from the first-class rolling stock that they had inherited from the British," Lutken remembers. "They rigged up trucks with flange wheels. Each truck would pull three to four goods wagons behind it. Since the trucks were beaten-up old wrecks, it was a miracle that the system operated at all."

When Mogaung fell, the British took over the operation of the undamaged portion of the railroad. Now supplies for the Allies rolled on tracks that only a few weeks before had carried supplies for the Japanese.

"The British ran a string of box cars without even a truck to pull them," says Lutken. "They knocked a hole in the end of the first one so that a guy could sit there and look out. Then they installed a truck engine in it. The engine was linked by a sprocket and chain to the front axle. The odd-looking contraption started out slowly. It stopped even more slowly, because the only way to apply the brakes was to run from car to car screwing down the hand brakes. Since there were fifteen or sixteen cars following behind the jerry-built locomotive, the train crew had to start stopping a mile ahead of time. The British also used a truck with flange wheels to pull from six to eight cars. They found that a Jeep was too light to be any good."

Large numbers of Japanese soldiers, according to 101 agents, had hidden in the jungles along the railroad line in the vicinity of Mayan and Pidaung. The tables had been turned. It was now the Japanese who were attempting to blow up British trains and wreck the railroad. The Kachins patrolled the tracks but, characteristically, they were not content with a defensive operation. American-Kachin Ranger patrols searched the jungles for their Japanese quarry, and by the end of June the last of the Japanese soldiers hiding in the jungle had been liquidated.

\* \* \*

The shadow war of the agents continued. The Japanese captured a Chinese who was purported to be an agent. He was a coolie, who helped to carry supplies. One day, unaccountably, he began to speak in Japanese, then English and Burmese, and a Japanese officer immediately became suspicious. A coolie does not speak in many tongues; he is not expected to say much even in his own language.

The Japanese officer questioned him. He directed that his sleeping place be searched. There was no evidence to indicate that he was anything other than a coolie. The officer showed a signal glass to him, and he proudly explained that he knew what it was. When shown a map, he proudly proved that he knew how to read it. Coolies do not understand about signal glasses, nor do they know how to read maps. Of course, he might simply be a very intelligent coolie, who had somehow learned these things and was trying to impress his Japanese masters with his ability in the naïve hope that this would somehow lift him out of the world of backbreaking labor into the privileged world of men of knowledge. The campaign had reached a critical stage. A prudent officer could not take any chances on a spy. He gave orders that the coolie be shot. His orders were carried out.

\* \* \*

Japanese agents desperately sought to learn about the dispositions of the American-Kachin Rangers. Where were these jungle phantoms? What were their plans? The Kempi Tai sent Shan and Burmese agents throughout the region, but they were poorly trained and easily caught. Some of the agents were persuaded to become double agents and report to 101. Others were confined in remote villages in the mountains until the war was over. They could do no damage from such out-of-the-way places. If a captured agent proved to be too dangerous to neutralize in this way, every effort was made to fly him out and turn him over to the British for imprisonment in India, where he could do no harm. Unfortunately, many of these men were not captured close to a 101 airstrip, and it was necessary for the Kachins to take them through the jungles to a point from which they could be evacuated. In almost every case the Kachins arrived without the agent.

"Duwa," they would report to a 101 officer, their eyes gleaming with satisfaction at how beautifully things had worked out, "the captive attempted to escape. It was necessary to shoot him."

If there was no American present when a Japanese agent, or even a soldier, was captured by the Kachins, they often saw no reason to trouble their American friends about the matter. They stripped the hapless man naked. It was amusing to see him standing, shivering with fear, in the middle of a circle of hypenlas or villagers. The Japanese conqueror no longer looked so formidable as he cowered there, covering his penis and testicles with his hands as best he could. Sometimes the Kachins adapted the Japanese trick of beating their naked prisoners on the spine with a wooden paddle, but they were morc likely to follow the time-honored custom of inserting a bamboo sliver into his penis and setting it on fire. When it came time to put the prisoner to death, the proper ritual was to pink him playfully with their dahs in order to encourage him in the business of digging his own grave. When the grave was the right depth, somebody would stab his dah into the prisoner's right leg, and then another person would stab him in the other. The next stab was in the stomach, with a last thrust into his heart. It was always considered something of a misfortune that the victim could not cover himself with dirt as he lay in his grave.

\*      \*      \*

As the fight for Myitkyina continued, 101 guerrillas set up roadblocks and ambushes along trails and rivers that led from the area. If the Japanese managed to break out, they would have to run the Kachin gauntlet. At the same time, 101 was establishing a new guerrilla force from one hundred to one hundred and fifty miles farther south so that the next move the conventional Allied forces made would also enjoy guerrilla support.

Reports of the near starvation rations on which the Japanese troops now had to fight filtered out through 101 agents working within Myitkyina. In late July the Japanese loaded their severely wounded on rafts and attempted to float them down the Irrawaddy River to safety, under cover of darkness. Then General Mizukami, the commander, committed hara-kiri. He had obtained General Tanaka's permission to withdraw, but the disgrace of having to make the request had to be assuaged. In small groups the Japanese began to slip out of the city. They followed hill trails and roads southward and descended the river aboard makeshift rafts.

Pete Joost's Kachins set up what he called "duck blinds" along the Irrawaddy River. The blinds were about a mile apart.

"When the Japs came floating along, eight to ten men on a raft, our Kachins had a field day shooting at them with machine guns and burp guns," Joost said afterward. "Then the Japs had a bright idea. They built their rafts higher up from the water so that the men riding on them could tumble off into the water at the first fusillade and take shelter on the far side. The Japanese swam beneath the rafts to safety. Then the Kachins in their turn figured out what they were doing and fired mortar shells just ahead of the rafts so that the underwater concussions killed them."

Joost's Kachins put an end to something like three hundred fugitives from Myitkyina as they fled down the river and annihilated about three hundred others on trails and roads.

Finally, Joost obtained Opero's permission to move his three companies about eighty miles farther south to Sima, where he set up additional blocks to destroy any Japanese units that managed to escape the traps closer to Myitkyina. The Kachins wiped out another four hundred Japanese, and during the entire operation at Myitkyina and Sima suffered no casualties at all. The demoralized Japanese, fleeing through the jungles, were no match for Kachin ambushes.

At the Namtu River the Kachins sat and waited patiently in the thickets on the bank for the Japanese to come down the trails in small groups. They watched the Japanese cut trees and build their rafts. When a worthwhile number, perhaps fifty, had gathered and were almost ready to launch their crafts, the Kachins massacred them. The bloody trap was sprung over and over again. When one group of raft-builders was wiped out, the Kachins would clean up the scene of carnage so that the next group of Japanese to come along would set to work filled with hope that they might build a raft, launch it, and escape successfully.

\*     \*     \*

As a boy, Wes Berry had delighted moviegoers as "Freckles," one of the original members of the Our Gang Comedies. Now he and Bill

Martin sat in wooden deck chairs on the verandah of a two-story Shan house beside the Irrawaddy, 35 miles below Myitkyina. They played the same record over and over on the RCA phonograph that they had found in the house. Previous Japanese occupants had smashed the other records against the wall, and their fragments littered the floor around the teakwood furniture. There were only three records left intact, and only this one played without any scratching.

"Faraway places with strange-sounding names," ran the song.

The two men swept the river with their binoculars in search of enemy troops floating downstream, hugging logs, trying to escape from Myitkyina.

"Wes Berry and I watched the river and listened to the song. When we saw the Japanese floating down the river, we first took a head count. We let them pass, then cut loose," Martin told me.

Their rifle fire alerted a company of Kachins who were in hiding fifty yards downstream. They had twenty Bren guns in position, and when these opened up the slaughter was fearful. When the gunfire was stilled, Kachins paddled out in the river in dugout canoes to search for bodies. They put to death any refugees from Myitkyina's impending fall who might have escaped. In this way Martin's American-Kachin Rangers killed 559 Japanese and captured 29. They also captured 19 Chinese deserters. Even the Kachins began to feel sorry for the Japanese, but this did not stop the slaughter. The Myitkyina garrison had been given many opportunities to surrender, yet their response had been to redouble their efforts to break out and escape. Zhing Htaw Naw now brought 400 new Kachin recruits from Nawbum to assist in the annihilation of the Japanese.

For a few days Skittles joined the shoot.

"The Japanese trying to escape from Myitkyina floated down the river beneath the surface, breathing through papaya stems," he remembers.

It did them very little good, because although they might escape the Americans, there was little chance that the Kachins waiting just below the house on the riverbank would miss them.

\*     \*     \*

In Myitkyina Colonel Maruyama had taken over after General Mizukami's suicide. Even as their comrades attempted to flee, the remaining Japanese kept up a furious resistance. Later, 101 agents informed Pete Joost that the colonel had managed the almost

\*     \*     \*

incredible defense by issuing his men a steady ration of opium. Drugged and oblivious to the fearful plight they were in, the Japanese fought like tigers.

On the night of August 2, Colonel Maruyama broke out of the town and led the remainder of his men across the river, heading toward the Chinese border. He hoped to move south along the border to reach the strong Japanese garrison that held Bhamo. It was Maruyama's misfortune that Joe Lazarsky and his Kachins picked up his trail. Lazarsky, who had helped to train the original group of 101 men in western Maryland, had chosen to come to Burma himself. He had joined Pete Joost at Kwitu, and now he was in command of a company of American-Kachin Rangers.

Kachin agents brought in the first word that a large group of Japanese was heading south. Lazarsky's company had been hard hit by malaria, and he had only fifty Kachins ready to fight, but this did not keep him from setting up an ambush. As usual, the Kachins let the Japanese get into the most vulnerable position and then sprang the trap. In the first ambush they killed about twenty-five and took one prisoner.

The remainder of the Japanese fled to a village where they set up defenses. Obviously they had a seasoned commander, who had somehow managed to rally them after the first terrifying attack. Lazarsky interrogated the prisoner, and he admitted that he had been carrying the litter of a wounded colonel. Lazarsky threw a cordon of Kachins around the village. There were still ten times more Japanese than Kachins, but he was determined to capture such a high-ranking officer.

The Kachins set up two-inch mortars about seventy-five yards from the village. The first shell fell into the headman's basha where many of the Japanese had gathered. It exploded with a loud whomp, and flames leaped up through the thatched roof. The few Japanese who escaped the basha were shot by sharpshooting Kachins. The next mortar shots torched the other bashas. Only a handful of Japanese managed to escape the village, but Colonel Maruyama was among them.

The remaining Japanese fled south toward Bhamo with Lazarsky and the Kachins in pursuit. They caught up with the Japanese three times in the next week, at an ambush, then at a river crossing, and finally when the Japanese stopped to bathe in the river. Maruyama finally arrived in Bhamo with only fifty to one hundred men. Against a well-led, well-supplied enemy in prime condition the Kachins had proven deadly. Now against a defeated Japanese army trying desperately to reach succor, the Kachins were proving to be nothing short of murderous. The stench of decaying corpses hung heavy over Myitkyina and everywhere in the jungle where the Japanese fleeing from the town had been ambushed. Ray Peers, flying into the Myitkyina airstrip, remarked that the fierce odor could be detected high in the sky. After a plane had been on the ground at Myitkyina, it had to be fumigated because the odor stayed with it for days afterward.

It remained for Ray Peers to extend an accolade to the defeated Japanese.

"The tenacity and capability of the Japanese as fighting men, as combat soldiers, never once wavered," he said of their performance at Myitkyina and during the bitter withdrawal. "Near the end they were fighting against strong odds, their supplies had long before been cut off, many of their personnel were sick or wounded, and their food was all but exhausted."

With the fall of Myitkyina, Detachment 101 had completed the first of the assignments it had been given by General Stilwell.

"Accordingly," says Ray Peers, "he thanked the unit for what had been accomplished and then, true to his promise, gave us the go-ahead signal to increase the size of the force to approximately 10,000 guerrillas with a commensurate increase in other activities."

Even as Detachment 101 was playing its bloody role in the fall of Myitkyina, it was recruiting Kachin guerrillas far to the south to lend the support that irregular warfare could give to the next advance of British, American, and Chinese forces.

With the successful conclusion of the half-year campaign, a few Marauder officers who had seen the Kachins in action volunteered for service in 101. In this way Phil Weld, Tom Chamales, Roger Hillsman, and Charles Scott joined the American-Kachin Rangers. Bill Brough, a British Quaker, who served with Seagraves's hospital unit, also came to Ray Peers and asked to be brought into the OSS. He, too, had taken a liking to the courageous Kachins, and he wanted to try and give them medical care.

\*    \*    \*

Only Saki, the British writer, who had been born and raised in Rangoon, could have invented a story like the one Ray Peers found himself caught up in. One day he went to the airstrip at Myitkyina, now firmly in Allied hands, to meet Red Maddox, who had flown in from Area IV for a much-needed rest. He was talking to Maddox when they heard a babble of excited voices a hundred yards farther along the strip. The two 101 men could not figure out what the fervid discussion was about, so they walked over to the crowd.

"What is going on?" asked Maddox.

"It is some Kachin talking about a gadget somebody gave him."

Suddenly Peers had an intuition that the gadget might just possibly be the watch that he had handed to Saw Judson long ago as A Group got aboard a plane to jump into the Koukkwee Valley. Saw Judson, it will be remembered, had given it to an old Kachin duwa in the Triangle who had led his party to safety when they were surrounded by Japanese. Peers and Maddox drew closer, and soon the old man and Maddox were talking and laughing together like old friends.

Yes, it was Peers's watch, and the duwa pointed out to Maddox that it was quite useless to him. He could not read, write, or tell time, and he would be very happy to trade it for a few pounds of rice or other food. With Stilwell's approval, 101 had set up awards for Kachins who helped in the rescue of Allied military personnel. They could take their pick of four hundred silver rupees or a muzzle-loading rifle. Maddox gave the duwa a choice between the money or the rifle in exchange for the watch. The duwa selected the rifle. He handed the watch to Peers. Peers wound it. A year of monsoons and jungles had done no damage. It began to tick. It not only ran again but kept perfect time.

# Lazum Tang

After the fall of Myitkyina on August 3, the Japanese regrouped for the defense of Bhamo and the Burma Road. The Mars Task Force, successor to Merrill's Marauders, was on the trail toward Bhamo, and the Chinese were also moving south in force. The American-Kachin Rangers went about their deadly business of harassing the Japanese wherever they attempted to establish themselves and ranged ever farther south behind their lines. Then on October 19, 101 men at base were stunned by the abrupt removal of General Stilwell from his command. Stilwell's relations with Chiang Kai-shek had never been good, and now they had deteriorated. When the Japanese army attacked and captured the American air bases in China, in 1944, the generalissimo blamed the loss on Stilwell and demanded that President Roosevelt recall him. With Stilwell's dismissal, Lieutenant General Albert Wedemeyer was placed in command of American forces in China, and Lieutenant General Daniel Sultan was placed in command in India-Burma.

*　　*　　*

As the purely military aspects of the campaign unfolded, there were also incidents during this period that highlight personalities and events which were to become legend in 101 history. The stories of Oscar Milton, Jim Luce, and others are told and retold.

Oscar established himself in the next village south of Myitkyina on the Irrawaddy River. There he set up a food rationing system to provide relief for four to five hundred Burmese who had been made destitute by the fighting. With his batman, Law Kaw the 'Nung duwa, at his side, he went about healing the wounds of war with the same sensitivity to people and their feelings that he had shown as an agent.

For the most part the Japanese in Burma were indifferent to the nutrition and health of the Burmese people, but OSS groups did their best to concern themselves with their well being. Oscar near Myitkyina, the Reverend Case in the vicinity of Mogaung, and Father Stuart in the Hukawng were all at work bringing relief to the people, who had been badly savaged by the war. Jim Luce might be Area I's commander responsible for 1500 Kachins, but he was a man of medicine to the heart, and he operated a dispensary at Ngumla that took care of 720 cases in a two-month period. He treated 537 individuals for wounds and diseases such as malaria, pneumonia, dysentery, tapeworm, chancre, and gonorrhea.

Some of the gunshot and shrapnel wounds required major surgery. At dusk one day, Gerry Larsen and Jim Luce were hiking a trail near Ngumla when they were met by some Kachins carrying a wounded hypenla on a litter. During an ambush, the Kachins had been fired upon by a Japanese knee mortar. A shell had burst nearby, wounding the man in three places—his left upper arm, his thigh, and his right forehead. Luce tells about the case:

"He had tied up his own wounds with strips of cloth torn from his clothing and walked a mile to a rendezvous point where he collapsed. He was carried by his companions to platoon headquarters, where his wounds were covered with battle dressings and eight coolies were obtained as litter bearers.

"For the next three and one-half days, these men carried him over steep and difficult trails, stopping only for rest and sleep as it became absolutely necessary. There was no further first aid or care other than to keep him as warm as possible and to offer him a little food night and morning. When we saw him, he was covered with dried blood, the bandages soaked and barely covering the wounds, and the man laboring to keep alive.

"On the surface it appeared that he could not stand to be transported to our camp. We realized that there was no other place for medical aid, so the coolies were turned about and ordered to carry him to the surgery with all possible speed.

"This term, 'the surgery,' needs a little clarification. It consists of one room in a bamboo shack. The operating table is bamboo with the supporting legs put through the floor into the ground for stability. The instruments and necessary equipment are laid out on a bamboo bench. Water is carried to the place in bamboo containers. Sterilization is obtained either in a small alcohol sterilizer or in a large pot set over an open fire just outside the surgery door.

"There was no time to lose and, although we did not know the extent of the injuries covered by the bandages, it was obvious that quick action was mandatory. We put up a shout for Pharmacist's Mate Dietz and Lieutenant Damen, and they arrived in a matter of seconds.

"Damen put a man on the generator to see that it was kept going and rigged a light over the operating table. The coolies willingly lent a hand and got a fire going for the sterilizing process. Dietz was preparing instruments and other paraphernalia like a veteran, although he had never had any previous experience in surgical work. Lieutenant Larsen was caring for the sterilization of towels and instruments as fast as Dietz could get them ready. The native interpreter was helping to cut away clothing and bandages, and several other natives organized a water-carrying group.

"On removing the bandages, we found the leg and arm wounds to be minor, but the head wound was extremely severe. The scalp and eyebrow had been torn away, and the skull was very well exposed and revealed a gaping hole through which destroyed brain tissue was oozing.

"There was only one course of action to be followed, and so, with the pharmacist's mate as main assistant, and with the executive and signal officer helping him and the interpreter reassuring the patient, a brain operation was started.

"For ninety minutes there was a lot of action but very little conversation. Occasionally, one of the lay help would step outside to get a little fresh air, but no one stopped working. The only anesthetic which could be used was local anesthetic and a little morphine. The destroyed scalp, muscle, bone, and brain tissue had to be removed, and the fragments of bone buried in the depths of the wound were exposed and carefully lifted out. There were times when all held their breath while a deep or particularly small blood vessel was clamped and tied.

"As each step was completed, a report in native jargon was relayed outside to the small group who had collected, and the exclamations were somewhat like those heard amongst the more sophisticated audiences at home. When the last bandage was in place, no one but the coolies who had patiently carried him in was allowed to touch the litter. It was their final gesture when they carried him from the surgery to the little shack that serves as a hospital.

"The patient lived and, although still very ill, is improving each day."

Luce also found time to study the types of malaria prevalent in the Kachin Hills and made bacteriological diagnoses employing microscopic methods. He planned and later established a system for evacuating American and Kachin wounded by light plane, and this materially improved morale in the field. A guerrilla fighter lives with the psychological burden that if he is badly wounded and if his group is hard pressed by the enemy, he may have to be put to death by his own people so that he will not be captured and tortured. For a man to know that he will have something of a regular soldier's chances for life if he is injured in a fight or crippled by disease means a great deal when he is fighting behind the lines.

Jim Luce became known throughout the Triangle for his medical concern for Kachin men, women, and children and for the fighting men of the American-Kachin Rangers. At the same time, this navy doctor proved himself time and time again as a military strategist who ranked among the best men in Detachment 101. As the 475th Infantry of the Mars Task Force prepared to follow obscure trails that led southward to the east of the Myitkyina-Bhamo Road, Luce furnished them with Kachin guides, interpreters, porters, and a security screen of scouts. Kachin agents went to see the duwas of the villages that lay along their route south to Bhamo to let them know the Americans were coming and to insure their help.

The Chinese 38th Division was also on the march along the main road to Bhamo. As they dug in for the defense of Bhamo, the next major Allied objective, 101 agents kept close check on the Japanese. Old Kachins, particularly those who had become semi-addicted to opium, hid by the trails and rivers so that they could observe every Japanese movement. Young boys were also put to work as trail and river watchers. Additional 101 men, some newly arrived from the States, jumped or infiltrated into the field to expand the intelligence and combat groups now operating between the Irrawaddy River and the China border east of Bhamo. I was one of these men, and it was during this climactic campaign that I learned firsthand about the Kachin people and the Americans who lived and fought by their side.

\*　　\*　　\*

As we Americans and Kachins sat about the fire on the mountaintop, from where we could see China far to the east and the shimmering band of the Irrawaddy far to the west, the jaiwa told a story in his reedy, trancelike voice. He told of Dumsa La Lawn, a Kachin villager of the eighteenth century, who had gone to sleep and dreamed of a village in which hereditary duwas with absolute authority had given way to elected duwas and a village council. In his dream village the people were far more prosperous and happy than in any village that he knew in the real world.

When Dumsa La Lawn awakened, he went to his village duwa to tell him of his dream. The duwa listened with amazement and then, convinced that the good nats had sent the dream to Dumsa, voluntarily surrendered his exalted position so that the villagers could elect the duwa they wished and form a council. When the village with elected leaders became as prosperous and happy as the village in Dumsa La Lawn's dream, other village duwas surrendered their authority to democratically elected councils and duwas. They, too, proved prosperous and happy, and what became known as the gumlao movement spread rapidly among the Kachin people. In the Jinghpaw tongue, "gum" means "bend down," and "lao" means "turn over." A somersault performed by a child is a gumlao; a revolution performed by a community is also judged to be a gumlao. In a gumlao village the villagers are free and equal. There is no "thigh" duwa such as Ngai Tawng's father, no hereditary overlord such as Zhing Htaw Naw in the Hukawng Valley.

"Each man is as good as his neighbor," says Edmund R. Leach, the Cambridge University social anthropologist, of the Kachins in a gumlao village. "There are no class differences, no chiefs."

Among the Kachins, boys and girls sixteen years and older who are considered old enough to experience sex may do so without any social disapproval. Usually there is a crude basha situated in the paddies. It serves for rice storage and as a place where boys and girls can carry on flirtations. They sleep together in a group, and only if a couple feels strongly drawn to one another do they pair off by themselves.

"The house of the young in a village is not just for sex," explains Z. Brang Seng, a Kachin scholar now living in the United States. "It is a place for debate and talk. Girls learn which boys are the most promising because the Kachins rank intellect above physical beauty. The intelligent boy not only is likely to get the girl, but in a gumlao village his male contemporaries are able to size him up for election as a future duwa."

The Southern Gauri people of the Sinlumkaba Hills live in gumlao villages. Sinlumkaba, which is Jinghpaw for "big town," is the leading Kachin town in the Sinlumkaba Hills and perhaps the most important of all Kachin towns. When I first walked into the town after a long trek up the trail from the Irrawaddy Valley, I thought it something of a Kachin Shangri-La. The Kachins of Sinlumkaba had long ago put aside the nomadic life and lived not only in their traditional thatched bamboo bashas but also in stone houses. They had built long walls of stone to support rice terraces on the mountainside and had constructed a sophisticated irrigation system. Most of the Kachins of the Sinlumkaba Hills were Christians. Some were Catholic and some were Baptist. The duwa kaba of Sinlumkaba, Lazum Tang, was a Catholic, diminutive of stature—about five feet three inches tall —but erect of bearing, and sinewy and strong. Lazum wore shorts, a short-sleeved shirt, boots, and a purple turban twisted around his head. He slung a dah over his shoulder and carried a submachine gun. This made him appear the very model of an up-to-date Kachin duwa kaba: traditional in his relations to his people, he had armed himself with weapons both traditional and modern.

\* \* \*

Lazum Tang, followed by two of his men, walked into Pete Joost's camp at Sima. For several days Kachin scouts had brought word to Joost that the important duwa kaba was coming to see him. Both of Lazum's men were named Labang La, which proved confusing to Joost and his men, but both were equally welcome, since they were seasoned guerrilla fighters with a great deal of experience in ambushing the Japanese. The duwa and the two Labang Las went to work for Joost immediately. They recruited Kachins into the American-Kachin Rangers and trained them. Only a short distance away from Sima, at Bhamo, there were seven thousand Japanese soldiers anxious to avenge the defeat farther north at Myitkyina, and it was highly critical that Joost build up his force as quickly as possible. Jim Luce had returned to Nazira to build a base hospital for Americans and Kachins who could be flown out from one of the many light plane strips that were proliferating behind the Japanese lines in Kachin-held territory. Pete Joost had taken Luce's place as Area I commander, and he had a huge job to do if the drive on Bhamo was to be given the irregular warfare support that the Myitkyina campaign had shown made the difference between military success and failure in the Burmese jungles.

Joe Lazarsky of Area I command hiked with Lazum Tang up the winding trail to Sinlumkaba to enlist several thousand Kachins who were volunteering to follow their duwa kaba into the Rangers. The men were available to fight the Japanese, but could 101 arm them? Pete Joost walked out to Myitkyina to arrange for arms to be sent in, and then he jumped back into the field near Sinlumkaba to meet with Lazarsky, Lazum, and several of the ranking duwas of the hills.

"One thousand men are only waiting for arms," Lazarsky reported to Joost.

Joost radioed base, and the very next day planes, taking advantage of a break in stormy weather, came roaring in to drop fifteen plane-loads of weapons. The Kachins quickly familiarized themselves with the American arms and took up positions around Sinlumkaba. News had reached 101 agents that a force of Japanese were about to advance on the town from Bhamo. Joost and Lazum Tang moved their headquarters into the building once occupied by the British commissioner to the border areas, and prepared to ward off the Japanese attack.

The next day twenty more planeloads of guns were dropped, and another one thousand Kachins were armed and deployed. On each of two successive nights Japanese forces of about four hundred men struck at Sinlumkaba, but both times they were annihilated to a man in the Kachin ambushes set up to protect the trails. When I came up the trail taken by one of the Japanese forces several weeks after the ambushes were sprung, a Kachin hypenla, who had been part of a group defending Sinlumkaba, showed me the pungyis still in place with the dried blood of their victims still darkening the wood. He described how he and the other Kachins had fired from this point and swept the Japanese column with a murderous enfilade fire. The Kachins had even dislodged huge boulders from the hillsides so that they rolled down on their enemies with terrifying effect. It was an unforgettable lesson from an expert as to how a jungle people could annihilate a fully equipped modern combat force.

The Japanese sent Shan and Burmese agents up into the hills to spy on the Kachins, but in their turn they were captured. For once the Kachins did not torture their captives; they set them free after letting them see the formidable number of well-armed men who were ready to defend Sinlumkaba. They hurried back to Bhamo to tell the

Kempi Tai that thousands of Kachins were now in arms. When Kachin forces began nightly raids on Japanese outposts in the valley, the alarming reports were confirmed. A Kachin agent reported to Joost:

"Duwa," he said, "I have learned that all the Japanese staff from Bhamo are to meet with the secret police officers at noon tomorrow in a village midway between Sinlumkaba and Bhamo."

Joost radioed base and requested an air strike the next noon. He gave the exact coordinates of the village. Then he sent the agent back to the village to warn the villagers to slip out unobserved. Just before noon several hundred Kachin hypenlas, Joost, and Lazum Tang were on a hill from which they could conveniently look down on the village. They waited with mounting tension for the air force. At exactly twelve o'clock, six P-51s came winging in low from China. They dived down on the village, and released two bombs that screamed down onto the bashas. The planes circled and streaked over the now-flaming bashas with their machine guns chattering.

After the raid was over, Kachin agents returned to the village and learned that sixty Japanese, including the colonel in charge of Japanese intelligence in Bhamo and high Kempi Tai officials, had been killed even as they were plotting countermeasures against Detachment 101's new base—so very close but so unreachable—in the Sinlumkaba Hills.

Whenever the weather permitted, more supply and arms drops were made to Joost's Area I headquarters at Sinlumkaba. Only two weeks after he reached Sinlumkaba, Joost had four thousand Kachins under arms ready to strike at the Japanese rear as the Bhamo garrison braced itself for the approaching Chinese 38th Division and the Mars Task Force.

\* \* \*

Lazum Tang was distraught. When the Japanese had conquered Burma, his wife and two small sons had been trapped in a village just outside Lashio, about one hundred miles south of the Sinlumkaba Hills. At first his wife and children were safe enough, but then somebody informed the Japanese of their identity. The Japanese put the duwa kaba's wife to death when she refused to reveal the whereabouts of her husband. Now they held the boys with the belief that the old tiger might be tempted to rescue his cubs. Oscar, having finished the work of a Good Samaritan at Myitkyina, was now working his net of agents deep into Japanese-held territory from the Sinlumkaba base. It was one of his agents who learned that Lazum Tang's sons were alive and in good health. Lazum Tang immediately set out for Lashio to rescue his sons despite the certainty that he was being lured into a Japanese trap.

"I had come to love Lazum Tang like a brother," Pete Joost told me, "and I thought I'd never see him again. I could scarcely blame him for wanting to rescue his kids. I would have done the same thing, particularly when you think of some of the cute little tricks the Japanese had in reserve for captured Kachin youngsters, but here was this man who had already made all the difference to us in our mission going off on a suicidal mission of his own."

Oscar was the one who flashed the word out to Ray Peers that, incredibly enough, Lazum Tang had appeared out of the jungles with both his sons at his side. Nobody knows how he managed it. Father and sons set out on the trail to Kwitu, from where a 101 liaison plane was to fly the boys out to India, to a new life in a British school. Their movements were traced by Oscar's agents as they traveled day after day through the jungles. When they were a day's march out of Kwitu, Ray Peers flew in to the strip, and he and Pete Joost waited for the Kachin leader.

Lazum Tang wore his purple turban and immaculate dress as he approached the strip.

"When we met him," remembers Ray Peers, "his two small boys, dressed in their native garb, were following along behind him. They were immaculate and presented a heartwarming sight."

There was a fervid conference at the airstrip, and Lazum Tang and his sons boarded a plane and flew out to India. Within ten days, Lazum had placed his boys in school and returned to 101 for duty. He flew back to Kwitu and walked to Sinlumkaba. Later in the year he received a letter from Luke, the oldest boy, who was fourteen years old. He recounted how his younger brother had become ill and despite a doctor's care had died. Luke had arranged for his brother's burial, represented the family at the funeral, and written his father.

"Luke was a very brave boy," said Pete Joost. "He described all the arrangements so his father would know. Here and there on the page, his father could see where his tears had splashed down so that the ink had run."

Lazum Tang was proud of his Kachin son. As Z. Brang Seng says, "Bravery is the virtue of the Kachin people." Later, after the war,

Luke was to come to America and study at Fordham University. Today Luke Lazum Tang is an engineer.

\*     \*     \*

The Chinese were not getting along well with the Kachins. They feared the jungle people almost as much as the Japanese did, and fear led to hatred. There had been brushes between Chinese and Kachins as far back as the first Burma campaign. When the Chinese retiring through the Triangle after their defeat by the Japanese came to the ferry at N'Bun, they wantonly shot a Kachin boy. Lazum Tu, a village duwa, and his men tracked the Chinese to the Chati Hka and there killed ten of them in revenge. During the Allied return to Burma, problems had also arisen, but 101 man Charles Scott, a resourceful Ohioan, and his company of Kachin Rangers were to learn firsthand that, while General Sun might write commendations concerning the Kachins' bravery and their service to Chinese arms, the rank-and-file Chinese soldiers held considerably different sentiments.

Twelve thousand of General Sun's division had arrived in Shwegu just as Scott's Kachins were preparing to receive a badly needed air drop. As soon as the parachutes finished falling and the rice had been free-dropped, the Kachins rushed out onto the drop field to gather up the supplies. The Chinese swarmed out too, and since their numbers were overwhelming, they soon had the lion's share of the equipment and supplies. It was necessary to radio base, which Ray Peers had now moved forward from Nazira to Myitkyina, for a second drop. This time Scott had his Kachins set up machine guns so that they could cover the drop field. This, he hoped, would dissuade the Chinese from stealing the second drop as well.

The Chinese, noting the machine guns in position and the Kachins ready to open fire, did not interfere with the second drop, but General Sun exploded in anger. He wanted to know why Scott would allow his men to menace his Chinese soldiers. Then one hot afternoon, when eight of the Kachins were swimming in the Irrawaddy, Chinese soldiers happened by. They playfully lobbed hand grenades into the water to kill the swimmers, and stole their clothing and weapons. It was Scott's turn to be angry. That night the Kachins quietly left their camp and went off into the jungles. They refused to risk their lives scouting and patrolling for the Chinese, who had killed eight of their number just to steal their clothing and weapons.

This was not the end of the episode. As the Chinese army advanced to the south, a lead element encountered an ambush. Scores of Chinese were killed, and there was not a Japanese within fifty miles. During the next month, the Chinese army struck ambush after ambush that 101 men would just as soon not admit that the Kachins had set. When the Kachins felt that they had evened the score, just as suddenly as they had turned hostile they went back to ambushing the Japanese and guiding the Chinese through the jungle to their next military destination.

\*     \*     \*

Oscar was now at Shwegu, on the Irrawaddy below Bhamo, where Roger Wolbarst, who had a characteristic antic flare, had become his friend. Wolbarst owed his life to Zhing Htaw Naw. The fact that he still wore his infantry helmet on the trail was testimony to his lack of adjustment to the special rigors of the arena in which he found himself. He stumbled with exhaustion into a swamp one night about three in the morning, after an all-night hike.

"I had already sunk to my shoulders and was too fatigued to care any more," he told me later. "I was the last man in our column, as far as I knew, and there was nobody to help me."

Zhing Htaw Naw, always a jungle man, was still farther behind on the trail, but he soon came upon the hapless American. He clamped his arms about Wolbarst's chest and heaved and pulled until he broke the sucking grip of the swamp. When he was at last on firm ground, Wolbarst threw away his helmet and an extra box of ammunition. He, too, was learning the 101 lesson that a guerrilla does not encumber himself with anything that is not absolutely essential.

Even so, the next day he found that he was walking the skin right off his feet.

"The calluses of a lifetime had gone," he remembered. "I had nothing but raw meat."

Wolbarst was suffering from jungle rot. The constant moisture of the jungle had turned his feet fish-white. He could run a knife a half inch into the flesh and not feel it. He had to hole up for two weeks before he could continue on the trail. Then he learned not to wear boots in the rainy season and always to make certain his socks were dry. He switched to canvas jungle boots as did most of us, put on a cool Kachin longyi instead of hot American fatigues, and affected an Australian bush hat.

Now Roger Wolbarst was a veteran American-Kachin Ranger and

Oscar's friend. On the trail to Mongmit, a Japanese agent had tried to lead the force into a trap. After two days of questioning established that the man was guilty, he was made to dig his own grave and then executed. A few days later a tall Burmese came to see Oscar at Shwegu. He had known Oscar at Steele Brothers in the days before the war. Oscar was delighted to see him. That night Law Kaw cooked and served a superb curry, and Oscar, Wolbarst, and the Burmese guest sat down to dinner together. The conversation was sentimental, old days were remembered, and the laukhu sipped between mouthfuls was a superior distillation.

"I went back to the radio to get the nightly message from headquarters," says Wolbarst. "It was a list of five dangerous Burmese agents, who were to be shot on sight. Our Burmese guest was at the head of the list."

When he returned to the dinner, Wolbarst handed the list to Oscar, who was recounting a story about the old Steele Brothers days. Oscar glanced at the message and continued to tell his tale without revealing the slightest trace of emotion.

"Would you show me the new trail to Shwegugale?" he innocently asked his guest when the dinner was completed.

The two men set off along the trail arm in arm. A little later Oscar returned, and the tall Burmese was never heard from again.

\* \* \*

The Japanese withdrew from Shwegu. In so doing, the Japanese commander left behind his two beautiful Anglo-Burmese mistresses. Oscar, Law Kaw, and Wolbarst decided to see for themselves whether the Japanese officer had good taste in women.

"They were luscious beauties with big boobs," remembers Wolbarst. "We were having a very satisfactory visit when three Chinese officers broke into the house."

The Chinese had just reached the area, and there had already been trouble between the Kachins and their presumed allies. Oscar talked in Chinese to the excited officers.

"We'd better get out of here," he said to Wolbarst.

"And leave these beautiful women for those guys?" rejoined Wolbarst.

"They're taking these women with them," said Oscar. "They're going to feed them to their troops."

Wolbarst was all for defending the two women with every drop of blood in his gallant, red-blooded American body, but when the 101 men stepped outside they discovered a hundred Chinese soldiers, their guns ready, waiting for the women to be "fed" to them. It was only discreet to abandon the women and leave the village quietly before feeding time began.

\*   \*   \*

Kachin girls with their jet black hair twisted up in braids, often with jungle jasmine festooned about their necks, sang love songs as they wove bamboo strips for baskets or the walls of a house. Many an American 101 man found himself falling in love with one of these dark-eyed beauties; many more, having been accepted into the village circle by the Kachins, took advantage of their standing by courting the girls with the same relish that the Kachin young men displayed.

Roger Wolbarst proposed to Oscar one night, as they sat beside the campfire in a company of Kachin Rangers, that they pay a visit to a nearby Kachin village, through which they had passed earlier in the day.

"The girls there are truly magnificent," said Wolbarst.

Oscar agreed, and the two men crept out through the camp's defense perimeter. They walked for several hours.

"Oscar carried no weapons," remembers Wolbarst. "He felt he'd survive better in the jungle without them. I had a carbine. He had a Kachin bag with opium in it."

When they at last came to the village, they went to the duwa's basha. The duwa immediately ordered up a feast to mark the occasion. A boy brought in a bamboo section filled with laukhu and poured each of the guests a liberal cupful of the fiery liquor. The council of elders joined the party, and everybody sat about and sipped laukhu and talked. When the first course was brought in, liberal servings of a gray substance on plantain leaves, Oscar drew his breath in through his lips with appreciation.

"Ah," he said to Wolbarst. "Raw monkey brains."

Wolbarst felt his gorge rise, and he stared with disgust at the unappetizing mess on the plantain leaf which a boy handed to him with such a winning look on his face.

"Never mind," said Oscar. "Eat it."

"I ate it," says Wolbarst. "It was awful. No salt and pepper. Just raw monkey brains."

Everybody else in the room was smacking his lips with satisfaction, but Wolbarst stepped out the door onto the platform. His stomach heaved, and he vomited over the railing, to the discomfiture of the pigs that were sheltering down beneath. The main course was a succulent curry featuring the flesh of the same monkeys whose brains had been served as hors d'oeuvres. When it was over, the duwa, selected village elders, Oscar, and Wolbarst prepared to relax over a pipe of opium.

"It is a great honor that they're offering us," said Oscar.

Wolbarst was not so sure. He watched as a Kachin heated a quantity of opium in a copper spoon by holding it over the fire. Then he dropped portions of the tarry substance that resulted onto plantain leaves. He waited for the opium to cool and then rolled the leaves into balls. He ignited a ball and put it in a wooden pipe with a V insert in it. When a pipe was ready for everybody, the smokers lay back with their heads on wooden blocks and prepared to enjoy a more or less congenial social hour or so.

"Don't put the stem of the pipe in your mouth," Oscar hissed to Wolbarst. "It's very rude. You hold the stem of the pipe up to your mouth as if it is a blowgun."

Oscar was Kachin gentility itself when he puffed on his opium pipe. With every inhalation the opium snapped, sparkled, and popped in the pipes. A Kachin boy brought each smoker a cup of tea.

"Take a sip of tea," explained Oscar, "after every inhalation. Inhale, then tea, then exhale. It's too abrasive if you don't drink the tea."

Wolbarst was terrified. The basha in the jungle, the Kachin faces, the opium in his lungs, and the terrible knowledge of what it could do to him filled him with fear. Opium smoking among the Kachins, for some unexplained reason, rarely becomes the grim problem it does among other societies, but any 101 man who tried a pipe with his Kachin hosts did so with great trepidation. The first pipe did nothing to Wolbarst. He was given a second pipe, and he smoked that too. Suddenly the opium struck. His head felt disembodied, and it floated around the basha by itself, looking down on his prostrate body and at the other smokers. That his head was functioning separately from the body up there in the rafters, where the smoke from the fire was eddying about seeking the fire hole in the thatched roof, did not keep it from carrying on a conversation with Oscar. Wolbarst felt all-wise, and he said profound and significant, eloquent and magnificent things. Oscar, for his part, it seemed to Wolbarst, was speaking sheer gibberish. Somehow Oscar and Wolbarst got back to camp. In the morning Wolbarst had a terrible headache. With his head throbbing as if ten thousand nats were warring within it, he decided that his first experience with opium was also going to be his last.

A few nights later when Wolbarst was recovered, Oscar had another plan.

"It's time to court the girls," he said.

"Yes, but let's avoid the headman," replied Wolbarst, who was confident that he would never survive another pipe of opium.

They slipped through the perimeter again that night and in a few hours had reached the village.

"What do we do now, Oscar?" asked Wolbarst.

Oscar spotted a young boy and caught him by the arm. He and the boy jabbered back and forth in Kachin, and the youngster went off.

"We're all set," Oscar explained. "It is the proper thing to send a young boy to tell the girls that some men have come courting."

Soon the boy came running back, panting. Everything was indeed arranged, and he led Oscar and Wolbarst to a basha almost one hundred yards long, where he stationed them beneath the n-ladap, the room of the unmarried girls.

"It is something of a free zone for any unmarried males," Oscar explained as they stood ankle-deep in the pig and buffalo muck beneath the basha. "Married males must beware. A married man who commits adultery is executed. The Kachins always assume that the man is at fault. If a girl gets pregnant by an unmarried man or boy, there is no problem. The village will raise the child.

"This is where I think the girls are," opined Oscar.

He jabbed a hand through a hole in the floor and spoke rapturously.

"I have a breast."

Wolbarst followed his mentor and thrust his hand through another hole in the floor.

"I think I have a stomach," he said.

"Move your hand a little," suggested Oscar.

Wolbarst did as told and he, too, held a firm breast.

"Now sing along with me," directed Oscar.

He began to sing a Kachin love song in a high-pitched falsetto. Wolbarst imitated him as best he could.

"We sang for half an hour with mosquitoes chomping on us, up to our ankles in manure," Wolbarst remembers. "My hand became so numb that I couldn't tell a breast from a foot. We were being eaten alive by the mosquitoes. I was about to tell Oscar that I didn't think it was worth it, when there came a pounding on the floor above us."

"There they go," cried Oscar. "After them!"

He sprinted out from beneath the basha as fast as he could run, and Wolbarst went running after him, his heavy boots clumping through the village street. Two girls, wraithlike, were just disappearing into the jungle at the far end of the village. The fair pursued and the amorous pursuers raced along a jungle trail.

"They all disappeared up a hill and left me behind," says Wolbarst. "Finally, off in the distance I saw a little light. It was the granary and young people's house in the paddies."

At one end of the large room in the house was a raised platform used to store the rice. When Wolbarst entered the lower part of the building, Oscar was sitting beside a fire, his arms around two cute Kachin girls.

"With their bangs and straight black hair, their breasts peeking from their jackets, black skirts, and dainty bare feet, they were very attractive indeed. Each had a fortune in silver coins sewed onto her jacket," says Wolbarst.

"Sit down," Oscar told him. "Which one do you want?"

Wolbarst put his arm around one of the girls, but she edged away.

"She doesn't like me," he told Oscar.

"Nonsense. Put your arm around her."

Wolbarst once again put his arm around the girl, and she edged away again. She laughed, showed her little white teeth, and said something in Kachin.

"You look like a goat," translated Oscar.

Oscar was clean-shaven, but Wolbarst had let his beard grow. Kachin men have very light beards if any beard at all.

"She's frightened of you," said Oscar.

"What shall I do?"

"When we get back to camp, shave it off. Now don't let it hold you back. She'll go for you. You have to subdue Kachin girls by force."

Wolbarst put his arm around the giggling girl again, but she broke free and leaped up onto the rice platform.

"Corner her," cried Oscar, as he hugged his own girl tight. "Grab her, but before you go up on the platform, take your boots off. You can't wear them on the grain platform."

Wolbarst furiously unlaced his boots and tugged them off. He dove up on the platform and made a grab for the girl. She sprang right through the wall and went running off. Wolbarst was about to dive after her.

"I'll run her down," he cried.

"No, it's not the sporting way," said Oscar.

There was nothing to do but hike back to camp. The next day Wolbarst shaved his beard off.

\* \* \*

The Kachin jaiwa looked at some chicken bones left over from the evening's dinner.

"Somebody is going to be shot," he said.

Louis Singleton, a 101 radioman, felt a chill run up his back. Charlie Scott's company of Kachins had worked around until it was south of Bhamo, where it was harassing Japanese troop and supply movements. The very next day as the company moved along a trail, Scott came face to face with a Japanese. He threw his Bren gun up to fire, but it jammed. The Japanese fired, and his shot dropped Scott with a bullet in the shoulder. The Kachins coming up chased the Japanese away. Scott was brought down to the Shweli River, where a few days later a 101 pilot landed on a sandbar in the middle of the stream. Singleton recalls that a knot of Kachins had to push the plane along the bar so that it could gather enough speed to take off. Scott flew out to Jim Luce's new hospital where he could get medical care.

Bill Martin had been taken out of the jungles on leave, and now he was ready for another assignment. Opero decided that he should take Scott's place. Where was he to be dropped? On a moutain peak? What were the coordinates? We just made a supply drop there, claimed Opero. We'll find it.

"I wasn't too happy about the jump when I learned I was to do it in the dark," says Martin. "They radioed that I was coming in. We reached the drop zone. Red light means an alert. Green means jump. First, red light. Crew chief says get ready to go. Green light. Out I go. I'm floating down into a sunset. Horizon is still light. Next thing I know, figures are running around down below. Fire flashes and bullets zip by me. I climb the chute and drop over a mountainside. Fall down. Walk down into valley. I'd started coming down on the Japanese army. It took two and a half days for the Kachins to make a contact. Fortunately they'd seen the plane too. It was a hell of a way for their new CO to arrive."

*        *        *

With Bhamo invested by the Allies, American-Kachin Ranger units were in action throughout the region. As the Chinese and Americans neared Bhamo, the Japanese attempted a flanking movement, a classical maneuver, which had won them many battles in the first Burma campaign. They were balked by the Kachins, who commanded the territory through which their movement had to be executed. The presence of the Kachins, raiding with impunity, forced the Japanese to increase their forces in the areas east of the road from Bhamo to Namhkam, where in peacetime Seagraves had once had his hospital.

At the same time, 101 units were leading the Chinese 22d Division in its march on Shwegu, except for temporary defections by Kachins who had been antagonized by Chinese cupidity and belligerence. Shwegu fell on November 6, and Bhamo on December 15. Once again the Japanese had been forced to fight the attacking regular forces on a wide front, while defending their rear from the Kachins as best they could. Once again, as they fell back to new defense points, they fell back through bloody ambushes set by the Kachins.

The pattern of Allied victory was established, and it began to become evident to General Tanaka and other top Japanese commanders that ultimately there would be no end to the humiliating defeats their soldiers were suffering short of the Thai border. To their credit, the Japanese continued to open up every conceivable avenue of military effort, to fight bravely and efficiently. Another army's morale might well have collapsed at this point as it confronted the Allied campaign to free Burma, but the Japanese acted as if victory and not defeat were still the daily outcome. They remained a redoubtable army, badly hurt but scarcely beaten.

# Sinlumkaba

Now 101 guerrilla bands were erupting behind the lines with what must have seemed to the Japanese command like appalling spontaneity. They provided an intelligence and guerrilla screen for the advancing British 36th Division. They secured the British left flank so that the 36th could concentrate its forces on Mohnyin and then attack down the railroad corridor to Katha and Indaw. They mined Japanese roads and disrupted communications. At the same time, 101 guerrillas were securing the entire right flank of the Northern Combat Area Command from Katha to the Chindwin River. They struck heavy blows at the Japanese forces to dissuade them from launching an attack on the engineers building the Ledo Road toward its ultimate rendezvous with the old Burma Road. None of this was spontaneous. It was the result of careful preparation by agents in the field, and of the close cooperation between Kachin and American leaders in the recruitment, training, and direction of guerrilla forces. Nothing whatsoever was left to chance.

The 475th Infantry and the 124th Cavalry made up the Mars Task Force. Their goal, assigned by the Northern Combat Area Command, was to reach the Burma Road and to link up with Chinese forces advancing along the road from Yunnan in the face of bitter Japanese opposition. The 475th struck out east of Tonkwa on a steep trail following the 101 Kachin scouts, led by Hiram Pamplin. What began as a road, fifteen to twenty feet wide, degenerated into a track just wide enough for a man and a mule, which led up and down across seemingly endless hills. It was a land where tiny villages clung to hilltops and where every valley seemed terraced into paddies. Each night the Kachins had to show the American soldiers to bivouac areas where water could be found. Army maps were poor. Bob Flaherty's company of Kachins had earlier been given the task of mapping the country into which the Americans were now advancing.

"Because the sheer fatigue of climbing the steeper slopes was formidable, march schedules went out the window, or rather, down the mountainside with quite a few steel helmets and an occasional mule," wrote Charles F. Romanus and Riley Sunderland of the Office of the Chief of Military History, Department of the Army.

"A screen of Kachin Rangers was preceding the American column. Speaking the local dialects and carrying radios and automatic weapons, the Kachins were an excellent screen which masked the Mars Task Force while reporting anything that might be suspicious."

The 475th crossed the Shweli River on bridges built of bundles of bamboo for pontoons and vines for cables. The river's swift current tore at the bridge so that Kachin bridgebuilders were busy repairing the structure even as the Americans and their heavily laden mules gingerly crossed. Beyond the Shweli the trails became even more difficult, and the men gasped for breath and sank to the ground in utter weariness.

The rains began, and the red clay of the trails became slippery. At first the men kept their feet by holding onto the mules, but after several mules slid over the cliffs, they decided to rely on their own nimbleness. The 124th Cavalry following the 475th found that the advance regiment, instead of breaking the way, merely churned up the clay, impeding their own progress still further. Watching men and mules slide off a trail and go slithering down a slope to the bottom sometimes moved the men to laughter, especially when the man who took the plunge was an officer; but since some of the skids ended up in serious injury or even death, laughter had a way of turning into grim silence.

Clouds swirled among the surrounding peaks so that it was impossible to make air drops. Men grew hungry when no supplies dropped from the sky. Each day grew interminable. At last the columns came down out of the mountains to Mongwi, where Dan Mudrinich and a battalion of one thousand Kachins who had been recruited at Sinlumkaba by Lazum Tang were waiting for them. Mudrinich, Joe Lazarsky, and Alvin Freudenberg, each with one thousand Kachins, had been dispatched by Pete Joost to block Japanese escape routes from the battle of Bhamo. Joost had wanted to take Bhamo itself with his hard-fighting Kachins, but Stilwell had decided that the Kachins would be better used in decimating the Japanese during their retreat once the city fell. Freudenberg's battalion, having taken up positions along the road from Bhamo to Lashio, the last route of withdrawal open to the Japanese, had inflicted especially heavy casualties on the enemy.

*    *    *

It was during this time when the Japanese were escaping from Bhamo as best they could that Father Stuart had another brush with death.

"On Christmas Eve, '44," he noted in his journal, "I had a very narrow escape. Bhamo town was still held until a short time before this by the Japanese, though the areas around it were in our hands for weeks. Even when the town was in their control, we could move around the outskirts in the daytime without any great fear. Now I was in the hills east of Bhamo. I had said mass on Sunday morning at Hkudung, the mission of old Father Gilhodes, who had been taken to Mandalay the previous spring. I had walked there from the plains. After mass I left for Sinlumkaba, Father Flatley's mission, to have midnight mass there. It was a sixteen-mile walk over hilly country. I went ahead, followed by two boys who carried my kit. A few miles from Sinlumkaba at a corner on the trail, I met three armed men. I paid no attention to their uniforms, rather worn, but took them for Yawyins, a more backward tribe of the Kachins. I addressed them in Kachin, but excited by suddenly meeting a white man face to face unexpectedly in the jungle, as I thought, they ran into the bush. Later along the trail I waited until my two boys caught up and asked them if they had met the three men. They hadn't seen anyone. The men must have abandoned the trail. That night these men were killed by Kachins, and their rifles and equipment brought to Sinlumkaba. They were Japanese soldiers."

I had been with Father Stuart just a few days before at Momauk, just east of Bhamo, and on Christmas Eve I, too, was hiking up the trail that leads to Sinlumkaba. Mike, the Hindu radio operator, and I had started out for an eighteen-mile hike, which we intended to finish that night so that we could spend Christmas Day at Pete Joost's headquarters. The trail from the Irrawaddy Valley to Sinlumkaba begins with a boulder-strewn ascent through jungled foothills. Mike and I climbed that first hour without a break, certain that we would reach Sinlumkaba in plenty of time. We stopped to fill our canteens in one of the many waterfalls which plash down from the rocky ledges overhanging the trail. The water in these falls is pure and good to drink. The loud screams of the jungle birds obscured the sounds of a party of Kachins coming down the trail, so we were surprised by several families when we rounded a bend. Secure within their own country, the Kachins were laughing and singing to make the miles go faster. They were enroute to one of the bazaars that Pete Joost had gone to great pains to have reopened in the hills so that people would have no trouble in getting salt, rice, and the other staples of life as well as what merchandise might become available. Bazaars in the North Burma hills are not only a source of supplies but a place where people go to learn the news or just to talk and have a good time.

"Kaja-ee," I said. "Is it good?"

The Kachins smiled with friendship.

"Kaja," answered the man in front. "It is good."

"Kaja-lo," said a lad. "It is wonderfully good."

We climbed higher past lofty cliffs until we had come out of the jungles into a meadow. We paused in Sinlumkajee, or "Little Town." Standing before the duwa's basha, we could look out over the Irrawaddy Valley. Japanese planes were bombing Bhamo, and we could see the burst of their bombs on the faraway town set in the middle of the pastoral serenity of paddies and villages. A girl pounding rice before the basha looked up from her work to gaze at the far-off military action in the valley. She smiled. What could war have to do with life in Sinlumkajee?

Once we rounded a boulder and came upon a large tiger. Mike and I looked into his eyes for a moment. Then he trotted off. I knew that my weapons were virtually useless against him, and somehow he just did not seem hostile. It was as if he, too, shared the peaceable kingdom of the mountainside inhabited by the young girl pounding rice at Sinlumkajee. In the war in Burma there were many such peaceable kingdoms where 101 men found that life was going on in its usual way despite the terrible things which might be happening only a few miles distant.

We passed through the next village, and it was then that we came upon the Japanese whom Father Stuart, ahead of us on the trail, had encountered. They were not in uniform at all, as he thought, but in ragged Kachin dress. One of them, I learned later, was a doctor, and the other two were soldiers. Mike and I also took the stragglers for Kachins from some remote tribe, perhaps from across the border in China.

"Kaja-ee," I said.

They did not reply but shoved on past. In the village below us, I learned later, Kachins immediately recognized the men as Japanese and attacked and killed them. They cut off their ears and dispatched them to Sinlumkaba as something of a Christmas present for Pete Joost.

Not long after meeting the Japanese, Mike and I took a wrong turn, which led us along another trail for some seven hours. It began to grow dark, and we regretted that we had eaten all the K rations we carried at lunch. It also grew cold, and we could not help but slump down on the ground from time to time for a rest. The barking deer came close about us, and their odd, doglike cries were companionable.

"I'd give anything to be in a village," said Mike. "I don't care if we ever reach Sinlumkaba."

We heard voices on the trail below us. Men were laughing and singing. We stopped and waited for a party of half a dozen Kachins to come up. The oldest gave some orders, and a boy took out some rice wrapped in plantain leaves from his bag. Mike and I squatted on the trail and ate some rice. I had learned enough of the Kachin ways by this time to drop a few crumbs on the trail as a gift for the nats. Seeing me do this, the older Kachin made the sign of the cross to indicate that he was not an animist but a Christian. But he immediately crumbled a bit of rice on the trail himself to show that, Christian or not, he had no intention of offending the nats, who might at this very moment be thinking of rolling a rock down the mountainside to crush us or sending a tiger to maul us.

We started up the trail together, but we could not keep up with the Kachins, who were on their way home from the bazaar, packing salt and other supplies. The Kachins stopped, and the older man again gave an order. The boy vanished into a thicket and soon returned with a bamboo section filled with laukhu. The Kachins place caches of laukhu here and there along their trails in case they want to have a warming swallow or so to help them on their way. The boy handed the laukhu to me, and I took a long drink. So did Mike, and we started up the trail again. Suddenly my legs went dead. Laukhu can have a drastic effect on people who are not accustomed to it. I sank to the trail. Mike took one look at me and slumped to the trail himself. We were a disgrace. The Kachins half carried and half dragged us to their village. We arrived in a drunken stupor amidst the barking of dogs, the laughter of children, and the sympathetic cooings of the women.

A curry dinner is a good antidote to laukhu, and we recovered quickly once we had eaten. We sat by the fire in the duwa's basha. A young hypenla, home on leave from one of Lazum Tang's battalions, shuffled off his Kachin dress and got into his new Rangers uniform to show me that he was one of us. His father, beaming with pride, embraced him and kissed him affectionately on both cheeks. The young soldier's sister came and sat by me. It was her task to see that I was not chilly in the night when the fire burned low.

I was sound asleep when a furious fusillade of shots broke out. Men shouted just outside the basha.

"It's the Chinese bandits," cried Mike.

We had learned before leaving base that Chinese irregulars had been raiding across the border east of Bhamo. They had looted Kachin villages and raped women until Pete Joost had deployed two battalions under Tom Chamales and Al Freudenberg. The hypenlas had the dual job of securing the border against Chinese attacks and attacking Japanese traffic on the road from Bhamo, which skirted the Sinlumkaba Hills to the south and ran to Wanting where the Burma Road crossed into China. The Chinese, under the command of a frontier warlord, attacked nine Kachin villages, burning bashas, stealing precious salt and rice, and carrying away girls and women.

It was unlikely that Tom Chamales and Al Freudenberg made any effort to restrain the Kachins under their command, but if they had it would not have made any difference. The hypenlas crossed into China to rescue their women. They caught up with the Chinese, and after a brief fight freed the captives. Before returning to Burma they also attacked and destroyed nine Chinese towns.

"To them it was an eye for an eye," commented Ray Peers.

Pete Joost, hearing of the incident, reported the matter to Ray Peers. Peers asked for an impartial commission to investigate the conflict, but the commission's work stalled in bureaucratic confusion and the utter failure of Chinese and Americans to agree on anything. Finally, four to five months later, Peers received a personal letter with the chop of Generalissimo Chiang Kai-shek affixed to it. Chiang demanded five hundred million Chinese Nationalist dollars in restitution for the damage done by the Kachins. At the exchange rate of twenty to one, this amounted to twenty-five million U.S. dollars. Chiang Kai-shek held Peers personally responsible for the debt.

"Although I was quite honored by his request, to think that a U.S. Army colonel would have that kind of money," Peers said after the war, "I was obliged to turn it over to NCAC with the recommendation that the generalissimo be advised as to the findings of the board."

The matter was dropped, but the Chinese raided across the border again as soon as they learned that most of the Kachin men were elsewhere engaged with the Japanese.

Listening to the gunfire and shouting outside the basha, I thought Mike was probably right about the Chinese bandits. I snatched up my carbine. The hypenla burst into the basha, shouting in English, "Merry Christmas, duwa! Merry Christmas!"

I put down my rifle and looked at him in incredulity. He rushed over and embraced me.

"Merry Christmas!" he repeated.

"Merry Christmas," I said at last.

It had grown quiet outside. Then the women and children began to sing. They sang timidly, softly at first, but their voices gained in volume and conviction. They sang in Kachin, but the melody was "Silent Night." The men's voices joined in. Mike and I followed the hypenla out onto the platform of the basha, and we looked down on the villagers, whose faces were lit by torches.

"Silent night, holy night," I sang in English. "All is calm, all is bright."

Together we sang other carols. The spirit of Christmas had reached halfway around the world.

In the morning the hypenla guided us to Sinlumkaba. We left before dawn, and we were there within a few hours. Two little Kachin boys, Taney and Smiley, brought me breakfast, which I enjoyed with a leader of their people who I soon learned was Lazum Tang, the duwa kaba. There were perhaps forty Americans at Sinlumkaba then. I remember one of them was Pete Joost, of course; others were Butch Brown, with his flaming red beard and peacock-feathered hat, who was one of our most effective jungle commanders; Bob Rodenberg, another one of 101's top commanders; Bob DeWeese, the softspoken medic, who had earlier organized guerrillas in Greece for the OSS; and Doc Franklin, whose skilled surgical hands had already saved the lives of many wounded Kachins and Americans.

The Americans had put up a Christmas tree, of what variety I cannot say, and made presents for the Kachin children who, eyes shining, were stand-ins for their counterparts at home whom the 101 men sorely missed on this holiday for children. Father Stuart had celebrated his midnight mass, and now, as everybody crowded around the tree, the children sang carols. A small boy with the face and voice of a choirboy sang, and Lazum Tang shook his hand with great solemnity when he was finished, which he imagined was the American way of showing approval, and then, laughing, hugged the child in his arms, which is the Kachin way. Ngai Tawng, the animist, looked on this Christian celebration with wonder. He took my hand, and his eyes asked for an explanation. I pointed to Father Stuart. He would be the one who could tell Ngai Tawng what all of this meant.

That afternoon we gathered in a high meadow from where we could look fifty miles over endless ranges of mountains into China. Lazum Tang made long speeches in Kachin and English about his people, their history and their hopes, their love for the Americans. Everyone ate curried dishes and drank laukhu, and as the afternoon grew late and shadows lengthened on the mountainside, we did not feel the chill.

Foot races were held for boys and girls, and packages of salt, wrapped in leaves, were distributed to village duwas and elders who were present. A group of young men and boys stood in a circle and tried to keep a small wicker ball in the air by kicking it aloft with their knees. They were incredibly agile. The ball would fly about for five to ten minutes at a time until somebody, usually an American who had joined the game, would miss. Then everybody shouted and laughed. The person who had made the error laughed loudest of all, except for one boy who, having missed the ball several times, was carried down to the icy pool where Pete Joost habitually took his morning dip, and dropped unceremoniously into the water. The boy emerged from the water spluttering and shook his wet self as a dog shakes in order to wet his tormentors, all the time jabbering and shrieking with laughter.

The moon was full that night. It turned the distant mountains to silver and lit up the Sinlumkaba Valley below us. The eerie sounds of rattles and gongs, drums, cymbals and bells, flutes and stringed instruments similar to violins came to us as we celebrated in the meadow. A procession came around the hill to join us. First boys came wearing loincloths, lighting the way with flares. Then came the musicians in fanciful costumes and rank after rank of hypenlas. The soldiers had stripped to loincloths, too, and their oiled bodies shone in the torchlight. Each carried a dah. After them came the girls in their best manau clothing, their eyes shining with excitement, and flowers in their black hair.

The girls danced while the musicians played music that pulsed and skirled in the night. Their movements were magic and grace. The musicians struck up an exultant song. An elder stepped forward with a live chicken and held it up. A soldier severed the chicken's head with a slash of his dah. He stepped forward holding aloft the knife, on which a few drops of chicken blood sparkled. He flung back his head and glared at the moon with demonic eyes. He stretched his muscles in supple grace for a moment and then gyrated, whirled, and leaped through a fantastic dance, his dah whirling about his head, his body, and between his legs. The moonlight glinted on his oiled body and on the flying steel, and the music went screaming down over the mountainside, all in honor of the Christ Child. Women watching the dancer broke into tears and shook with frenzy. The dance ended, and everybody cheered and applauded. All became silent except for the weeping of the women.

There were more dances by the girls, a torch dance by men and boys, and stick dances, in which half-grown boys laid into one another with staves. Ngai Tawng, in a style befitting a wild boy from the Hukawng, whirled and struck with his stave in such a savage way that he bested opponent after opponent, driving them cringing into the shouting crowd. Once he dropped a boy with a resounding blow in the ribs. He stood over the fallen youth, his eyes suddenly grown gentle, and held his hand down to him to help him to his feet again. The Kachins are this way—a mixture of gentleness and ferocity.

There were songs of the heroic past sung by the jaiwas in their reedy voices, and love songs sung by the girls. Unmarried men and boys, Americans as well as Kachins, drifted off into the shadows with the girls. Could such a Christmas celebration have ever been imagined? The evening's festivities ended with carols, sung by children. Last of all, everybody stood up and sang "God Save the King." In spite of everything that had happened in Burma, the Kachins at Sinlumkaba still accepted the ruler in faraway London as their supreme duwa. We Americans brazenly sang "My Country 'Tis of Thee," but no one else knew the difference.

It was only a few nights later that the weretiger came to our hut door and scratched his claws on its worn wood. New Year's Eve, 1945, arrived. We sat on our mountain and looked out across the lower summits to a faraway mountainside where a Kachin village was burning. The Chinese bandits had crossed the border again. The last of the hypenlas had left after the Christmas manau to go south to fight the Japanese. We expected an attack on Sinlumkaba all night and slept little. No attack came. We learned that a force of Kachin boys, too young to be counted as hypenlas, had come from the villages and attacked the Chinese. They had driven them back across the border. For several days after that the mountains were wrapped in mist, and sometimes it rained with incredible fury.

On January 9, with the trail a morass, several of us Americans walked down into the Irrawaddy Valley. At last I could keep up with the Kachins on the trail, and I felt proud of myself when I arrived at the airstrip at Momauk. From Momauk, 101 liaison planes flew us down to Mongwi, where we arrived some time before the Marsmen came toiling over the hills to our rendezvous. Both Ngai Tawng and I soon found ourselves with a company of Kachins, who were to provide an intelligence and guerrilla screen for the 475th Infantry which, once it had been given a brief rest and a supply drop, was to cross the Loilun Range to surprise the Japanese who were holding the Burma Road along the stretch where it ran through the Hosi Valley.

\* \* \*

Red Maddox and Pete Lutken arrived at Dum Dum Airport in Calcutta. After close to a year and a half behind the Japanese lines they were on leave. Maddox, although a bona fide British major, wore no insignia, and was dressed in a tropical helmet and an American uniform—true to form for a 101 man. Lutken wore a captain's bars on his American uniform. They walked into the cool lobby of the Grand Hotel with the great whooshing fans.

"You had to be an officer to stay at the Grand," Lutken recalls, "so I lent Red a set of my captain's bars and a pair of extra crossed rifles that I had."

The 101 men registered, dropped their duffle in their room, and started down Chowringhee. They had not gone a block before an American MP stopped them. Lutken did not have bars on his cap. The MP took the friends to the station.

"You'll have to show me your orders," said an MP noncom.

Lutken had no orders, but he did manage to dig his dog tags out of his shirt and wave them at the noncom. He kept Maddox behind him

as best he could. Then the noncom demanded to know Maddox's serial number.

"438," replied Maddox confidently.

"Nobody has had a serial number that low since George Washington," remarked Lutken. "The truth had to come out, and Red admitted that he was really a British major."

"My name is Santa Claus," said the disbelieving MP.

When Maddox and Lutken insisted that they were OSS men and
above such nonsense as wearing the right rank and uniforms, the MP
ushered them in to the provost marshal. After hearing their story, he
called Harry Little at the OSS Calcutta office. He gave Little the
names of the prisoners.

"Have you heard of either one of them?" he asked.

"I don't know who they are," said Little, probably more than a bit
tired of bailing out troublesome 101'ers from the field.

The provost marshal ordered the two 101 men locked up.

"After two years in the Burma jungle and the first time out, I'm
arrested in fifteen minutes," recalls Lutken sadly. "I didn't behave
too well in the jail that night. The next day Harry Little got us out."

Maddox stayed on in Calcutta, but Lutken took the Bengal and
Assam train for Assam. He felt more at home in the jungle.

On leave in Calcutta, Simla, Darjeeling, or wherever else they happened to go, 101 men were not known for either their sobriety or
their good behavior. One group brought the reigning madam of a
Calcutta whorehouse to a fancy ball given by the British governor
general, much to the dismay of the gentlemen present. When word
ran through the room with the speed of lightning that the handsome
lady with the young Americans was the famous madam, wives stared
at her in amazement. Their stares turned to angry glares as the
madam blithely greeted almost all of their husbands by name.

The only occasion that surpassed this in the fond recollections of
101 men was the night that Butch Brown rode a horse up the stair-
case of the Grand Hotel in Simla and cantered into another ball, his
Robin Hood's feather-in-the-cap as jaunty as ever. All in all, both
their commanders and the remainder of the Allied military estab-
lishment agreed that 101 men were at their best out in the jungle.
Jim Luce, who naively assumed that 101 men were being taken out
of the field from time to time for necessary rest and recuperation,
had to welcome the jungle warriors back to Nazira when they returned from wherever their predilections took them. Tom Moon re-

members how Luce would fix a fine professional eye on the wilted soldier.

"Young man, you'll learn that it's best for you to give up women and drinking," he would remark.

"Commander, I don't deserve the best," was the usual sardonic reply. "What's next best?"

\* \* \*

Pete Lutken and two Kachins, Mahka and Ting Bam, who had served with him in the field in previous assignments, jumped just south of Sinlumkaba. They headed south across the Bhamo-Wanting Road. They sent foot messengers back to Pete Joost with periodic reports until Curtis Schultz, a radio operator, could be dropped in. As he continued on, Lutken recruited Kachins. He had only about fifteen when he was almost surprised by a strong detachment of Japanese coming down the Bhamo-Wanting Road that they had just crossed. Carrying their packs and equipment, they had to race to cover across a quarter mile of open paddies to beat a column of Japanese cavalry which soon emerged from some trees.

"We did the distance in one minute flat," claims Lutken.

Lutken was now in a country where Palaung and Kachin villages were interspersed. The Palaungs are an exceptional people, who are famous in Burma for the tea they grow, the Buddhism they profess, and their odd concept of what makes a beautiful woman. When a girl is very small, they place brass rings around her neck, never to be taken off. They add successive rings so that the child's neck is progressively elongated. The longer a neck a young woman has, the more beautiful she is considered to be. Missionaries among the Palaungs insisted that any converts to Christianity among the giraffe-necked women must remove the rings. When they did so, the long necks of the unfortunate girls could no longer support the weight of their heads, and they undulated like serpents.

Lutken and his Kachins tried to sneak around the Palaung villages because they were feared to be pro-Japanese. They stopped in the Kachin villages. To make their transit of this dubious country safer, Lutken divided his group into two. He and Schultz went with one party, and Ting Bam took the other. They were to rendezvous again atop Loi Pang Ngoum Mountain, from where Lutken proposed to commence guerrilla raids on the Japanese.

Lutken's group dodged the Japanese all the way, with narrow es-

cape following upon narrow escape. Lutken and Schultz came to a
Chinese mud village named Ho It, way up among the pine trees on
the slopes of Loi Pang Ngoum. The headman was a horse herder,
and when he joined Lutken he brought with him two hundred and
fifty horses that would solve any future transport problems. Finally,
at eight thousand feet Lutken reached the cool refuge at the top of
the mountain.

"It was a magnificent hiding place," recalls Lutken. "There was a
spring for drinking water, and apple trees with branches filled with
fruit. Apples were all over the ground. We cooked them, roasted
them over the fire. We lived off apples."

Lutken contacted Likun Zaw Seng, a Kachin duwa kaba. He
began to recruit Kachins for a new 101 battalion. He also learned
that the Japanese had trapped his other group and that all but Ting
Bam had been killed. A bullet had pierced his cheek, but he had escaped to a Kachin village.

Some 101 men preferred to jump into an area where they were to
work, but Pete Lutken was not among them.

"I always walked into an area," he told me. "I never dropped
right into it. As I walked along through the countryside, I'd feel my
way along, get known, make friends. If I met a Kachin, I'd pump
him, learn what's up, who's reliable. I knew whom I was going to
talk to long before I got to a village."

Kachins told him that Dashi Yaw, a duwa, would be helpful.
Lutken and a few of his Kachins walked down the mountain to Dashi
Yaw's village. It was his intention to talk to Dashi in the security of
the jungle to learn if he would help him recruit a new American-
Kachin Ranger Unit. As they came near the village, dogs began to
bark their warnings. They certainly could not get any closer without
revealing their presence, and it was likely that there might even be
Japanese soldiers or agents there, since Japanese regularly patrolled
the village.

That night Lutken sent a Kachin from the vicinity into the village
to invite Dashi Yaw to meet him in the jungle. Dashi Yaw soon appeared where Lutken lay hidden.

"He was very anxious to help fight the Japanese," recalls Lutken.
"That was the true beginning of recruiting the 7th Battalion. There
were forty homes in Dashi's village, and each home was to send one
man. Other villages in the vicinity sent men, too, so that we ultimately had fourteen hundred."

Dashi and Lutken arranged for a time when all the men were to meet atop the mountain. Some would have to sneak out of villages occupied by the Japanese, so the time and place of the meeting had to be kept secret. Lutken radioed to base at Myitkyina to ask for a drop of rifles, ammunition, and uniforms for one thousand men at a precise time. He was counting on the drop to arrive on schedule so that he could arm the new volunteers. Armed, they would be able to keep the Japanese from storming the mountain; unarmed, they would be a thousand or more men in a trap.

Kachin boys slipped from village to village with their message that men and boys should go to the top of the mountain. At the appointed rendezvous Lutken waited.

"That night men came from all directions," he remembers. "The mountain lit up with cooking fires. I was confident that the Japanese in the valley below would see the glowing fires on the mountain and attack us by dawn. Fortunately, a fog screened the fires from the valley."

In the morning Lutken and his men put out his recognition panel and built bonfires. Kachins threw green branches on the fire to make smoke to attract the planes. The Kachin volunteers squatted down by the edge of the mountain meadow where the drop was to be made and waited for the miracle to happen. Lutken sweated. Then just after daybreak four planes droned in from the north. They reconnoitered the drop area until they spotted the smoke, waggled their wings to indicate their satisfaction, and then poured down a cascade of supply parachutes. The Kachins broke open the boxes and dug out the rifles. They set up rifle ranges, and those who knew how to shoot taught the others. In only three days Lutken's newly formed 7th Battalion of the American-Kachin Rangers attacked Japanese-held Mong Tat.

"It was only a practice attack," says Lutken. "We had a dozen bazookas, and I wanted the Kachins to get used to their big noise. For the next three weeks we did our on-the-job training by striking out at the Japanese in all directions."

Lutken's Kachins erected a stockade at their mountaintop headquarters. Every captive they took, or any Shan, Palaung, or Burmese who wandered into the area they now controlled, was placed under guard in the stockade.

"We'll turn you loose when we leave the area," promised Lutken.

"If we let you go now, the Japanese would only catch you. They would torture you and make you talk about us."

Lutken decided to send an agent into Namtu to spy on the Japanese army holding the town. He could not send a Kachin in Kachin's clothing, but he could send a Kachin in Shan's clothing. There were plenty of Shans in the stockade. Why not dress the Kachin spy in clothing borrowed from one of them? Without delay the Kachin agent prepared for his mission, leaving one dead Shan in the stockade. The Kachins had an explanation that made sense to *them* at least:

"Duwa," said their spokesman, "we went in to get Shan clothes. We took the clothes off the Shan, but it is not proper for a Shan to wear Kachin clothes. He also cannot just be naked. That is not right, so it was necessary to kill him."

*　　*　　*

Bill Martin was uncertain what to do with a Burmese who brought packets of rubies from the celebrated mines at Mogok into his camp. Each package might include a few dozen to a hundred stones. The ruby dealer was happy to trade them for parachute cloth, food, and medicine. Ed Conley, who had joined Martin, accepted a few of the rubies in trade even though Martin pointed out to him that they were probably just bottle glass.

"After all," claimed Martin, "that stone there is as big as a fingernail and three-sixteenths of an inch thick. It can't be real."

The dealer had a whole sack of what he claimed were blue sapphires. Obviously, he was trying to cheat the 101 men. Martin finally had the Kachins run him out of camp, and they obliged with their usual zeal. At the end of the campaign in Burma, Conley brought his rubies to a gem dealer in Calcutta, who appraised one of them alone at five thousand dollars.

Fighting behind the Japanese lines in the land of jade, amber, rubies, and sapphires, 101 men should have become rich; but they were so intent upon winning the war that they missed their chances. They also had such doubts about the stones that they muffed their opportunities. Bill Martin was not the only 101'er who doubted the genuineness of the sacks of stones that might have been his for a song. Several times I, too, turned down the opportunity to buy gems for practically nothing. But none of us had any experience as strange as Roger Wolbarst's.

Before the war Swede Olson was the manager of the ruby mines at Mogok. When they captured the gemstone town, the Japanese placed Olson in a concentration camp. There he stayed until the war swept ever farther south and he was rescued by the American-Kachin Rangers. Noah Levin, another 101 doctor, who spent part of his time healing bodies and the rest dodging bullets behind the lines, treated Olson, who was in poor shape, dying of a failing heart. His legs were swollen, and he sat on a veranda of the 101 basha at Shwegu and yarned about the old days in Burma. Not only 101 men but British and Chinese from Allied forces that had captured the town brought stones to him for his opinion. In gratitude for his rescue and the medical care, he promised to evaluate them. At the time, stones were being traded to Allied soldiers for everything from food to cigarettes to medicine. There was a steady procession of men coming to show their gems to Olson. He looked at each stone carefully.

"Any ruby or sapphire with a star in it is defective and not worth anything at all," he opined.

He showed his contempt for such unworthy objects by throwing them over his shoulder into the nearby river. Wolbarst sat and talked to Olson as he scrutinized stones.

"He threw hundreds and probably thousands into the drink," he recalls. "He had no idea that star sapphires and rubies bring premium prices in the West, as we learned when we returned home."

Perhaps Swede Olson's mind had broken in the Japanese concentration camp. Whatever the reason, he tossed away hundreds of thousands of dollars worth of gems, and Wolbarst watched him do it.

1945

# The Burma Road

Two giant hills that resembled women's breasts rose on either side of where our Kachins were camped at Mongwi. Later on, when Pete Joost moved his headquarters from Sinlumkaba to Mongwi, 101 pilots called flights to the landing strip he built among the paddies between the hills "the milk run," out of appreciation for their suggestive shapes. Some of the Kachins moved with us into the tin-roofed houses of Buddhist monks close to a large temple. The monks, favoring the Japanese cause, had fled with the approach of the Mars Task Force. The rain rushed down on the tin roofs with a cataract's roar as we waited for orders to move out.

On January 8 we said good-bye to the comely pair of hills and headed up over the trail that snaked through the Loilun Range. Lt. General Daniel Sultan had ordered the Mars Task Force to strike at the Wanting-Hsenwi section of the Burma Road and disrupt Japanese supply lines. The Marsmen were to establish a roadblock. This promised to be a difficult task. The Japanese had the 56th Division plus the 168th Regiment of the 49th Division in the Hosi Valley north of the point where the Marsmen were expected to reach the Burma Road. The 4th Regiment of the 2d Division and the crack Yamazaki Detachment were positioned just south and northwest of Namhpakka immediately to the south. The Japanese had a major munitions dump at Namhpakka, and they undoubtedly were not going to give it up without a fight. Since they could easily throw 11,500 men into the struggle, the two American regiments of the Mars Task Force were up against formidable odds.

The impending battle promised to be critical. If the Burma Road could be cut, the Japanese would be forced to withdraw from Namhkam over mountain trails through another terrifying ordeal by ambush. The Chinese who were advancing with their customary timid-

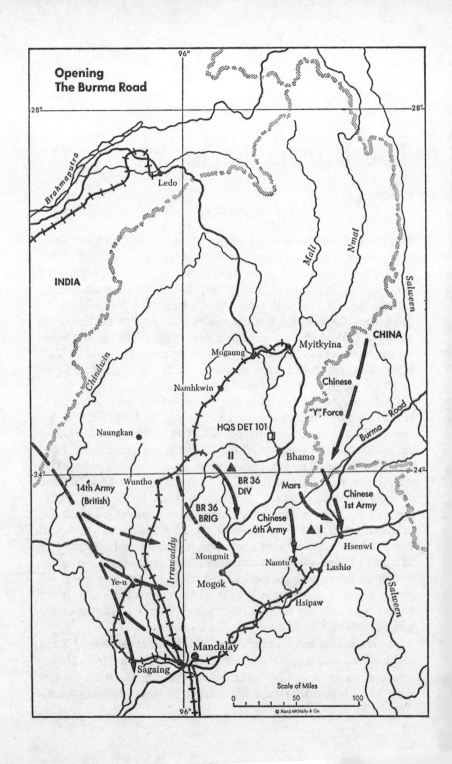

ity, both along the Burma Road from China and in support of the Mars Task Force, might be encouraged to make a more strenuous effort. Lashio might fall, and the Burma Road, the lifeline to China, would be reopened to Allied traffic. Stilwell's goal for the entire North Burma campaign would at last be realized.

Our American-Kachin Ranger company was to provide the usual intelligence and operational screen for the advancing Americans, and our scouts ranged far ahead. Hiram Pamplin, Stan Spector, and I moved about freely in the jungled mountains ahead of the Americans. Elsewhere 101'er Pinhead Adams and his Kachins were providing additional coverage for the advancing Americans. From the start the trails over the Loilun Range, which peak at over ten thousand feet, proved to be more devastating than anything the Americans had encountered. We watched from higher ground as their weary column inched upward toward us. The men would climb for a minute or two and then rest.

Only seventy miles or so separated the strike force from the Japanese, but the trail led up to the summit of one ridge only to drop down to a dark, narrow valley and then up again to a point still higher. At last, two miles east of Hopang village, we came up on a high ridge that ran east and west. We were able to follow this ridge with relative ease. It was also the watershed through which streams rippling down its sides ran off into both Burma and China. When Pamplin informed Ngai Tawng of this salient geographical fact, he mounted a rock just off of the trail and spat into two streams, one bound for China and the other for Burma.

"Duwa Dick," he cried. "I so spit in the streams and take possession of them and all the lands that their waters reach for the Kachins."

It might have been just the feckless action of a larking boy, but some hypenlas, hearing his brave words, seized him from the stone and carried him in triumph down the trail.

"They scare me sometimes," Pamplin told me. "Look at that! Will we be able to hold them back when the war is over?"

Each day was much like the others, with long marches on precipitous trails made slippery by the rains. We set up our camps and put out our perimeter defenses. Spector would send and receive his messages with Ngai Tawng or another Kachin boy called "Slim" turning the hand generator. When dysentery struck both Pamplin and me, we munched on some of the opium that we carried. I improved rapidly, but Pamplin was near collapse. One night a Shan spy infiltrated into our camp, but a GI scout dog named King, whom we had borrowed from the American canine corps together with the soldier who had trained him, discovered the interloper and gave the alarm. The Shan escaped into the jungle, and the Kachins were disconsolate. Ngai Tawng buried his face in King's side.

"You are a true Kachin dog," he said. "You give the warning when we are careless. The Shan might have murdered one of our American friends where he slept, and how could we ever explain this to the duwa kaba?"

Pamplin was somewhat better on the morning of January 16 when we broke camp at five in the morning and started on the trail. It was just as well, because Colonel Esterbrook, who led the operation against the Burma Road, had given orders for the 475th Infantry to undertake a forced march in order to surprise the Japanese. The Kachins were everywhere in the jungles, checking out this trail or that, climbing to viewpoints from which they could scout the mountains for miles in every direction, searching for any sign of the Japanese. We climbed through a succession of high mountain passes that taxed the strength of the Americans so that they began to fall with exhaustion. Kachins following the column would come upon soldiers collapsed by the trail and gently but firmly get them back onto their feet so that they would not be left behind. The Kachins knew that Shans and Palaungs who lived to the south of the mountains might well find them if they did not keep up. At the very least they would take them as prisoners to the Japanese.

It grew dark, but there was no stopping. Despite the best efforts of the Kachins, the 2d Battalion of the 475th wandered off the trail and was lost for two hours. The delay was costly. About nine o'clock in the evening, our vanguard of Kachins reached a Kachin village. The Japanese had come there that morning, and they had killed and tortured the villagers who had not managed to escape into the jungle. A young mother sat in the door of a basha and held her crying baby in her arms. Her face, lit by firelight, was the embodiment of grief and horror. A dead boy, bloody and mutilated, lay close to the basha wall. Smokey, the Kachin cook from the Triangle, was just ahead of me as we came up. He drew his dah and slashed a sapling that grew by the village street. He swore vengeance. Ngai Tawng appeared out of the dark. He burst into tears and clung shivering and weeping to me.

"Why do they have to kill in that way?" he sobbed. "If they have to kill us, why don't they just kill us?"

"You Kachins torture your captives too," I reminded him.

"We do not torture children," he said angrily. "I do not want to be a hypenla any longer. I want to go home. All of us want only to go home."

He slumped down by the basha and stared at his jungle boots. Many of the hypenlas tied their jungle boots together with the laces and suspended them around their necks. They walked barefooted along the trails, but when they came to a village they put their boots on so that the women and girls in the village would see how important and well-off they were, walking in shoes as Americans did. Ngai Tawng went barefoot more often than he wore shoes, but now he had put them on.

Pamplin came up with the village duwa, and he and I talked to him. A Kachin interpreter helped us ask him to join us as a guide. He might be able to help us reach the Hosi Valley unobserved over a safer back trail. As we stood talking, the Americans began to come by. They were men walking through a nightmare. Their haggard faces registered shock as they saw the mother's face and the dead child. They noticeably strengthened.

As we resumed the long march through the night, Stan Spector, Hiram Pamplin, some Kachins, and I were hiking along with an American company. Ngai Tawng walked moodily ahead of me behind a small Kachin mule on which Spector had packed his radio equipment. Ahead of us the big American mules from Missouri stumbled and slipped on the trails and plunged over the cliffs. During the night at least forty mules stumbled to their doom, and a mule does not choose to do this quietly. There was a terrified scream as he felt himself going, a furious scrabbling of hoofs, and then the horrible sounds of the poor beast striking the valley below. The fall of the mule was usually followed by merciful silence, but sometimes we could hear the animal screaming in its agony way down below us in the dark.

Our small Kachin mules were much more surefooted, and we did not lose any of them. We almost lost Pamplin, weakened by dysentery and the long march, who tumbled over the brink and saved himself only by hanging to a bush. Spector, a hypenla, and I pulled him to safety. He was trembling, but he laughed and said, "A fellow ought to wear a parachute on this superhighway to heaven."

Ngai Tawng had recovered his spirits.

"You will fall over the cliffs if you do not hold onto the tail of the mule as I do," he told me. "He can see in the dark better than you and I can."

When a Kachin makes a suggestion in the jungle, it is a good idea to take it. I grabbed hold of the mule's tail, and we went on along the cliff's edge, following the beast. Colonel Esterbrook was somewhere ahead of us. With the trail so narrow and dangerous, he took to passing commands to the rear guard by word of mouth instead of sending back a messenger. The rear of the column was straggling badly, and when the colonel learned of it, he sent back orders, "There's a gap in the column. Stop the column." By the time this command had been passed down the column from one tired soldier to the next, the message had been corrupted to, "There's a Jap in the column. Stop the column." Some uncomfortable moments ensued while we stared suspiciously at our neighbors.

In the middle of the night we came upon a mountain stream. The water was bitter cold, but there was nothing to do but splash right in and wade across with the current surging up to our waists. I've never heard such deep-hearted cursing as the soldiers indulged in when they staggered wet and chilled up onto the far bank. Colonel Esterbrook and his ancestry figured in almost every curse. Not long afterward mules in our party brayed, and from across the valley on another mountain slope, other mules answered.

"They're probably the Japanese army's mules," said Pamplin.

We expected mortar shells at any moment, but nothing happened. About five in the morning, just as it was getting light, we flopped down where we were by the trail and slept until seven. Then we forged ahead. The first fighting began at ten o'clock in the morning of January 18.

Nawhkam, a Palaung village of about forty bashas, spread on either side of the ridge trail. One mile east was an alluvial valley, three miles long and one mile wide, where the villagers had their rice fields. Beyond the valley three hills rose for about nine hundred feet. Loikang hill to the south was at the end of the ridge which we had followed through the night. Atop its crest was the Kachin village of Loikang, at least four hundred feet higher than the surrounding countryside, from which the villagers looked down on the Burma Road, another mile and a half east of the hills. The Burmese town of

Namhpakka lay behind the hills on the road, hidden by jungles even from the Kachin vantage point.

Esterbrook's plan was to cross the valley and its paddies to seize Loikang Ridge. I Company of the Third Battalion and the Kachin Rangers were sent about five miles north with orders to block the road from the Shweli Valley to Namhpakka and prevent the Japanese from moving up reinforcements. We moved swiftly to execute our role. As our force came up on Nawhkam from the north, a Japanese soldier standing in the door of a basha caught a glimpse of a U.S. soldier and fired the first shot of the battle for the Burma Road. He missed, and the fight was on. The Americans and the Kachins stormed into the village as the Japanese sprinted up a knoll, about seventy-five yards away to the south. Their rear guard in the village fought hard, and before they could be silenced the bashas were smoking ruins.

The Japanese in Burma did a remarkable job of digging in, and their outposts were extremely difficult both to discover and destroy. Despite the best efforts of the Kachins one outpost escaped notice until the next morning when it was finally discovered and destroyed. The valley below Nawhkam was now secure enough that an ammunition and supply drop could be made there around 2:30 that afternoon. By late afternoon the 612th Field Artillery had taken up its postion in the valley and began to fire on the Burma Road, lobbing its shells over the hills whenever Kachin scouts reported by radio that Japanese trucks or small tanks were coming.

The Kachins, probing farther south, encountered a force of about one thousand Japanese moving up on our flank. Their report arrived just in time to allow Colonel Esterbrook to counter the move.

We shifted our American-Kachin Rangers headquarters over onto a mountainside beyond the valley which the Kachins said could be easily defended. It was not the best plan. The Japanese had mounted heavy artillery atop the tip of the Loikang Ridge, and their 150-mm howitzers laid down a furious bombardment on the valley where GIs and villagers were trying to smooth out a landing strip. L-1 pilots of the 71st Liaison were expected to fly in to the strip and evacuate the wounded. A bitter battle broke out on the afternoon of January 18, and American casualties were very heavy. The Japanese shells screamed over our heads toward their ultimate destination in the valley, but since the enemy's aim was a bit haphazard some of them burst perilously close to our position. At first both Kachins and

Americans dug foxholes just because it seemed a good idea, but after the first Japanese bombardment, there was not one of us who didn't dig with true conviction.

We often speculated about what would happen if the Kachins were ever pinned down in the sort of fixed-position battle that had now developed for the control of the Burma Road. None of us doubted the jungle people's bravery, but their entire history of warfare had trained them over countless generations to fight as guerrillas. Would they remain firm under shellfire or would they slip off into the jungles during the first night never to be heard from again?

From our foxholes midway between the American guns and the Japanese howitzers we were able to watch the artillery duel. We hugged the floor of our holes whenever a Japanese shell screamed our way. The Kachins seemed totally unperturbed by the shelling. They chattered among themselves and played cards and other gambling games. Ngai Tawng went right on asking English words for this or that object even when death seemed to be heading his way. The Kachin boy had taken a liking to King, the canine corps dog, who had somehow attached himself to our headquarters. Once King broke out of a foxhole where Stan Spector had been holding him and dashed after a shell which had passed immediately over our heads. The shell had landed perhaps thirty yards away, and in some macabre way it skidded to a halt among some bushes where it lay ominous and sinister, ready to blow up at any moment. King dashed right up to the shell and nosed it, barking excitedly.

"My God," cried Spector. "He'd bring it to us as if it were a stick, if he could get his mouth around it."

Ngai Tawng leaped out of the foxhole and called for the dog in his newfound English, "King, King! Come here, boy!"

He knew that the dog, as he put it, did not "speak" Jinghpaw. The shell was a dud. Its twin came roaring in and blasted a huge hole, throwing dirt and debris over Ngai Tawng, who leaped back into the foxhole.

"King has no sense," he complained as he landed on me.

"Neither do you," I told him.

"I like that dog," he said in explanation.

For a Kachin there was nothing more to be said. King escaped the second shell and trotted back to the foxholes.

At night the skies were lit by flares and thundered with the muzzle blasts of the contending artillery and the exploding shells. A force of miniscule Japanese tankettes tried to force its way through the road-block, but it was shot apart in a nighttime battle of fiery tracer bullets and exploding mortar shells.

The transports made regular air drops into the valley, despite the hazards involved. As I watched the fearless pilots bringing their big planes in over the valley, a Japanese sniper shot a kicker right out of one of their doorways. He tumbled down to earth, and the Kachins went hunting for the sniper.

One night at dusk some dozen Kachins and I went down into the Hosi Valley along the Burma Road. We headed out past the Japanese positions. Spector had received a message that we should contact a British guerrilla unit which was said to be in the vicinity. No contact was made, but we may have been the first group to set foot on the Burma Road. Under foot, it felt like any other blacktop road, and the jungle birds along it called as if nothing unusual was taking place. The next night some of the Kachins blew a hole in the road.

The battle continued on for days as the Japanese moved up their vastly superior forces over the Burma Road from China to the north and from Lashio to the south. The Yamazaki Detachment, which on the night of the 18th had withdrawn to the vicinity of Namhkam, attacked with bloody effect. They dug in atop a razorback with machine guns and 82-mm mortars, and defied the Marsmen to attack in turn. For five nights in a row Japanese soldiers struck the Americans with violent shelling and infantry. The 475th's 2d Battalion suffered especially heavy casualties.

Once the light plane strip was completed in the valley, L-1s came in to fly out the wounded. Every time a plane came into view, the Japanese began to shell the strip. Word had reached us that the Mars Task Force officers were allowing Kachin wounded to lie by the field while less seriously wounded Americans were being flown out. I went down to the strip to see whether this was true, and I saw one of our planes taking off with a pattern of mortar shells marching up the strip after it as it raced for its life. The plane escaped. Vince Trifletti, a 101 pilot, remembers a pilot's-eye view of what the strip was like:

"When Rocky Reardon sent John Kessler and me to assist three L-1 pilots of the 71st Liaison in evacuating wounded of the 475th Infantry Regiment, he didn't realize what he was getting us into. He figured it was a casual run that would take part of the day.

"The 475th was fighting in the Hosi Valley just west of Namhkam and the Mu-se Valley, over a six-thousand-foot ridge. When I flew over the ridge and dropped down, there were so many fires burning that the whole scene looked like it was being seen through a diaphanous curtain. The place was devastated. Every village, every basha was in flames or was a smoldering pile of ash.

"A C-47, hit by Jap mortar fire a few hours before while attempting an airdrop, lay on a narrow road, its tail angled in the air. The small strip that I had to land on was pocked with mortar craters. Several wrecks of light planes were strewn about. Angry puffs of white mortar fire jetted out of the surrounding foliage. It was apparent that the strip was the focal point of the fighting.

"No sooner did my L-1 touch ground, than the wounded were rushed out from distant tree cover. 'Feller, you got it wrong,' a GI told me when I asked if he had a dozen or so wounded. 'We got over a hundred right here to evacuate and there's lots more on the way.'

"They loaded five, and even before I was revved up, they disappeared back into the trees. The plane was built for two, including the pilot. We moved so slowly up out of that valley that we seemed to be hovering. I sat with dry mouth and tense thighs, expecting a mortar shell with my name on it to zoom up any minute and hit me in the can.

"The threat from outside was bad enough. Inside the plane, I was whipped by another emotion. The bouncing and tossing in rough air currents brought groans, cries, sobs, and curses from my passengers. One baby-faced kid lay with his head just to the right of my shoulder, in great pain, his moist eyes fixed on me like my conscience made visible.

"With each slam of an air current, I'd offer the only thing I could, a consoling word. He gave back a tortured smile of understanding. He badly bruised my psyche, that lad.

"On one stop that first day, as they loaded the wounded, I dashed over to a nearby stream to douse my face. I kneeled on a rock and bent down. A mortar shell landed to my left, sent rocks and shrapnel whistling over my head, and struck some mules tethered a few feet from me. One's head was crushed, and it died instantly. If I hadn't bent down, I'd have had it too. I ran back to my craft, my enthusiasm for the mission waning."

*    *    *

After about three weeks of battle, I received a message by radio recalling me to Mongwi for an urgent assignment. I was told to fly out on one of the 101 liaison planes, but I refused to do so since a wounded man would have had to remain on the strip while I, who was in perfect health, went flying off unscathed. On the other hand, as Pamplin pointed out, it was extremely dangerous for me to head back over the mountains which we had crossed. Japanese die-hard units were reported to be raiding the area, and the Shans and Palaungs could not be trusted. To compound the dangers, the Chinese army was coming up, and we could never be sure how they were going to get along with the Kachins.

Finally, with a small group of hypenlas who could scarcely be spared from the battle, and Ngai Tawng, who refused to stay behind me, I set out over the mountains. It was morning, and the previous night the Japanese had pressed home one of their bloodiest attacks. An artillery barrage came in just as I was leaving our headquarters area. Neither Pamplin nor Spector would come out of their foxholes to say good-bye, so I stuck my hand down for a last handshake and ran. When a shell came roaring in as we crossed the valley near the airstrip, I had the narrowest escape of my Burmese adventure. Our small party dropped behind a paddy dike, and we were saved as the shell threw dirt all over us. For once even the Kachins were scared. We lost no time in crossing the open valley and starting back up into the hills. It was eerie how rapidly the sounds of the battle died behind us.

Only four hours later we came upon two Kachins on the trail. Ngai Tawng, at my request, asked them if they would guide us to Mongwi. They refused because with the Japanese near they did not want to leave their village. All able-bodied men and boys were needed for its defense.

We compromised. We would go with them to Hopak, their village, and talk to their duwa. The duwa had a son in the American-Kachin Rangers, and he was anxious to do anything that would help defeat the Japanese. He ordered the two men to act as our guides. He also explained that villagers from nearby Chinese settlements had been looting the dead mules that had tumbled over the cliffs during the night march. I sent a runner to Pamplin and Spector with a message describing the situation, and we set out again over the Loilun Range.

Ignoring the pass, we went right over the tallest mountain on a trail known only to the Kachins. The guides were anxious to return home, and I was equally anxious to reach Mongwi. That evening we arrived at the Chinese village, Maliseten. How we had arrived there so soon I had no idea, since my map showed me that it was almost halfway to Mongwi. As we approached the village, the Chinese fled into the jungle, gabbling in their fright.

"I will go and talk the Chinese into coming back," said Ngai Tawng.

He went into the woods where he soon found an old man hiding and caught him by the sleeve. Perhaps ten minutes went by as the boy argued with the old man. Still clutching the old man's sleeve, Ngai Tawng at last came back to where we were standing on the outskirts of the village. He was laughing.

"He thinks we are Japanese," he said.

He pulled the very reluctant old fellow up to me and pointed at my very Caucasian nose. He asked a question in Kachin and laughed. He was all too obviously having a very good time. The Chinese studied my nose seriously. Then he smiled a toothless smile and spoke to Ngai Tawng, who laughed aloud again.

"What did he tell you?" I asked the boy.

"He said, Duwa Dick, that I am right. No Japanese could ever have such a big nose. It is a marvel that any human being can have such a big nose. You are an American by the nose."

"Megwa bing?" asked the Chinese in his own language.

"Megwa bing," I said. "American soldier."

The villagers returned, and soon we were settling down in a mud house for a meal of C rations. We were still trying to get used to the hard bricks of the bed oven on which we were to sleep when the elderly Chinese entered the room. He shouted something to Ngai Tawng.

"There is a Chinese soldier outside," the young Kachin told me.

"Have him brought in."

Soon the soldier was standing with a sheepish look on his face, staring at the Kachins who had each grabbed for his weapons. The soldier handed me a note written, much to my surprise, in English. I no longer recall the exact wording of most of it, but a Chinese captain who was staying at another village about three miles away with ninety soldiers, had heard of our arrival and wished to invite me to a roast-pig dinner.

"You are also cordially invited to a Jap hunt in the morning," he concluded.

"You must not accept his invitation," urged Ngai Tawng. "The Chinese hate the Kachins, and it will not be safe."

The Chinese detachment was looking for a Japanese group which that morning had terrorized the very village where we were preparing to sleep. I penned a note back to the Chinese captain.

"I regret that I cannot accept your kind invitation, but I am on an urgent mission," I wrote. "Happy hunting."

Then we devoured our miserable C rations and after posting necessary guards went to sleep. The next day we had trouble on the trail with Japanese stragglers whom we shot. They were beaten men, dressed in rags, but they still put up a respectable fight. Once we had taken care of them, we went on our way toward Mongwi.

"Are you not proud of me, Duwa Dick?" Ngai Tawng asked. "I did not even want to cut off their ears. When I am at school in America, you'll be very proud of me. No one will ever guess about me. I'll be an American too."

He grinned with the idea. Within six hours after he so confidently spoke of his future, he was dead. Perhaps he had become too American already, and had become careless in the jungle. As he scouted ahead on the trail when we took a break, he was captured by Shan villagers. They had no idea that the hated Kachin boy was beginning to think of himself as an American. They bound him helpless and cut him with their knives. It must have been the hardest thing of all for the tortured boy to be emasculated by one of the knife cuts. Ironically, he had survived the massacre in his home village in the Hukawng only to die in the same agonized way in the Loilun Range.

Ngai Tawng was still alive when we reached the Shan village. We had found the marks on the trail where he had scuffled with the men who had captured him. The Kachins had no trouble following the trail to the village, but we were too late. I tried to stop the flow of blood from his terrible wounds, but he feebly pushed my hand away.

"I do not want to live any more," he said in English.

Then he died as a Kachin boy in the jungles, which is to say that he died bravely with a slight smile on his face and a last look of friendship in his eyes. His hand in mine grew limp, and even to this day many decades later I cannot write of this without feeling again the tragedy of war. Once years later I asked the sawbwa of Hsipaw, a Shan prince, who had become a friend of mine, how these usually peaceful and kindly villagers had been able to torture and kill a mere boy.

"Have you heard the old Kachin saying?" he asked. "It is only natural for a Kachin to eat a good curry, make love to a beautiful girl, and kill a Shan."

He felt that no more explanation was needed, and I suppose he was right. Sometimes simplicity is best.

\* \* \*

The struggle for the Burma Road continued. On February 26 four Kachin companies captured a hill overlooking the road between Hsenwi and Lashio and held it against frontal attacks from five hundred Japanese. The Japanese suffered heavy casualties. Joe Lazarsky and his Kachins played a vicious game of hit and run on the road north of Lashio. They hop-skipped over the road, hitting from the west and then vanishing into the jungles to the east only to return from the east for another foray and vanish again into the west. They destroyed a complete Japanese convoy and ambushed a column of infantry and then a motorized column. When the Japanese hurried a formidable force into the area to destroy Lazarsky's company, Lazarsky, instead of moving north to security as the Japanese expected he would do, followed a classic American-Kachin Ranger maneuver and cut even deeper into the enemy's territory. He turned up south of Lashio and commenced another destructive series of attacks on Japanese military traffic on the road to the Bawdwin mines at Namtu.

Joe Lazarsky and his men built another 101 behind-the-lines airstrip by knocking out the dikes between paddies in a valley. The strip was in dangerous proximity to a large Japanese garrison, which hurried to the attack. Just as the last dike was leveled and the strip prepared for planes, the Japanese hit a Kachin patrol on the far side of the field. The patrol fought the Japanese to a standstill, but then fell back, leaving several wounded. Bill Brough, the conscientious objector who had left Seagraves to join 101, was with Lazarsky as a medic. Faithful to his pacifist beliefs, he still refused to carry a gun or take a life. This did not mean that he was short on nerve. Brough slipped out of the Kachin position to rescue the wounded, who were lying in an open paddy where they had fallen. He reached the first wounded hypenla without trouble, but as he was carrying the soldier back to cover, a Japanese sniper fired and killed the wounded man in his arms.

Brough put down the dead man and returned for a second wounded soldier. Once again as he ran for cover, carrying the hypenla, a second Japanese shot struck this man in turn and wounded him further. Again Brough put down his burden—this time with his fellow Kachins in a safe spot—and ran back for the third and last wounded. He picked him up and raced for cover. A third shot cracked, and the third soldier was shot dead in his arms.

"That does it!" cried Brough.

He dropped the dead man and tore off his medic's armband. He snatched up a fallen soldier's rifle and joined the battle. Bill Brough turned out to be a skillful and imaginative fighter who, later in the campaign, commanded a company of Kachins.

*       *       *

Dan Mudrinich had received a message from the Shan sawbwa of Hsenwi state. Early in the war the prince had been forced to give support to the Japanese conquerors, but now that 101 guerrillas were nearby, he was refusing to carry out Japanese orders. Japanese retribution was inevitable. Could Mudrinich and his Kachins guarantee safety for his family?

Winning the friendship of the Shans had become an important goal for 101. The war was moving southward out of the Kachin country, and Opero realized that the remarkable success of the American-Kachin Rangers could not be expected in a country where the Kachins were no longer the native people. The Shans must be won over from the Japanese. Ted Barnes, an enormously capable 101'er, and two other men were dropped into the field to raise a force of Shan laborers to build an airstrip capable of taking a transport. Skittles had already made the initial contacts with the Shans and vouched for the feasibility of the project. There were strong Japanese forces in the vicinity, but things had changed with the Shans and nobody hurried to inform on the 101 men. The sawbwa saw to that.

In only a few days Barnes had the strip ready, and a transport came winging in to a dusty landing. Not only the sawbwa, but the mahadavi, his principal wife, and several lesser wives, several children, and relatives, a total of twenty-seven people, all boarded and were flown to safety in India.

Betty, an agent whose slight build and pretty face had impelled Skittles to give him a feminine code name, was anything but feminine in action. A 10th Air Force air-rescue helicopter had flown him to a point west of Hsipaw. He was the first OSS agent to be put into the field in Burma by helicopter. Betty worked overland to the Namtu area where he soon was in contact with old friends. He radioed in significant reports. The Bawdwin mines were now closed; the workers were terrified of the Japanese who had turned cruel as their authority weakened. Not only Kachins but Shans and Pidaungs in the vicinity would gladly join the 101 guerrillas. Joe Lazarsky and his men were operating east of Namtu, but Opero decided to send Pete Lutken into the vicinity to recruit a mixed battalion of Shans, Pidaungs, and Kachins. Lutken succeeded in doing this, and despite the antagonisms among his recruits, he soon operated west of Namtu.

Lutken also took a hand at rescuing a sawbwa. Burmese soldiers were keeping the sawbwa of Taung Pang in a cave outside of Nam San. Lutken's guerrillas went to the rescue. They brought the sawbwa, his six wives, and twenty-three children to safety. When Lutken offered to have the entire group flown out to India, the sawbwa was delighted, but when the plane landed to pick them up, he left his family behind. The only person that the sawbwa saw fit to take with him was his grand vizier.

Lutken's men later came upon the mahadavi of Mongmit, a beautiful Swiss girl who had been hidden by her loyal subjects in isolated villages and caves for two years to keep her from falling into Japanese hands. A 101 liaison plane landed at the strip that Lutken hacked out of the paddies to fly the princess out. She had no baggage except for four cigar boxes, which she chose to hold in her lap. When she reached Bhamo, where the 101 forward headquarters was now situated, she cheerfully showed her rescuers what the boxes contained. Each was filled with rubies, blue sapphires, white sapphires, and emeralds. One star sapphire alone, big as a hen's egg, was worth one hundred thousand dollars.

\*     \*     \*

Detachment 101 units harassed the Japanese who were by now retreating from Namhkam. By early February, 101 forces operating about forty miles south of the battleline were probing Lashio itself. Pete Joost's Area I battalions were moving in on the key Burma Road city from all directions. Joost's Kachins had already killed over thirty-five hundred Japanese soldiers in the fighting. They had suffered about a hundred casualties, most of them when the American air force mistakenly attacked a Kachin column.

When there were about sixty-five-hundred Kachins in position around Lashio, all tough and resourceful fighters, organized in nine battalions, Joost asked for permission to take the city. He flew from Mongwi to General Sultan's headquarters to make his request. Sultan turned Joost over to General Cannon, his chief of staff.

"The Kachins have led the whole advance south from Myitkyina," Joost told Cannon. "I'd like to let them have the honor of capturing Lashio."

The Kachins in the hills around Lashio were two hundred and fifty miles south of Myitkyina. They had come a long way. Lashio was the last important Japanese base in northern Burma and the key to the Burma Road. Cannon listened to Joost, but he decided to give the two Chinese divisions approaching from the north the task of capturing the city. They had the numbers to do the job without a question. The Kachins, for their part, were to capture the airfield and the railroad station as soon as possible.

The Kachins had to be content with the capture of Imailong, a town on the Namtu-Lashio Road. They surrounded the one thousand Japanese defenders on three sides and, after shelling it with 4.2 mortars, they charged. The assault swept the Japanese defenders from Imailong.

"We had Imailong by four, but an hour later I decided to withdraw my men," Joost told me.

As the Kachins pulled back about two miles for the night, the enemy moved back into the town in force. Presuming that the Kachins were still in the town, a large number of Japanese came up with the purpose of surrounding and destroying them.

"They were licking their chops at the thought of having trapped the Kachins for once in a town where their wily jungle ways would do them no good," Joost said.

The newly arrived Japanese forces attacked what they thought were the Kachins. The Japanese in the town returned their fire, and the two Japanese contingents fought a hard fight with one another, both showing the implacable zeal for combat that few armies can muster. The Kachins watched the Japanese slaughter their own from a nearby hill until dawn the next day. They then joined in the fray themselves. After a heavy mortar barrage, they attacked and drove both of the Japanese forces out of Imailong. The town had fallen, and the Japanese losses were very heavy.

Lashio itself now came under assault. Butch Brown and four battalions crossed the river and operated to the southeast of the city. Joost remained with three battalions at Imailong, but another two battalions cut to the east of Lashio. The battalions, each numbering around 750 Kachins and Americans, launched their attack on the airfield and railroad station from three sides. The Japanese fought with suicidal fury, but after three days of direct assault, the Kachins had won. They had not only captured their objectives, but they had proved that they were a formidable force in a fixed battle in city as well as jungle. They held the positions against every Japanese counterattack. The Chinese divisions from Yunnan came up on the next day, March 7, and Lashio was soon in Allied hands.

The entire Ledo-Burma Road was now open to Allied traffic. The Kachins moved on south and southwest to prepare the way for future triumphs in the last campaigns of the war in Burma.

# The Last Campaign

The American-Kachin Rangers threw an intelligence and guerrilla screen out in front of the British as they crossed the Chindwin River and attacked the railway at Wuntho. The British 36th Division crossed the Irrawaddy at Katha and Twinnge on February 14 and advanced up the Shweli Valley. It was up to Detachment 101 guerrillas to close the gap that opened between the main force advancing up the Shweli and the 29th Brigade to the west. All the 101 groups that were operating west of the Irrawaddy now crossed over to join those working east of the river. They established intelligence checks on the Japanese 18th Division from the Namhkam area, where the Chinese and Americans were advancing southwest to the Myitsen-Moo sector, where the British were breaking through Japanese defenses. The Kachins set up roadblocks on the roads behind the Japanese lines in the British sector, and 101 combat patrols harassed the enemy as far behind the lines as Kyaukme, Maymyo, and Mandalay.

Chuck Roberts and his company of Kachins entered Kyaukme ahead of the British and carried away a few souvenirs from the town hall as proof of their exploit. Pete Lutken set up a roadblock on the road south to Na-mon and held it for a week as the retreating Japanese tried desperately to get through. The Japanese continued to fight hard and again proved themselves brave soldiers. The Kachins killed them by scores, but every night would see another Japanese attempt to break the block.

When the Chinese passed through Hsipaw, they came up the road to Na-mon in pursuit of the Japanese. There were none. They were either dead or had safely infiltrated around the roadblock. In the dark of night the Chinese in turn came upon the Kachin roadblock and, thinking it was Japanese, attacked.

"There was something so hysterical about the firing, we thought the attackers might be Chinese," says Lutken. "We backed off after inflicting casualties. In the morning we discovered that our opponents were indeed Chinese."

\* \* \*

A British weapons carrier raced down a road ahead of the advancing army. Bill Martin had written a note to advise the British that his Kachins were in the vicinity and placed it on a stake driven into the road, but the driver ignored it. When a Kachin stepped out of the jungle, the Englishman took one look at the brown-skinned warrior and spun the weapons carrier around to make his escape. The vehicle plunged into a ditch, and the driver jumped out and hotfooted it down the hill and out of sight.

Bill Martin, coming up the trail to the road, sent for one of his eighteen elephants and pulled the vehicle out of the ditch. He used the weapons carrier to shuttle his company of Kachins some three miles down the road to a strong position. He left a second message fixed to a stake in the road.

"We're Americans and Kachins. We have your vehicle. Don't fire on us."

In a few days the British army came down the road, and a red-faced driver reclaimed his weapons carrier.

\* \* \*

A special group of thirty Kachins had been training under Billy Milton, an Anglo-Burmese operator from the original O Group. It was now time for them to take to the field. One dark night they were dropped between the roads leading to Mongmit and Mogok from the west. The Japanese were falling back along these roads before the advancing British. Billy Milton and the Kachins soon were engaged in another, by now classic, Kachin maneuver. One night they ambushed one hundred Japanese on the Mongmit Road, leaving only a few survivors. The following night they attacked a Japanese army detachment on the southern road and killed nearly fifty. In two weeks they killed about three hundred Japanese by attacking first one road and then the other from a position in the jungles somewhere in between.

\* \* \*

The Kempi Tai won a victory. Hate Group was covering Japanese movements from a base near Kyaukme. The Japanese secret police discovered their whereabouts, and they were captured. At first they were imprisoned in Kyaukme, but then the Japanese took them to Lashio, which was still in their hands at the time. Outside the jail in Lashio, 101 agents could hear their friends screaming in agony within as the Japanese tortured them. They radioed word out to base, and a flight of three fighter bombers was sent to the rescue. They flew over the jail and placed their bombloads directly on it. The jail was blown to pieces, and as Ray Peers puts it, "The men placed beyond torture."

*       *       *

Mandalay fell to the British on March 20. The campaign in northern Burma was ending in victory. The American-Kachin Rangers were then at their height. There were 10,500 guerrillas organized in seven battalions, 60 espionage agents operating deep in Burma, and 400 short-range agents providing behind-the-lines intelligence. Additional agents were carrying out psychological-warfare assignments. Already in March 4,000 Kachin Rangers in Area I had been flown to Bhamo by the U.S. Air Force. The pilots of the transports that flew the hypenlas northward to their home hills stared at the by now legendary fighters. One minute the young Kachins were all discipline and military purpose; the next minute they were joshing and pushing one another. They were still boys despite all their victories over one of the world's most powerful armies. Two battalions had remained in the field to assist the British in South Burma in the campaign to free Rangoon. From Bhamo the Kachins marched in triumph up the trails to Sinlumkaba.

At the Kachin capital a huge manau was held in their honor. Many of the soldiers were rewarded with hunting rifles and shotguns, and the CMA medal was given to the bravest by Lazum Tang and Pete Joost. The dancing, singing, and feasting went on night and day in the meadow aerie overlooking both China and Burma. A final payroll totaling about five hundred thousand dollars in paper rupees was airdropped to Sinlumkaba. The bales of money broke when the parachutes failed, and the wind blew the bills all over the mountainside.

Kachins from nearby villages searched the mountain for the lost money. All that day rupees were brought to Pete Joost and Lazum Tang in Kachin bags clutched in the hands of men, women, and children. That night 101 men sat up late counting the money that had been turned in by the Kachins. Of the five hundred thousand dollars, all but three hundred dollars was accounted for. The return of the money was really no surprise; 101 men already knew that anywhere in the Kachin country a man could leave his belongings beside a trail and never have them disturbed, though nearby villagers might erect a shelter over them to keep off the rain. Even so, this last example of Kachin honesty seemed almost overwhelming.

"I will never forget the day of the big rupee search," Pete Joost told me later. "The way those people brought all that money to us. One old lady walked in. She was dressed in rags, but the expression on her face when she plumped down a bag full of rupees was so proud that I'll always remember it. The Kachins are the most beautiful people I've ever known even if they do have a penchant for collecting their enemies' ears."

\*     \*     \*

The manau at Sinlumkaba was not the only manau the American-Kachin Rangers celebrated in April, 1945. We celebrated wherever we were—Americans and Kachins together in an outburst of fraternal triumph. At Namtu, Pete Lutken's 7th Battalion gathered on the tennis courts of the prewar British Club for three days of drinking, singing, gambling, stave fighting, and listening to the battalion jaiwa sing the ballad of their exploits.

"We drank great quantities of laukhu, ate copious quantities of rice and curry. The women danced 'like saadse das,' as the admiring Kachin men said, 'like winnowed grass.' We fired our BARs at the sky to punctuate our conversations or our swallows of laukhu," remembers Lutken.

Lutken, who had earned a reputation as the "meanest man in Burma," had lived on the beetles that inhabit bamboo shoots, had learned to relish ants and the larvae discovered beneath a decaying log. He had dined on elephant, monkey, jungle fowl, and wild pig, intestines and all. He was the hero of the celebration. The jaiwa had given him the name of "Ka Ang Zau Lai," which is Kachin for "He who has been through from the beginning to the end." The jaiwa flicked a bamboo clacker as he stood before the circle of triumphant hypenlas to get the tempo, and in a high nasal tone he sang the newly composed saga of the 7th Battalion. He sang with his eyes closed, and the magic of his poetry held the Kachins spellbound. The epic poem went on for hours, each phrase in perfect meter and rhyme, for the Kachins have a great appreciation for the beauty of their spoken tongue. The saga was intended to take its place with the other great sagas of the Kachin people so that it could be sung around campfires and at manaus hundreds of years later, just as the great songs telling of the descent of the people from the Himalayas and of their ancient victories over the Shans, the Burmese, and the Chinese are sung today.

"I felt like a Homeric hero," recalls Lutken.

Lutken had learned to speak Kachin even if his grasp of the language was a bit on the loose side. He rose, his feet unsteady from the laukhu, and made a long, flowery speech in response. The Kachins listened to Ka Ang Zau Lai. They laughed at his mistakes, but their eyes glistened with tears as he warmed to the subject. When he sat down, fourteen hundred soldiers and all their relatives and families cheered and stamped their feet until the hills rang.

The Kachins stacked their arms. When the celebration was over, Lutken and his men loaded the weapons on a DC-3 that had flown in to pick them up. Working in the plane, Lutken whipped off the hat that had weathered the campaign from the beginning to the end and plunked it down on a box. When the job was done, the plane took off.

"The plane flew away with my campaign hat," said Lutken. "I knew that the adventure was over when that happened."

\*     \*     \*

Ray Peers emerged from his experiences as commander of Detachment 101 of the Office of Strategic Services as America's greatest authority on guerrilla warfare. Peers and all other 101 men agree that the Kachin people were mainly responsible for the almost incredible success of the American-Kachin Rangers, but the OSS men who served behind the Japanese lines in Burma had made an outstanding record as well. What kind of men were they? Ray Peers has some ideas on the subject:

"Within the detachment we were always greatly concerned about what type of U.S. personnel was most effective in behind-the-lines operations. Jim Luce and I talked this over at length, but we came to no specific conclusions. Just about the time we thought we had the answer, something would happen to negate it. For example, we thought that perhaps the best type would be somebody such as Lieutenant Ted Barnes, who had been raised on a farm in Wyoming, had had extensive outdoor life and a fairly good education. Generally, this analysis worked out correctly for the initial period behind the lines, since such persons were sure of themselves, did not panic, and could do most anything. Later, however, we found that many of these desirable characteristics were showing up in the city-born personnel who had spent some time with the unit. Thus, it could be generalized that initially the farm-boy type was more adept than the city boy, but after a period of familiarization they tended to equalize.

"There were certain things that could be stated specifically. A boy who had stayed with scouting and had attained a high rank, up to Eagle Scout, almost invariably was well equipped for the job. On the other hand, the sheltered boy, the mama's boy, was almost useless until the mama could be taken out of the boy and he could become one of the group. We salvaged several such boys, but under hostile conditions it was very costly in training time and effort.

"Another type of individual we learned to treat cautiously were the braggarts. When alone in the thick jungle they tended to become tense and panic. They needed companionship to buoy their spirits. For a time, we thought this was typical of the paratroopers as there were several cases wherein this was evident. However, as we analyzed this situation the thought lacked validity. It was not because they were paratroopers, it was because of their recruitment in OSS. They were recruited by a person who was somewhat eccentric and, since like attracts like, some strange characters came into OSS. The airborne troops were probably glad to see them go. As we received additional paratroopers, they proved highly successful, perhaps some of the best personnel in the detachment.

"Another thing we found concerned education. It didn't necessarily take a college degree to do this type of work, although it helped, and certainly a high-school education and possibly a year or two of college were highly desirable. Those with lesser intelligence capabilities were limited in where they could be assigned. They simply could not cope with the continuing mental demands and the requirement for a high degree of flexibility."

*     *     *

The war had gone south, and life was settling down in the Kachin villages. Ah Tha, the ten-year-old son of a duwa, was playing with the other boys in his village. Close by, they found a strange round thing made of metal. It was just the thing to toss into a fire. Ah Tha watched the flames lick around it. There was a blinding flash and a roar, and the fire blew in every direction. Ah Tha screamed and lay crumpled with dozens of shrapnel wounds in his small body.

It is hard to kill a Kachin. Jerry Genaw of Butch Brown's 3d Battalion was preparing to get into Vince Trifletti's L-5 for a flight back to Nazira when some Kachins came running carrying Ah Tha. Genaw and Trifletti gave the boy first aid and administered morphine to deaden the pain. They gently placed him in the plane beside Genaw, and Trifletti took off.

Bill Bostwick was at Nazira when Ah Tha was brought to Jim Luce's hospital.

"More dead than alive, he was rushed into surgery for the first of a long series of operations," Bill remembers.

"During the four months or so that he was a patient at Nazira, he became the darling of the entire detachment. That infectious smile could turn off the blackest grouch in a moment. When he was able to walk again, he seemed less a patient and more a mascot. And never did any military hospital have a more endearing mascot.

"But young bones knit quickly. After an epic series of reconstructive operations and lots of tender loving care by the Burmese nurses, he was a whole boy again. He was flown back to the hills and his most grateful Papa."

Only a few weeks later Ah Tha and some other Kachin boys were playing when they found an interesting thing made of metal. One of the boys thought it would be amusing to throw it in the fire. He did. There was a blinding flash and a roar, and the fire blew in every direction. Ah Tha screamed and lay crumpled with dozens of shrapnel wounds in his small body. Even a Kachin is made of flesh and bone. This time he was dead. Just as the discarded Japanese grenade blew up as it hit the fire, the legacy of bitterness that was left behind by the war in North Burma would erupt in many grim ways in the years to come.

\* \* \*

The war in Burma suddenly came alive again as a result of the brilliant drive by two Japanese divisions in China during November and December, 1944. They smashed through thirty poorly armed, poorly trained, and poorly led Chinese divisions to capture the 14th Air Force bases at Hengyang, Luichow, and Kweilin. If the Japanese resumed their offensive, they might conceivably capture Kunming, the northern terminus of the Hump route, as well as the Burma Road,

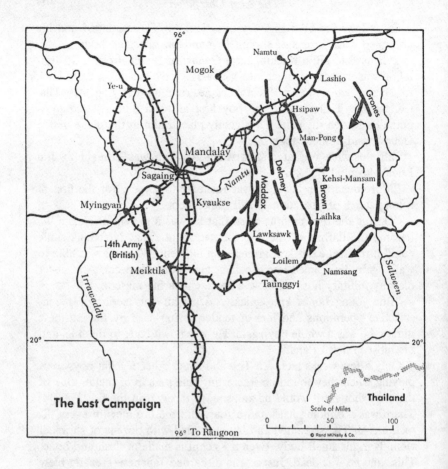

The Last Campaign

just when it appeared the road might be reopened. Chiang Kai-shek asked General Sultan to return two American-trained and equipped Chinese divisions fighting in Burma to China as soon as possible, and the 14th and 22d divisions were immediately dispatched.

When General Donovan appeared in New Delhi for a rendezvous with Ray Peers, 1945 was only a few days old. Donovan wanted his man in Burma to brief him in detail on 101 operations in preparation for a meeting to be held a few days later in Myitkyina. Lord Mountbatten and Generals Sultan, Wedemeyer, Davidson, and Donovan all sat in Sultan's office to discuss what should be done about the dangerous weakness of the Chinese armies in China. The generals agreed that all Chinese troops in Burma should be returned to China as soon as Lashio and Mandalay had fallen. At Myitkyina and at subsequent meetings with Ray Peers held at Mountbatten's headquarters at Kandy, Ceylon, Donovan worked out OSS contingency plans for the uncertain future that Burma would face once the Chinese had withdrawn.

Back at his headquarters, now moved forward again to Kawmahut, a Shan village near Bhamo, Ray Peers put the plans into action. Deep-penetration agents had to be sent into the field. Skittles, one of the best 101 agents, and his radio operator were dropped to Grones and his Kachins east of Lashio. From there they hiked for two hundred and fifty miles along the Shan Plateau beyond the road over which the Japanese would one day have to withdraw into Thailand. A last trap was being set. Skittles, harbinger of Japanese disaster, was on his fifth mission. In no time he had established himself in the commodious palace of the sawbwa of Mongnai, whose subjects had received their ruler's word that henceforth all the information they gathered was to go not to the Japanese but to Skittles.

"I had carte blanche to do what I wanted," remembers Skittles today. "I was watching the Taunggyi-Kentung Road and also the Thai Border. Sometimes base would ask me a specific question, which I would try and answer, but mainly I collected general intelligence information."

Skittles kept regular radio schedules with base except for one night when he was chased by the Japanese.

The nephew of the sawbwa of Hsenwi had also become an OSS agent, and he was dropped in to Kehsi-Mansam, a Shan state capital and a center of Shan culture. The Japanese falling back from Lashio could only pass through this region, where Shan agents, once their friends, were now spying on them and reporting to their ruler's nephew.

By April the situation in China worsened. The Japanese divisions had resumed their attack and were driving the Chinese before them. Chekiang and Kunming were their goals. The Chinese divisions still in Burma must be sent to China immediately, along with the Mars Task Force.

"General Sultan called me in and informed me of the plan," says Ray Peers. "He was deeply concerned because this would deprive him of his last combat soldier, and he felt the newly opened Stilwell Road would be exposed to possible Japanese action north of Lashio. His main concern was the area south of Hsipaw-Maymyo where there were an estimated five to six thousand Japanese, mostly of the 56th Division. He was also concerned about the road from Taunggyi to Kentung which the Japanese, retreating before the 14th Army's drive toward Rangoon, were using to escape to Thailand."

General Sultan wanted to know if 101's ten thousand rangers could drive the Japanese out of the Hsipaw-Maymyo area and cut off the escape route into Thailand. With some of his best ranger units already disbanded, Peers could promise only to employ the remaining battalions and implement them with volunteers from the demobilized units. American officers were given a month to get the battalions reorganized and into action.

Bob Delaney, Butch Brown, Dow Grones, and Red Maddox fell to work with customary 101 zeal, and well before the deadline the four battalions moved into position for 101's last campaign. By the early part of May, the 10th Battalion, which Bob Delaney had created out of Lutken's unit, was moving down the long ridges through the Shan States to take up a position in the hills along the Taunggyi-Kentung Road. They set up a sanctuary in the hills from which they soon were carrying out the sort of raids and ambushes that had so tormented the Japanese farther north. They killed about three hundred and fifty Japanese and ambushed a number of motor columns.

Stung repeatedly in an area that they had, until then, considered entirely secure, the Japanese hastened the withdrawal of forces farther north before the Kachins could establish an even more deadly grip on their escape route. By early June the 1st Battalion, which had been reformed in the vicinity of Lashio by Dow Grones, moved south along the Salween River to the Taunggyi-Kentung Road on which they fastened a roadblock to prevent any eastward movement by the

Japanese. The retreating enemy had waited too long, and bloody punishment now awaited any units that attempted to quit Burma.

As it turned out, there were over ten thousand Japanese still showing fight in the area south of Maymyo and Hsipaw. Two battalions of Rangers under Red Maddox and Butch Brown went into action against them. An OSS Detachment 101 report describes the operation:

"The battalions employed a combination of normal infantry and guerrilla tactics. In each case, about half of the force applied frontal pressure, while the remainder of the force worked twenty to fifty miles in the enemy's rear. Within three months these small forces were able to push a force of nearly ten thousand Japs out of an area over one hundred miles in depth and to control all of the road except a small strip in the area of Taunggyi. All battalions experienced heavy fighting, but the brunt of the fighting was in the western zone. The Japanese suffered heavy losses—over 1,200. The ratio of guerrilla losses to Japanese was one to five, which was the greatest percentage of guerrilla casualties suffered by the unit during any phase."

In addition to their numerical superiority over their guerrilla opponents, the Japanese had the advantage of well-prepared fortifications, heavy artillery, tankettes, and motor transport. Unfortunately for them, their intelligence provided very little useful information about their shadowy foes, whereas, in contrast, the 101 units knew virtually everything about their adversaries, sometimes before they even made a move. The battle was between a muscular Goliath, who had become blind, and a slender David, whose sharp eyes saw everything. The 101 assault on Kehsi-Mansam was typical. A 101 Shan agent operating in the heart of the town radioed out every Japanese move and critical details about their defenses. During the fight that ensued, Butch Brown, he of the peacock plume, was struck in the butt by a Japanese bullet.

"You can sure see which direction he was going," remarked one of his irreverent men.

Brown's wound served to make him mad as hell, and he led the last charge into the town by several lengths.

With the fall of Laihka came the end of two large supply dumps, dug in and camouflaged with the usual Japanese care. Each dump was over a square mile in size. One contained ammunition and the other medical supplies. The ammunition was turned over to the British, but

101 kept the medical supplies for its own use and distribution to the Burmese people. Once Laihka was in Kachin hands, John Raiss set about putting the captured Japanese airfield into shape. Even though the enemy had carried out a thorough demolition, Raiss had the field in working order in three days. A large roller had been left behind.

Dennis Cavanaugh notes that "John gathered a lot of Shans and set them to work carrying dirt and rocks night and day, frantically trying to meet the impossible deadline. As time ran out, headquarters received a petulant radio message from John, 'I am getting awfully tired pulling that damn roller. Please send me a jeep.'

"The picture was pitiful. They sent the jeep, and two days later the strip was ready. John named it 'Paddy's Raiss Field'."

When the field was in condition the 10th Air Force agreed to 101's request that six P-38s be stationed on it. Laihka was still behind the Japanese lines, and it was an oddity of the last big struggle in Burma that American air-force planes were actually operating from such a position. From their base, protected by guerrilla forces, the planes attacked Japanese defense positions in and around Loilem to support the Kachins in their siege of that important target. The Japanese fortifications at the tops of volcanic peaks rising over the lesser hills appeared to be impregnable to the guerrillas. But they were far from invulnerable. A 101 man on the ground talked on a walkie-talkie to a 101 pilot in a liaison plane, which would then drop smoke grenades on the target. The P-38s swept in to hit the marked targets with napalm. The guerrillas could then charge in for the kill.

\*    \*    \*

Palmer Hansen, better known as "Slug," Doug Martin, Pete Meade, and Paul Froberg were with their Kachins as 101 reduced the Japanese defenses at Loilem, one by one. Here is Hansen's report to Butch Brown, in whose battalion he was serving:

"I'll give you a report here of what happened yesterday, and then if they want a full formal report later I'll do so.

"We knew the Japs were in this area up there, and we knew also that they were dug in and that it would be foolish to try to chase them out. So we planned on going up and nosing them out and worrying them with a few mortar rounds.

"About a mile and a half from Loilem (southeast) near Maungya Hsai village (LN 2532), we came upon a hill that we suspected Japanese to be on. We flanked both sides and sent a section up the middle to see if they were there. The section sighted them and started to withdraw. Then our Brens and their MGs opened up. Back in defilade position Froberg and I opened up with mortars. After firing a few rounds we told the jemadar to withdraw both platoons and we would go back to a greater range and give them a few more mortar rounds.

"Our route of withdrawal brought us across an open spot which was in view of another section of the hill from which the firing came. We were almost completely out of it when they opened up on five of us behind a big tree.

"The tree and protection were big enough, but somehow or other Froberg showed himself for a moment and he caught a bullet through his left side.

"He died in less than a minute.

"The rest of us remained in that position for nearly a half hour, so I was certain that he was dead when I left.

"Two attempts to recover his body were made in the afternoon, but we were beat back both times. Villagers agreed to remain there and try to recover the body after dark. Most of the company was up there by that time so we moved back to camp.

"Villagers came back this morning and reported that the Japs had moved down to that area at dusk, so they could not get back in.

"A coolie and one hypenla were injured at the same time that Froberg was hit. But neither wound was very serious."

This was on June 5. Four days before he was killed, Paul Froberg had earned the silver star for gallantry in action against the enemy. Pinned down by enemy fire, Froberg and Hansen saw their machine gunner knocked out of action.

"Paul and I ran to his side, and as I manned the machine gun, Paul administered aid to the gunner," reported Hansen. "We decided we had better withdraw, so Paul picked up the wounded man and retreated under fire while I provided cover with the machine gun."

Each strong point held by the Japanese at Loilem could only be regained with American and Kachin blood. This was not the sort of warfare that was second nature to the Kachins, but neither Kachins nor Americans flinched. The 2d Battalion succeeded in taking Loilem by the middle of June.

\* \* \*

The Japanese air force was no longer more than a nuisance. Airmen flew in to Paddy's Raiss Field just for the novelty of landing behind

Japanese lines. Lieutenant General Dan I. Sultan, Theater Commander, stopped in to see if it was true that there actually was an airbase operating behind enemy lines. John Raiss rose to the occasion; he presented General Sultan with a "ten thousand mission" air-corps cap, which was as filthy as it was bedraggled. The general could only wear it with pride. Raiss, the self-proclaimed "sawbwa" of Laihka, also managed to have extraordinary leaflets printed in the town.

"Your trip to Burma is not complete without visiting—Paddy's Raiss Field," they announced. "At the immediate front. And sometimes behind Jap lines. Where else in Burma can you find these features at such amazingly low prices? Hurry! Hurry! Hurry! This may not last!

"Note: We have good connections with the Citations and Promotions Board. If rotation is accelerated because of malaria or dysentery contracted in this area, all charges will be doubled. Purple Hearts at no extra charge."

There were a full, six-course Burmese dinner at $2.50, native music, and dancing girls under the Burma moon. Photography at the front with Jap prisoners at $2.50, flying over an area where there might be Japs at $15, and flying over an area where there *are* Japs, $17. Recreation was touted as: "Hiking jungle trails, with guide and armed guard, per hr., $1.00." Accommodations: "Sleep out in the open in front of the perimeter at no extra charge." A picture of the sawbwa of Laihka on his throne was also included on the brochure that Raiss had printed. The throne was, of course, his royal seat in a jungle latrine.

\*     \*     \*

Larry Grimm was one of the most redoubtable 101 commanders and at the same time the kindest.

"When it is necessary to fire mortar shells into a village, you must always be sure there are no women and kids there," he explained to his men. "I'm a pacifist at heart."

Larry Grimm spoke for us all when he told what it was like to wait in the jungles for something to happen.

"I am lying on the perimeter in the moonlight. Nothing moves," he told me. "There's a log in the moonlight, or is it a Japanese who has been creeping up and who is playing possum? The walls of the jungle close in. You fight the tension. You're ready to squeeze off a shot. The first shot is the one to get off. There may never be a second if you wait too long. Once the fight starts, it's a relief.

"It is that enemy country in the Shan States. A fourteen-year-old Kachin kid wearing a little turban puts a flower behind his ear and beams at me with the sweetest smile imaginable, then puts a knife between his teeth and slips into the river waters like a playful muskrat, and goes swimming out to a raft occupied by a Jap soldier. He cuts the head off the soldier.

"I am walking down the trail. Two Kachin scouts are out in front. Behind me walks a little Kachin boy carrying his shoes. I'm wearing high boots. There was this little snake. A krait, and it's deadly. I stop. I don't want to panic the little kid behind me. He skips past me, plants a little bare heel on the snake and grinds the life out of it, and then skips around back of me. He had endangered his life without the slightest hesitation to protect mine."

Larry Grimm is a Texan who knows much about life on the American frontier, and he again speaks for all 101 men when he makes a comparison.

"We weren't far removed from pioneer times," he says. "We had the same love of courage, the same rugged spirit, and the pleasure in doing manly things."

\* \* \*

The Japanese who had retreated from Mandalay and Maymyo had fallen back into the Heho area, which had once been the heart of the Japanese air control of Burma. There were strong forces at Taunggyi, too, and if these forces were to be driven eastward through the gauntlet of ambushes into Thailand, Red Maddox and his battalion must strike directly at the strategic key to the situation. This was Lawksawk.

Maddox slipped south from the Burma Road and crossed the Namtu River. Monsoon rains had swollen it, and it rushed through a deep gorge. The Kachins had to string a rope taut across the river to keep them from being swept downstream as they waded and swam. The Namtu was the Kachins' Rubicon, and they knew that they could never retreat back over it if they were defeated and pursued closely by the Japanese.

The battalion moved south, killing Japanese in ambush as they fled from the British victory at Mandalay. By the end of April Maddox and his Kachins had reached their destination. Only two hundred

Japanese soldiers, according to 101 intelligence, held Lawksawk. If two companies of Kachins could block the road leading to the southwest and Pangtara, a village about twenty-five miles away, and two more could block the road leading to the southeast, the four remaining companies could attack the city from the north.

But unfortunately, the Japanese moved seven hundred additional soldiers into Lawksawk, and at two A.M. on the morning of May 7, their artillery bombarded the Kachin positions. The Japanese swarmed to the attack. Banzai charges followed banzai charges until two that afternoon, when the guerrillas, their ammunition nearly exhausted, fell back. There were 9 Kachins dead and 15 wounded. Agents later learned that the Japanese suffered 280 dead. Over 80 bullock carts of wounded were counted. Lawksawk remained in Japanese hands, and elements of the Japanese 15th and 18th Divisions could still move back through the town toward Taunggyi and the escape route.

Neither could the Japanese afford to lose Pangtara. Two companies of Maddox's Kachins attacked the village and occupied it, but six hundred Japanese succeeded in driving the Kachins out after a bloody battle. The Kachins did not go far. They set up a massive ambush outside the town so that when the Japanese resumed the attack, they were caught in a deadly cross fire. The Japanese lost heavily, but the Kachins' losses were the heaviest of any engagement of the entire Burma war: thirty dead, several wounded, and about twenty missing.

While Roger Hillsman and a company of rangers raided and ambushed the Japanese between Lawksawk and Taunggyi, Red Maddox withdrew to regroup. He built an airstrip so that light planes could fly out his critically wounded and they could receive supply drops. The first the Japanese knew that Maddox's men were back in action was when Kachins shot up motor transports and blew up bridges. By now the Japanese in Lawksawk were feeble from lack of supplies, and the city fell to the Kachins on June 1. Pangtara fell on June 8. Within less than ninety days the Kachins had killed over six hundred Japanese and broken their line of retreat.

"This action completed the mission of Detachment 101 to seize the Taunggyi-Kentung Road," noted Ray Peers. "On 1 July orders were issued to inactivate the unit as soon as possible."

On July 12, Detachment 101 of the Office of Strategic Services was inactivated. The last of the Kachin hypenlas went home to their villages. We Americans went off to new assignments with the OSS in China, in Ceylon, and in Indo-China and Malaysia.

\* \* \*

Lieutenant General Dan I. Sultan, Commanding General, United States Forces, India-Burma Theater, said of the Kachins:

"The American-Jinghpaw Rangers have made an immensely valuable contribution to the success of the campaign in North Burma. Operating entirely behind enemy lines, their complete knowledge of the jungle has enabled them to disrupt Japanese communications and harass their rear areas. They have given the Japanese no respite even where they should feel the safest. Their operations form one of the most colorful chapters of the war in the Far East.

"The contribution which the Jinghpaw Rangers, operating under American leadership, have made in defeating the Japanese and driving them from North Burma has been out of proportion to their relatively small numbers. Their skill in jungle fighting, in the use of the modern weapons of war, their knowledge of the terrain and their fearlessness has made their service of great assistance to their allies, the Americans, the British, and the Chinese."

\* \* \*

A citation issued in the name of the president of the United States reads as follows:

"*Service Unit Detachment No. 101, Office of Strategic Services* is cited for outstanding performance of duty from 8 May to 15 June 1945 in capturing the strategic enemy strong points of Lawksawk, Pangtara, and Loilem in the Central Shan States, Burma. This unit, composed of approximately 300 American officers and men, volunteered to clear the enemy from an area of 10,000 square miles. Its subsequent activities deprived the Japanese 15th Army of the only East escape route and secured the Stilwell Road against enemy counterattack. Although Detachment No. 101 had been engaged primarily in intelligence and guerrilla activities, it set about the infantry mission of ousting a determined enemy from a sector long fortified and strategically prepared. These American officers and men recruited, organized, and trained 3,200 Burmese natives entirely within enemy territory. They then undertook and concluded successfully a coordinated 4-battalion offensive against important strategic objectives through an area containing approximately 10,000 battle-seasoned

Japanese troops. Locally known as the "Kachin Rangers," Detachment No. 101 and its Kachin troops became a ruthless striking force, continually on the offensive against the veterans of the Japanese 18th and 56th Divisions. Throughout the campaign, the Kachin Rangers were equipped with nothing heavier than mortars and had to rely entirely upon air-dropped supplies. Besides a numerical superiority of three to one, the enemy had the advantage of adequate supplies, artillery tankettes, carefully prepared positions, and motor transportation. Alternating frontal attacks with guerrilla tactics, the Kachin Rangers remained in constant contact with the enemy during the entire period and persistently cut him down and demoralized him. During the vicious struggle for Lawksawk, 400 Rangers met 700 Japanese veterans supported by artillery and, in a 12-hour battle, killed 281 of the enemy while suffering only 7 casualties. They took Loilem, central junction of vital roads, despite its protecting system of bunkers and pillboxes after 10 days of unremitting assaults. Under the most hazardous jungle conditions, Americans of Detachment No. 101 displayed extraordinary heroism in leading their coordinated battalions of 3,200 natives to complete victory against an overwhelmingly superior force. They met and routed 10,000 Japanese throughout an area of 10,000 square miles, killed 1,247 while sustaining losses of 37, demolished or captured 4 large dumps, destroyed the enemy motor transport, and inflicted extensive damage on communications and installations. The courage and fighting spirit displayed by the officers and men of Service Unit Detachment No. 101, Office of Strategic Services, in this successful offensive action against overwhelming enemy strength, reflect the highest traditions of the armed forces of the United States."

Dwight D. Eisenhower,
Chief of Staff

# Glossary

**bashas** – huts
**bum nats** – evil spirits
**chang** – sour, soupy home brew
**chaung** – river
**chinthe** – stone lion-headed dragons
      that guard temples
**dah** – swordlike knife
**duwa** – leader
**duwa kaba** – grand leader
**Ga Shadup** – earth spirit
**gaungpaun** – turban
**godown** – rice storage
**gumlao** – revolutionary movement
**hkas** – rivers
**hku** – headwaters
**hypenlas** – soldiers
**jaiwa** – soothsayer
**Jinghpaw** – Kachin
**kahtaung** – village
**Kempi tai** – Japanese secret police
**lathis** – sticks
**laukhu** – fermented drink
**longyi** – wrap-around skirt
**lweje** – market
**mahadevi** – principal wife
**manau** – celebration
**nadai-hap** – sacred compartment
**nats** – Kachin spirits
**n-ladap** – room of the unmarried
      girls
**pongyi** – Burmese monk
**pungyi** – bamboo stake
**sawbwa** – Shan prince
**stupas** – solid votive shrine
**tongyaw** – itinerant rice culture
**uma** – headman's youngest son

# Bibliography

## Manuscripts, Letters, Pamphlets, and Documents

Baker, Col. Robert H. "Cooperation of Detachment 101 with ATC." Headquarters, Assam Wing, August 20, 1944.

Brown, Newell. Letter in 101 Association Archives, Tustin, Cal., n.d.

Bupp, Betty Jane. Letter to author, December 19, 1977.

"Burma Campaign." Office of Strategic Services Detachment 101, Nazira, India, 1945.

"Burma: the Golden Peninsula." Embassy of the Union of Burma, Washington, D.C., n.d.

Cavanaugh, Dennis. "Taro Tales." MS. 101 Association Archives, Tustin, Cal.

Clower, Lt. Freeling H. "Narrative," given in hospital, January, 1944. 101 Association Archives, Tustin, Cal.

Coughlin, John, Col., USA, Ret. Letter to author, September 9, 1978.

Cummings, William. Letter to author, October 21, 1978.

Davidson, Howard C., Maj. Gen. "Contribution of Detachment 101, OSS, to USAAF in Northeastern Assam and North Burma." Headquarters, Tenth Air Force, August 1, 1944.

Davidson, Howard C., Maj. Gen., Ret. Letter to Harold Miner, Chief, Division of Middle Eastern and Indian Affairs, Department of State, n.d.

Donovan, William J. Letter to Harold Miner, Chief, Division of Middle Eastern and Indian Affairs, Department of State, October 21, 1946.

Eisenhower, Gen. Dwight D., Chief of Staff. "General Orders No. 7." War Department, Washington, D.C., January 17, 1946.

"First 50 Years of Pan Am, The." Pan American World Airways, 1977.

Genaw, Gerald L. Letter to author, July 7, 1978.

Georges, Capt. Michael P. "OSS-SU 101 Schools and Training." Nazira, Assam, November, 1944.

Goodfellow, M. Preston. "How 101 Was Created." MS. 101 Association Archives, Tustin, Cal.

Grimm, Laurence H. Letter to author, May 22, 1978.

Luce, James C. MS. in the 101 Association Archives, Tustin, Cal.

Moree, Irby. "Scrapbook." Collection of Mrs. Irby Moree, Mundelein, Ill.

"OSS Detachment 101 Operations." Compiled by the 101 Association, n.d.

Peers, William R., Lt. Gen., Ret. Letter to author, October 9, 1978.

Peers, William R. "OSS." MS. 101 Association Archives, Tustin, Cal.

Peers, William R. Report to Brigadier General William J. Donovan, Office of Strategic Services, February 29, 1944.

Peers, William R. "To the Headman and People of the Village of Hu Hson." Detachment 101, Nazira, Assam, n.d.

Powell, Libbie. Letter to author, December 27, 1977.

"Pyidawtha." Economics and Social Board, Government of the Union of Burma, Rangoon, 1954.

Saw Dee Htoo. Letter of July 23, 1976, in 101 Association Archives, Tustin, Cal.

Staudacher, Rosemarian V. MS. about Father James Stuart and memoranda about Father Stuart.

## Periodicals

Aitken, Robert G. "Twenty Years Ago and Today." *101 Association Newsletter*, Fall, 1965.

Bostwick, William. "Ah Tha." *101 Association Newsletter*, October, 1974.

Brown, Newell. "Paddy's Raiss Field." *101 Association Newsletter*, April, 1975.

Cavanaugh, Dennis V. "Airdrop, Part I—Three Tragedies." *101 Association Newsletter*, March, 1976.

Cavanaugh, Dennis V. "Airdrop, Part II—People, Parachutes, Problems." *101 Association Newsletter*, June, 1976.

Cavanaugh, Dennis V. "Citation for Military Assistance." *101 Association Newsletter*, March, 1976.

Cavanaugh, Dennis V. "The God Fathers." *101 Association Newsletter*, April, 1975.

Cavanaugh, Dennis V. "How Our Airforce Began." *101 Association Newsletter*, April, 1975.

Cavanaugh, Dennis V. "Myitkyina to Afghanistan to Japan: Friends and Foes." *101 Association Newsletter*, December, 1973.

Duncan, Lt. Col. Harry N. "Combat Intelligence for Modern War." *Army Information Digest*, June, 1962.

"Eyes, Ears, Daggers for Stilwell's Return to China." *Fort Point Salvo*, Presidio of San Francisco, Cal., May, 1977.

Hansen, Palmer. "The Death of Sergeant Paul Froberg." *101 Association Newsletter*, January, 1977.

Henderson, Ralph E. "Jump-In to Adventure." *Reader's Digest*, June, 1945.

Hopper, Jay. "Twelve Medics from Nazira." *101 Association Newsletter*, October, 1974.

Lazarsky, Joseph E. "The Death of Lieutenant Berg." *101 Association Newsletter*, June, 1976.

Luce, James C. "Jungle Medical Surgery." *101 Association Newsletter*, July, 1978.

McCarthy, Rev. E. J. "Breaking New Ground." *Far East,* October, 1941.

O'Brien, Walter E. "Affair with China." *101 Association Newsletter,* October, 1974.

Peers, William R., Lt. Gen., Ret. "Guerrilla Operations in Northern Burma." *Military Review* 28, No. 4 (July, 1948).

Peers, William R., Lt. Gen., Ret. "Intelligence Operations of OSS Detachment 101." *Intelligence Articles,* IV 3, n.d.

Power, Stuart E. "The Wit and Wisdom of John Raiss." *101 Association Newsletter,* April, 1975.

Rosson, Maj. Gen. William B. "The U.S. Army in Special Warfare." *Army,* November, 1962.

Schreiner, Sam A. "The Lovable Psychologist." *101 Association Newsletter,* August, 1975.

Tegenfeldt, Rev. H. G. "To 'Shing' for Christmas." *Ex-CBI Roundup,* October, 1957.

Trifletti, Vincent J. "Rocky Reardon's Airforce." *101 Association Newsletter,* April, 1975.

Tuchman, Barbara W. "If Asia Were Clay in the Hands of the West." *Atlantic,* November, 1970.

"Wayne 'Pop' Milligan." *101 Association Newsletter,* July, 1963.

Wolbarst, Roger. "A Stroll in the Jungle." *101 Association Newsletter,* October, 1974.

## Books

Ba Maw. *Breakthrough in Burma.* New Haven, Conn., 1968.

Belden, Jack. *Retreat with Stilwell.* New York, 1943.

Bixler, Norma. *Burmese Journey.* Yellow Springs, Ohio, 1967.

Boulle, Pierre. *My Own River Kwai.* New York, 1967.

Chamales, Tom. *Never So Few.* New York, 1957.

Churchill, Winston S. *Closing the Ring.* Boston, 1951.

Collins, Larry, and Lapierre, Dominique. *Freedom at Midnight.* New York, 1975.

Collis, Maurice. *Last and First in Burma.* New York, 1956.

Dorn, Frank. *Walkout: with Stilwell in Burma.* New York, 1971.

Douglas, William O. *North from Malaya.* Garden City, N.Y., 1953.

Dunlop, Richard. *Burma.* Garden City, N.Y., 1959.

Dupuy, Trevor Nevitt. *Asian and Axis Resistance Movements.* New York, 1965.

Dupuy, Trevor Nevitt. *Asiatic Land Battles: Allied Victories in China and Burma.* New York, 1963.

Fisher, Charles A. *South-East Asia.* London, 1964.

Ford, Corey. *Donovan of OSS.* New York, 1970.

Girsham, Jack, with Lowell Thomas. *Burma Jack.* New York, 1971.

Gump, Richard. *Jade: Stone of Heaven.* Garden City, N.Y., 1962.

Hart, G. H. Liddell. *History of the Second World War.* New York, 1970.

Henderson, John W.; Heimann, Judith M.; Martindale, Kenneth

W.; Shinn, Rinnsup; Weaver, John O.; and White, Eston T. *Area Handbook for Burma*. U.S. Government Printing Office, Washington, D.C., n.d.

Hillsman, Roger. *To Move a Nation*. Garden City, N.Y., 1967.

Hunter, Charles Newton. *Galahad*. San Antonio, Tex., 1963.

Kingdon-Ward, Frank. *Return to the Irrawaddy*. London, 1956.

Leach, Edmond R. *Political Systems of Highland Burma*. London, 1970.

Lewis, Norman. *Golden Earth*. New York, 1952.

Liang, Chin-Tung. *General Stilwell in China, 1942–1944*. Jamaica, N.Y., 1972.

Lovell, Stanley P. *Of Spies and Stratagems*. Englewood, N.J., 1963.

Matthew, Geoffrey. *The Re-Conquest of Burma, 1943–1945*. Aldershot, Hampshire, England, 1966.

Miles, Vice Ad. Milton E., USN. *A Different Kind of War*. Garden City, N.Y., 1967.

Moon, Thomas N., and Eifler, Carl F. *The Deadliest Colonel*. New York, 1975.

Newhall, Sue Mayes. *The Devil in God's Old Man*. New York, 1969.

Ogburn, Charlton. *The Marauders*. New York, 1959.

Olschki, Leonardo. *Marco Polo's Asia*. Berkeley, Cal., 1960.

Peers, William R., Lt. Gen., Ret., and Brelis, Dean. *Behind the Burma Road*. Boston, 1963.

Read, Katherine L., with Robert O. Ballou. *Bamboo Hospital*. Philadelphia, 1961.

Romanus, Charles F., and Sunderland, Riley. *Time Runs Out in CBI*. Office of the Chief of Military History, Department of the Army, Washington, D.C., 1959.

Rooney, D. *Stilwell*. New York, 1971.

Rowan, Carl T. *The Pitiful and the Proud*. New York, 1956.

Scott, Col. Robert L. *God Is My Co-Pilot*. Garden City, N.Y., 1943.

Seagraves, Gordon S. *Burma Surgeon Returns*. New York, 1946.

Smith, Donald Eugene. *Religion and Politics in Burma*. Princeton, N.J., 1965.

Smith, Nicol, and Clark, Blake. *Into Siam*. New York, 1945.

Smith, R. Harris. *OSS*. Berkeley, Cal., 1972.

Stevenson, H. N. C. *The Hill Peoples of Burma*. London, 1945.

Stevenson, William. *A Man Called Intrepid*. New York, 1977.

Stilwell, Gen. Joseph W. *The Stilwell Papers*. New York, 1948.

Sykes, Christopher. *Orde Wingate*. London, 1959.

Taylor, Edmond. *Richer by Asia*. New York, 1964.

Thiesmeyer, Lincoln R., and Burchard, John E. *Combat Scientists*. Boston, 1947.

Thomas, Lowell. *Back to Mandalay*. New York, 1951.

Tuchman, Barbara. *Stilwell and the American Experience in China*. New York, 1970.

Turner, F. St. John. *Pictorial History of Pan American World Airways*. London, 1973.

Wedemeyer, Gen. Albert C. *Wedemeyer Reports*. New York, 1958.

# Index